# WE ARE AN
# INDIAN NATION

# WE ARE AN INDIAN NATION

*A History of the Hualapai People*

Jeffrey P. Shepherd

## FIRST PEOPLES
*New Directions in Indigenous Studies*

The University of Arizona Press    Tucson

The University of Arizona Press
© 2010 The Arizona Board of Regents
All rights reserved

www.uapress.arizona.edu

Library of Congress Cataloging-in-Publication Data
Shepherd, Jeffrey P., 1970–
    We are an Indian nation : a history of the Hualapai people /
    Jeffrey P. Shepherd.
        p.  cm.
    Includes bibliographical references and index.
    ISBN 978-0-8165-2828-8 (cloth : alk. paper) —
    ISBN 978-0-8165-2904-9 (pbk. : alk. paper)
    1. Hualapai Indians—History.  2. Hualapai Indians—Social conditions.
    I. Title.
    E99.H75S53 2010
    970.004'975724—dc22
                                                            2009039073

Publication of this book was made possible, in part, with a grant from the
Andrew W. Mellon Foundation.


Manufactured in the United States of America on acid-free, archival-quality
paper and processed chlorine free.


All proceeds from this book go to a college fund for members of the
Hualapai Nation.

Dedicated to the people of the Hualapai nation,
past, present, and future

and

in memory of Monza J. Honga,
September 25, 1963, to July 10, 2009

# Contents

# Illustrations

# Foreword

*Lucille Watahomigie*

This book on Hualapai history is very important to the Hualapai Tribe. Most books on Native people rely too much on the histories stored in libraries, which frequently represent the views of the Bureau of Indian Affairs and the superintendents overseeing life on reservations. These stories also stress the views of anthropologists and others who came to our lands to examine and research our way of life. Their work tends to be superficial because the researchers do not understand our cultures, or they leave out values and mores that are important to our people.

This book written by Jeffrey Shepherd is one of the first books for the Hualapai tribe that was reviewed by a committee appointed by the Hualapai Tribal Council. This committee, along with other tribal members, gave input to Dr. Shepherd that he tried to incorporate into the book. Moreover, Dr. Shepherd sought out and received approval from the Hualapai Tribal Council long before he began conducting his research. Because of his willingness to listen and his attempt to tell a story that takes the perspectives of Native people seriously, we have a document that can be used by future generations. This book will be best read and discussed with elders or Hualapai families who experienced or were told about the events and incidents covered in the book.

There were many injustices and traumas that happened to the Hualapai people in their fight for their land and territories and maintenance of their language and traditions. In the present day, it is still a struggle to pass on the knowledge of the tribe to all generations of the people. Today, the tribe has been forced to believe that their way of life (language and culture) is not acceptable, and therefore it is not being actively practiced. Almost all of the tribal members are assimilated into the mainstream culture and other minority cultures of the United States.

We hope that this book will point out how colonization negatively impacted our culture and, in the process, help to heal the people so that they can begin to revitalize the Hualapai language and culture.

Lucille Watahomigie
Director of the Hualapai Education and Training Department
and Native Languages Activist

# Foreword

*Wilfred Whatoname, Sr.*

Gum u? (How are you? in Hualapai)

My name is Wilfred Whatoname, Sr., Hualapai Tribal Chairman, son of Gladys Butler Whatoname and Howard Whatoname, both of whom are deceased. My mother lived to be 100 years old and passed away in December 2002, and my dad passed away in 1967.

I have been given the honor to write the foreword of this book, which tells the history of my people and how they have survived despite incredible odds.

This book tells of what the Anglos did to my people and why my people did what they did to survive. History tells us of how the colonists and pilgrims immigrated from Europe and settled in the eastern part of the continent, and how they trekked out to the western part of the country. However, it does not always explain in detail how lands were taken, and how the Indians were eventually removed from lands they had inhabited from time immemorial.

This book starts with important oral histories that explain the origins of our people along the Colorado River, and then describes the painful experience of removal from our homelands in the 1860s and 1870s. It also talks about the role of the U.S. Cavalry in the Hualapai Wars and the creation of the reservation in 1883. It goes on to discuss other important issues such as cattle ranching, the court case with the Santa Fe Railway, and the creation of the modern Hualapai government and tribal constitution. The book even attempts to explain our history along the Colorado River and our struggle for water rights. These are crucial issues for our community.

Today the reservation population is 2,225 and continues to grow. The elder generation, like my father and mother, who were born in the late 1890s are not alive anymore. The ones that we consider the elders are of the generation born to my parents who are now in their 70s and 80s. They continue to tell the old stories and keep the oral traditions alive by participating in cultural events and speaking with the younger generations. The stories about our origins, kinship relations, and ties to the land are very important for our identity today.

Some things, however, have changed since the days when my grandparents were young. This change is reflected in the growing use of drugs and alcohol, especially among our young people, who have easy access to them. In the time of my parents they were very hard to obtain. But times are different now. Our parents were against the use of drugs and alcohol and preached against their use because of their terrible effects on families. The use of drugs is also tied to the presence of gangs on the reservation, which also causes a problem in the community.

On the brighter side, the language, the culture, and traditional ways of the Hualapai people are still being taught, though it is difficult to compete with television and movies. Many organizations such as the Boys and Girls Club, the Cultural Department, Natural Resource Department, Hualapai Elders, and Hualapai Tribal Council all contribute to the preservation of the Hualapai language and traditional cultural activities. This work has led to many positive efforts, such as involving the very young in Bird Singing by fathers and grandparents. Also, there are various Hualapai dance groups who are participating in community events and off-reservation activities, which also involve grandparents, parents, and children coming together. The Hualapai Tribal Council assists these dance groups with monetary support, and the tribal departments sometimes provide help when there is a need for transportation. Thus, maintaining culture and language is a community responsibility that we try to take seriously.

Overall, I think this book educates non-Hualapais about our struggles and our successes as a tribal nation. Even though it cannot cover every story that has been told by or about us, it offers a good glimpse into our history.

Wilfred Whatanome, Sr.
Hualapai Tribal Council Chairman

# Acknowledgments

Since my first visit to the reservation in late 1997, numerous people from the Hualapai Nation have provided support and encouragement for this project. The Hualapai Tribal Council listened to updates on the book, gave critical commentary on content, and offered administrative and financial assistance that was crucial for the completion of the manuscript. The Hualapai Department of Cultural Resources, Tribal Court, Grand Canyon Resort Corporation, River Runners, Health Department, Peach Springs Public School, and other entities opened their doors and facilities to me, hoping that this book would represent their history with fairness and accuracy.

Several Hualapai community members went far beyond anything I could have expected in their generosity, knowledge, and willingness to endure my endless questions. When I first met Lucille Watahomigie at the University of Arizona's American Indian Language and Development Institute, she greeted me by saying, "So you are the one interested in Hualapai history." Apparently, she had learned of my participation in the institute and research into the history of her people before I had actually approached her. Since then she has shared her knowledge of tribal history and introduced me to many members of the community. She has been a supportive mentor and, if necessary, a gentle critic when I have misunderstood Hualapai history. I am also especially indebted to Monza Honga, past director of the Hualapai Cultural Resources Department and tribal judge, and to Chief Judge Joseph T. Flies Away for their support and endless conversations about Hualapai history and contemporary Indian affairs. Your tenacity and dedication to the Hualapai people are inspiring.

I also want to thank the following individuals for their contributions to the book. When Loretta Jackson-Kelley became the director of the Cultural Resources Department, she inherited a complex array of issues ranging from flight paths over the Grand Canyon to the protection of traditional cultural properties. In between her endless work she somehow found the time to assist me with my research. She helped create the Hualapai History Review Board, whose members read and commented on several versions of the manuscript, and she made important observations on the text. The entire Cultural Resource Department, which has consisted of several people over the past decade, has been my home base for the innumerable hours I spent on the reservation. In particular, my appreciation goes out to Marcie Craynon for her endless support and friendship; Cheryl Beecher for her assistance with interviews and identification of band identities; Drake Havatone for his knowledge and good humor; and Dawn Hubbs for her comparative knowledge of Australian Indigenous peoples and her uncanny expertise organizing meetings. I would also like to express my gratitude to past chairman Charles Vaughn for reading the manuscript and offering detailed and extremely important comments on band identities and family relationships. Camille Nighthorse, thank you for the wonderful photographs of your grandfather, Fred Mahone. A heartfelt thanks goes to Sandra Irwin, director of the Health Department, and to the present chairman, Wilfred Whatoname, both of whom have talked with me about Hualapai history for several years and whose support for this project has made the process incredibly rewarding.

I would be remiss if I did not mention some of the other community members whom I interviewed or who somehow made this book possible: Benedict and Lydia Beecher, Robert Begay, Robert Bravo, Emmett Bender, Louise Benson, Earl Havatone, Carrie Imus, Greg Glascoe, Mille Grover, Linda Havatone, Delores Honga, Waylon Honga, Verna Kopelva, Monique Mahone, Elvira Otten, Floranda Powskey, Melinda Powskey, Joe Powskey, Sylvia Querta, Dallas Quasula, Juliete Steele, Ruby Steele, Ron Two Bulls, Philbert Watahomigie, Lonnie Wilder, Sharon Wilder, Wiletta Wilder, Candida Yazzie, and Sheri Yellowhawk. It is difficult to express my respect and admiration for all of you.

There are many mentors and colleagues I would like to thank for their intellectual support and personal contributions to this project. My deepest appreciation goes to Peter Iverson for his patience and interest in what began as a dissertation under his direction at Arizona State University. I could not have asked for a more knowledgeable and judicious mentor, who, despite my anxiety and doubt, remained convinced that I could do a decent job on an increasingly complicated endeavor. During my doctoral studies I am also grateful to Edward Escobar, Robert Trennert, and Octaviana Trujillo, whose collective expertise in race relations, American Indian history, and Southwest history gave me a solid foundation on which this book is based.

I also appreciate friends, colleagues, and mentors who helped me throughout graduate school and during the final phases of this manuscript. Matt Dennis, Jeff Ostler, Todd Lundgren, Nicolas Rosenthal, and Gray Whaley made my experiences at the University of Oregon intellectually and personally rewarding. I am thankful that we have been able to keep in touch after all these years. The Departments of History and Native American Studies at Arizona State University provided a rich community of friends who stimulated me intellectually and urged me to do forward-thinking work. In retrospect, I am perhaps one of the few people who can say I had a truly wonderful experience as a doctoral student. For that I want to thank Lynn Abieta, Steve Amerman, Laurie Arnold, Brian Collier, J. Wendell Cox, Andrew Fisher, Brad Gills, Leah Glaser, Patricia Harms, Gary Owens, Jr., Doug Seefeldt, Tara Travis, and Lolita Whitesinger for countless laughs and wonderful debates about history, life, and the future. Special thanks go out to Karen Leong, Amy Lonetree, Susan Miller, Jennifer Nez Denetdale, and Waziyatawin Angela Wilson for their patience and endless discussions with me about American Indian studies, colonialism, and decolonization. In particular, I want to express my deepest respect for Myla Vicenti Carpio, an Arizona State University alumna, wonderful mentor, and fellow racquetball fanatic, for her friendship and inspiration. Several other colleagues have commented on parts of this monograph or through their own scholarly work helped me think more deeply about the history of Native peoples: Juliana Barr, William Bauer, Ned Blackhawk, Joe Graham, Alexandra Harmon, Brian Hosmer, Martha Knack, Eric V. Meeks, Colleen O'Neil, Cynthia Radding, Margo Tamez, Sam Truett, and Marsha Weisiger. Your scholarship is impeccable, and I look forward to years of learning from your work. Christian McMillen and I have shared a friendship and mutual interest in Hualapai history, and our conversations have sharpened my understanding about the nature of history in general and the specifics of the Hualapai past. And finally, I would like to thank my students and colleagues at the University of Texas at El Paso: Cristobal Borges, Ernesto Chavez, Yolanda Chavez Leyva, Scott Comar, Paul Edison, Maceo Dailey, Gary Kieffner, Dana Wessel Lightfoot, Antonio R. Lopez, Cheryl and Charles Martin, Gina Nunez, John Paul Nuno, Nicol Partida, Michael Topp, and Edith Yanez.

Several archives, institutions, and individuals helped bring this project to fruition. Patti Hartmann at the University of Arizona Press has given me invaluable guidance and support, urging me to complete a book that she truly believed in. Mary M. Hill's meticulous copyediting and insightful advice have streamlined the manuscript and made it much more readable. I am indebted to the staff at Hayden Library; the Arizona Historical Foundation;

the State of Arizona Archives; the University of Arizona; Northern Arizona Special Collections; the Mohave County Community College; the Arizona State Museum; and Prescott College. I also want to recognize the Museum of Northern Arizona in Flagstaff and Pat Foley of the Mohave Museum of History and Arts in Kingman, Arizona. Paul Wormser and Lisa Gezelter at the Pacific Branch of the National Archives and Records Administration and staff in Washington, D.C., also assisted with the labyrinthine files of Record Group 75. I am indebted to financial support from the Hualapai Nation; the Department of History at Arizona State University; the Associated Students of Arizona State University; the Fort McDowell Yavapai Nation; the American Indian Studies Department at ASU; the Max Millett Fund; the Arizona State University History Associates Award for Excellence; the American Philosophical Society; and the History Department, College of Liberal Arts, and Graduate College of the University of Texas at El Paso. In addition, the Hualapai Tribal Council provided much-needed financial support to defray the costs of research and make the book affordable to a larger audience.

Since 1997 I have enjoyed two research fellowships at the D'Arcy McNickle Center for the American Indian at the Newberry Library in Chicago, Illinois, which provided a supportive and stimulating environment for the study of American Indian ethnohistory and the relationships between Native peoples and capitalism. It also introduced me to the following colleagues and friends: David Anthony Tayame Clark, Loretta Fowler, Jane Hafen, Alexandra Harmon, Brian Hosmer, Fred Hoxie, Martha Knack, Colleen O'Neil, Malea Powell, Paige Raibmon, and many others. Finally, I want to thank the anonymous reviewers who commented on and improved the overall quality of the manuscript.

More than anyone else I want to thank my family. Cynthia Bejarano, the examples you set as a scholar, intellectual, and activist are inspirational and astounding to watch. I'm blessed to be your husband. I also want to recognize the support of my in-laws, Felix, Elvira, Debbie, Rich, Daniel, and Santana; my parents, Walt and Sharon Shepherd; my sister, Stephanie; and my brother, Christopher. You have given me faith and countless hours of laughter, and although you never badgered me about how long it took to complete this book, I know that you were always wondering, "Is it done yet?"

# WE ARE AN
# INDIAN NATION

# Introduction

## *The La Paz Memorial Run*

Every April, as the desert prepares for the blistering summer heat, several dozen Hualapais wake up in Parker, Arizona, nearly two hundred miles away from their reservation. They are participants in a commemorative four-day run that marks a traumatic turning point in the history of the Hualapai nation. In 1874, several years after the United States waged a campaign of ethnic cleansing against Indigenous groups in the region, the military rounded up hundreds of Pais and forcibly relocated them to the Colorado River Indian Reservation in Parker, Arizona. Children, the elderly, and the sick died on the two-week march, but more died of disease and starvation during their yearlong internment in the place referred to as La Paz at the sweltering northern tip of the Sonoran Desert. Nearly one year later, in 1875, the surviving band members escaped imprisonment and returned home to northwestern Arizona. The annual La Paz Run memorializes these experiences by allowing Hualapais to retrace the steps of their ancestors from the point of internment northward to the Hualapai Reservation.

The trauma of internment and the subsequent escape from La Paz are important turning points in Hualapai history. Akin to the Navajos' Long Walk to and return from Bosque Redondo in eastern New Mexico, the Hualapais' imprisonment and liberation from La Paz work as metaphors for their larger experience with American colonialism. Just as the march and concentration represent in microcosm the century and a half of violence committed against the Hualapais, the escape and return home represent their perseverance in the past and their hopes for the future. Moreover, the annual reenactment has become an important site of community commemoration and a key signifier of Huala-pai historical identity. While the runners make their way north, Hualapais on the reservation learn about La Paz through elders recounting stories about the difficult times in the nineteenth century after the arrival of Anglos. Such inter-generational storytelling helps Hualapais retain their identity and traditions. "We are trying to instill in our children a sense of the history and the hardship the Hualapai People have endured," recalled Vice Chairman Edgar Walema during an interview about the La Paz Run. Community members discuss the importance of family, band responsibilities, and the roles of men and women in the community. Hualapai Bird Dancers sing songs with members from neighbor-ing nations who join Hualapais to celebrate their survival. At the end of the run community members meet the runners as they enter the reservation to engage in an act of remembrance that honors past, present, and future generations.[1] In the words of Jean Parker, whose ancestors fled internment, "We are the survivors of the ones who escaped."[2] By refusing to forget the past while daring it to imprison them, Hualapais rewrite their history and strive for a better future. To quote Edgar Walema, vice chairman in the late 1990s, "Even though this happened in the past, we are trying to have a meaningful life."[3]

The La Paz Run and associated community events work as a counter-narrative scripted by the descendants of Pais who were the targets of American colonialism and ethnic cleansing. Although the run and related events invoke painful memories of violence, Hualapais have a chance to recast the trauma of history and write their own stories of survival in the face of ongoing marginalization and oppression. Similarly, this book offers a narrative of survival and resistance that challenges dominant beliefs of Hualapais as a conquered people who, after confronting the U.S. military and the invasion of Anglos in the nineteenth century, slid into the shadows of history. Nothing could be further from the truth. Just as the La Paz Run and tribal commemoration wed stories of death and disease with survival and resistance, this story balances historical violence and community resilience to illuminate a little-known history of a people who, when assaulted by colonialism, racism, poverty, and disease, forged a new place for themselves as an Indigenous nation in modern America.[4]

## The Significance of Hualapai History

The Hualapai who run in honor of their ancestors' escape from La Paz offer an implicit critique of the American nation-state and its alteration of the geography of Indigenous peoples in the territorial Southwest during the mid- to late nineteenth century. Frequently known as "the Indian Wars," the period between the end of the Civil War and the "capture" of Geronimo in the 1880s witnessed brutal campaigns against the Yavapais, Hualapais, Paiutes, Chemehuevis, Mohaves, and other groups along the lower Colorado River basin. Though not as well known as the campaigns against the Apaches, the ethnic warfare against these nations yielded equally horrifying acts of carnage and inhumanity. Little more than hunting expeditions against people who had lived in northwestern Arizona for centuries, the campaigns of Col. William Redwood Price, for example, between 1865 and 1869 allowed an invasive settler society to transform purportedly "vacant land" into outposts of empire. Quickly thereafter, the military, acting in concert with the Indian Office, the territorial government of Arizona, cattle ranchers, miners, and land speculators, helped dispossess Hualapais of nearly six million acres of land. In less than twenty-five years after first encountering Anglo-Americans, Hualapais had lost more than half of their population and nearly all of their land, and they found themselves living on the fringes of a new society that cast them aside as vestiges of the past.

Such radical transformations characterized life for most Indigenous peoples by the late nineteenth century. Colonization and empire building marked much of American society at that time, and as scholars such as Amy Kaplan, Mathew Frye Jacobson, and NoeNoe K. Silva have shown, much of American history before and after the Indian Wars was a history of conquest and dispossession.[5] These processes reflected a larger constellation of beliefs about nonwhite peoples, their status within the nation-state, and the ways in which America expressed its power at home and abroad. As Hualapais confronted the traumas of military conquest and marginalization by Anglo settlers, the broad thrust of American empire had worked its way into Central America, the South Pacific, and Alaska, linking northwestern Arizona with U.S. expansion more generally. When "concerned citizens" in Mohave County demanded the allotment of the Hualapai Reservation in the 1880s and 1890s for cattle ranching, American fruit corporations waged a proxy war for the state by dismantling Hawaiian sovereignty. And when a pernicious system of blood quantum and racialization trapped Native people in a confusing limbo of noncitizen wardship during the early twentieth century, nativist fears barred Chinese, Japanese, and myriad "others" from entering the United States. In essence, expansion into the territorial Southwest was part of a larger expression of American power on the national and international stage.

Although stories of dispossession and subjugation are central to Hualapai history and the experiences of people of color caught in the maelstrom of empire, they challenge dominant beliefs about America's past, forcing us to reconsider the dominant narratives of American history. Well-known and patriotic histories of immigrant achievement, the progressive impulse to protect the weak, the ever-expanding access to voting and civil rights, and the liberal visions of a multicultural nation contribute to the pervasive and popular view that the United States stands as a beacon of hope and possibility in a world of failed nations and international rivalries. These heroic narratives are rooted in a vision of American history characterized by westward expansion and the growth of democratic institutions, rugged independence, and the ability of hard-working individuals to improve themselves without the weight of Old World customs or the state. Best articulated by Frederick Jackson Turner, a professor of history at the University of Wisconsin, in his 1893 speech at the Columbian Exposition in Chicago, these themes constitute an American imagination that if it acknowledges violence against Native cultures, it construes it as a necessary and acceptable byproduct of settling the West. Constructing physical violence against Indigenous nations as inevitable to expansion is tightly interwoven with the concomitant denial of sovereign peoplehood and the existence of Native communities as historical actors. Thus, the popular belief that Native peoples had to make way for the spatial expansion of the nation-state justifies the historical basis for contemporary inequalities.

According to Turner and the advocates of American exceptionalism who believe that progress justified Native dispossession, the Hualapais should not have survived what were nothing less than campaigns of ethnic cleansing and cultural genocide. And yet they did. Looking at westward expansion from the perspectives of Native people, we see an "invasion" that vaulted many smaller Native groups, especially those in the Southwest, Great Basin, and Colorado River region, into complex situations that strained their cultures, economies, religious beliefs, and political structures. Physical conquest preceded the creation of a colonial bureaucracy that sought the near total management and transformation of Indigenous peoples from independent nations into isolated individuals competing in a liberal capitalist society. Stripped of their autonomy and uncertain of their future, Hualapais managed to weather the racial violence of the nineteenth century and reconstitute their cultural values and institutions of government in the twentieth century while simultaneously preserving a shrunken land base and a language under attack.

Hualapais' emergence onto the regional and national political landscape is nothing short of astounding when considering that their numbers had dwindled by roughly 60 percent between 1850, when Anglos appeared, and 1902, when the Bureau of Indian Affairs established a subagency in Valentine, Arizona, near their reservation. A few examples bear out the significance of their story. In the 1880s, after suffering a generation of warfare and internment, Hualapai leaders convinced the military and federal government to create a reservation for them within their traditional homelands. Though one-sixth of their original territory, the 997,000-acre reservation ran along the Colorado River near their place of origin and rooted them in the landscape of their ancestors. However, within a few years Anglo ranchers and the Santa Fe Railway monopolized the springs on the reservation, and the railway claimed nearly a third of the Hualapais' land base. Living largely off the reservation, Hualapais sought wage labor jobs in new industries, maintained cultural ties with neighboring Mohaves and Chemehuevis, and eked out an existence on the margins of a new society. Hualapais reacted to these uncertainties by crafting political institutions such as the Walapai Indian Association to protest segregation in the schools and theft of their natural resources while fighting against ranchers and the Santa Fe Railway. They sought political support from organizations as diverse as the Mission Indian Federation and the Indian Rights Association, wrote letters and sent petitions to numerous presidents, and solicited legal aid from the famed legal scholar Felix Cohen in an attempt to protect their homelands. Nearly sixty years after the creation of the reservation, their activism bore fruit in 1941 when the U.S. Supreme Court ruled against the Santa Fe Railway and validated Hualapais' long-standing claims to their land.

As they moved to the reservation in greater numbers, Hualapai families and bands negotiated a new political identity as a tribe or, in the modern vernacular, a nation. Though not everyone embraced this conceptualization of themselves, the Hualapai nation was encoded in a new constitution and government that became an important marker of collective political identity. Hualapai leaders worked with other Native people during the post–World War II era to oppose termination and relocation legislation, participate in statewide economic development, and influence federal policy via the National Congress of American Indians. By the turn of the twenty-first century this small community had tried to build a dam on the Colorado River, rejected numerous overtures for uranium mining, established an internationally recognized bilingual education program, elected numerous women to office, and fought against diabetes, alcoholism, and youth gangs to carve a place for itself within a nation-state that generations before had displaced it. These and other astounding stories form the core of this book.

Based on more than a decade of archival research, interviews, and participant observation, *We Are an Indian Nation: A History of the Hualapai People* charts how thirteen bands of extended families known as the Pais confronted American colonialism and in the process recast themselves as a modern Indigenous nation. It is a story about a relatively little known community that confronted modernity and imperial projects that sought to displace it from the national landscape and erase it from the American imagination. The book takes a broad historical scope and uses colonialism and nationhood as its analytical lenses to emphasize survival and resistance during a two hundred–year confrontation with foreigners and the American nation-state. Such an approach offers a critical perspective on the long-term mechanics of Indigenous nation building and the institutional and cultural adaptations of one Native people to a colonial settler-state economy. This narrative structure allows for analysis of progressive shifts in band identification and the discursive boundaries of national identity as Hualapai social structures and political traditions adapted to changing circumstances. It illuminates enduring cultural traditions, connections to the landscape, and sustained acts of resistance and thus ties nineteenth-century freedom fighters such as Wauba Yuma and Schrum and recent tribal moves toward sovereignty and self-governance. Finally, it traces Hualapais' search for a national identity across multiple generations and their confrontations with American empire and modern colonialism from a perspective that typically might be circumscribed by a book with a narrower chronological scope. Though it is not the final word on their past, *We Are an Indian Nation* is grounded in Hualapai voices and agendas while simultaneously situating their history into a larger tapestry of Native peoples' confrontations with colonialism and modernity.[6]

## Conquest, Colonialism, and Nation Building

Most Americans do not like to think about their history in terms of colonialism, conquest, or empire, but these realities explain relationships between Hualapais and the individuals, institutions, and groups that took Native land in the nineteenth century and sought to control Hualapais' lives and resources in the twentieth. Much ink has been spilled over the precise meaning of these terms and the extent to which such expressions of power are susceptible to forces of resistance, but they nonetheless serve as key elements to this narrative of Hualapai history. While this book cannot resolve these disputes, it uses them in conjunction with nation building as organizational frameworks and analytical tools to narrate the history of one Indigenous community and offer insights into the ways in which power is expressed, contested, and reconstituted over time.

I argue that the broad processes of conquest and colonization that washed over the tribe in the mid-1800s—and continue to do so today—structure but do not wholly define the emergence of the Hualapais as a modern nation in the twentieth century. Conquest involves the physical and psychological domination of one group by another combined with the objective of controlling that subjected group through traditional means such as military force as well as more complex means such as political, biological, and cultural strategies.[7] Conquest frequently results in the destruction of Indigenous populations and their ways of life, or, at bare minimum, it profoundly compromises their social fabric, family relations, gender identities, and cultural productions. Colonialism stems from conquest and is defined by an exploitative relationship that perpetuates the inequalities ushered in by conquest through the presence of "colonies" of foreigners consuming Indigenous land and resources, and in the process it rearranges the political and cultural geographies of Indigenous peoples.[8] Colonial powers extract labor and tribute from subjected populations and denigrate Indigenous knowledge, religion, and spirituality. In addition, European American conquest and colonialism targeted Native gender roles and kinship networks in an attempt to assimilate men, women, families, and bands into European American social and cultural structures of radical individualism. Although both are typically associated with the initial contacts between European Americans and Native people, scholars such as Andrea Smith and Jennifer Nez Denetdale argue that conquest and colonialism are ongoing processes that transcend temporal and spatial boundaries. They continue through the twenty-first century in new forms and modern guises such as boarding school education, English-only laws, uranium mining, termination and relocation policies, and the theft of Indigenous knowledge about plants, medicines, and ecosystems.[9]

The conquests and cross-cutting colonialisms of European powers formed a tangle of interests and loyalties in what some scholars term the "New World" of post-Columbian America. In addition, the sometimes contradictory tendencies of colonialism—such as competing bureaucracies and the simultaneous validation and negation of Indigenous rights—created spaces for resistance, manipulation, and redefinition of the boundaries of colonial projects. Divergent political and economic interests within the colonizing society sometimes worked against each other as aboriginal people diverted the institutions of the colonizer, thus weakening the ultimate impact of the settler societies.[10] Simultaneously, colonialism created new identities as Pai bands cooperated against common threats of Anglo penetration into their lands, while in other scenarios some groups broke away and splintered into identities with ambiguous relationships with other Pai bands. Reactions ranging from resistance to submission press scholars toward a multidimensional interpretation of colonialism and conquest.[11]

Although this book views colonialism as an enduring force with manifestations in new and less physical forms such as modern liberalism and the attractive language of civil rights and integration, colonialism can be overly broad and difficult to connect to the internal dynamics of tribal communities. True, conquest and colonialism destabilized the micropolitics of Native communities, but claiming that the differences between Hualapai bands and families are the solitary function of the disruptive power of colonialism can deny those same families their diversity and individual agency. For example, many Hualapais wanted to build an eight-hundred-foot-tall dam on the Colorado River to generate electricity and to capture water for their reservation. A purely colonial analysis would argue that regional developers manipulated the Hualapai government into supporting the dam, but closer scrutiny reveals several important dimensions to this controversial project. First, some tribal members opposed the dam because it would flood twenty thousand acres of the reservation; second, Hualapai leaders saw few other viable solutions to the lack of water and electricity on the reservation. Hualapais disagreed about the dam because it was a drastic solution to their dire conditions and because Pai families and bands had the potential to respond differently to changes around them before the arrival of Europeans and Americans. Differences between tribal members and the tribal government had as much to do with traditional decentralization as with the neocolonial conditions in which Hualapais lived in the twentieth century. Thus, if colonialism is used to explain all internal community differences, it implies that preconquest Native peoples agreed upon everything, or, at bare minimum, it means that the structures of conflict mediation always resolved the same dilemmas. While acknowledging colonial dominance, a nuanced interpretation is necessary to recognize the multiple voices of the Hualapais.[12]

Focusing on colonialism and nation building also shifts attention away from old debates about agency versus victimization and assimilation versus cultural persistence that have occupied scholarship in American Indian history.[13] These important debates have nonetheless obscured other issues and frameworks that are central to understanding Indigenous histories such as imperialism, nation-state formation, globalization, liberalism, and racialization in the modern era. Colonialism and nation building also foreground the history of Indigenous peoples' struggles to reclaim the cultural sovereignty and political independence that came under assault with European American expansion into Native homelands. These new frameworks retain analytical room for enduring questions while stressing the "hidden transcripts" *and* public articulations of self-determination and Indigenous peoplehood.[14] The point of this book, then, is that colonization and persistence can exist in the same geographical and interpretive space.[15]

Such a reevaluation of American Indian historiography owes much to decolonization scholarship and decolonial narratives. At least since the 1980s a growing chorus of intellectuals have been formulating a critique of colonialism by drawing upon traditional Indigenous knowledge and a diverse range of postcolonial, subaltern, and "Fourth World" literatures. My understanding of decolonization is informed by scholars such as Vine Deloria, Jr., and Frantz Fanon as well as Native American, postcolonial, and subaltern studies intellectuals, all of whom have traced the historical and contemporary implications of colonialism upon oppressed peoples. Their work unmasks the economic, political, religious, and social institutions of colonialism. It calls into question various myths propagated by the West such as the inevitability of progress, racial hierarchies that privilege European Americans, the superiority of Christianity, and notions of scientific fact and objectivity. Decolonial scholarship argues that they are social constructs used by European Americans to facilitate and justify conquest and colonization. The expansion of the West into Indigenous lands was not ordained by a higher power but was a function of historical forms of capitalism and the accumulation of land, resources, and wealth into fewer and fewer hands. Notions such as progress made conquest seem more palatable in its alleged inevitability, even as the Europeans who wielded the concept also wielded the tools of Indigenous dispossession. Decolonization, then, reverses many of the dominant notions of the modern era and interrogates them from the perspectives of the people who were victimized by centuries of violence and upheaval. This angle of analysis also casts doubt upon the related notions of unbiased truth in history and universal knowledge. Finally, decolonization reveals the often unseen ways in which colonialism undermines Indigenous ways of thinking about and conceptualizing history, space, culture, and identity.[16]

More than a critique of the West or an illumination of victimization, decolonization points to the struggles of Indigenous peoples to reclaim lands, traditions, and a sense of collective purpose. It seeks a place of healing from historical trauma and violence while at the same time carving a space for indigeneity in the modern world.[17] In arguing for this decolonial approach, Dakota scholar Waziyatawin Angela Wilson in her pathbreaking *Remember This! Dakota Decolonization and the Eli Taylor Narratives* offers a powerful example of how Indigenous narratives challenge the "colonizer's" view of the world. She notes, "Colonial dominance can be maintained only if the history of the subjugated is denied and that of the colonizer is elevated and glorified." Elaborating on Wilson, Cree scholar Winona Wheeler claims that decolonization offers a "strategy for empowerment" that "entails developing a critical consciousness" about the cause(s) of oppression, the distortion of history, Native collaboration, and the degrees to which some tribal members have internalized colonialist ideas and practices.[18] Decolonization requires the awareness of the origins of conquest, the implications of exploitation, resistance to that oppression, and a recovery of traditions and memories that define Indigenous identity. It replaces the silences of history with clear demands for justice and new relationships of power that structure the ostensibly neutral world of academia.[19]

To the extent that this book, written by a non-Hualapai, non-Native scholar, can employ decolonization theory and help undo the long trajectory of colonialism, it seeks to make a small contribution to that effort. By providing a forum for listening to the voices of Hualapais as they adapted to and resisted changes around them, We Are an Indian Nation stands as a project of historical recovery and a hopeful story of Indigenous resistance to conquest and colonialism.[20] These narratives of anticolonial survival and the Hualapai nation's struggle with the conquests that began washing over them nearly two centuries ago form the core of this project.[21]

## Historiography and the Hualapai Nation

More than a century of scholarship on American Indian peoples has only hinted at the themes of colonialism and nation building. Numerous books employ "nation" in their titles but fail to evaluate the nature, scope, power, and significance of nationhood as it is historically constructed and contested. Similarly, scholars interested in nations and nationalism generally overlook these developments within Indigenous populations of the United States. This is striking because the number of monographs on non-Western nationalism is immense.[22] As noted earlier, scholars have typically focused on agency, victimization, resistance, and adaptation within the methodology of ethnohistory, which blends anthropology's interest in culture with the historian's concern for change and continuity over time. This approach is related to what has become known as the "New Indian History," which is less a distinct school of interpretation than an analytical sensibility that says Native people, rather than savages or victims, are complex historical actors who shape their own histories and have unique perspectives on the past. These two trends in the scholarship have made important contributions to the broader public's understanding of Indigenous people and their interactions with Europeans, but they are limited by an inattention to the internal political culture of nation building and the colonial context of domination within which nations construct themselves.

Beginning with thirteen Northeastern Pai bands composed of extended families in the mid-nineteenth century and tracking the twentieth-century embrace of the term "Hualapai Indian Nation," this book focuses on the crossroads between band identities, the notion of a tribe, and the popular term *nation*. "Indian nation," in particular, indicates Hualapais' sense of themselves as a politically, legally, culturally, and geographically distinct people. *We Are an Indian Nation* interrogates the historical development and construction of identity among the Hualapais in part by highlighting the ways community members have identified with each other and represented themselves to outsiders. This book makes an important contribution to the scholarship because only a few books have drawn from the literature on national identity and nationalism and applied it to Native peoples.[23] By national identity I mean an active sense of and investment in being a nation, which is a unit of social organization that includes political and cultural loyalties to a common group identity, top-down dictates and policies, and the bottom-up influence of the masses. Nations are products of memory, political structure, cultural artifact, and historical invention, common language, territoriality, and ancestry.[24] Moreover, the discourse of national identity can be rooted in traditional "face-to-face" relationships maintained by kinship ties or extralocal sociocultural networks or even impersonal "imaginings" of community facilitated by modern technologies.[25]

I see nations as products of historical moments and trends that reflect powerful internal and external forces, which in the case of the Hualapais involve their reorganization from decentralized peoples into more centralized entities with layered identities. Indigenous nations do not necessarily possess large populations, standing militaries, or bureaucratic states, but they do include literal and figurative boundaries and cultural borders, common origin stories, a mother tongue, and the assertion of some superiority over surrounding groups. Nations are modern constructs that gain power from their ability to explain and organize the world as it is perceived by groups subscribing to the common threads binding them together. This sense of being a nation is tied to nationalism, which is a politicized movement employing the rhetoric of the nation and the implicit commonality of interests to mobilize people for various purposes. Finally, nation building is the complex process of gaining control over the cultural, human, and natural resources of a people and using them in ways that further the survival of that nation.[26]

Whereas American Indian history and ethnohistory rarely address these issues, scholars of Native American and Indigenous studies, especially authors engaged in decolonization, have. Indigenous scholars such as Taiaiake Alfred and Jeff Corntassel only cautiously apply European-based definitions of nationhood to Native cultures. Rather, they offer the concept of "peoplehood," which is rooted in an "oppositional, place-based existence, along with the consciousness of being in struggle against the dispossessing and demeaning fact of colonization by foreign peoples. . . . [This] fundamentally distinguishes Indigenous peoples from other people in the world."[27] As such, Hualapais have faced modernity through the workings of colonial law, liberal democracy, capitalist development, and Western time to construct identities that reflect and reimagine preconquest relations with the land. This is not a primordial or essentialist vision of themselves but an organic sense of peoplehood articulated in lived experiences and ongoing struggles to hold onto land, history, and cultural homelands. They might agree with Partha Chatterjee, who reminds scholars using national identity to frame Indigenous histories that modern nationalisms rest on bifurcations of the religio-spiritual and material-physical worlds. Because colonizers have used strategies to "divide and conquer" the worlds of Indigenous peoples, scholars should not recolonize Native histories by making the same mistakes.[28]

Simultaneously, this book recognizes the liabilities of nationalism and nationhood, such as the growth of statelike characteristics within the Hualapai nation. Neocolonial constitutions and bylaws, ordinances, penal systems, police forces, multi-million-dollar budgets, and the bureaucracies that accompany them anchor Indigenous nations within a problematic global political landscape. As institutions that enforce the literal and discursive boundaries of the nation, modern states shape the histories of Indigenous communities. To quote Anthony Smith, "The ideal of the nation, transplanted across the globe from its Western heartlands, has brought with it confusion, instability, strife and terror, particularly in areas of mixed ethnic and religious character. . . . [N]ationalism offers a narrow, conflict-laden legitimation for political community, which inevitably pits culture-communities against each other."[29] Thus, scholars must confront the liabilities inherent within the status of nation, even as it serves an important analytical function.

Similar concerns come from Loretta Fowler's *Tribal Sovereignty and the Historical Imagination: Cheyenne-Arapaho Politics*, which hesitates at the adoption of colonial structures embedded within nationalism. Drawing from John and Jeanne Comaroff's notion of the "colonization of consciousness," Fowler argues that hegemony involves "the unconscious, unspoken, naturalized systems of control and dominance rooted in beliefs and assumptions about how the world works." She sees Indigenous nationhood as resistance to hegemony in that "subordinated peoples do not accept dominant economic, political, and religious structures passively. They may accommodate imposed institutions and absorb them into a reinvented tradition. They may also reconstruct dominant institutions in ways that are locally meaningful and that serve local ends. And they may contest and overtly resist dominant structures." Nationhood enables tribes to resist oppression just as easily as it reconstitutes new forms of domination.[30]

Historicizing Hualapai nationhood within their ongoing confrontation with colonialism requires multiple angles of analysis, from federal-Indian relations, to the interactions between Hualapai community members, to the tense and sometimes constructive meetings between tribal members and the surrounding settler society. The chapters that follow move back and forth between these overlapping narratives and competing voices. Some chapters rely almost entirely on non-Indigenous sources such as military reports and government documents, although these sources frequently include the words and impressions of Hualapai people. Many of the sources stem from the colonial relationship between Hualapais and the federal government that was and is epitomized by the Bureau of Indian Affairs. Despite the strained context of these sources, I have found numerous letters, speeches, petitions, and other expressions of Hualapais' views on contemporary reservation affairs. Other chapters draw from Hualapai materials such as Tribal Council minutes and the tribal newspaper, *Gum-U: The Hualapai Newsletter*, first published in the 1950s. Documents from court cases, affidavits from the Indian Claims Commission, and census reports have proven valuable sources for reconstituting Hualapai history. Finally, numerous oral histories offer Hualapais' views on the past.

Although this "national history" of the Hualapais follows some of the conventions used in tribal histories, I situate the chapters and issues they address within the historical particularities of the Hualapai people. Some mirroring of national events and shifts in policy is inevitable, but I have anchored the chapters to the political, cultural, social, and economic trends of the Hualapai nation. Chapter 1 starts with Pai origin stories and offers a sketch of their sociopolitical organization and leadership traditions, with an emphasis on decentralized band structures, land tenure, and relationship with the environment. In the 1850s the emergence of an Anglo settler-society bolstered by the might of the U.S. military radically altered the world of the Pais. Pai-Anglo confrontations exploded in 1865 with the murder of several prominent band leaders and the scorched-earth policies of Col. William Redwood Price. The violence continued despite an 1869 agreement ending the Hualapai Wars, as the military rounded up Pais and marched them to La Paz on the Colorado River Indian Reservation, where they remained until their escape in 1875.

The postinternment years, the focus of chapters 2 and 3, were marked by the colonization of Hualapai space, as band members adjusted to and resisted non-Hualapai laws and sociopolitical and economic institutions. Before the federal government established the reservation in 1883, Hualapais lived in a cultural borderland where competing laws, social expectations, bureaucratic institutions, and interest groups jockeyed for power and influence. Hualapai bands made decisions about their political identity as decentralized networks of families that were increasingly treated as a singular people by non-Indians in the region. Pais violated new laws as they practiced old ceremonies and hunted for food in spaces categorized as private property or public domain. They adjusted to industrialization and the market economy by seeking wage labor, using the new railroad to visit family and friends, and staking claim to old rights via new laws and relationships. With the creation of the reservation Hualapais could point to a protected space where they could build a collective economy, but the dual realities of Anglo monopolization of land and water on the reservation and the refusal of some band members to move there revealed interband political differences and the reality of an unusable reservation.

Chapter 3 focuses on the social and cultural implications of the colonization of Hualapai space. Although reservations draw the attention of most scholarship, this chapter analyzes the creative ways in which Pai bands nurtured ties to traditional territories by seeking allotments on the public domain and through the process of "recolonizing" emerging towns and Anglo settlements. Though never accepted by the settler society as racial equals, Hualapais negotiated relationships with ranchers and the Santa Fe Railway, which had penetrated their reservation one month after its creation in 1883; they avoided the full gaze of the Bureau of Indian Affairs by remaining beyond the jurisdiction of the superintendent; and they selectively took part in boarding school education while allying with Anglos who supported their claims to the reservation. Alternately, several bands remained uninterested not only in moving to the reservation but in subsuming their identity under "Hualapai," a term that stemmed from Anglo mispronunciation of the name of the Amat Whala Pa'a band east of Kingman.

Chapter 4 highlights Pai leaders fighting for land rights and self-determination as symbolized by Hualapais' critique of Indian Office policies and the actions of the Santa Fe Railway. Drawing upon theories of Native self-determination and nationalism, this chapter argues that Hualapais created hybrid political organizations to advocate for Indigenous land claims by using the language of tradition within a modern framework of law and private rights. Hualapai leaders such as Fred Mahone and Philip Quasula moved into the discursive spaces between band decentralization and the modern trend toward unified and hierarchical political action symbolized by the Walapai Indian Association and the allied Mission Indian Federation. These political developments marked a turning point in modern Hualapai national identity.

Chapter 5 covers Hualapai political culture in relationship to questions of citizenship and the discourse of national belonging. It charts the debate between Hualapais as individuals and as a collective and between Hualapais and the surrounding nation-state to reveal uncertainty about where Hualapais belonged in the early twentieth century. By integrating recent scholarly debates over citizenship with Hualapai peoplehood, this chapter analyzes the colonial contradictions of Hualapai status as individuals, as citizens of the American body politic, and as members of their own semisovereign nation spanning multiple spaces in Arizona, itself a territory of the United States until 1912. Tracking these complexities through the status of reservation and nonreservation Hualapais, their expectations of service during World War I, their ability to vote and gain access to public schools, and, later, the significance of the 1924 Indian Citizenship Act on Hualapai status forms the core of this chapter. I thread questions of status and national belonging through the 1930s and the imposition of an Indian Reorganization Act (IRA) government upon Hualapais who only recently were able to move to the reservation. This latter section analyzes how the neocolonial IRA government became the official framework of reservation government even though a minority of Hualapais voted for it. The deep post–World War II suspicions that Hualapais have toward their government are rooted in these developments of the 1930s.

Chapters 6 and 7 provide powerful examples of Hualapai nation building in local, regional, and national contexts. Starting with the 1941 Supreme Court victory against the Santa Fe Railway, chapter 6 traces the political and economic trends of a community that wanted to control its resources and, to quote one of its leaders, "move into the modern era." Western nations, shaken by global war and decolonization, entered into new relationships with marginalized populations such as Indigenous peoples. And Hualapais, like other Native nations in the United States, looked skeptically at overtures toward civil rights and integration because such agendas threatened their semiseparate status. Moreover, anti-Communist agendas, coupled with deepening individualism and cultural homogeneity as manifested in termination and relocation legislation, again placed Hualapais on the defensive. New generations of leaders such as Sterling Mahone, Rupert Parker, and Dallas Quasula confronted complex questions about economic development, unemployment, and the relationship between the booming Hualapai population and the Tribal Council, but they revised the constitution, expanded the powers of the government, opposed privatization of their lands, and worked toward more permanent sources of water and energy.

Throughout the 1960s and 1970s the Hualapais endured deepening poverty even as the Great Society expanded its reach. These new federal programs brought wages and services to the reservation but failed to alleviate the structural sources of underdevelopment caused by colonialism. Rather, the system of grant writing and the requirement that government programs be administered by "qualified" individuals increased dependency on "educated" non-Indians. Simultaneously, Hualapais waged a three-decade-long campaign to build Bridge Canyon Dam across the Colorado River in an effort to bring water and electricity to the reservation. Such confrontations revealed their exclusion from regional water compacts that allocated the water, which Hualapais could not use despite their reservation running along one hundred miles of the river. Despite congressional passage of "self-determination" legislation in the late 1970s as a reaction to radical activism and political lobbying, Hualapais continued to struggle with the local realities of colonialism.

The final chapters analyze recent Hualapai history with an eye toward the limits and possibilities of sovereignty and self-determination. Building on the critique of Great Society programs and legislation of the 1970s, chapter 7 highlights the importance of Hualapai women in tribal government and Native politics across Arizona and New Mexico. Women such as Lena Bravo, Lydia Beecher, Louise Benson, Lucille Watahomigie, and others managed the Hualapai government, made important decisions about the economy, and served as role models for Hualapai youth. Bright spots in the Hualapai economy emerged in the creation of the Hualapai River Runners, the only Native-owned and -operated rafting business on the Colorado River, and a world-renowned Hualapai language program. At the same time, the tribe came into direct conflict with the Grand Canyon National Park as the park asserted its perceived power along the Colorado River and into the Hualapai Reservation. This dispute highlighted ongoing colonialism because the Grand Canyon National Park, much like the Santa Fe Railway, ignored Hualapais' claims to Indigenous spaces, despite origin stories and tribal memories. Devaluing Hualapais as legitimate owners of the land while deploying the powers of the state to alienate them from the river and their cultural identity revealed the hegemonic powers of contemporary American governance.

Chapter 8 connects the local changes of the post-self-determination era with the regional and national political economy of a globalizing world. By situating Hualapais' struggles for independence within the twin processes of decolonization and the "new federalism" of the Reagan-Clinton-Bush eras, this chapter balances the perspectives of Hualapais coping with deregulation and privatization while addressing the efforts of the Hualapai government to navigate a global economy. Environmental racism, regional development, and the implications of NAFTA were part of the neoconservative attack on Native sovereignty that accompanied the election of President Ronald Reagan and typified the work of Secretary of the Interior James Watt and Washington Senator Slade Gorton. Hualapais rejected privatization and creeping federalism as well as overtures for uranium mining and fought for a local economy based on government employment, increasing education, and the often volatile tourist industry. In particular, Hualapais embarked on a controversial relationship with David Jin, a Chinese American business-man, to build the Hualapai Skywalk on the western end of the reservation. Completed in 2007, the Skywalk represents the complexities of Native life in the twenty-first century: it was an unpredictable alliance created from economic desperation and bold decision by a tribe that has surmounted incredible obstacles.

The conclusion reflects on the significance of Hualapai history for Hualapais, the academic community, and the larger American imagination. While returning to and reframing the importance of Hualapai nationhood, the conclusion evaluates the frameworks at the core of this book: nationalism and national identity. Both concepts stress commonalities and converging identities through the process of boundary making, yet they implicitly mute the internal historical diversity of the Hualapai people. The conclusion meditates on the structural inequalities created by a colonial economy and an American political system that alternately tried to assimilate, marginal-ize, and erase Indigenous people. Moreover, it investigates the process of writing this book and relationships with the Hualapais, keeping an eye on the politics of writing across cultures and from positions of privilege and inequality. By emphasizing the limits of historical narrative while also analyzing the parameters of representation, the conclusion offers a measured sense of optimism for future collaborations between Indigenous peoples and academic researchers.

# From Origins to La Paz

So, each family left one by one, they came out of the canyon and
. . . they roam[ed] across this country. There were twelve people
and this one Indian settled in I guess it was Peach Springs right here
and said, "Well, I'm going to be a Walapai, I'm going to be here
and multiply." And the others, they went on saying they were Hopi
Indians now, and the Navajos and the others they went on and they
call themselves different tribes of Indians.[1]

## Origins and Homelands

The white granite bluffs of Spirit Mountain rise from the desert floor at the
Colorado River near what today is known as Davis Dam. Just north of the
point where Arizona, Nevada, and California meet, Spirit Mountain is the
place of origin for the Hualapais. In one account of Pai origins narrated in
Hualapai by elder Paul Talieje, when time began, water flooded the earth
and washed away the homes and gardens of the People. After the torrent
subsided, one man remained atop a mountain called Wikahme', or Spirit
Mountain. The man grew old and believed his death was imminent until
Dove brought instructions from Matavila, the Creator, to drain the ocean
with the horn of a mountain sheep and then dig a hole in the ground. As
the man did this the water drained away, and slowly the hills, plains, and
deserts emerged into the sunlight.[2]

After the old man passed away the Doer of Things, Giver of Life created
the Earth-Brothers to care for the land. Madvil, the older brother, was the
Steward of the Old, while Judaba:h, the younger brother, was known as the

Steward of the New. One night Madvil had a dream that instructed them to gather canes from the Colorado River, scrape them clean, and then place them in a large pile on the riverbank. They did this and went to sleep but were awoken by laughter the following day. Seeing dozens of people milling about, Madvil addressed them: "Thus it has happened; this has come about; and thus you are, you have come about. Be good; live a proper life; you be good; since you are related to each other, be friends with each other." Madvil continued by instructing them to cooperate, avoid confrontations, resist vengeance, and think positive thoughts. Judaba:h then told the people to find good places to live where the soils were fertile and water was plentiful. Talieje recounted the Creator's words:

> You Hualapai, you, Hualapai
> This is what your name is going to be.
> Nowhere, no far away lands, different lands
> Some strange lands belonging to others,
> You are not to go or be anywhere.
> Here, the water that lies here, the land here
> The land along this river, here you roam here
> Be around here, you are to be here, it is destined.

He told them to use the water for their plants and cut the wood for their homes. Yet the lands became crowded, and Pais moved around, never far from Madwida, their birthplace on the Colorado River.[3]

Whereas Paul Talieje talks of the creation, Elnora Mapatis recounts stories about the differentiation of the people in the region. Mapatis was born in 1903 in Hackberry, Arizona, where she learned Pai stories, songs, and traditions from her elders. In her recounting she says that many people remained in Madwida. They grew corn, squash, and beans and gathered agave, yucca, and piñon nuts for food, but life for the People changed when a fight broke out one day. A small disagreement grew after an individual lashed out at someone, their relatives became angry, and someone died in the ensuing melee. As punishment, the Creator told the people to leave their homes in Madwida. "From now on our language will not be one, from now on we all will leave and scatter one by one. When we come out at the rim, just continue on your way by foot. You will settle throughout the land." Some made their homes in Supai, while others journeyed on to present-day Tuba City or farther east, as did the Zunis and Acomas. Apaches went to White River, and Yavapais went south with the Cocopas and Maricopas. When they reached their homes they announced their arrival: "Mah, I will remain Hualapai, I will be Havasupai, I will be Hopi, I will be Navajo." The people built homes, hunted, grew crops, and looked for water. "The people went and settled throughout the land," Elnora asserted. "Do you understand this? This is the way it was."[4]

As these stories denote, Spirit Mountain and the Colorado River are sacred places for the Hualapais, Havasupais, Mojaves, Dieguenos, Yavapais, Quechans, Maricopas, and Pai Pais, all of whom claim the area in their origin stories. The stories have an important literal and metaphorical place in Pai society because they deemphasize linear time and teach people about Pai worldviews. The stories refer to unique places in both the past and present and in doing so create cultural landscapes that explain behavior, impart morals, and often mark the boundaries of the community itself.[5]

The stories suggest that Pai peoples inhabited a vast cultural homeland that encompassed six million acres of land in northwestern Arizona at the southwestern edge of the Colorado Plateau (see fig. 1.1). As reflected in their origins and symbolized by Pais' refusal to be relocated, the landscape is striking in its combination of high desert plateau, mountains covered in pine trees, and deep canyons cutting into the Colorado River. Mountains and volcanic cones such as the San Francisco Peaks rise above the plateau, which falls precipitously at the Mogollon Rim and cuts across Arizona, dividing the plateau in the north from the Basin and Range Province of the south.[6] These features contributed to the cultural borderlands of the Pais in northwestern Arizona. To the north the Colorado River and Grand Canyon divided Pais from Southern Paiutes, although the two groups did trade extensively across the river. The Peach Springs–Diamond Creek runoff system combines with other gorges and streams to feed into the Colorado River. To the west the Black Mountains and Colorado River bordered Northeastern Pais and Mohaves and Chemehuevis. At the southern edge of Pai territory the Bill Williams River system receives water from the Big Sandy and Santa Maria rivers and divides the Northeastern Pais from their linguistic relatives, the Yavapais. The eastern stretches of Hualapai territory cross the Little Colorado River and overlap land of their allies, the Hopis and Navajos, with whom Hualapais share a common reverence for the San Francisco Peaks.[7]

Low levels of rainfall characterize the American Southwest and shape the social, cultural, and economic institutions of the region. Northwestern Arizona straddles three climactic zones: a mountainous, snow-covered mountain region; a canyon land region; and a high desert region. Despite spring thaws and summer cloudbursts, the northern sections of Pai land receive less than fifteen inches of rain per year. Altitudes in the region range from one thousand feet at the bottom of the Grand Canyon to seven thousand at the highest point on the reservation. Summer temperatures exceed

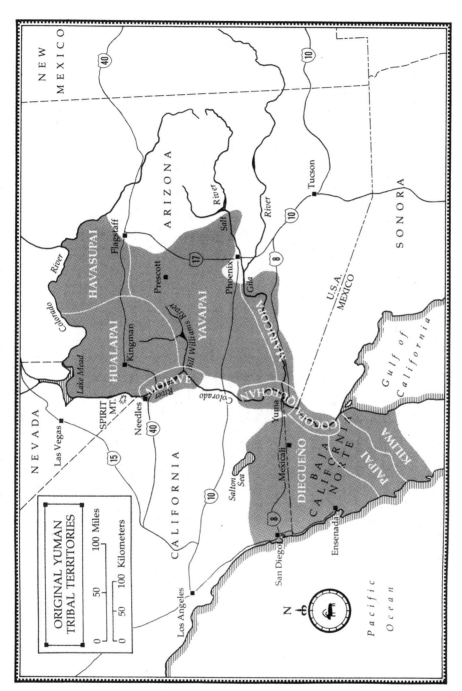

FIGURE 1.1. Original Yuman tribal territories. Hinton and Watahomigie, *Spirit Mountain*, 4.

one hundred degrees, and winters drop into the single digits. Chaparral and high desert grasslands cover most of the valleys and basins. Prickly pear, saguaro, barrel cactus, and agave as well as southwestern species like mesquite, creosote, and paloverde provided people with food and fuel. Juniper, pine, oak, and walnut covered higher elevations.[8]

Utilizing and revering this stunning landscape, Indigenous peoples in the region inhabited a dynamic world of trade and cultural exchange. Precontact anthropological evidence is scarce, but the triangulation of ethnographic materials, oral histories, and secondary sources paints a picture of a large network of Indigenous peoples living across the modern American Southwest and northern Mexico.[9] Evidence of Pai habitation in northwestern Arizona stems from excavations along the Colorado River that reveal numerous styles of pottery and objects of material culture originating from other societies. Bits of vessels resembling Puebloan pottery from northern New Mexico indicate that they traded with people who traded with the Pais. Tools and objects indicate that Pais obtained goods from Chemehuevis, Mohaves, people from southern California, and Hopis. Evidence also places Pais in the center of a trade network extending from the Pacific Ocean to eastern New Mexico and from Nevada and Utah to Mexico.[10]

Pais maintained their own local economies through light agriculture and seasonal migration around a tightly defined landscape. Thirteen Pai bands comprised of extended families enjoyed a range of wild game and plants, roots, and berries. Hualapai elders in the late twentieth century recalled eating agave, yucca, and *sele'*, three favored plants common to the region. During the hottest days of August families woke up before sunrise to gather the fruit of the prickly pear cactus, which they used throughout the year. In the fall Pais gathered piñon nuts to roast and store for the winter. As winter ended and the spring thaws arrived, the people began the yearly cycle again.[11] Men hunted game as the primary source of protein for Pai dietary needs. Pais enjoyed a diverse diet, coupled with physical activity and intimate knowledge of local medicines and herbs.[12]

The Pai bands that lived across present-day northwestern Arizona are the ancestors of the modern Hualapai nation, which is part of the Pai language group (see fig. 1.2). The name Hualapai comes from an English translation of the name of a Pai band, Amat Whala Pa'a, which Anglos used to identify all Northeastern Pai bands. Linguists place Hualapais in the Yuman language group, which is divided into two groups called the River Yuman Family, which includes Mohaves, Maricopas, and Quechans, and the Delta–California Yuman Family, which includes the Dieguenos and Cocopas. The Yuman language group covered a vast territory, encompassing

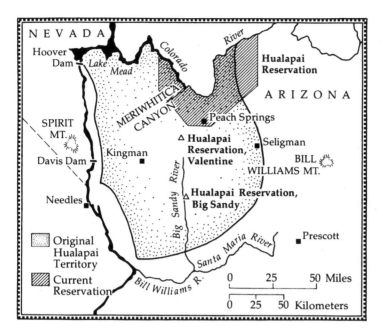

FIGURE 1.2. Aboriginal Hualapai territory and current reservation. Hinton and Watahomigie, *Spirit Mountain*, 12.

several states and crossing the current international border.[13] Despite the linguistic similarities, Northeastern Pais perceived themselves as different from Yavapais based on territorial occupancy, social behavior, competition for land, and belief systems. Pais constructed an ethnic boundary around themselves that consisted of particular traits, institutions, behaviors, beliefs, and geographic spaces. Self-references even denoted this sense of superiority to others, as seen in translations of the word *pai* and its derivations, *paya* and *paia*, all of which mean "the People."[14]

The sociocultural and political structure of the Northeastern Pai had elicited considerable debate among scholars in the late twentieth century. Henry F. Dobyns and Robert C. Euler in their 1970 publication *Wauba Yuma's People* claimed that thirteen bands (including the Havasupais) of Northeastern Pais "conceived of themselves as belonging to one of three sub-tribes," which encompass several bands in a specific region. Bands in turn centered on topographical features such as a spring, mountain, or plateau. In this schema the Middle Mountain subtribe lived at the bend in the Colorado where the river turns southward from its western course. The Red Rock band

and Cerbat Mountaineers constituted the people in this subtribe, which covered approximately 1,850 square miles of cliffs, plateaus, and high desert country. The much larger aggregation, the Plateau people, lived east of the Middle Mountain subtribe and covered an immense area past the point where the Little Colorado River branches southward from the Colorado River. This group was comprised of the Grass Springs, Clay Springs, and Hackberry Springs bands, just south of the Colorado River. They lived in the canyons for part of the year and often met with Southern Paiutes on the Colorado River. Other bands were the Milkweed Springs band, the Peach and Pine Springs bands, and the Cataract Canyon band to the east. The northeasterly bands constituted part of the Havasooa Pa'a, or people of the Blue Green Water, who became known as the Havasupais and who split from other bands as Anglo encroachment increased in the late 1800s. These easterly bands had the greatest contact with Hopis.[15] The Yavapai Fighter subtribe lived farthest to the south, extending all the way to the Bill Williams and Santa Maria rivers. They received their name from their role on the front line of contact with the Yavapais. The Juniper Mountaineers lived slightly to the east, while the Mahone Mountaineers lived west of them. The Big Sandy band lived in a strip of territory between the Mahone Mountaineers to the east and the Walapai Mountaineers to the west.[16]

Dobyns and Euler's rigid configuration of band, subtribe, and tribe is problematic on several levels. First, it is rooted in a long-critiqued structuralist theory of anthropology that fails to explain the highly decentralized nature of Pai society. Second, it uses evidence and points to events from the Hualapai Wars, in particular, the ability of leaders such as Schrum to coordinate large-scale attacks against Anglos, to support its hierarchical model. Dobyns and Euler argue that Schrum's marshaling of men would have been impossible without the subtribe category of social organization. Yet their schema has elicited critiques from scholars and Hualapais themselves because it rests on a singular moment in postconquest time and ignores the diverse agendas of Pai bands.[17] It does not, however, obscure the reality that individual bands had particular affinities toward each other that they did not have with other bands that, for example, lived some distance from them. For example, the Burro Creek band was, arguably, part of the South people (Koowev Kopai) and lived at the southern tip of Big Sandy band territory. They farmed and lived along streams and throughout canyons and plateaus on both sides of Burro Creek. They even intermarried with the Yavapais, with whom they were mistaken by Anglos entering the region during the 1850s.[18] The Big Sandy band lived in a region shaped by the river and parallel to mountain ranges draining water into the river. The Aquarius Cliff escarpment of the plateau on the east and the Hualapai Mountains on the west shaped the cultural ecology of this band.[19]

Dobyns and Euler's configuration also does not properly account for Pai ties to the land and the violence of conquest. West of and including the Hualapai Mountains was the Amat Whala Pa'a band, the name of which became associated with all Northeastern Pais. This band lived from the Hualapai Mountains east of Kingman, west to the Mohave bands straddling the Colorado River. As testimony of the enduring attachment of Hualapais to these preconquest homelands, one man testifying to the Indian Claims Commission in the 1950s recalled: "There was a lot of Hualapai families that lived in this area. South of Beale Springs . . . before the white man came there was a lot of Indians . . . Hualapai Indians."[20] Auggie Smith reiterated memories of his father regarding Whala Pa'a life: "When they got their food in the basin on the right side of Kokame', they went down to the Colorado River to get their water. . . . They went there because they owned that country, too, and they have a right to it without any fear from anything."[21] Numerous Pais today recall the memories of their grandparents who had direct ties to the ancestors living in these stolen lands.

To the northeast the Pine Springs and Peach Springs bands contained roughly ninety people each in the late 1860s after the military decimated many of their relatives to the south. Havasooa Pa'a (Havasupai) bands have been estimated at 175–250 people, a number similar to the Big Sandy band before the Hualapai Wars. The latter suffered high casualty rates during the 1860s and lost members to disease, while the former remained relatively unscathed during the height of Anglo invasions. In turn, they began a steady process of ethnic splintering that the Indian Office facilitated when it created a different reservation for the Havasupai band in the early 1880s. Cerbat Mountaineers to the west apparently coalesced with the Red Rock band during this volatile period, thus reducing its population.[22] Such examples demonstrate the breadth and scope of Pai living patterns and the depth of attachment to the land before the arrival of Europeans and Americans.

## The Spanish Colonial and Mexican Eras, 1530s–1848

This sociopolitical and cultural world was indirectly impacted by the emergence of Spain and Mexico. Few Spaniards actually ventured into the Pai homeland, but trade with Hopis, Yavapais, Mohaves, and groups along the Colorado River introduced the Pais to European material goods, tools, and animals. By the seventeenth century Spanish colonial society was a market for Indigenous goods and labor, and this altered the flow of trade across the region.[23] Europeans also impacted Pai society as smallpox, influenza, and measles ravaged Native populations, and pigs, sheep, goats, and cattle transformed land-use patterns for centuries. Guns and horses altered old forms of movement and methods of providing food and sustenance for Native families. These forces transformed Pai culture before the first American trappers and explorers entered Pai homelands.[24]

Spanish records provide limited documentation of Native peoples and their reactions to European colonists. Explorers skirted the Pai homelands, favoring the lower Colorado River and regions south of the Gila River or east of the Little Colorado River. In the wake of Álvar Núñez Cabeza de Vaca's penetration into Texas in 1528, a few non-Natives ventured into present-day Arizona. The *entrada* of Cabeza de Vaca into perhaps the southeastern section of Arizona fueled ensuing explorations into the region.[25] Francisco Vásquez de Coronado in 1540 led nearly three hundred Spaniards and one thousand Indians out of the present-day Southwest as far north as central Kansas. Several lieutenants branched off to extend the reach of Coronado's exploration. Melchor Díaz crossed the Colorado River into California, García López de Cárdenas became the first Spaniard to see the Grand Canyon, and Hernando de Alarcón entered the Colorado River Delta and probably reached the Gila River. During this excursion Southern Yumans most likely saw their first Europeans in Alarcón and his men. Alarcón questioned the Yumans, peoples he labeled "Quicama and Coana," about their sexual practices, healing methods, and warfare, built a crude chapel at the mouth of the river, and left the region in 1542, ending the Spanish presence for another forty years.[26]

In the 1580s Antonio de Espejo, a wealthy *peninsulare* merchant, led a dozen soldiers and one hundred Zunis to find minerals in north-central Arizona. After trading with Hopis he claimed the region for Philip II of Spain and then went in search of silver and copper deposits east of Prescott. Piqued by the possibility of wealth, the Spanish initiated a more organized expedition across northern Arizona led by Marcos Farfán de los Godos, who traveled with Juan de Oñate to northern New Mexico in 1598. Farfán and his Hopi guides traveled west across the Little Colorado River until they met people he referred to as "Jumana Indians," possibly Yavapais, the Juniper Mountain bands of Pais, or northwestern Apaches. They led the explorers to the Verde River, which Farfán said had "splendid pastures, fine plains, and excellent land for farming." Farfán then traveled southward to the silver mines near present-day Jerome.[27]

With a foothold in northern New Mexico, Oñate wanted to establish a route to the "South Sea" past the mines Farfán visited in 1598. In 1599 Oñate sent Vicente de Zaldívar on an unproductive journey, but a more fruitful trip began in 1604, when Oñate ordered Father Francisco de Velasco to find the South Sea. Eventually, Oñate himself went through Yavapai territory and then down the Bill Williams and Colorado rivers to the Gulf of California, where Alarcón had visited sixty years ago. Oñate's party noted five "tribes" between the Gulf and the Gila River (the Kohuanas, Halyikwamais, Coco-pas, Halchidomas, and Amacavas), but he quickly returned east.[28]

Interaction between Yuman peoples and Europeans would not occur again for generations as Spanish missionaries focused on the Sonoran Desert to the south. A second wave of Spanish penetration into the Colorado River region came in 1694, when Jesuit priests such as Eusebio Kino left the Pimería Alta to convert Indians along the Gila and Colorado rivers. In 1702 he made contact with the O'odhams, Maricopas, Quechans, and Cocopas, baptized the sick, discussed diplomatic relations, and asked about geography. Kino never reached Yavapai or northeastern Pai homelands, but in 1743 Father Ignacio Keler ventured into Yavapai lands long enough to provoke a brief skirmish.[29]

Franciscans inherited the Jesuit missions in the 1760s and continued efforts to make contact with Colorado River peoples. Francisco Garcés became the most well known due to his travel along the Colorado River in the 1770s. In 1776 people whom he called "Jaguallapais" led Garcés to Havasupai Canyon, where they introduced him to several families. Garcés was one of the first Spaniards to spend time with Pai bands in the Grand Canyon, but he did not suggest missionary activity among them. After leaving, he reached Hopi villages but turned around and founded a mission in Quechan homelands in 1780.[30] Garcés's journal entries for his time in Pai country indicate that he camped in territory claimed by the Truxton Canyon or Hackberry band northeast of present-day Kingman. He seems to have discriminated between Western Apaches and various Pai groups by referring to the latter as "Yabipai," rather than some derivation of Apache. He also distinguished the "Yabipais" from the "Coninas" (the Hopi word for the Havasupais, or the most northeastern band of Pais) and "Walapais." He used the term "Yabipais" to refer to southern Pais, probably the Juniper Mountain, Big Sandy, and Mahone Mountain bands, and "Jaguallapais" for the Hualapai Mountain band to the north.[31] Despite Garcés's experiences in northern Arizona, he and other Franciscans built missions across the Colorado River, south of the Gila junction. In 1780 local groups rose up and killed Garcés and ended eighteenth-century Indigenous-Spanish interaction in northwestern Arizona.[32]

The failure of Spanish colonialism in northwestern Arizona did not limit the spread of European horses, guns, tools, food, and religious beliefs across the region.[33] The ripple effect of these transformations did not, according to Edward Spicer, fundamentally change the "aboriginal ways of life" for communities along the Colorado River. One dynamic that did considerably alter Indigenous communities was their integration into a vast system of horse raiding and human trafficking. To acquire horses, Indigenous communities often cooperated with the demands of Catholic missions. Raiding parties north of the O'odhams, who had stronger ties with the Spanish, stole horses from the missions, brought them north, and "traded" them for captives to bring south. By the 1820s Yavapais were raiding horses from Sonoran ranchers, one hundred miles to the south, and, not unlike the Navajos, Comanches, and Apaches, took the animals back home, only to have them stolen by Mohaves or Northeastern Pais. In return, Yavapais stole cattle and horses that Northeastern Pais had acquired from Hopis.[34]

The search for horses and cattle involved human captives as leverage to acquire an increasingly valuable commodity and marker of wealth. In *Captives and Cousins* James Brooks discusses a vast slave trade that had emerged by the 1740s, when Spanish communities demanded Indian labor in northern Sonora.[35] Their need for workers increased as European diseases killed off Indigenous people. This stream of human labor flowed southward along the Colorado River through Quechan and O'odham lands and then to the Spanish markets farther in the interior. The Spanish demand for labor far outstripped the preexisting practices of Native people as slave raiding became a goal itself rather than a byproduct of territorial disputes.[36]

While Spain tried to strengthen its claim to its northern frontier, a borderland that it destabilized through its acceptance of the slave trade, it had already begun to experience vast convulsions that ended in independence.[37] As land switched hands from colonial empire to new republic in the 1820s, the borderlands witnessed an even greater polarization of resources as Indians suffered the most, falling to the lowest rung of the economic ladder. Native communities once associated with missions experienced greater poverty and alienation and, in turn, fought back against liberalization policies promoted by the Mexican republic. Moreover, events in the United States also began to impact Indigenous people in the borderlands.[38]

With the Spanish empire in tatters, Thomas Jefferson sent Lewis and Clark to the recently purchased Louisiana Territory, an area that doubled the size of the United States. Trappers and mountain men crisscrossed land recently claimed by the new republic, and several of these individuals, now enshrined in the American imagination, traversed in and around Pai lands. James O. Pattie, a trader from Missouri, ambled through central Arizona and went northward along the Colorado River. After angering Mohaves in 1824, Pattie approached the site of present-day Parker Dam and, after turning eastward, reported encounters with Yavapais or Havasupais. In 1826 Jedediah Smith spent several weeks with Mohaves on the Colorado River, while William "Old Bill" Williams, born in North Carolina and raised in Missouri, spent time in northwestern Arizona during the 1830s before wandering through northern sections of the Little Colorado River.[39]

By the mid-1830s, as individual speculators and explorers crisscrossed Mexico's northernmost frontier, the region experienced another convulsion in the form of Texan independence. Mexico suffered a cataclysmic blow when an American military force crossed into its territory in 1846 and sparked the U.S.–Mexico War. After a brief yet bloody war that ended in 1848 with the Treaty of Guadalupe Hidalgo, hundreds of thousands of Mexicans citizens became American citizens. However, many of these people were culturally and ethnically Indigenous, though Mexico's inclusion of them as citizens of the nation erased their legal and political nationhood. Now in the United States, their status, rights, and identities underwent radical changes.[40]

## Anglo Invasions and the U.S.–Hualapai Wars

With the signing of the Treaty of Guadalupe Hidalgo, Pais confronted succeeding waves of westward-bound immigrant trains, military expeditions, miners, trappers, and traders interested in the resources of this new territory of the United States.[41] U.S. Army mapping explorations out of Santa Fe, such as the one led by Capt. Lorenzo Sitgreaves in 1851, foreshadowed a new era of conquest. Sitgreaves entered Pai lands to determine their amenability to a possible railroad, and his guide received a welcome befitting the party's objectives. Men from either the Cerbat Mountain or Hualapai Mountain band shot the guide. In November the expedition camped in the area around Truxton Springs, which was one of two main springs used by the band of the same name. Members of the band tried to take mules from the party but were confronted by one of the men in the expedition. The camp erupted into activity, and roughly a dozen Pais fled as the Anglos shot at their backs. Other military explorers, such as François Xavier Aubry in 1853 and Lt. Amiel W. Whipple in 1854, elicited similar reactions.[42]

Despite Pais' rejection of these frontline representatives of empire, in 1857 Lt. Joseph C. Ives, an engineer for the Department of War, entered Pai country to determine if a recently created wagon road named after "pioneer" Edward F. Beale would suffice as a train route. Ives's Mohave guide made reference to the Amat Whala Pa'a band of Pais, also known as the Pine

Mountain people, who lived in the vicinity. Ives misunderstood the reference and thought Amat Whala Pa'a was the name for all Pais, not just one band. When Ives submitted the *Report: Colorado River of the West Explored, 1857 and 1858* in 1861, he set the foundation for the false premise that the term "Hualapai" applied to all Pai bands.[43]

And yet, as he stumbled through Pai lands in 1857 Ives requested help surveying canyons leading to the Colorado River. Once his Mohave assistant, Ireteba, found "some Hualpais tractable enough to enlist for a few days in our service," Ives described the men in ethnocentric terms common to the era: "They were squalid, wretched looking creatures with . . . large joints, and diminutive figures but had bright eyes and cunning faces, and resembled a little the Chemehuevies." Dr. Mollhausen, the group physician, suggested that they take one of the men and "preserve him in alcohol as a zoological specimen." After the guides and Ireteba talked, Ives thought they were "recounting their personal histories from birth to the present date," but when the conversation ended, the assistant told Ives that the Hualpais knew little about the region. After Ives offered gifts "one of them recollected where he was" and led them to water.[44]

Upon reaching the Colorado River, Ives observed cliffs, chasms, and canyons that would have been dangerous for the group had it not been for the Pai guides, who may have been from the Milkweed Springs, Grass Springs, or Peach Springs band. Ives followed the men, which he now thought "were of great assistance," since they seemed "perfectly at home" among the blind turns and precipitous drops. When the group entered a Pai camp near the river, Ives was surprised that the women, probably from the Peach Springs band, "went on with their work without taking the slightest notice of us." Around the fifth of April Ives walked to the bed of the Diamond River (Diamond Creek) and stood in awe at the thousand-foot cliffs, which Ives thought "perhaps the most splendid exposure of stratified rocks that there is in the world." A week later Ives went eastward, never to return.[45]

Pais confronted other Anglos, most of whom brought with them the institutions and force of an expanding nation. Perhaps the most influential was Lt. Edward F. Beale, who in 1857 first brought a caravan into Pai lands while building a wagon road from the Upper Rio Grande Valley to California. The wagon road was based on a trail used by Pais and Mohaves, and it became a major artery for immigrants. But by 1858 west-bound travelers on Beale's wagon road forced Mohaves, Yavapais, and Northeastern Pais into a defensive war to protect their villages and crops. A man in Beale's caravan by the name of Rose wrote in his journal that "from there to the Colorado River we were continually harassed and shot at by them. Many of our horses and cattle were wounded, also one man, whom I sent back from Savedra's spring." In another incident in August 1859 a group of Mohaves killed eight migrants in retaliation for the deaths of band members. When a military detachment attacked, the Mohaves backed off.[46]

Conflict between immigrants and Indigenous peoples was not uncommon, but sometimes the depravity of the intruders was. The case of Lieutenant Beale proves illustrative especially because he inhabits a revered position in the historical memory of non-Indians in the region. In late 1859, after two years fighting with Pais and Mohaves opposed to the wagon trail, Beale decided to "play a good joke on the Indians." After Pais killed a mule from one of his caravans, Beale had several men hide and attack the individuals as they went for the dead animal. He recorded the incident in his journal: "Just as we had expected, our red brothers came down to see the mule they had killed, and what damage besides they had done to us, when our party fell upon them and killed four, returning to camp before it was ready to start in the morning, bringing bows, arrows, and scalps as vouchers." One of the icons of Mohave County then noted that "it was a good practical joke—a merrie jest of ye white man and ye indian."[47]

These initial conflicts brought the military into the region in an attempt to end resistance to westward expansion. In 1859 the army established Fort Mohave at Beale's crossing on the Colorado River in the middle of Mohave country, adjacent to Pai lands. Fort Mohave was the central command for western Arizona, situated at the crossroads of the Colorado River and the trading routes connecting the Southwest to the nation.[48] After a brief lull in the military buildup at the fort, the end of the Civil War portended great changes for Native peoples in the Southwest because it enabled the federal government to concentrate on conquest and because ex-soldiers and civilians moved west in greater numbers, hoping to find land as compensation for service. To this end Union troops established Fort Whipple outside of Prescott in December 1863, and in early 1864 officials for the new territory reached the outpost. Crews constructed a wagon road between Prescott and Fort Mohave, linking the capital with the Colorado River and the Gulf of California and the Pacific Ocean. Steamboats traveled along the Colorado River and landed at Hardyville, a port near Fort Mohave, as wagons hauled supplies to Prescott and other emerging towns.[49]

By the mid-1860s the cultural landscape of the Northeastern Pais was a racially charged and fluid ethnic frontier. Pais, Mohaves, Chemehuevis, and Yavapais would have been concerned by the emergence of strangers into their lands, but these people brought tools, wagons, horses, guns, and other implements that were useful to them. Moreover, some non-Indians established trade relationships and learned Native languages and cultural practices, while some Native leaders tried cooperating with the newcomers. Pauline Weaver and Hualapai Charley were examples of "cultural mediators" and diplomats between the groups. A Tennessean, Weaver worked for the Hudson's Bay Company and arrived in the region in the 1830s, working as a trapper, scout, and "Indian negotiator" between the military and western Arizona Indians such as the Hualapais. Hualapai Charley was the half-brother of Schrum, a prominent band leader, and he tried to convince his people not to attack wagon trains in the region.[50]

But these moments of cooperation died a quick death as violence engulfed the region, as recollected by Hualapais a generation removed from the events. A member of the Whala Pa'a band, Auggie Smith was born at Walnut Creek (Tak Tadapa) in 1876. His father was Amutoo' and was related to "Chief" Leve Leve. Perhaps the eldest living member interviewed for the Indian Claims Commission in the 1950s, Smith narrated conquest as told to him by his father Smith: "When the white people first came in, they came with soldiers, and they shot down every one of them. . . . [T]his was the first time white men came. They came from the east killing from water to water until they came to this place. The white people did this."[51] Echoing Smith's story, another Hualapai recalled stories from his mother: "The first settlers came to Big Cane Springs [in the Big Sandy region to the south]. These first settlers were friendly, they don't molest us very much. But finally other white families and white ranchers came and took over this whole valley, our gardens, our homes. We didn't give this country up voluntarily. We were just overrun by white people taking up the springs, the grass, the gardens and all of this territory. We never gave up anything: these people just overran us."[52] These two sets of memories demonstrate that frontiers as sites of cultural cooperation can easily yield violence and intimidation.

In this landscape of uncertainty the growing power of the state tipped the scales against Native peoples and ushered in military conquest. Post–Civil War Indian policy emphasized the relocation of Indians from ancestral homes to reservations so non-Indians could better colonize the land. One series of meetings and agreements illustrates a deepening pattern of tentative peace followed by violence and force. In early 1864 the superintendent of Indian Affairs for the territory of Arizona met in La Paz with what may have been the largest gathering of Native people in the region. Superintendent Charles Poston said that Chemehuevis, Mohaves, Hualapais, and Yavapais agreed to a 75,000-acre reservation on the river where they would all relocate and make way for non-Indian settlers. Poston claimed that the agreement would "be the best both for the whites and the Indians" because the Indians would receive assistance with farming. Although it is difficult to determine the reactions of Native representatives, it is hard to believe that 10,000 Indians whose ancestral territory covered western Arizona and southeastern California would agree to farm on 75,000 acres of land. Moreover, there is no evidence that Yavapais or Northeastern Pais moved to the recently established Colorado River Indian Reservation.[53]

Other incidents, such as a contract to allow Anglos to travel through the region on a toll road, reflected the changing social and demographic geography of the region. Like Poston's vision of concentrating Indians onto a reservation and thereby imposing a colonial geography upon dispersed peoples, the newly constructed Mohave and Prescott Toll Road, also known as the Hardy Toll Road, signified a new division of space that marked some lands as white and some as Indigenous. The contract, signed by William H. Hardy and Schrum, Hitch Hitchi from the Plateau people, and Wauba Yuma of the Yavapai Fighters on 15 July 1865, allowed non-Indians passage through Native lands and included "the right to build houses at the several watering places on the road . . . and the right to fence and improve said grounds . . . and the right to graze stock along the road and also to cut timber, use water, and make use of whatever is necessary for the convenience of the traveling public."[54] As a contract enforced by the state, it reflected the penetration of capitalism and the attendant settler society as well as a new legal regime that segregated Indians from lands that they had inhabited for centuries. It marked the first of numerous geographical conquests that excluded Native peoples from their own lands through a process of racialization and boundary making. These changes criminalized Pais for "trespassing" into territory that had once been theirs, making them strangers in their own land.[55]

Combined with the failed relocation agreement and the dubious toll road treaty, the presence of a growing military contingent brought the region to the precipice of war. When squatters killed a well-known Pai leader, Ana:sa, northwestern Arizona erupted in violence.[56] Anglos accused Pais of retaliating for the death of Ana:sa by killing a prospector at the Willows near the toll road, so the population of Hardyville demanded vengeance. Contributing to the tensions, the U.S. Army declared that all Indians seventy miles east of the Colorado River—Yavapais, Pais, and Apaches—were subject to extermination.[57] This "official" declaration emboldened a citizens' posse to kill the closest Pais, including nine innocent women and children.[58]

If the deaths of the women and children were not enough, the final straw for Pais was the murder of respected headman Wauba Yuma and his sons by either a drunken teamster or one of several vigilante groups. The death of Wauba Yuma ignited conflict between the southern Pai bands most impacted by colonization and Anglos seeking revenge.[59] Wauba Yuma's murder and the proclamations of whites about an "Indian uprising" yielded something of a self-fulfilling prophecy: non-Indians near Fort Mohave and Hardyville demanded soldiers to protect them, and the *Arizona Miner*, a paper in Prescott, called for the extermination of all "hostiles" in the region.[60] This emboldened whites to attack Indians with little cause, which made the Native people in the region increasingly angry and defensive and thus more likely to shoot first and ask questions later. The situation finally exploded in 1866, when, according to a report from Arizona Superintendent George Leihy, on 12 August a group of "Hualapais and Apache-Mohaves" intercepted a wagon train near Skull Valley on its way to Prescott. Between seventy-five and one hundred Native men approached the group but, speaking in Spanish, told the lead teamster, Mr. Freemen, that they did not intend to attack. A spokesperson told Freemen that "the water, the grass, and the corn and the country were theirs, and they wanted them back." Freemen apparently took this as a threat and with the assistance of several soldiers took the "chief" of their party hostage.[61]

A larger group referred to as Mohave-Apaches (probably Yavapais) and Northeastern Pais again confronted the Anglos but then laid down their weapons and promised not to attack. Rather than listen, a soldier rode back to the fort and returned with Lieutenant Hutton, who ordered the troops accompanying the wagon train to approach the Indians. The Indians repeated their demands that the water, the grass, the corn, and the country were theirs, and they wanted them back, but they added that the whites had six days to leave the valley and that the wagon train was free to move on. Hutton responded by saying that ten Indians would be arrested, upon which the Indians reached for their weapons. The military opened fire and killed over thirty men.[62]

The ethnic warfare continued for years, as growing numbers of soldiers from Fort Whipple participated in the conflict. In turn, Schrum and Hitch Hitchi sought justice for the murder of Wauba Yuma, and Pai bands killed teamsters and miners in the Black Mountains near the Colorado River. Hardyville citizens convinced a group of Mohaves to kill two dozen men and capture nineteen Pai women along the Colorado River. Soon an Anglo posse joined fifty Mohaves in exterminating twenty-one Pais in a *ranchería*. During an attack on mail carriers riding toward Fort Rock Station, Pais suffered nearly twenty casualties in a day-long fight.[63] A full-blown racial war had begun in northwestern Arizona.

Unaware of the arrival of five hundred troops from the Eighth U.S. Cavalry and Infantry in early 1867, Pai leaders aggressively defended their lands against non-Indian colonists and the military.[64] One such assault took place in May, when Schrum organized nearly 250 Pais and Southern Paiutes to attack the Camp Beale's Springs mail station. The mail station represented the incursion of foreigners into Pai lands, but it also provided communication between northwestern Arizona, the territorial capital, and the string of military forts across the Southwest. The attack reflected Pais' knowledge of Anglo communication systems, but it also revealed the ways that small bands of Indigenous peoples attacked institutions crucial to the process of colonization. Importantly, Schrum recruited, organized, and commanded fighters from bands across the region, something that demonstrated his authority and leadership. In the wake of the assault, the commandant of Fort Mohave reported that "the most hostile band is led by Chief Chesora [Schrum]," an observation that fueled the belief that he was a chief of the "Hualapai Tribe."[65] Schrum's skill and the tenacity of his band led officers from Prescott to claim that they "would rather fight five Apaches than one Hualapai."[66]

After the May siege soldiers from Camp Beale's Springs set out after the group and killed fifteen Pais commanded by a "half-breed" and supported by several Yavapais and Paiutes near Peacock Springs. It is difficult to determine if this group or the group killed by Captain Williams near Cottonwood Springs was responsible for the mail station incident, but it probably struck most white settlers as just compensation. Such killing of "Indians" reflected a level of racial violence that failed to discriminate between bands or Native groups. All Natives, with the exception of compliant Mohaves at La Paz, were criminalized by the non-Indian population.[67]

The new protagonist in this tragedy was Col. William Redwood Price, who in June 1867 entered his new position as commanding officer of the District of the Upper Colorado with the central goal of crushing the Pais and marching them to La Paz or another reservation in southern Arizona. With clarity of purpose characteristic of few men, for several years he penetrated Pai territory, "driving and harassing" the "degenerate" Hualapais until they were "thoroughly whipped."[68] Writing to Maj. John P. Sherburn within a month of his arrival, Price recalled how "Genl Gregg and a party had come on to a rancheria, charged it, killing four Indians, Capturing a large lot of Buckskins, Furs, and food." In correspondence to superiors he wrote with pride of individuals such as Captain Williams who repeatedly killed Hualapais. During a ten-day excursion in July, Price traveled down Diamond Creek and killed nearly a dozen "Indians," most likely members of the Milkweed or Peach Springs band.[69]

Price and his military command claimed to have killed over one hundred Pais and injured twice that many, while Anglo posses claimed more in acts of vigilantism. For example, on 8 November 1867 a lieutenant under Price "surrounded and attacked a rancheria of Hualapai Indians . . . killing nineteen Indians, and capturing Sixteen Squaws and children" while they roasted agave.[70] Price used the freezing temperatures and howling winds of an early winter to his advantage by increasing the number and frequency of excursions against the Pai. On 2 December he reported that a lieutenant "surprised a rancheria of Hualapais . . . killing three Indians and capturing four children and one horse, also destroying a large quantity of seed and Indian property," while on the following day another detachment "destroyed two rancherias and a large amount of property, captured one squaw, [and] killed one Indian." On both occasions the ranking officer noted the cold and desolate conditions facing the people in the camp but did not express remorse for the killings.[71] One Lt. P. Hasson used the same matter-of-fact tone when reporting the death of principal band leader "Hitch-Hitchie," an action for which Hasson received promotion to brevet captain. January brought much of the same: an attack on a large ranchería with nearly one hundred people led to the death of sixteen Pais and the capture of thirty, while another attack killed nearly twenty-five individuals.[72]

The collective toll of military pursuit, weather, and destruction of their food stores crippled Pais' ability to resist colonization. The physical loss of life and the spiritual trauma of the violence pushed the Big Sandy, Juniper Mountain, Mahone Mountain, and Hualapai Mountain bands to the edge of annihilation. The Clay Springs, Peach Springs, Cerbat Mountain, and Red Rock bands, which inhabited the central and western portions of Pai territory, also experienced campaigns against them, but the more northeasterly Pine Springs, Havasu Baja, and Grass Springs bands remained beyond the full force of Colonel Price and his men. The warfare destabilized Pai social bonds and kinship networks while simultaneously forcing multiple bands to cooperate in an unusually frequent manner. Conversely, attacks on the southern and central bands distanced them socially and culturally from the bands far from the worst fighting. Military leaders had also imposed their own categorizations upon the Pais, referring to Northern and Southern bands split in half by the Hardy Toll Road. Those below the toll road were targeted for death.[73]

The warmer months of 1868 allowed Pais to regroup, but Colonel Price directed troops to destroy every wickiup and garden they encountered. Price also whipped up the fears of Mohaves to the west by informing them that if they assisted the Pais and their accomplices—some Yavapais, a few Mohaves, and several Paiutes—the military would reduce their rations and place them under arrest. Pais were moving in and out of the Colorado River Indian

Reservation to take food and weapons from Mohaves, some of whom assisted them openly. Price played on the fears that Mohaves had of some Pai bands and added disincentives to their furtive support of the anticolonial rebellion.[74]

The end of the resistance began when Leve Leve, head of the Hualapai Mountain band, signed a peace agreement on 20 August 1868 with Colonel Price. Leve Leve brought over thirty armed men into Camp Willow Grove and said that nearly eighty Pai men had died in combat, while double that were injured. Leve Leve reminded Price that the military and Anglo vigilantes had nearly wiped out several bands of Pais and in the process practically destroyed a generation of tribal members. In return for an end to the campaigns, Leve Leve gave Price several men to accompany Price throughout the region to explain his peace offering. Price wanted Pais to meet him at Fort Mohave, but no headman could enforce such an order, so the situation during the late summer of 1868 remained in flux. Quamalapoca, nephew of Hitch Hitchi and headman of the Milkweed Springs band, emerged as a negotiator to reduce the death toll among his people, and he met Price on 10 September with several warriors and Leve Leve. He would again meet with Price on 4 October, when he, Schrum, Leve Leve, and others came to listen to the colonel.[75]

Price was especially interested in meeting Schrum, whom he held responsible for "all the murders and villany [sic] that has been committed by the tribe during the last two years." Schrum appeared in September on the outskirts of a camp Price pitched near Hualapai Springs but refused to speak with Price because he feared imprisonment. After this failed meeting Schrum told Price that he would meet him at Fort Mohave on the Colorado River to discuss peace plans.[76] Leve Leve, on the other hand, brought in forty of his men and informed Price that Schrum and his half-brother, the equally stubborn Hualapai Charley, refused to enter the camp. Price decided that he would arrest Charley and Schrum and send them to prison in California. Only afterward would he consider creating two military reservations for the Pais, one on either side of the toll road, citing the case of the Paiutes as a positive example. For nearly two weeks, however, Schrum and Charley refused to enter the fort. Leve Leve continued to stall for time and discuss peace with Price, who had become agitated at the delaying tactics of the three leaders. Finally, on 3 October Schrum and Hualapai Charley entered Fort Mohave with nearly 250 Pais and an estimated 50 Paiutes to discuss peace.[77]

The agreement lasted as long as Schrum remained in the custody of the military: roughly three days. Schrum and Charley escaped the fort with most of their men but returned several weeks later. On 7 November Schrum again entered the fort, this time with fewer men and practically no chance of escaping. The guards placed him in shackles and stationed several guards to watch him until troops arrived to escort him to Alcatraz. But, much to the consternation of Price, Schrum escaped yet again on 12 November and remained "at large."[78] Schrum's repeated escapes made a mockery of the troops at Fort Mohave, so Price destroyed six rancherías and killed another twenty-three Pais while he searched for Schrum.[79] In February 1869 Price received word that Schrum refused to surrender and that he preferred to live in the mountains away from the white people.[80]

The anticolonial resistance of Schrum represented a response to conquest that bands following Leve Leve had rejected. Now known as the "Peace Chief" of the Hualapais, Leve Leve sought an end to the fighting in January 1869. This left roughly two bands and a few groups of Paiutes, Yavapais, and Mohaves holed up in the canyons with Schrum. Perhaps out of sheer desperation Price promised Schrum an honorable end to the wars if he would help Price defeat the Yavapais. This combination of waning Hualapai resistance and an emphasis on conquest of the Yavapais reduced the pressure on Schrum, who outlasted a military assault of profound dimensions. In the spring of 1869 Brevet Brig. Gen. Thomas C. Devin declared an end to hostilities against the Pais. All the while, Schrum neither surrendered to military force nor signed a peace agreement.[81]

Schrum's victory notwithstanding, five years of warfare inflicted a heavy toll on the Pais. Headmen such as Wauba Yuma and Hitch Hitchi died in the conflict and took with them wisdom and skills that would have enabled the bands to better negotiate the changes around them. Death, disease, dispossession, administrative pressures, and other factors fractured some bands and caused others to merge. The Red Rock band merged with the Cerbat Mountain people, and the Truxton Canyon, or Hackberry, band merged with the Peach Springs band to the north. The concentration of warfare in the central, southern, and western sections of Pai homelands spared the Havasupai and Pine Springs bands from the brunt of the violence, but many of them distanced themselves from the military and nearby forts.[82]

In the wake of warfare Pais tried to return to their traditional camps, gardens, and homes. For some in the northern areas of Pai country this did not pose great difficulties. Bands from Pine Springs, Milkweed Springs, Grass Springs, Peach Springs, and Cataract Canyon—nearly all of the so-called Plateau people along the east-west axis of the Colorado River—had some success reconstructing their lives. Far from the toll road, mining camps, forts, and Anglo population, these families maintained some semblance of a familiar routine. The Havasooa Pa'a began favoring the Grand Canyon, though they continued to live part of the year on the plateau. For members of the Big Sandy, Juniper Mountain, Hualapai Mountain, Mahone Mountain, Cerbat Mountain, Hackberry, and Clay Springs bands life on this still volatile racial frontier would prove difficult.[83]

Some Pais assisted the U.S. military as scouts against the Yavapais and Apaches, hoping to find stability during this new era. Pai warriors and American infantry joined forces in mid-1869 to begin campaigns against Yavapais between Prescott and Aubry Landing to the north and the Gila River and Fort Yuma to the south. Leve Leve volunteered assistance after Colonel Price threatened Schrum with another military campaign. Price cajoled the leaders to supply him with more scouts, and eventually nearly fifty assisted. In September 1872 Capt. J. W. Mason led another contingent of Pais, including Schrum, Hualapai Charley (recently released from Alcatraz), Sukwana, Koara, and Chief Navajo of the Cataract Canyon band against Yavapai rancherías. By the time the military discharged the scouts in the spring of 1873, over one hundred had helped conquer the Yavapais.[84]

The use of Native scouts marked an important turning point in the region because it undermined the possibility for a multitribal resistance to Anglo domination. This does not mean that Native peoples in northwestern Arizona should have automatically shared interests, but the military used divisive policies to encourage Pais to fight against the Yavapais, even though some Yavapai bands had cooperated with Pais in defending the region against white aggression. The military offered Pais tools, horses, and rations as well as the right to return to their territory if they supported excursions against the Yavapais. Military records and enlistment papers do not cast much light on Pais' perspectives during the campaigns in the early 1870s, but the larger significance of the colonial tactics seemed clear. By 1873, less than one decade after the Pais confronted military conquest, armed resistance was futile, a regional resistance movement had ended, and the time for making treaties had passed. The future of the People was indeed tenuous.

## Internment at La Paz

After the final subjugation of the Pais the War Department redoubled its plan to force them onto a military reservation. It was this last attempt in the early 1870s to control Pais that led to the "Long Walk to La Paz."[85] In March 1871 Capt. Thomas Byrne established his Twelfth Infantry Unit at Camp Beale's Springs, a few miles from the small town of Kingman, to gain control over the Pais. Gen. George Crook charged Byrne to protect the Pais from the Anglos just as carefully as he protected the Anglos from the Indians. While Byrne settled into northwestern Arizona, Agent Vincent Colyer arrived at the camp, having just established reservations for the Apaches. Colyer tried to help Byrne transform Camp Beale's Springs, a desolate one-mile-square location graced by a single spring, rough terrain, and little farmland, into a military reservation. In late 1871 Byrne issued rations to the growing numbers of Pais congregating around the camp, banned them from their "old haunts," and ordered them to submit to his authority. Crook noted that "any failure to feed them would not only destroy their confidence in me . . . [it] would cause frightful consequences should these Indians break out."[86]

Contradictions within colonialism facilitated the Pais' manipulation of new social, cultural, and political changes around them. On the one hand, the small military presence made it easy for men to avoid the surveillance of Captain Byrne and other soldiers. Pais who had assisted Captain Mason and General Crook in the Yavapai campaigns used this service to demand more rights and privileges. And Schrum, emboldened by his refusal to sign a peace agreement or surrender to Colonel Price, ignored repeated calls to settle in or near the fort. On the other hand, the roughly two hundred Anglos in the region viewed the Pais ambivalently. Some despised them for allegedly stealing cattle, while others offered Pais employment as ranch hands and in the mines. Anglos expressed concerns about an "Indian uprising" when they were not praising the Pais for their service in the Apache campaigns. But just as the colonial situation opened spaces for Native adaptation, it revealed the growing inability of the Pais to live as they always had.

Many families grew dependent on rations, and several Pais agreed to serve in an Indian police force charged with monitoring the bands near the camp. The police force and the people seeking rations illustrated the colonial situation facing Pais in the region, as employment in the force provided men with money and resources for their survival and created a buffer between the military and Pai bands. Working for the military, however, represented a degree of co-optation that caused resentment among some band members. The cash as well created economic divisions between families. Similarly, accepting rations reflected the desperation and poverty caused by the destruction of Pai hunting grounds and gathering places and kept people from starvation, but it simultaneously implied dependency.[87]

Situating the camp within the northwestern section of Pai homelands had an uneven, though important, impact on the bands. The camp served as a magnet for the bands most weakened by military conflict and Anglo appropriation of Pai lands. The Burro Creek band, which lived at the southern tip of Big Sandy territory and sometimes intermarried with Yavapais, merged with larger bands that interacted with the military outpost.[88] Kate Crozier remembered when they established the camp: "They made a little reservation and they surrounded us and put us [there], two miles from Kingman called Beale Spring, Ha Koome' where all of the surrounding territory of Beale's Springs was Hualapai home." He also recalled the experiences of his parents, who heard a rumor while visiting the Cerbat Mountain band: "Short time after that rumor . . . it must be from the military authorities to gather all these Walapai Indians around the country here, they did. All these Walapais around the country. At that time the parents went, too, and they all got together at Beale Spring. They were kind of scared. Looked like something going to happen to us. During that time, the army officers gave them some flower [sic], some things to eat, some meat, beef, while they stayed there at Beale springs."[89] In contrast, the Juniper Mountain, Pine Springs, and Havasupai peoples were able to remain outside the sphere of influence created by the military and, to a greater extent, the growing Anglo population.

This situation grew more problematic in late 1873, when the Office of Indian Affairs began discussions about moving Pais to the Colorado River Indian Reservation. J. A. Tonner, the Indian agent in charge of the southern reservation, informed Crook, Byrne, and the Indian Office that relocation to La Paz would benefit the bands and remove them from the growing number of mining operations in the area. Moreover, Tonner argued that farming on the reservation would help them make the transition to agriculture.[90] The Hualapais learned of their relocation, which was scheduled for January 1874, and fled the immediate vicinity of the camp. Byrne tried to convince Pai families that the new reservation would provide them with farming opportunities that were unavailable to them in the high desert.[91] Allegations in February of an attack upon white citizens in Truxton Springs stoked anti-Indian sentiments and confirmed the military's resolve to march the Pais south. General Crook's threat of a military attack and Byrne's promise of farming equipment convinced families associated with Leve Leve to surrender on 22 March, beginning the early phases of relocation.[92]

Reconstructing the actual removal is difficult, but memories of surviving Pais and stories passed down by ancestors provide a window onto a traumatic experience that was fully under way by April. Kate Crozier, a boy during removal, remembered how "all Walapai Indians we skipped off, going down into Grand Canyon [to] get out of the way. So they left Beale Spring and gone into the Grand Canyon." His group stayed there for "must have been two weeks," until Captain Byrne convinced them to return to Beale's Springs. A few days later Crozier and his family began their march to La Paz.[93] Bob Schrum, son of the Pai leader Schrum, survived the march as a child. Speaking in 1944, he recalled traveling south along the Hualapai Mountains down Cito Wash and then Mojave Wash to Bill Williams Fork. He stated that the military forced them west through Chemehuevi Valley and then south to La Paz. When the group began the journey on 6 April, Byrne forced them on excruciating hikes of up to fifteen miles a day. Bob Schrum recalled how "the young and very old Indians [were] unable to continue the march," which ended two weeks later. Estimates of the number of Pais relocated range from four to six hundred, but all accounts agree that dozens died in the removal.[94]

Indian Honga, who was roughly seven years old when "the Indians were gathered up to go there," recounted his memories of La Paz during an interview in 1943. Honga recalled: "My family got away with the other Indians belonging to the Pine Springs group and we went to the mountains." Similarly, a Hualapai named Koara who was related to Jim Fielding, an important tribal leader during the early twentieth century, recalled in 1900 that he took rations at Camp Beale's Springs when Agent Tonner told him about the planned removal. Koara and his family ran away into the Hualapai Mountains, using guns taken from the military. They remained in hiding for over a year.[95]

Pais who survived passed the stories down through the generations so that future members would not forget the suffering. In a 1967 interview Tim McGee, a Hualapai from Big Springs, recalled stories from her grandparents about Hualapais gathering seeds around Hackberry when removal began. All of a sudden "they see the dust, so one of them goes to meet them, he runs towards them and finds out it was just a white army coming down. So they ran up the boulders and rocks, and they went to get the horses and climb up back of those boulders, so the army shot them." Many Pais resisted, according to Tim's grandmother, "and then Serum [Schrum] was there too, but he got away somehow he was ready for it I guess. He cut a hole in the ground and built a little shack over it. We were sitting in there and he shot at them too. He got some kind of pistol [and] they kept shooting and shooting."[96] Another Hualapai, this one born in the 1880s, recalled the stories of his father:

> The Walapais were gathered at Beale Springs, and then the soldiers drove them south. They came by Yucca and straight on to Ookwatagijo . . . where they crossed the Bill Williams Fork. When they drove them, they just whipped them and made them come. A lot of them got sick from the water and food and died on the way. My father had a horse and was riding. Some of them had shoes, and some not. The children had shoes, and they didn't have much food to bring with them. So they suffered a lot on the way and many lives were loss.[97]

Uprooted from their homes, families lost contact with their birthplaces as the military interned them in La Paz. Forced to endure oppressive heat, Pais tried to grow crops and raise stock, but many died of heatstroke and exhaustion. Others died of new diseases, and men who used to hunt had to rely upon worm-infested rations. A Hualapai talking with Henry Dobyns in 1950 attested to the cultural impact of the march, which, though smaller in scope than the Cherokee Trail of Tears and the Navajo Long Walk, had similar results. Again, Tim McGee recalled stories told by her grandparents: "They took all the Indians to La Paz. Whites took all loud Indians, got cold, no good shelters, got measles and died. My father's mother died with measles." When the Supreme Court heard a case in 1941 between the Hualapais and the Santa Fe Railway, it called internment a "high-handed endeavor to wrest from these Indians lands which Congress had never declared forfeited."[98]

Sparse reports during the year-long internment at La Paz paint a picture of heat, malnutrition, and discontent. Within days of their arrival Pais asked Agent Tonner when they would leave the reservation. They lived in small, poorly constructed wickiups and tried to remain close to band members and their leaders. They lacked clothing and blankets, food, and medicines, and ditches built to deliver water to small gardens failed. Indian Office orders for beef fell below the normal allowance for the agency, and the addition of the Pai bands exacerbated allegations of corruption.[99]

By the spring of 1875 the Indian Office and the military disagreed about what to do with the Pais at La Paz. Captain Byrne left the reservation temporarily and placed an enlisted officer in charge, but orders from the Indian Office demanded the relocation of Pais northward to the main agency on the Colorado River Indian Reservation. Official reports reveal contradictory statements: one has the Pais moving north to work on farms, while another report has them moving to facilitate the distribution of rations. Once they arrived, Tonner ordered the presiding officer to reduce rations, and several band members died in early April.[100]

Pais responded to the confusion and the promise of another sweltering summer by escaping the reservation. Reports to the commissioner of Indian Affairs state that, "owing largely to bad influences from without," Pai bands left the reservation on the morning of 20 April. External influences are unlikely to have caused them to leave, since they had never wanted to relocate in the first place, although there is some indication that Hualapais who refused to live on the reservation were coaxing them to escape.[101]

Pai bands had survived a year interned, and their escape was a profound act of rebellion. Much like their resistance to military subjugation and their rejection of life at Camp Beale's Springs, the escape from La Paz indicated a refusal to live in a colonial situation dominated by the military and the Indian Office. Their traditional lands pulled them back northward even though their future remained uncertain. To punctuate their desire to live beyond the surveillance of the state, Schrum took a message of resistance to Territorial Governor A.P.K. Safford. Governor Safford wrote to Gen. August V. Kautz that Schrum and his people "have unanimously agreed not to return again to the Reservation; that they have also agreed . . . to live in peace." Safford added that he thought they were "fully determined to fight rather than return to the reservation." The Pacific Division commander of the U.S. Army thought that the Indian Office treatment of Pais was an "injustice [carried out in] bad faith . . . a disgrace to any civilized country."[102]

The Long Walk to La Paz and internment on the Colorado River Indian Reservation marked a turning point in the history of Pai bands and families. Military conquest and settler colonialism had wrenched most Pais from their homelands and threatened their very existence as a people. Their escape from La Paz, however, was a fitting reminder that colonized peoples do not submit fully to the state. Pais indicated to Americans that they would meet the challenges of colonization with a variety of tactics and responses. Their refusal to remain beyond their aboriginal territory speaks to cultural resilience and the persistence of band identities. This combination of resistance to colonialism and the desire to remain in their homeland would prove crucial to their survival in coming years when Pais confronted new assaults on their land and identity.

2

# The Colonization of Hualapai Space

Hualapais' escape from La Paz and their trek northward were expressions of anticolonial resistance that indicated Pais' attachment to their homelands and their refusal to follow the dictates of the military and Indian Office. As rebellious as the flight was, it highlighted a complicated historical moment in the relationships between Pai bands, the settler population, the military, and the Indian Office. Pais escaped after Congress ended its treaty-making process and at the end of presidential mandates known as the Peace Policy. The bands lacked a reservation, but Congress had not yet enacted the allotment policies of the 1880s. So the bands stood at a tenuous moment where their connections with their aboriginal landscape had been disrupted by war and relocation but had not been fully terminated. For the next twenty-five years Pais lived in a fluid and shifting cultural landscape that defied standard notions of "frontier" life. This changed when the Indian Office created an agency in Valentine in 1900 to oversee the Pai bands, but even this surveillance was limited to the few Pais in the vicinity. In this multivalent setting no stark line existed between "savagery and civilization" in the manner articulated by Frederick Jackson Turner. The world that the Pais navigated at the end of the nineteenth century was one of great contestation over and (re-)creation of Hualapais' spatial homelands.

## The Changing Hualapai Landscape

Removal, internment, and the escape from La Paz were defining moments in Pai history, as illustrated by the memories of Pais discussing life during the late nineteenth century. These memories demonstrate how Pai bands tried to return to traditional territories, sacred sites, band homes, rancherías, and springs after removal. They also offer glimpses of life in a time of great transition before and after the creation of the reservation in 1883.

Jane Huya was born near Peach Springs and lived there all her life with her parents as well as band members Mike Sue, Jim Smith, Prescott Jim, John Smith, Hatame, Honga, Matuck, and Young Beecher, all of whom lived in *wachude*, or "Indian homes" made of juniper trees and cedar bark. Of the days before removal she recalled that "there were also sweat houses, a place where arrows were made and places where there were grinding stones for grinding seeds." She survived the Long Walk to La Paz and internment and recalled how these events "scattered them around" and made it difficult for them to return to their traditional sites. Bob Schrum's wife, Nora, remembered Peach Springs as the home of her extended family: "I was born at Peach Springs Water, on the Wallapai reservation, in 1870." She added: "When I lived there as a little girl and a grown woman, there were Indian homes, sweat houses, places where the Indians cooked mescal, places where the Indians ground seeds . . . and I can find the places where a number of these things were, and show them to anybody, even now."[1]

After internment Hualapais tried reclaiming their homelands in an anticolonial restructuring of their landscape. Bands competed with non-Indians for access to springs and grazing pasture, while mining operations and white homesteaders threatened to appropriate their lands as well. Kate Crozier, whose father was born near Merriditica and whose mother was born at Cowarrow Springs, was a boy when the military relocated the Pais to La Paz. Crozier said that during relocation "some stayed in the Walapai country in groups, some went toward the river and lived along the Colorado . . . because they lived there and did not want to leave it." He too did not want to leave and went back to the Milkweed Springs area, where there were "lots of deer on that part of the reservation there in the old days." Crozier remembered how some of his relatives tried to return to Clay Springs, Tinnekah Springs, and Diamond Creek, but miners and ranchers surrounded the first two locations.[2]

Nora Schrum recalled how after internment she and her husband, Bob, fled to Pine Springs, where they lived for several months before moving around in search of work in the ranching industry. Like members of other families, they lived a hand-to-mouth existence that frequently teetered on starvation.[3] Queen Imus recalled how her family, which included her father, Coyote Jim from Tinnekah Springs, also left and returned home: "They returned there to live just as they had lived before they had been taken down [to La Paz]." In her testimony decades later Queen stated that she and her husband replanted their old garden and rebuilt their irrigation ditches after La Paz, but when they came home after a trip to Merriditica, non-Indians had moved onto their lands near the spring. She noted that if "I want to go back there and live there, I know that the whiteman who lives there will try to run me off." Her father had tried to negotiate with the settlers, but "a white man came and told him, my father, he would shoot him if we didn't move away," so Queen and her family relocated to the homes of extended family members. Relatives who lived near Tinnekah Springs, Dick and Jim Bennett, and the parents and grandparents of Dave Grounds and Indian Sampson all had to adjust to non-Indians there.[4]

The year at La Paz allowed Anglo newcomers to take Hualapai land, especially near springs. One Big Sandy band member recalled his father's attempt to return to land occupied by Anglos: "My father used to have a place down there before I was born. I saw that when I was old enough. They can't stay [at] that place without anything to eat, have to go out to mountain to hunt deer, antelope, Indian food. The white man come in and take them all away, the land—land down on the Sandy. I never heard about trading off the land to white man, or sell the land to white man. They came in themselves and took it away." Another band member recalled a similar series of events after La Paz and the return to Big Cane Springs: "The first settlers came to Big Cane Springs. These first settlers were friendly, they don't molest us very much," he said. By the late 1870s "other white families and white ranchers came and took over this whole valley, our gardens, our homes. We didn't give this country up voluntarily. We were just overrun by white people taking up the springs, the grass, the gardens and all of this territory. We never gave up anything: these people just overran us."[5] Such stories were common for tribal members trying to adjust to life in a post–La Paz era.

As Hualapais tried reconstructing their lives, the military attempted to control Hualapai movement. When Agent Tonner from the Colorado River Indian Reservation sent word to General Kautz at the Department of Arizona headquarters in Prescott that Hualapais fled from La Paz, he noted that "troops here are useless. Send cavalry unit in pursuit if possible." Tonner was alarmed at the escape and feared that it was the first step in a larger uprising of the Native population.[6] After Captain Byrne rejected Tonner's demands for cavalry because Byrne believed that the Pai bands simply wanted to return to their "old haunts," Tonner acknowledged that it was "advisable not to take any coercive steps at present to force these Indians upon a reservation." General Crook, Captain Byrne, and General Kautz all blamed Tonner for the Pais' escape because he wanted to move them closer to the agency and reduce their rations, but the Pais' escape from internment reflected a larger context of military conquest and Native rebellion that Kautz, Byrne, and Crook could not control.[7] Pais left the reservation not because of any choices or mistakes by Tonner but because they wanted to return to their homelands and live as they had before Anglos entered the region.

As they tried to evade the military and the Indian Office, most band members settled near their old homes and band territories or they congregated near settlements such as Kingman, Peach Springs, Chloride, Hackberry, Mineral Park, and Seligman. This attempt to reclaim their aboriginal homelands sparked concern among the non-Indian population: two dozen citizens of Mohave County petitioned the military to relocate the Hualapais back to the Colorado River Indian Reservation. Writing to General Kautz and Colonel Morford, the acting agent at the Colorado River Indian Reservation, citizens complained that Hualapais killed their stock, but they ignored how their own use of springs and grasslands undermined the Pai economy, which only made the cattle look more attractive. At the same time that some Anglos expressed outrage at the property loss and a potential "Indian uprising," others admitted to "claiming land formerly occupied by Walapai Indians," and a few acknowledged that the families did not "appear hostile to the whites." Yet they still wanted the Indians moved to "some portion of this county and restricted to that locality, or be removed to some reservation entirely out of the county" in order to "serve the best interest of all concerned."[8]

Such disputes over land and laws reflected in microcosm larger confrontations over space as settler societies moved into Native territory. Most accounts of westward expansion focus on military battles and physical struggles, but European notions of land and topography privileged private tenure and bureaucratic definitions of space, while the science of geography, techniques of mapping, and the power of surveying worked as tools of conquest. Physical conquest and colonial settlement redefined Indigenous lands in terms that made sense to non-Natives: latitude and longitude, township and block replaced familiar Hualapai names for the landscape. These foreign conceptualizations of space altered Pais' interaction with the landscape and forced them to adapt new strategies of movement. Lands newly classified as public domain and private property looked no different, but they were integrated into a new field of knowledge and a matrix of laws and symbols that marked them off from the old lands. The new forms of power expressed by the settler society tried to monopolize space and relegate Hualapais to less desirable landscapes. Politicians and surveyors redefined Pai spaces as non-Indian territories and extracted aboriginal homelands from the reach of

Native peoples by new maps, new modes of power, and the very real growth of an economy and legal system that devalued Native territories and valued capitalist economies.[9]

Yet Pais did not entirely lose contact with or knowledge of these newly defined lands and spaces as they crossed into and tried reclaiming them in ways that reflected their own memories and traditions. Pais challenged boundaries and laws by denying charges of theft and trespassing on white private property. When headmen Schrum, Little Captain, and Hualapai Charley met with Lt. H. L. Haskell in the summer of 1878, they questioned ranchers such as William Grounds, who claimed that Pais killed his cattle. Little Captain retorted that white thieves or Tonto Apaches killed the stock, not Pais, and several whites did admit that they could not confirm exactly who stole the cattle. After Little Captain harangued them about invading their lands, a few praised the work of Hualapai women in their homes and restaurants, admitting that the Indians "were of more good than harm to white people." Such condescension notwithstanding, the admission that whites could not blame Pais with certitude reflected both the permeability of the legal borders demarcating Native land from white private property and the flexibility of racial borders between Indian and white. Whites were not the victims of marauding Pai bands, and room did exist for cultural cooperation and understanding.[10]

This growing non-Indian population and its attendant laws, perceptions of the land, political relationships with the territorial government, and larger linkage with the southwestern economy sparked transformations that altered Pais' sense of themselves as a people. The social, economic, and cultural geography of the region had begun to change as bands of Pais competed with non-Indians for access to land, water, and space in northwestern Arizona. The perceptions of the land were not always diametrically opposed, but they tended to differ on the basis of ethnicity and historical experience in and with the region. In particular, the Pai lands witnessed the emergence of multiple communities, towns, villages, and "settlements" that were sometimes based on race but included multiracial outposts where Indian, Mexican, Irish, African, and "white" interacted within a larger array of cultural and ethnic frontiers. Non-Indians established these towns because they thought the lands were unoccupied or "vacant," lacking the marks of "civilization" or progress they believed indicative of permanent settlement. This vision required "improvements" such as roads, barns, European American towns, agriculture, water wells, branded cattle, and so on. Native peoples such as the Pai lived a different but equally legitimate existence that involved seasonal migrations to specified places, light agriculture, rancherías, and hunting. This lifestyle left a lighter footprint upon the land that many non-Indians either failed to perceive or failed to deem worthy of protection. Either way, the region became host to an array of land-use patterns, overlapping settlements, and confusing racialized spaces.

In particular, non-Indian towns emerged on top of Native rancherías, hunting grounds, and sacred sites throughout the county and threatened Pais' access to resources and their homes. When Mohave County was created in 1864, one census estimated that less than two hundred "citizens" lived within its area of 8.4 million acres. Few official towns existed, but those that did included Mohave City (the onetime county seat), Hardyville, Aubrey City, Hackberry, and a few others. The vast majority of the region was not occupied by whites, and the main economic activities were cattle ranching and mining. Most of the new population gravitated near the Colorado River adjacent to Fort Mohave, while very few whites lived in the eastern and northern sections of the county. Anglos began establishing institutions throughout the county in the 1870s: a public school "system" began in 1872, and a new courthouse was built in the new county seat of Mineral Park in 1877.[11] Important sources of water, such as Peach Springs, which were the nexus of Pai rancherías, had attracted non-Indians as far back as the 1840s. Although tax records for the 1870s do not indicate anyone filing property claims near this particular spring, by the early 1880s it had become "a place of about twenty rough buildings and tents, all business places" associated with a railroad stop for the Santa Fe Railway. By 1886 the spring and the nearby depot had become a hub of activity with stores and houses owned by Anglo residents.[12] In 1887 a small school served non-Indian children, a post office maintained communications for the community, and the Santa Fe Railway built a Harvey House near its depot.[13]

The colonial layer of Anglo settlement and reterritorialization included industries such as cattle ranching and mining, both of which had a tremendous impact on Pai landscapes. Mining gouged large craters in the land near and on Native sacred sites and, if hydraulic methods were used, demanded excessive amounts of water. Mining also disrupted the ecological systems and human-land relationships that Native peoples constructed because deer, elk, rabbits, and other staples of the Pai diet lost valuable sources of water. Ranching had similar, if not more devastating, impacts on people, plants, and animals. Thousands of cattle immigrated with Anglo settlers and consumed vast quantities of grama and other grasses, compacted the dry soils, and denuded topsoil so that rain or strong winds led to erosion. As ranchers "improved" the springs, cattle congregated around the water and further destroyed the range to such an extent that during first decade of the twentieth century officials observed the poor state of the ranchland in some parts of Mohave County.

The combination of growing towns and settlements, new institutions and laws, imported animals and plants, foreign industries such as mining, and other impositions placed upon the Pais a troubling set of circumstances.[14] The efforts of Pai band leaders to assure non-Indians of their friendly intentions, for instance, and the reactions of non-Indians to the Pais' flight from La Paz hinted at a colonial relationship of unique dimensions. Local whites reacted with ambiguity to Pais and their efforts to reclaim their Native spaces within a new context marked by complex racial, ethnic, and cultural relationships. Some wanted the Pais returned to the Colorado River Indian Reservation, while others wanted them to remain in the region. In the late 1870s stories of "savages" attacking stagecoaches and wagon trains permeated the country as the so-called Indian Wars became seared into the collective consciousness of the nation. The manifestations of these fears in northwestern Arizona compelled many whites to repeatedly demand roundups and relocations far into the twentieth century. In contrast, military leaders occasionally defended Indigenous lands, while Indian Office officials intimidated and neglected tribal members.[15]

The colonial experience had different effects on Native peoples. Some Pai leaders demanded a reservation immediately upon returning from La Paz, while other bands refused to move if offered a choice. The common experience of internment and flight from La Paz may have increased cooperation between bands and families, but those who escaped internment had different memories of the experience. For all Pai bands, new geographies of property rights and capitalist extraction created areas of contention as they tried returning to familiar locations but found them occupied by ranchers, miners, and small towns. Thus, conquest threatened to divest Pais of their identity, but bands negotiated new relationships with each other since they could no longer remain highly independent. These fluid and sometimes hardening cultural boundaries and shifting identities revealed the complex social and economic worlds of Pais and non-Indians negotiating competing senses of place.[16]

These quickly changing circumstances forced Pais to forge alliances with and in some cases become dependent on non-Indians in the region. One such individual was Charles Spencer, who came to Pai country in the early 1860s as a mail carrier and scout for the military. He met numerous Northeastern Pai bands and slowly learned the language well enough that the Indian Office and the military employed him as an interpreter. In the late 1870s he began ranching in Matawidita Canyon near the Colorado River, an important religious site and one of the few locations with level fields and ample water, and he married a Hualapai named Synje, with whom he had two children. Hualapais had mixed feelings about Spencer despite his value as a mediator. He helped the government compile statistics on population, health, and band dispersal, but he also promoted farming and would even receive credit for helping with the creation of the reservation in 1883.[17]

When Pais could not readily forge alliances with whites such as Spencer, they courted military officers and government officials after La Paz. Upon hearing reports from Crook and Byrne, Arizona Territorial Governor John Charles Frémont visited the region in 1878 to investigate its economic potential and bring the territory into the "modern era." Schrum informed Frémont about tensions in the area but assured him that the Hualapais would "struggle with starvation rather than take a step which looked in that direction" of La Paz. Schrum invited other leaders who also seemed intent on governing themselves and carving out a niche in the changing region.[18]

The growing settler society frustrated Hualapais' self-determination as non-Indian cattle operations cordoned off springs and white developers filed claims to Pai land with the territorial government in Prescott. The increase in cattle and non-Indians threatened Pais' ability to survive off the land, so bands had to rely increasingly on rations in Hackberry and Kingman. Captain Byrne, a reluctant participant in the La Paz ordeal, issued food and supplies to Pais from Camp Beale's Springs, a few miles northwest of Kingman, the final seat of the county and the eventual economic hub of the region. Ration days were bittersweet moments that revealed the frustrations and indignities of life in a radically altered landscape. At one rationing 573 Hualapais arrived, while at another only 497 came to the agency. Byrne thought that the decline had been caused by an illness that recently struck the Big Sandy band, although this is difficult to confirm. These days also afforded a glimpse into the concerns of some Pais about their uncertain future. In the fall of 1879 Byrne noted an interaction with several Pais who stated that there was "a rumor amongst them that my only object in issuing them rations was to get them together, surround them with Cavalry, and then drive them upon a reservation." Such rumors revealed the Pais' fear that the military was luring them to the camp for removal to La Paz.[19]

Ration days also afforded officers a chance to critique the Indian Office and the non-Indians in the region for their treatment of Pai bands. Officer George Wilson, who worked with Byrne, observed that Pais had a difficult time surviving in the area because they lived in constant fear that non-Indian citizens would convince the Indian Office to relocate them or, according to one Hualapai Wilson talked with, that Anglo posses would attack Pai camps. He learned that non-Indians had already surrounded the springs in the region, leaving many Hualapais without access to water. He concurred with Lieutenant Haskell, who observed that there was "little water in this region, and it is usually taken up by the whites whose cattle roam near," and an 1879 military report stating that Pais lived "in poverty, which is due in large part to the occupancy of their country by white people."[20]

The need for rations represented one facet of the larger shift in Pai subsistence patterns and economic activities that had been disrupted by outsiders. Not all Pais took rations, but they constituted one element of their new situation, which included hunting, gathering, and small gardens where they could find access to water. Their situation also resulted in several letters and correspondence between local and territorial officials with the War and Interior departments. In 1879 Colorado River Indian Agent Henry Mallory received a petition from Anglos in the county for the removal of Pais around Kingman and the Big Sandy Region.[21] Another letter expressed "concern" about the tribe and its condition, especially the women recently impressed into prostitution. The petition, signed by several residents of Mineral Park, said that "the Indians are at present favorably disposed, but trouble is at any time likely to grow if their intercourse with the whites continues, particularly through their women. . . . [T]hey are willing to work and are useful in many ways, but too many of them crowd in the towns." The letter resembles the thousands of letters written by "concerned" citizens across the West about the "plight of Indians." It regrets their poverty without noting its origins, expresses surprise at their willingness to work, and yet contains fear about "too many" Indians in town. The text of the letter narrates a racialized geography that marks towns as "white spaces" and the countryside as "Indian spaces," even though the boundaries resided more in the imagination of the author than on the landscape of northwestern Arizona.[22]

Although many whites new to the area expressed similar fears, astute observers understood the sources of Pai marginalization. The U.S. representative for the territory, John Campbell, wrote to the commissioner of the Indian Office in 1880 acknowledging the "stream" of letters coming from Mohave County regarding "Walapais" and their condition. An odd sense of comprehension permeated his letter, which recognized Pais' need to take cattle from Anglo ranching operations: "As soon as the government ceases to provide for the Indians . . . they would from necessity be forced to steal stock from the settlers." While admitting that "Hualapais have been in large part self-supporting," although the "country where they have lived has within the past few years been settled by miners and stock raisers to such an extent that the former resources of the Indians has in a great measure been destroyed," he failed to comprehend the decentralized nature of Pai social structures, which allowed for diverse reactions to colonialism. Pai headmen, even those as well respected as Schrum, could not force other Pais to abide by their wishes. Yet Campbell and his peers continued to homogenize the bands and assume that they followed a single "chief" who ruled over everyone. On the other hand, Campbell seemed to understand that "precautionary measures [needed to] be taken by furnishing the needed supplies for the Indians, and thus avert[ing] the loss of property and life," rather than simply punishing them for "theft." He believed in the colonizers' laws and was not about to defend the aboriginal residents in an Anglo court of law, but he implicated Anglos in the poverty of the Hualapais.[23]

## Establishing the Reservation

The enclosure of aboriginal territory by Anglo property lines and the related loss of the Pais' land base compelled Pai headmen to protest to the Indian Office and the military for a reservation. This was a bold move that marked an important turning point in Hualapai history because it signaled the possible preservation of a piece of their aboriginal homelands, even though reservations across the American West conjured images of disease and poverty. Although archival documentation and oral histories fail to reveal what band members thought in the days leading up to its creation, we may infer through their actions that headmen understood what a reservation was. Schrum and Hualapai Charley had been to the Colorado River Indian Reservation and sought a similar land base in discussions with Colonel Price and Col. O. B. Willcox in 1875. Moreover, Schrum and Charley's tour as scouts in southern Arizona would have also introduced them to the Apache reservations. Communication with Pais in the eastern portions of their territory as well as interaction with Hopis would have revealed that the railroad was headed into Pai lands, further piquing Pai interest in a protected land base.

The most serious discussions about creating the reservation began in 1881, when Colonel Price, the main purveyor of violence against Pai bands, met with Schrum, Hualapai Charley, Soskourema, and Cowarrow, Pai headmen. It is difficult to determine the thoughts of the dozens of band members attending the gathering, but the group, assisted by Charles Spencer, urged the officials to set aside land since ranchers and now the railroad jeopardized the tribe's survival. Speculation abounded regarding the motivations of Spencer, who owned a ranch on the land and may have won contracts to supply beef to the new agency. Yet there are no records of conflicts between Spencer and one of the largest Pai groups, the Milkweed Springs band, in whose territory Spencer established his ranch in Milkweed Canyon. The mystery surrounding his intentions go back at least to the late 1870s, when Spencer laid out a stone monument near Peach Springs and when he allegedly marked off sections of the reservation boundary as it was first discussed in 1875. Whether or not his actions reflected spatial conquest, philanthropic desire, or some mixture of both, tribal memory has it that Spencer acted in the best interests of the people. In the 1930s the prominent Hualapai leader Jim Fielding remembered how he accompanied Spencer in the region that became the reservation to preserve "a piece of land as an Indian Claim against the newcomers."[24]

With or without Spencer, Pai leaders borrowed from their experiences with the military and promises ostensibly made by Crook and Willcox to preserve their relations with the land. Schrum in particular reminded Price that he and his people had frequently talked about the need for a reservation since 1875, the year Hualapais escaped from La Paz, and that the 1881 meeting was an extension of that ongoing conversation about Hualapai space.[25] A particular discussion from 1875 became an important point of reference for tribal land rights struggles far into the twentieth century. For example, in a 1928 letter to Secretary of the Interior Hubert Works, Jim Fielding and "Chief" Bob Schrum claimed that in 1875 several Hualapais, with assistance from whites, marked lands that would become the reservation in 1883. Fielding stated, "We believe that our claim was staked out by Captain Mike Burns, Charles Spencer, and Mr. J. Smith, all citizens of the United States in the year of 1875."[26] The Indian Office disputed the existence of that meeting, but in 1881 the military supported the boundaries set by Spencer and Fielding six years earlier. Colonel Willcox issued General Order no. 16, reserving land for the tribe, upon approval of the president.[27]

The order wound its way up the bureaucracy and was eventually approved by President Chester A. Arthur in January 1883. But why establish the reservation at that particular place? Schrum, Charley, Soskourema, and Cowarrow supported the location of the reservation on the Colorado even though it did not seem promising for agriculture. At least one of them noted that the Big Sandy band had irrigable gardens that produced a variety of crops, but Schrum reminded them that several people had died there due to smallpox and other illnesses. There also may have been some tension between the Big Sandy and other bands over the location of their future home. Although the Big Sandy band would hesitate moving to the proposed reservation, it nonetheless ran along the Colorado River and placed the band near their point of origin, Spirit Mountain, and this was an extremely important characteristic of the reservation. Moreover, it contained a sizeable stand of timber, and its grazing lands and springs promised to support a new economy of ranching. It also encompassed the land of the Pine Springs, Peach Springs, and Milkweed bands while abutting the territory of the Hackberry and Havasoo bands. Finally, it was one of the few tracts of land that whites had not fully colonized, even though ranchers used many of the springs. Considering the aforementioned internal choices and external limitations, the executive order seemed to protect the bands' land from the railway lurching toward the reservation. And with these conditions structuring conversations about the reservation, Colonel Price, following the general order articulated by Willcox, sketched the proposed reservation boundaries:

> From a point on the Colorado River, 5 miles eastward of Tinnakah Spring, south 20 miles to crest of high mesa; thence S. 40 degrees East, 25 miles to north point of Music Mountains; thence East 15 miles; thence north 50 degrees, East 35 miles; thence 30 miles to the Colorado River; thence along said river to the place of beginning—the southern boundary being at least two miles south of Peach Springs and eastern at least 2 miles east of Pine Spring, all bearings being approximate.[28]

Immediately after the executive order became law, the future of the land remained unpredictable as Congress, the president, territorial politicians, and local communities debated the meaning of the reservation in light of land claims made by the railroad, Anglo ranchers on the reservation, and myriad band reactions to the executive order. Affirming support for the reservation, Pai leaders, Colonel Price (a surprising ally on this issue), and Commissioner Hiram Price noted that the Hualapais had a better claim to the local springs than the Santa Fe Railway, which held a grant to land and asserted water rights in the region. Commissioner Price knew "the Indians have no title to the lands occupied by them" but admitted they had "possessed" several springs "for a great many years." Commissioner Price wanted the secretary of war to "notify the railroad parties referred to that the Indians have the prior right to the water, and that it must not be diverted to the injury of the Indians." No records indicate that the secretary talked to the railway company, but had the conflicting claims to the water and land evolved into a lawsuit in the 1880s as they would in the 1920s, it is unlikely that any entity would have defended the interests of a few hundred Indians in northwestern Arizona.[29]

Adding to the precariousness of the situation was the role of Charles Spencer, which cast a shadow over the birth of the reservation. William F. Grounds, a well-known if disliked rancher in the region, alleged that Spencer convinced Schrum and other headmen to create the reservation so he would have free grazing land for his cattle. The accusation appears elsewhere, but it is difficult to substantiate. When Herbert Welsh, the head of the Indian Rights Association, visited in the mid-1880s, Spencer told him that with government agricultural assistance most of the roughly seven hundred Pais could move from their camps along the railroad to safe homes on the reservation. Spencer implored the government to improve the land or "provide a place for them where they can sustain themselves and be removed from the contaminating influences of the small frontier towns and mining camps, where there are always enough low, disreputable characters to furnish their men whiskey and debauch their women," but the Indian Office did little to improve the reservation until the public works programs of the 1930s.[30] Ultimately, it mattered little, because a business associate of Spencer shot him, and any devious plans to monopolize the land went with him to his grave.[31]

But Spencer's demise failed to calm discussion about the reservation, as many people continued to voice opposition to the protected land base. Jonathan Biggs, the agent at the Colorado River Reservation, who at the time had jurisdiction over the Pai bands, wanted all Indians in the region relocated to his reservation. A group of Mohave citizens could not have agreed with him more. In contrast, Colonel Willcox as recently as June 1882 wanted to issue cattle, sheep, and farming implements to Hualapais at Peach Springs, where he thought the government should locate a new agency for them. The materials would entice Pais to the springs and draw them away from the small settlements in Chloride, Kingman, and Mineral Park, where the bulk of the non-Indians lived. The disagreements caused much consternation among the leaders and "Captains of different bands," who, according to Charles Spencer, worried that the government had forgotten their claims and would capitulate to the non-Indians who were still promoting relocation. Before his death Spencer noted that the tribe was "entirely destitute" due to settlers monopolizing springs on Pai lands.[32]

In the midst of discussions about the reservation, General Crook ordered Maj. Julius W. Mason to survey the population dispersal of Pai bands in the region. Mason traveled around northwestern Arizona, visited more than a dozen rancherías, and interviewed Little Captain, Hualapai Charley, and Cowarrow, who said that they supported themselves by herding cattle, working for wages, and hunting small game. The socioeconomic changes obstructed traditional land-use patterns, but if Mason's survey was remotely accurate, it demonstrates some continuity in the extended family networks and the geography of Pai settlements. Each ranchería included several families led by a principal leader or headman. The largest concentration of Pais gravitated around Spencer's Ranch in Matawidita Canyon, with more than two hundred people led by Sinyeoga, Captain Jim, and Capoo. The second largest group lived on the Big Sandy, with roughly one hundred people under Oculowat, Lehi, Pat, and Watpo, all of whom were members of the band named after the location in which they lived. The third largest group was in the Pine Springs and Peach Springs region. The Pine Springs band, led by Cowarrow, who was negotiating with the military to create the reservation, and Captain Jinks, was arguably the farthest from the disruptions caused by non-Indians, the Hualapai Wars, and internment.[33]

Other well-known leaders such as Hualapai Charley, Leve Leve, and Schrum were members of the Mahone Mountain or Hackberry band, both of which were hit hard by the growth of the non-Indian population. Leve Leve had a camp with forty-two people in the Hualapai Mountains, where timber and minerals attracted newcomers. It was also a short distance from the budding town of Kingman, the eventual county seat. The impact upon his people from this demographic growth may explain his interest in creating a reservation to preserve land for the bands. The same could have been said for Hualapai Charley, who had a smaller group with him near Truxton Canyon, and Schrum, who had twenty-four people with him near Camp Beale's Springs (see fig. 2.1). These settlement patterns reflected the location of traditional band sites as well as Pais' desire to use the small towns as sources of employment and materials. Ultimately, it is difficult to precisely determine the rationales motivating every decision to live in a particular place when the cultural and economic landscape was in such flux.[34]

This brief survey of Pai landscapes could not have done justice to myriad forms of economic and cultural adaptation, nor could it have conceivably decoded the changing familial structures and merger of bands and villages. Major Mason did not live with or remain near the bands for any length of time, so his observations must be absorbed with caution, as should comments that the "Indian is a homeless wanderer in his own land" with "no place to call his own." Mason may not have understood the social changes wrought by the events of the past two decades when he and most non-Indians were guided by a linear view of human development that placed Indians at the bottom of a social hierarchy. His perception of culture was rooted in Victorian notions of civilization that disparaged communal landholding and oral cultures. This mental world would surely have influenced his survey and subsequent assessment that Hualapais were homeless and wandering rather than trying to maintain ties to traditional territories. The impact of the wars, removal, internment, and other recent upheavals does not appear in the authoritative narrative created for and by the federal government, yet it does give a glimpse of the changing landscape of Pai camps and families.[35]

FIGURE 2.1. Hualapai Charley, circa 1906. Photograph
taken by H. H. Watkins, #108, Mohave Museum of
History and Arts, Kingman, Arizona.

Despite such ambiguities, when President Chester A. Arthur signed the
executive order creating the Hualapai reservation, he affirmed Hualapais'
right to a portion of their homelands and implicitly recognized the territorial and political basis for Hualapai sovereignty. The reservation included
lands occupied by the Grass Springs, Milkweed Springs, Hackberry, Peach
Springs, Pine Springs, and possibly the Cataract Canyon bands. In contrast,
it excluded territories of the Red Rock, Clay Springs, Cerbat Mountain,

Hualapai Mountain, Mohone Mountain, Big Sandy, and Juniper Mountain bands farther to the west and south. Yet this 997,000-acre reservation would profoundly alter the identity, cultural landscape, and political-legal status of the people the government wanted to move there.[36]

## Life on (and off) the Reservation

While it is difficult to determine the reactions of all Pais to the creation of the reservation, its establishment raised important questions, ranging from basic concerns with food and shelter to more complex issues such as Hualapai identity, cultural landscapes, and band relationships. Native peoples in the region relied on a wide territorial area from which they hunted, grew small gardens, gathered food, and traded with each other, but by the mid-1880s this cultural ecology and interethnic economy had been weakened by non-Indians and their laws, land tenure, and transportation routes. Reservations emerged in this changing milieu as colonial spaces where the Indian Office could strip Indigenous people of their cultures and transform them into modern citizens of the state, but Native communities like the Pais subverted, rejected, and complicated these goals in various ways. Many of the people confined on reservations by the Indian Office and the military saw those reservations as prisons that insulted the people with disease, poverty, and limits to their traditional migration patterns and ceremonial sites. Reservations reminded Indigenous communities of conquest and the people's lack of control over their own lives. Indeed, reservations symbolized the power of the American nation-state and the futility of resistance. On the other hand, for other Native people a reservation in their aboriginal homelands was an important victory in light of the terrible options of landlessness and marginalization.[37]

Contributing to the problems created by Anglo ranchers on the reservation was its failure to encompass some bands and their specific territories, and thus it did not appeal to them as "their space." Northeastern Pais consisted of thirteen semiseparate bands of extended families that did not recognize a centralized political leadership. They lived in rancherías and migrated throughout the year for food, yet they relied on fairly fixed destinations and seasonal homes. They spoke a common language and shared similar beliefs about the world, their origins, and their cultural landscape, but the central core of their identity remained rooted in the band and extended family, not the modern sense of a nation. This structure had implications for their reaction to the reservation. Overlaying the reservation upon a few band territories and attaching the name "Hualapai" to it acknowledged spatial and symbolic boundaries that included and excluded some bands. This new bureaucratic colonization of Indigenous space overshadowed Pais' use of band names and geographical monikers to describe themselves, racializing Pais as a single group in the minds of non-Indians. Bands continued to refer to themselves in traditional ways, but the new identity of "Hualapai," tied to a reservation, altered internal and external processes of identification. The common experiences of internment and escape also reconceptualized the Pais from dispersed bands to a people with an increasingly similar fate. Nonetheless, the conflicting trajectories symbolized by the reservation and the dichotomization of identities in the region into "white" and "Indian" on the basis of race, language, culture, and place caused the similarities among Pai bands to overshadow—but not replace—the spatial divisions caused by the reservation and the decentralized structure of the bands.[38]

These trends highlighted the tensions between band identities, racial constructions, and the implications of coding the reservation as a Hualapai landscape. As noted previously, the term *Hualapai* came into usage before the Hualapai Wars when non-Indians mispronounced the name of the Amat Whala Pa'a band (Hualapai Mountain band) of Pais who lived between King-man and the Colorado River. Non–Amat Whala Pa'a bands did not identify themselves with this term because no such umbrella identity existed that incorporated all of them. But the frequent usage of the term *Hualapai* and its coupling with the reservation space demonstrated the power of colonization to rename and recategorize peoples along racialized lines. More broadly, the naming process reveals the blindness of "the West" in its classification of societies and peoples into hierarchies, its reduction of complex stories into simplistic systems of representation, and its use of foreign criteria to define and oppress non-Western others.[39] Non-Indians had little concern for diversity throughout Indigenous America because they viewed non-Europeans as deficient in the characteristics that Westerners ascribed to themselves as indicative of their own superiority. By labeling the Northeastern Pai bands as "Hualapais" the Anglos fueled the conceptual colonization that marched along with the political colonization of the Indigenous peoples of northwestern Arizona. Thus, the reservation revealed a double-edged sword for band members: it served as a potential refuge from racism within their traditional cultural landscape, but its spatial implications tied the bands to the dubious signifier "Hualapai," itself a result of racialization.[40]

Despite its historical inaccuracy and origins in colonialism, "being Hualapai" had a literal and symbolic utility because the Indian Office had marked the reservation as a protected space within the Pai cultural landscape and because Pais themselves changed the meaning of both. Though never equal to past possessions, the reservation became a focal point for a collective—or national—identity that the bands would tentatively accept and elaborate upon. More precisely, Hualapainess became part of their layered identity as members of families, bands, and now a nation increasingly known as the Hualapai. This notion of being Hualapai also became fixed to residency on the reservation, although Hualapainess was not fully confined to living within that space. Many of the southern Pais, such as the Hualapai Mountain, Juniper Mountain, Red Rock, and Big Sandy bands, had never spent much time in the area assigned to them, but they had the land and few other options. These bands could have found some cultural solace knowing that because the reservation sat along the river it met their practical need for water and placed them near their place of origin.[41] This struggle to preserve some land reveals how "places are saturated with the fixtures and fittings of power . . . [yet] particular places may play host to a variety of cross-cutting arrangements of power," as evidenced by Hualapais' ability to retain a section of their homeland.[42] It indicated that power does not emanate unilaterally from one locus such as the state: it may be concentrated in particular places, and it must contend with multiple sources of countervailing power. In the Hualapai case no single group held political power to force them to the Colorado River Indian Reservation, so Hualapais and federal officials negotiated a spatial truce symbolized by the reservation.[43]

Creating the reservation raised additional questions about divergent views of the past and competing visions of the spatial future of the Pai bands. Hualapai leaders who struggled for the protected reservation hoped that it would help them maintain traditions and build a tribal economy. They also saw it as compensation for the service of Hualapai scouts during the campaigns against the Yavapais and Apaches. In contrast, Anglos thought the "free" land was ripe for development in the hands of citizens seeking to fulfill the industrializing nation's "Manifest Destiny." After 1883 they believed the reservation "locked up" valuable resources. Thus, northwestern Arizona was in this respect a microcosm of the larger belief that the American West was a tabula rasa upon which enterprising individuals could (re)write their future. History mattered less than exploiting tomorrow's possibilities through development and industrialization.[44]

The Indian Office similarly rejected the vision of the reservation as a cultural homeland or racial refuge and instead viewed it as a temporary laboratory to teach Indians "civilization" and progress, two supposedly forward-looking concepts. Their vision involved wrenching the Pais from their past and pulling them into the future with industrial labor, private property, Christianity, and individual citizenship.[45] This linear view of history and human development rested on the premise that reservations would insulate Indians from the "civilized life" they were not prepared for while teachers, superintendents, missionaries, and other "Friends of the Indian" paradoxically transformed them into darker versions of the people they were supposed to emulate: people who did not accept them in their "present state." Reformers believed that assimilation policies pulled Hualapais *into* history by placing them in a temporary state of tutelage, symbolized by the reservation, where they were magically prepared for the Western world.[46] Once properly transformed, they could enter civilization—and history—on par with Anglos and the West. Worse, superintendents chided Hualapais for refusing to move to the reservation. Missionaries and other observers in the 1880s worried that Hualapais in town and working for ranchers were learning terrible habits from lower classes of people, yet some of those same agents accepted payments and bribes from ranchers illegally occupying tribal lands. Thus, Hualapais faced marginalization and poverty off the reservation if they wanted to remain close to their traditional homes, but if they moved to their protected reservation, they became subjects of colonial policies seeking to erase their culture and identity.[47]

As bureaucrats and Hualapai leaders debated the past and future of the reservation, Anglos resided on unallotted land that was held "in trust" for Hualapais. These ranchers and miners invaded Pai lands in the 1860s and 1870s as the military waged a scorched-earth campaign of removal against them, and after the creation of the reservation in 1883, dozens of ranchers moved onto the tribal land.[48] Even as it opined for the improvement of the Indian race, the Indian Office did little to challenge the usurpation of lands that Hualapais needed to survive. Situated under the jurisdiction of the Colorado River Agency, Captain Byrne and Lieutenant Haskell, now agents, worked out of a ramshackle subagency alternately located in Kingman and Hackberry (fifty-five and twenty-five miles, respectively, from the reservation) and lacked powers of enforcement despite their mandate to bring tribal members to the reservation and initiate farming and cattle operations. Even military men such as General Crook, who believed the reservation was a "barren waste, from which nothing whatever can be procured for subsistence," contributed to the contradictions facing Hualapais.[49]

This landscape became increasingly tenuous as Hualapais nearly lost the reservation due to local pressure for allotment. Military and some civilian officials still wanted to relocate Hualapais to the Big Sandy, where they felt the tribe had a better chance of growing crops and establishing a small farming community. In an 1884 investigation by Capt. F. E. Pierce, ten non-Indians farmed 850 acres in the Big Sandy area, but most seemed willing to sell the land since they lacked markets for their crops. Pierce counted one hundred

Hualapais working for the farmers or raising their own food and figured that they could grow crops for subsistence if not sale at the market. He claimed that the rest of the tribe could move there and have abundant pasturage "if procured by the government for their use." Perhaps, Pierce thought, "in two years they can become self-sustaining, under suitable management."[50]

A local movement to allot the reservation compounded discussions of relocation to Big Sandy. Federal allotment policy began in 1887 with the Dawes Act and attempted to accomplish several objectives: break up Native communities, encourage individual initiative, further the "progress" of Indian farmers, reduce the cost of Indian administration, secure a portion of reservations as Indian land, and open "surplus" land to non-Indians.[51] Demand for Indian land occurred across the West and resulted in a massive transferal of territory from Native communities to non-Indian businesses, states, and individuals. Estimates place this loss at between 80 and 110 million acres, hitting the plains and Indian Territory the hardest. The Southwest escaped the worst of allotment since little of the region was suitable for agriculture, but by 1934 portions of the Navajo, San Carlos, and Salt River reservations experienced allotment. By the time Congress passed the Indian Reorganization Act and ended allotment, Arizona tribes had 243,000 acres allotted; Idaho Indians 629,000; Washington 1.2 million; Montana 6.5 million; and Oklahoma Indians nearly 19.5 million acres.[52]

The dissolution of tribal lands would have erased the boundaries between federally protected tribal lands and state lands susceptible to taxation and alienation. Following these national trends, a group of "concerned citizens" offered their solution to the "Hualapai problem" in 1888, when the Mohave County Board of Supervisors sent a petition to the secretary of the Interior demanding he open the reservation. Under the chairmanship of local rancher Sam Crozier, two dozen petitioners claimed that the Hualapai lands contained gold, silver, lead, and copper and argued it was senseless to hold the territory in trust, since few Indians lived on a reservation without water. Allotment advocates pointed to the lack of clear surveys as justification for settlers "unknowingly" occupying Hualapai land, and superintendents such as Oliver Gates proclaimed that the Hualapais owned "some of the most valueless land on earth" that comprised the "wildest, roughest country that ever lay in God's out-of-doors." His views and those of others made it difficult to keep the reservation, since "Indians couldn't live on it if they wanted to. The reservation—if it is regarded as a reservation—is a farce and only makes trouble for the superintendent in charge, while doing the Indians no good what so ever." He added, "The sooner it is abandoned, the better."[53]

Vague boundaries fueled jurisdictional disputes because Mohave County claimed that it policed the reservation even though it did not receive property taxes. This lack of clear borders between state, private, and reservation land resulted in numerous allegations of boundary moving and tampering with monuments that denoted reservation territory. County officials pointed to rock markers that conflicted with the executive order creating the reservation, and ranchers moved cattle freely between reservation land and allotments on the public domain. The board also argued that the distribution of rations in Hackberry kept the Hualapais from moving to the reservation. Ironically, the petitioners ignored that most Hualapais could not live on the reservation because non-Indians monopolized the water.[54]

Schrum addressed threats to his people by confronting the military and Indian Office about boundary disputes and rumors of relocation. He refused to move to the Big Sandy, and he resisted efforts to allot the reservation, but he asserted that Hualapais could adapt if they could choose where they wanted to live and when and how they worked. He admitted living on Charles Spencer's old ranch, but he also noted that he went into town during the winter for wage-labor positions. At the ranch he had a "first rate year" with "plenty of grass, seed, etc." He also pointed to the women, who "wash clothes and gather hay [and] make plenty of money, so they don't get hungry, as they once did." He continued, "Before the whites came the Hualapais lived on rabbits, mesquite, etc. Now the whites have come and the Indians are comfortable—have horses, cattle, and work. As children we lived here, and we don't want to move. If the President could see us, he would think so too."[55]

In an apparent acknowledgment of Hualapais' insistence on the permanence of the reservation, the government appointed them an industrial teacher and special disbursing agent named Henry P. Ewing. Ewing began in 1895 under the jurisdiction of the Colorado River Indian Reservation with oversight of the Hualapais, Yavapais, and Havasupais. Lacking support from Washington, he distributed rations from Hackberry and Kingman to elderly or sick Hualapais and tried to monitor Hualapais on and off the reservation. He also had responsibility for the small boarding schools that the Indian Office built in Hackberry, Kingman, and eventually Valentine.[56] The Indian Office appointed him to serve as a full superintendent and agent for the Hualapais and Havasupais in 1898, when President McKinley signed an executive order approving land for the agency in Valentine, roughly fifteen miles southwest of the Hualapai reservation. Two years later the federal government set aside one square mile for an enlarged agency and boarding school. Hualapais now had the dubious honor of receiving their own superintendent who was fully dedicated to the project of colonization.[57]

Hualapais greeted their new superintendent with numerous demands, such as access to springs, better jobs, and improved health care for tribal members. Their biggest demand came in 1898, when Ewing investigated a Hualapai-controlled cattle business for the reservation. Nothing came of the initial inquiries, but it planted in the mind of the tribe the idea to establish a cattle operation. Ewing agreed with Cowarrow, Hualapai Charley, and Schrum that they should tax ranchers using their land. As cattle became a central objective of the tribe and because it simply seemed more feasible, Ewing implied that they should forfeit their interest in agriculture because the government refused to irrigate the reservation. Even if it did, Ewing predicted local whites would demand access to the newly watered areas. Ewing even warned tribal members that the reservation was still vulnerable to allotment, and he even obstructed development in its present state. Someone, he urged, had to survey the land and Hualapais had to live there, or the bureau could still allot it.[58]

Hualapais held onto the reservation in the midst of federal neglect and allotment pressure. By 1900 the combination of interest in the land, vocal leadership, and, oddly, bureaucratic neglect enabled the Hualapais to resist these and other challenges. Moreover, non-Indian interest in the land for mining and forestry waned in the early twentieth century. Finally, future agents in charge of the reservation worked with ranchers to give them access to tribal lands without worrying about allotment or acquisition of jurisdiction by the county. Despite Hualapais' opposition to allotment, ranchers won unfettered access to rangelands and water on the reservation. Yet the twentieth century brought some permanence to at least the idea of a Hualapai reservation. After the initial campaigns of allotment and the eventual mapping of portions of the reservation border, the federally protected portion of their aboriginal homeland seemed secure. While future challenges to their jurisdiction on and possession of the entire reservation would cause concern, the reservation had become a permanent fixture in northwestern Arizona.

3

# Society and Culture in the Early Twentieth Century

The restructuring of Hualapai space after conquest, internment, escape, and the penetration of the Anglo settler society transformed the reservation into a locus of contestation between colonialism and Indigenous nation building. Hualapais confronted the halting and uneven expansion of colonialism in Arizona territory at the same time that American empire expanded its reach throughout Latin America and the Pacific Basin. The power expressed by the American nation-state across the globe had a unique yet similar trajectory in Indian Country at the turn of the century. As the era of ethnic warfare and relocation yielded to concentration on reservations, the Indian Office initiated a new series of policies to "assimilate" Native peoples into the mainstream of American social, political, and economic life. Assimilation stood for many things, but most of all it was a sanitized term for modern colonialism without the unpalatable imagery of the British in India, Ireland, and Australia or the French in Algeria and Morocco. These nations, like the United States, used terms such as *assimilation* to mask larger processes that included boarding schools, prohibitions on Native religious traditions, and land allotment. These practices formed the core of a sustained attack on tribal cultures that continued through the mid-twentieth century.[1]

In the early twentieth century reservations were manifestations of oppressive policies and sites of resistance, but they were not the only location of protest. Hualapais' struggles against colonization frequently took place beyond the borders of this federally administered space. They confronted capitalist marketplace economics, negotiated boarding schools, and accepted or rejected transformations in their religious beliefs. Some Hualapais sought allotments of land near their traditional village sites, some entered the migrant labor stream, and others crafted relationships with Anglos in towns such as Kingman. These reactions to colonization point to the persistence of Pai ties to the land and their ability to adapt to changing circumstances. And yet the spatial, political, economic, and cultural pressures of colonialism had paradoxical impacts upon Pai bands and identities because wage labor brought individuals together across band lines, yet applications for allotments off the reservation strengthened group differences across the greater Pai landscape. The penetration of the railroad typified industrial capitalism and the commodification of Native space, but Hualapais used it to travel across their homelands and maintain connections with each other and with neighboring peoples. Thus, "conquest" remained a contested and indeterminate process with multiple negotiations over power and change in northwestern Arizona.

## Labor, Capital, and the Commodification of the Hualapai Landscape

By the 1870s Arizona Indians were familiar with the economic realities created by industries such as ranching, mining, agriculture, and the Anglo towns that cropped up in the territory. Pais' decisions to work for wages as ranch hands, wood cutters, and domestic servants or in other "menial" positions unsettled standard stereotypes of Indians as mired in the past, as nomads, or as nonmodern peoples. In fact, Hualapais accepted wage labor as a potential pathway for cultural survival by incorporating it into the social context and economies of their camps and kin networks.[2]

Reports from the Bureau of the Census in the Department of Labor gave a snapshot of these labor patterns across the United States. By 1900 there were 51,218 laborers out of 237,196 Indians in the United States. Roughly 96,522 lived in the "Western Division," while 34,319 lived in the statistical area known as "Basin and Plateau." In Arizona Indians constituted at least 10 percent of the total population, a percentage equaled only by Nevada. Of the number of Indian workers nationally, 36,895, or 72 percent, worked in "Agricultural Pursuits": 11,414 were laborers, 20,890 were farmers or planters, and 3,385 were stock raisers, herders, or drovers. The others were lumbermen, draftsmen, woodchoppers, or "other." Of the 14,232 individuals not in agricultural industries, some were professionals, domestic or personal servants, industrial workers, or mechanics.[3]

Hualapais' motivations for work reflected beliefs partially at odds with the capitalists and managers for whom they labored. Whereas managers viewed employees as resources to integrate into industrialization, Hualapais perceived wages as "resources" to integrate into their cultural landscape. Hualapais and managers created a continuum of relationships rooted in two contending labor value systems. At the extreme embraced by capital, Hualapais represented a racialized labor pool managers could exploit by paying low wages, relegating them to the most difficult work, and firing them before non-Indians. Cultural and economic self-determination, family cohesion, and survival represented the other end embraced by Hualapais. Interactions with regional industries fluctuated between employers exploiting Hualapais and Hualapais' use of the work for wages, clothing, food, and necessities they could no longer easily acquire. Indeed, if Hualapais wanted to survive, they had to embrace aspects of the new economy.[4]

Newspaper reports and the memories of Hualapais themselves shed light on the relationship between wage labor and subsistence patterns as well as the maintenance of traditions in a modern context. As industrialization attenuated hunting parties that enabled men to provide for their people, capitalist economic development weakened multitribal trade networks that generated wealth for the community. Leaders found new ways of maintaining authority and prestige, so Hualapais became "labor contractors" or "crew leaders" by recruiting workers for employers.[5] Crew leaders gathered men and women from outside their own bands to work in a labor group composed of multiple bands and families. Membership in these "labor gangs" was fluid because it was highly influenced by the demands of managers, landowners, and ranchers rather than intraband responsibilities and obligations. Thus, the dictates of capitalist labor weakened distinctions between bands by increasing interband relations and reinforcing a modern national identity. In the 1880s, when Maj. Julius W. Mason surveyed Hualapai camps, he noted that Schrum, Hualapai Charley, Sookwana, Mocohone, and Wathutama coordinated dozens of members from various bands to work for ranchers and mine owners. Schrum had one of the largest followings, "with a [large] band of Wallapais whose services he farms out to the mine owners." Schrum contracted men to work as baggage handlers and maintenance men for the railway and as wood cutters and laborers for the Grand Canyon Lime and Cement Corporation, jobs for which they received needed income.[6]

Although the crew leaders had to meet the needs of capital, Hualapai workers maintained some independence and movement around the region. What must have looked like aimless wandering to Anglos was in fact an adaptive strategy to avoid the gaze of the Indian Bureau and simultaneously preserve connections with their cultural landscape. Rather than submit to relocation to the south or, for some, concentration on the reservation to the north, Hualapai workers moved around their aboriginal territory with surprising freedom. In reaction to their spatial rebellion, Agent Henry P. Ewing tried to control his "wards" and bring them to the reservation by punishing crew leaders through the withholding of rations to their family members.[7] And yet Ewing recognized that the arid conditions in northwestern Arizona made it difficult to convince Hualapais to farm on the reservation. Some agents even ignored the policy of concentration because Anglos controlled the best springs on the reservation and admitted that their prospects as workers seemed brighter than as farmers, so they fostered Hualapai wage labor off-reservation.

By 1899 even Ewing had converted to this line of thinking as he helped Hualapais find work as cowboys, wood-haulers, and hay-packers, estimating that 75 percent of the men supported themselves with wages from industries in the region. This was a fairly large percentage of the tribe, but the pattern continued into the twentieth century. In 1910 Superintendent Charles E. Shell contracted with J. W. Wood from Needles, California, to provide him with Hualapai men. Wood owned property in Hackberry near the reservation, and Shell hoped they would live there and take up agriculture. When they accepted the jobs around his farm but refused to relocate, Shell ruminated that they would never "come to their senses and take hold while there is opportunity."[8]

Some employment took Hualapais outside of the region, but all the jobs provided Hualapais with income that helped them survive the vicissitudes of a market economy. In 1912 Superintendent Shell noted that several Hualapais picked cotton in southern Arizona, more than a dozen left for California's Imperial Valley, and a few boys went to work in the Colorado beet fields. At least six people joined the Barnum and Bailey Circus.[9] By the second decade of the twentieth century most Hualapais lived free of rations and earned $1.50 a day in various industries, while some Hualapai cowboys received a monthly salary of $35.00. In the mid-1920s twelve Hualapais worked in local mines earning $5.00 a day, while others in Kingman found employment as a chauffeur, in a saloon, and in a barbershop. The railroad employed Hualapais in the baggage department at an astonishing $160.00 a month, and a utility company employed Hualapais as laborers. Even a slaughterhouse employed one Hualapai, who the manager claimed was "as good a beef skinner as any white man," paying him $7.50 a week. Hualapais also worked in a hotel and department store, cleaning rooms and washing dishes.[10]

Hualapai women played an important role in the adaptation of bands and families to economic change in northwestern Arizona. While many scholars have investigated the intersection of labor and gender for women of color, few have analyzed the role of Indian women as wage laborers in the United States.[11] Hualapai women provided income to their families by working as domestics in the homes of Anglo women, echoing national statistics on employment at the turn of the century. A 1904 Department of Labor Census Report estimated that out of 11,716 female Indian workers in the United States, 5,565 were in agricultural pursuits, 276 were in professional services such as teaching and nursing, 2,421 held positions as domestic workers, housekeepers, or waitresses, while 3,391 had manufacturing positions. Women also tended to the gardens of Anglos and worked in the fields as migrant laborers with their male counterparts.[12]

Hualapai women often earned more than men since they worked in the migratory labor camps and for wages in nearby towns. In 1905 Superintendent Gates noted that some women made more money than men and that the infusion of cash provided them with new opportunities and increased personal mobility. Hualapai women used wages to purchase food and household items, but they also used the cash to visit camps and attend social gatherings and ceremonies held by Mohaves, Chemehuevis, and other tribes in the region. Numerous observers commented on the Hualapai women taking the train back and forth from Needles, California, through Kingman, eastward to Seligman, and as far as Flagstaff.[13] Some were even able to purchase luxury items that were becoming increasingly available through mail order catalogs in the late nineteenth and early twentieth centuries. These economic changes altered Hualapai gender roles and opened up new spaces for personal freedom and individual expression (see fig. 3.1).[14]

These labor and demographic changes were directly tied to the intrusion of the railroad and the expansion of cattle ranching, two key economic developments in Hualapai history. Both industries ambivalently impacted Hualapais because they consumed Hualapai land and monopolized water, but Hualapais used them for employment and mobility. Working as wage laborers for ranchers allowed tribal members to gain valuable skills that they used to initiate their own ranching endeavors in the twentieth century, but working for the railroad led to a colossal lawsuit and legal battle between the Hualapais and the Santa Fe Railway. Cattle ranching in particular represented an important shift from wage labor to Native economic development for many communities in the American West. Ranching reminded many Indian men of previous cultural activities such as hunting and appealed more to them than farming, which some felt was women's work.[15] After several decades working for ranchers, Hualapais wanted to start a livestock operation on the reservation in the late 1890s, but this endeavor failed due to lack of capital, economic competition, hostility from non-Indians, and

FIGURE 3.1. Margaret Parker, late 1930s. Photographer unknown, #3662, Mohave Museum of History and Arts, Kingman, Arizona.

restrictions imposed by the Indian Office. More than anything else, the presence of Anglo ranchers on the reservation prohibited Hualapais from building their own cattle industry.[16]

Despite complicit superintendents who facilitated non-Hualapai use of the range, in 1914 Superintendent Shell began individual and tribal stock programs for Hualapais on the reservation.[17] For Shell and the Indian Office, the cattle industry represented a positive economic endeavor and an instrument of cultural change. Cattle sales slowly generated income, and by 1916 an expanded tribal herd of nine hundred cattle and one hundred horses covered the range. These developments, however, revealed persistent conflicts over Hualapais' control of their own land.[18] Hualapai rancher Tom Susanyatame complained that the Sanford Cattle Company grazed stock on the reservation without paying fees, and he noted that the Carrow brothers, two Anglo ranchers, received a grazing permit for land he claimed. Susanyatame also observed that Shell refused to allow tribal members Tom and "Broncho Jim" to graze cattle and horses, claiming that Shell "was not a good" man and he "never helped us out." Shell ignored Susanyatame even as he admitted that "no [Anglo] applicant has been denied a permit except where it was thought that more stock would over-graze and injure the range." While Shell approved permits for ten thousand head of Anglo-owned cattle, he admitted that "the reservation is not fit for an Indian reservation but it belongs to the Indians," an ironic point, since he helped Anglos monopolize the water, thus undermining Hualapai survival.[19]

As Anglo ranchers expanded their holdings throughout the Southwest, the penetration of the Santa Fe Railway as a manifestation of larger processes of industrialization, mechanization, and modernization brought more people into the area, pressuring tribal land-use traditions and forcing Native people to take wage labor employment. Beyond any entity outside the federal government itself, the Santa Fe Railway would haunt the Hualapai tribe for more than a century. The railway arrived in Peach Springs one month after the creation of the reservation, but its history dated back to the 1860s, when it received its charter from the government. In 1866 Congress gave a multi-million-acre grant of land to the Atlantic and Pacific Railroad, the precursor to the Santa Fe, for a transcontinental line along the thirty-fifth parallel. The law prescribed the potential route and provided a 100-foot right-of-way and twenty alternate sections of public land on each side of the track for every mile of railroad completed. When the company began construction in the late 1870s and reached the towns of Flagstaff, Seligman, Peach Springs, and Kingman in the early 1880s, it strengthened the connection between northern Arizona and transportation routes extending from the Pacific Ocean to the Atlantic seaboard and, in turn, the global economy.[20] As the first truly transnational corporations, railroads consumed vast forests for railroad ties, stimulated the coal and mining industries, and moved people and goods across the country with an unprecedented speed and efficiency.[21]

The entrance of the Santa Fe Railway into Hualapai lands symbolized an especially important set of transformations as Americans faced a crisis of identity caused by modernity. Science, immigration, industrialization, and other global trends shook the foundations of nineteenth-century Victorian ideals and in the process enabled Americans to move west, closing the alleged frontier and ostensibly ending an important chapter in American history. Into this teleological narrative the Southwest witnessed a curious marriage of technology, colonialism, and nostalgia best symbolized by the Santa Fe Railway. As it conquered the land and brought thousands of new residents and tourists, the Santa Fe Railway marketed southwestern culture and the Indigenous people with advertising techniques propounding idyllic landscapes inhabited by Indians living in harmony with nature—a stark contrast to an age of mechanization. Images of the "Santa Fe Indian" and trains named the Chief, Super Chief, and Navajo blended technology, advertising, and "traditional" Indian cultures into a single package for tourists. Indian detours gave visitors a glimpse of "authentic" and "primitive" Native ceremonies long forgotten, and, coupled with Fred Harvey's restaurants, dining cars, and the "Harvey Girls," the Santa Fe profoundly shaped images of the Southwest. In Peach Springs the railway allowed tourists to leave the train and amenities of modern life to explore one of the most "remote" regions of the country. As the first tourists on the Hualapai reservation, easterners climbed into Harvey Cars, drove the automobiles along a twenty-five-mile bone-jarring road interwoven with Diamond Creek, and parked on the beach, where they looked with awe at the red and gold stratified walls that rose from the frigid waters. After a few words about the geology of the canyon, they returned up the trail and left the reservation.[22]

Hualapais reacted to the colonial nostalgia and economic imperialism of the Santa Fe Railway in surprising ways. Just as the railway facilitated immigration into Hualapai country and introduced new institutions into northwestern Arizona, the train enabled Hualapais to move around the region with greater speed and frequency. Hualapais had become such frequent riders that the superintendent of the Santa Fe allowed them to ride for free during certain times of the year from Needles, California, to Seligman, Arizona.[23] Yet the Santa Fe still angered the Hualapais because it claimed much of their land and usurped the natural springs on the reservation, even if it provided them with jobs and the means to move around their aboriginal homelands. Indian Office employees reacted ambivalently but for different reasons: the railway offered employment, but it enabled them to avoid the gaze of the state.[24]

Various reactions to the railroad notwithstanding, it surely altered the cultural geography of the region. Hualapais sold art and crafts at depots, sought employment from the company, took rides into towns to purchase goods and trade with people, and visited friends and relatives (see fig. 3.2). The railroad also impacted Hualapai residency patterns and band relationships. Seligman, thirty miles east of the reservation, became a regular stop for the railway, but it was coincidentally situated at the territorial border of the Cataract Canyon and Pine Springs bands. These were the bands that historically avoided Anglos, but in this new context band members brought vegetables and other products to sell at the depot in the new settler community. As the town grew, it became an important factor in blurring band differences because increased interaction fostered a common set of experiences.

FIGURE 3.2. Hualapai women at the Santa Fe depot in Kingman, Arizona. Photographer unknown, #3634, Mohave Museum of History and Arts, Kingman, Arizona.

The growth of the rail stop in the center of Pai territory and the land of the Peach Springs and Pine Springs bands in particular had more negative impacts than it had in Seligman. When the railroad arrived in early 1883, roughly 250 Pais lived on the land that became the reservation, with most on or near Spencer's Ranch, and roughly 90 lived near what became the railroad depot. Some families left and set up small encampments elsewhere, hoping to gain access to water, while others worked as woodcutters or baggage handlers at the depot.[25] Going west, the railway established depots in Hackberry, Kingman, Chloride, and into California. The town now known as Hackberry had been a traditional site for the band of the same name, but the railroad depot transformed it into a multicultural site of interaction between Pais, Anglos, and Mexicans.[26]

Roughly thirty miles west in the Hualapai Valley, between the Cerbat and Hualapai mountains, the railroad helped create a small population boom in Kingman, which was becoming the economic hub of the region. The local *Mohave County Miner* reported: "There is hardly a train [that] comes into Kingman" without "a lot of Indians, who jump on and off the train while [it is] in motion, with a perfect disregard for their personal safety." The paper noted Hualapais working in saloons, barbershops, and motels for daily wages or food. The railroad allowed more women to travel into Kingman, where they received wages for domestic work or sold baskets to whites. Though Pai women enjoyed great freedom of movement to gather food and meet with women from other bands, the railroad simply altered, rather than transformed, Hualapai gender relations.[27] Thus, the railroad facilitated preexisting changes, and it ushered in new sociocultural and economic dynamics for Hualapais.

## Families and Bands in a Colonial Geography

The arrival of the railroad contributed to the legacies of internment, removal, and modernization as seen in wage labor, family structure, and band dispersal by raising questions about the ability of Pais to remain connected to traditional sites and territories. Hualapais adapted to these changes by returning to sacred sites, springs, and rancherías, even if they were claimed by towns such as Seligman and Kingman. Although non-Indians referred to the Hualapais as squatters, their anticolonial reoccupation of space represented an interesting fusion of tradition and adaptation because Pais historically lived in the areas that became towns such as Kingman. The Amat Whala Pa'a, or Hualapai Mountain band, lived across a large swath of land from the Hualapai Mountains in the east, west to the Colorado River. As Pais returned to their camps after internment, Anglos recoded the landscape and rewrote the regional history of human settlement in the area, silencing Indigenous voices. In their colonial narrative, intrepid settlers tamed the frontier and built towns as "Indians" wandered across the landscape and squatted in camps on the edges of civilization. This geographical and discursive restructuring of social relations reflected racial and class divisions in Arizona, but it also symbolized Indigenous adaptations to the settler society rooting itself in Native homelands. According to Hualapai visions of the land and past, the camps represented continuity with their spatial history within the context of modernity, despite the violence of the Anglo narrative, which cast them as homeless squatters.[28]

Tribes throughout the Southwest faced similar situations living off their reservations in a variety of settings. Laguna Pueblos had colonies in Albuquerque, while the Tiguas of Isleta del Sur inhabited a tenuous location on the outskirts of El Paso, Texas.[29] Yavapais to the south of Hualapai territory lived in and around Prescott, and Navajos lived off-reservation and found employment in various border towns.[30] The Tohono O'odhams made homes for themselves in a wide variety of settings in southern Arizona and northern Sonora, Mexico.[31] Since the 1870s Maricopa County had had a visible Indian presence, while Los Angeles, Denver, and Minneapolis noted Indian families moving in and out. Western Shoshones refused to move to the Duck Valley and other reservations in Nevada, while Shivwits and Moapa Paiutes evaded relocation to lands in southern Utah.[32]

Despite their spatial adaptations to colonialism, the legal status of nonreservation Hualapais was problematic for Anglos who viewed Indians as "wards" on the road to disappearance. Indigenous peoples inhabited a contradictory legal world, especially if they had not accepted allotments, which the Hualapai generally did not. They were not citizens, because citizenship in the late nineteenth century rested on racist assumptions of white supremacy and narrow definitions of Americanism. Thus, the local authorities did not respect the land or rights Hualapais were demanding attention to. Along with their use of the tribal language and retention of Native customs, few Hualapais were fit for entrance into "civilized" life. These conflicts resulted in several attempts to remove them from the homes and communities they established around Kingman. In what seemed comparable to *colonias* of the twentieth century, Hualapais "illegally" diverted water from the city for cooking, cleaning, and irrigation and sought access to amenities such as cloth, canned food, and farming equipment.[33]

Despite social tensions, towns like Kingman did reveal surprising relationships indicative of larger patterns throughout the American West. Indians and whites sometimes cooperated with social events such as rodeos and patriotic commemorations. Though ironic, a hint of goodwill toward the Indian community resulted in Fourth of July celebrations in town. In 1895 two hundred Mohaves traveled from Needles to visit Hualapais for Fourth of July celebrations. The tribes joined whites in a week-long festival during which Hualapais played Mohaves in a game called shinny. In 1910 Schrum and Leve Leve even asked Agent Enos B. Atkinson for supplies for a "big dance" they planned to have in Kingman to which Anglos and Mexicans were invited.[34]

The town also became a hub of political activity where Hualapai leaders demanded adherence to tribal rights. In 1893 Schrum visited Kingman authorities to tell them about stockmen who refused to grant Hualapais access to water. Two years later Hualapai Charley gave a letter to an official from the Indian Office and told him to deliver it to President Cleveland. Charley described the difficulties of life on and off the reservation, recounted the deaths of his children, and appealed for more rations. Not to be outdone,

Schrum contacted the *Mohave County Miner* and told them that his people were not getting their fair share of rations.[35]

Amicable cross-cultural interactions notwithstanding, the night curfews, segregated services, and racial hostility caused personal trauma and economic instability. Mohave County Judge Redman sentenced a Hualapai man to forty days in jail for assault on another tribal member. And Hualapai Charley complained to Superintendent Shell that several of his sons received sentences on the chain gang from Judge Redman for "drunken and disorderly conduct." Other Hualapais received hard labor for various alleged crimes. None received proper legal counsel, a chance to defend themselves, or a trial by a jury of their peers.[36]

As they navigated the unpredictable relations with whites, Hualapais retained their ties with other tribes in the region. They rode the train to visit Chemehuevis and Mohaves along the Colorado River. Pai bands traditionally walked and then rode horses to visit their neighbors to the west, but the railroad increased the speed and frequency of their travels. The railroad enabled them to attend celebrations and ceremonies, but it also helped them continue another aspect of interethnic socialization: gambling. With access to cash and rations, Hualapais and Mohaves had more commodities of value to spark heated games of luck and skill. Celebrations and feasts brought old friends together and rekindled relationships jeopardized by rapid demographic change and colonial bureaucracies that limited the movement and behaviors of Indian people.[37]

These public events hide the fact that in small towns across northwestern Arizona Hualapais confronted numerous personal and familial challenges that revealed the complexity of life in a quickly shifting world. In 1913 George Wakayuta and Indian Beecher wrote letters to Superintendent Shell complaining that the other repeatedly became drunk and harassed members of their respective families. Wakayuta, who worked on the McGuire Ranch in Kingman, also said that he spoke for the "Kingman Indians" who had been neglected by the superintendent and unfairly imprisoned by the local sheriff. He was accused and arrested once for drunkenness, but other grievances were apparent in his letter. Wakayuta criticized Indian Beecher for lying to him about where he and his family could receive rations. Wakayuta claimed that Beecher told him the Indian Office would disperse food and annuities in Kingman, but, as Shell informed him, he had said nothing of the sort to Beecher. Shell speculated that Beecher may have disliked Wakayuta for Wakayuta's apparent abuse of alcohol, but in Wakayuta's letter to Shell he states, "If Beecher has told [you] that I have been causing a lot of talk, he is not telling the truth." He went on to tell the superintendent, "I will be in Kingman all the time during this term of court and I would be glad to see you and then we can talk about the whole matter [alcohol use] and I can explain to you that I have not been causing any talk." Wakayuta may also have been mad at Beecher's allegations because "we other Indians" had evidently pooled their money to pay for his bail from "the Penitentiary."[38]

The rifts between Beecher and Wakayuta represented variations between bands and families adapting to a new colonial geography. Some bands and families relied more than others on the rations and goods provided by the Indian Office, and these differences may explain some of the complaints to the superintendent. Other issues may have been at work, however, as Wakayuta noted that some "old Indians talk like if Indian Beecher stay in there and not tell lies, he all right," which leads one to believe that there may also have been generational divisions within the tribe or leadership tensions between bands. He criticized Shell for employing an Indian as a police officer on the reservation because, according to Wakayuta, "you should not have an Indian for policemen, who has been in lots of trouble and killed one man."[39] Comments like this raise several issues. Wakayuta felt free to criticize Shell and tell him how to react to the allegations of other Hualapais. Wakayuta may have even threatened Shell when he said he would be in Kingman during a session of the court. Second, such discussions should not be mistaken for the stereotypical factionalism that scholars see in Native communities, because such debates complicate assumptions of tribalism and cohesion in Indigenous settings. Rather, such letters are everyday forms of resistance by Native people to colonialism.[40]

If living in and at the edges of the new towns represented one end of the settlement spectrum while living on the reservation represented another, petitions for allotments on the public domain rested somewhere in the middle. With 450 Hualapais enumerated by the census at the turn of the century, no more than a tenth applied for allotments in the twentieth century. These requests drew upon the 1887 allotment legislation, which proposed the dissolution of reservations and stipulated that Indians could apply "under certain circumstances" for parcels of land on the public domain.

Indian Grover, for instance, was a member of the Big Sandy band, and he and his family scratched out an existence with small gardens, a few cattle, and sporadic work for nearby whites. Grover's homeland was hot and characterized by rugged hills and rock outcroppings interspersed with cacti and small creeks and springs. In 1919 he applied for title to land on the Big Sandy, and in his testimony to the Department of the Interior he stated, "I have resided on this land practically all my life; since 1905 I have had possession of it and had lived continuously on the land, and have cultivated about eight acres of it each year." Grover wanted the land "as an Indian allotment," declaring that he was an "Indian of full blood, and a member of the Walapai tribe." On his land he hoped to use wage labor temporarily to supplement his long-term goal of farming. Of particular interest was his identification as a full-blood member of the Hualapai tribe, not the Big Sandy band, thus supporting the contention that individuals were increasingly accepting the term *Hualapai*, at least when negotiating with non-Hualapais.[41]

The 1910 annual report of the superintendent stated that more Hualapais would take allotments on the public domain if white people did not harass them. The report informed the commissioner of a Hualapai who wanted an allotment on the Big Sandy, but "a white man came and ran the Indian off." The superintendent reminded the commissioner of two pending requests for allotments and then went on to describe the most recent dispute over land: "The Indian came to me and I advised him to stand up for his rights under the law," even though the white man told the individual that he could not file for his own land. With his "allotment papers partially filled out," the individual complained of intimidation from whites. After repeating his previous statement that other Hualapais reported hostility from Anglos, the superintendent added, "The impossibility of securing an allotment for an Indian on the public domain when white men are concerned is the reason I recommend that an executive order be secured which would take into the reservation a portion of the public domain which would eliminate the white man rancher in allotment matters."[42] In support of this assertion, a 1911 report from Superintendent Atkinson claimed that not a single Hualapai held an allotment on the public domain, even though "several Indians had tried to do so." The Indian Office was even willing to consider exchanging other federal land so that it could turn the Big Sandy into a reservation.[43]

Not all superintendents shared such sentiments. The example of F. E. "Butch" Clarke, who applied for land on the public domain outside Kingman in 1916, illustrates how bureaucrats rivaled civilians as obstacles to Native survival. Superintendent Shell sent Clarke's request to Assistant Commissioner E. B. Merritt and noted that Clarke was a "full blood Walapai Indian" who "maintains tribal relations" with his band. Throughout March the commissioner corresponded with Shell about Clarke's living habits, clothing, language use, and relations with his people. Shell noted that Clarke "has taken up his residence at Kingman, off the reservation, has adopted the habits and customs of civilized life but maintains relations with his tribe."[44]

Clarke did not receive an allotment, but, based on the language of Shell and Merritt that Clarke was a "full blood" who "maintained relations with his tribe," the two probably concluded that he could not handle private property. Stipulating that his "Indian blood" was a liability and that owner-ship of an allotment required Clarke to sever all ties with his people revealed a policy that sought to destroy Indigenous cultures through assimilation. Although allotment divested many Indigenous communities of their land, new legislation increasingly based decisions about land on biological notions of race. Following similar logic, citizenship and property ownership equaled whiteness, while "Indianness" equaled backwardness. As Melissa Meyer and Circe Sturm note in their respective work with the Anishinabeg in Minne-sota and the Cherokee in Oklahoma, "civilized" and "full blood," tropes that dominated the racial thinking of the era, created hierarchies within Native communities and provided resources on the basis of skin color, language proficiency, and acculturation.[45]

## To Kill the Indian: Education and Hualapai Children

The racialization of Indian identity and the colonization of Native lands constituted larger disruptions following the Hualapai Wars, internment, and escape. Although it would be too rigid to say that Hualapais faced a choice between the past and present worlds, the turn of the century looked grim for the People. Disease had depopulated huge swaths of Indigenous lands across the West, and alcohol and Christian conversion pressured and trans-formed Native communities on a regular basis. Wage labor, an ambiguous status as wards and noncitizens, and blatant racial segregation accumulated upon years of outright warfare. As "strangers in their own lands" Hualapais confronted these assaults upon their identities in the form of a colonial education backed by the force of the state and the zeal of reformers.

Beginning with Christian reform groups in the 1700s and gaining focus and the weight of policy after the Civil War, the federal government embarked on a program of removing children from their homes and sending them to boarding schools across the country. Sparked by Col. Richard H. Pratt's experiment at Carlisle Indian School in 1879, federally funded schools sought to assimilate Native children into the dominant society by erasing Indian cultures and immersing them in the values and behaviors of white society.[46] The experience of Hualapai families with this process of cultural genocide was both similar and unique to schools across the country as the Indian Office confronted Hualapai parents about the education of their children in the early 1880s, when the first boarding school in the region was located at Fort Mojave.[47] Parents resisted efforts of School Superintendent S. M. McGowan to enroll their children with Mohaves and Chemehuevis due to the deaths and illnesses of Hualapais attending the Albuquerque Indian

School. Hualapai Charley and Schrum refused to send any Hualapais to the old fort, but they did agree to a school within their territory so parents could monitor the children and the actions of the instructors.[48]

Hualapais' refusal to send their children to Fort Mohave yet enroll them in a school that was closer reveals the complex terrain of colonial education. Families might lose rations or other assistance if they refused to submit to the dictates of the Indian Office. School principals and reservation agents harassed Native families about the future of their children, their families, and their race. If they sent their children, they exposed them to alien institutions that sought nothing less than their cultural annihilation. Yet schools offered parents and their children a chance to learn about the language, laws, customs, and institutions of the dominant society.[49]

After moving the school to Hackberry, in 1898 an executive decision set aside land for a "Hualapai Indian School Reserve" at the Truxton Canyon Agency in Valentine, roughly fifteen miles west of the reservation.[50] In 1899 the Santa Fe Railway traded land surrounding the old Hackberry Day School for land surrounding the agency at Valentine to the federal government. The agency was in a tiny hamlet named Valentine, which caused confusion because people referred to the school as both the "Valentine Boarding School" and the "Truxton Canyon Boarding School."[51] The school and agency occupied nearly six hundred acres of land adjacent to the Santa Fe Railway, where impressive buttes and mountains surrounded by striking vistas and wide-open plains formed a beautiful backdrop. When the school opened in 1901, it consisted of a two-story brick structure with two large classrooms on the first floor and two classrooms on the second, though officials eventually built additional wings as more students enrolled.[52] The Indian Office completed the student dormitory in 1901; it had a capacity of 215 children. The compound had a small hospital that could hold twelve students until the Indian Office expanded it in 1931. The campus also had a detention house, a laundry building, offices for instructors and administrators, and several cottages for the faculty and staff.[53] Coursework followed the Indian Office's basic model for Native students across the country. All students took math and English, but girls enrolled in domestic science courses such as cooking and sewing, and boys learned agriculture, mechanics, and leatherwork. Keeping in line with the industrial aims of the schools, children worked half a day on ground maintenance, with stock, or indoors cleaning the facilities.[54]

Information about the teachers and those who worked at the school and agency is scarce. Miss Frances Calfee, who worked as a field matron and taught the English and composition classes, filed for leave of absence in 1899 due to exhaustion and isolation. Shell praised her for "mother[ing] these children for years" and claimed that they "regard her with veneration and love that no other could for years obtain."[55] Flora Gregg Iliff also worked at the school and agency for several years. Iliff was born in Iowa in 1882 and graduated from the Oklahoma Territory Teachers' Institute at the age of seventeen. After completing a Civil Service test in 1899, she received her appointment to the Hackberry Day School for the Hualapai.[56] She recorded her observations in letters to her family that she eventually compiled in a book, *People of the Blue Water*. Iliff made observations on the social life and dynamics of employees and students in Hackberry, where she first met Miss Calfee, Henry Ewing, and a Mr. Graham, an Indian from the northern plains who was the head teacher at the school. She also met Sam Swaskagame, a Hualapai who joined the army and whose actions and untimely death in France made him a regional war hero. She became the principal teacher on 1 January 1901.[57]

Iliff romanticized her experiences with the Hualapai as she filtered them through a cultural lens shaped by a Scottish-American middle-class upbringing. She appeared concerned with the health and education of the children, and the deaths of tribal members due to illness saddened her. She provided one of the earliest reports of peyote on the reservation and commented on its role in southwestern and Mexican Indigenous cultures, while conversations with female Mexican workers offer a glimpse of the interracial dynamics of northwestern Arizona. Finally, she was one of the few people to document important events in the area such as the first day of classes in 1901. Despite biases and naïveté about Hualapai culture, her story offers an interesting sketch of agency life.[58]

The social and cultural dynamics at the school mirrored some aspects of Indian education across the nation. Hopi, Navajo, Havasupai, Hualapai, Yavapai, Chemehuevi, and Mohave children attended the school and struggled to survive their surroundings. The first report from Truxton in 1902 noted 160 children enrolled, and it reported 535 Hualapais in the region, though few actually lived on the reservation. A 1905 report noted that for several years after its initial operation the school functioned well: most of the students were Hualapai, but others came from various reservations across the Southwest.[59] Oliver Gates, the superintendent from 1904 to 1910, claimed that in 1905 there were 116 children between six and sixteen years old in the tribe, and he hoped to enroll them the following year. Superintendent Shell claimed that attendance exceeded two hundred in 1916.[60]

When students grew too old to attend the institution, the Indian Office typically sent them to the Phoenix Indian School, a few days' trip from the reservation. Superintendent Atkinson noted that Johnnie Heneta and Tommy Clark, "the two best boys in the school," had been transferred to Phoenix along with Mack Tokespeta.[61] Eddie Wakayuta and Roger Havatone won the praises of Superintendent Atkinson, who said they were "among the most advanced pupils of this school and they were allowed to sign their own consent as their advancement and ages were sufficient to warrant their doing so." They left in 1910, while three years later a larger group of students were poised to leave northwestern Arizona. Hayney Crozier, Philip Huya, Will Hunter, Pete Imus, Pedro Piema, Frosty Querta, Wesley Sullivan, Dan Suathajame, Agnes Honga, and Daisy Tokespeta completed eighth grade and seemed prepared to move on in their studies. Their departure, however, raised important questions about their education in Valentine and their role in helping run the school. In a 1913 letter to the Phoenix Indian School, Superintendent Shell admitted:

> The situation that confronts every superintendent of a small school when the matter of transfer of large pupils is suggested confronts me. There is the usual work of the school to be done such as dish washing, cleaning, sewing, farm and repair work, care of the fires, care of the stock, etc. It is impossible for the employees to do all of this and those who are left are too small. I do not claim that the good of the children should not receive first consideration. Indeed it should, but who will do the work?[62]

Such candor revealed the colonial nature of boarding schools: they indoctrinated students into the mainstream of American life, stripped them of their heritage, physically abused them, and conscripted them for labor.

Several examples bear this out. In 1913 Hayney Crozier ran away to avoid whippings at the hands of the school engineer. When Hayney did not return for several weeks, Superintendent Shell wrote a letter to Kate Crozier, Hayney's father. Shell admitted that Mr. Hart, the school engineer, beat Hayney because he refused to clean a sewer pipe, but Shell did not question the punishment. Hayney returned at the urging of his father despite the problems with the engineer, but when Hart told him to clean out the stables, Hayney again refused. Superintendent Shell again wrote to Kate Crozier, complaining that Hayney was "always troublesome and it is hard to know what to do with him." The superintendent eventually sent him, without the approval of Kate Crozier, to the Phoenix Indian School.[63]

The conditions at the school continued to provoke controversy and investigations like the one conducted in 1917 by L. F. Michael, an inspector for the Bureau of Indian Affairs. In his summary to the commissioner of

Indian Affairs, Michael noted that in November 1916 Augustus Walema, William Honga, Bert Cook, and Dickson Saujiname were stripped of their clothes and whipped for leaving school. Based on interviews with employees and several students, Michael learned that these degrading practices were typical. In October Lodema Butler, Elizabeth Cook, Glada Pakatata, Olive Keho, and Maud Augge were locked in a basement washroom and fed bread and water for ten days. As punishment for speaking with other children, school employees whipped two students. Superintendent Shell admitted that worker J. A. Jamison was guilty of the whippings, but Shell responded defiantly, "No denial is made as to the allegation; they had plenty of bread and water and that they lost no weight during the months of their period of confinement." Shell's comment was surprising, if not for its insensitivity, then for the unsolicited information to Michael about the treatment.[64]

These conditions caused parents to express concerns about the policies of the school. George Wakayuta sent several of his children to the Truxton boarding school, roughly thirty-five miles from his camp near Kingman. In 1913 he contacted Superintendent Shell to inform him that he wanted his children to return home when they were sick because he felt that they had not received proper health care at the school. George Wakayuta also expressed his concern about the punishment of children at the school. He said that his son brought a "club or billy" home one day, and Wakayuta wondered "what these clubs are used for at the school and if they are used to hit the Indian boys with." Wakayuta continued corresponding with the superintendent to let him know that he would not allow his children or those of any tribal member to receive corporal punishment for what they did at the school.[65]

While the schools played a central role in the colonial education system, other practices characterized its attack on Native culture. The Indian Bureau took schoolgirls and placed them in the homes of non-Indians across the United States. Known as the "outing system," it targeted Indian girls between the ages of ten and eighteen and forced them to work for middle- and upper-class families without pay. Those accused of "poor behavior" were especially good candidates for the program because it supposedly inculcated "proper" gender roles into its participants. Indian Office officials and reformers believed that the sexual abuse that sometimes accompanied the outing system was unavoidable in light of the larger goal of transforming Indian girls.

In 1902 the Indian Bureau began sending female graduates from the Valentine school to white households in California through the Sherman Institute in Riverside. Girls and their parents protested and sought support from tribal leaders and sympathetic whites in the area, many of whom employed these girls in their own homes. Even the *Mohave County Miner* noted how the policy demoralized the girls and their families, and it chastised superintendents for the program.[66] In March 1915 letters between Superintendent Shell and Mrs. Ovington Jewitt, the field matron at the Sherman Institute in Riverside, California, revealed one conversation in a larger discussion on sending girls to wealthy Anglo families. Shell and Jewitt debated the future of two Hualapai girls, Edna Hunter and Ora Schrum, both of whom had completed fifth grade at Truxton. Shell claimed that the girls were in their midteens and ready for work but feared going to Kingman presumably due to racism. Jewitt and Shell agreed that the girls would work for a family and live at the house of their employers, but they did not seek consent from the girls' parents. Shell reminded Jewitt that the girls would still "belong" to Truxton Canyon, regardless of the length of their stay or the wishes of their new employers.[67]

Though Shell and Jewitt decided that working for a wealthy California family would discipline and indoctrinate the girls into white culture, they failed to consider the feelings of Edna and Ora or their families. Indeed, many girls in the outing program faced hostile and abusive employers who forced them to live in closets and eat starvation rations. Sexual assault was also a constant possibility. One such incident ballooned into a case that required a federal investigation to determine whether or not a teenage boy raped a Hualapai girl. The inquiry took place between 1911 and 1913 and involved the son of the California businessman for whom the young Hualapai woman worked. The parents noticed her unusual behavior, caused by the rape and resulting pregnancy, while she was home for Christmas. They contacted the superintendent and demanded an inquiry, which led to an investigation involving law officers and medical doctors in two states as well as agents from the Indian Bureau and Justice Department. A special investigator compiled a large file of information on the incident but exonerated the young man and blamed the young girl for becoming pregnant. The pain and trauma associated with such sexual violence are important parts of the Truxton school and its program of colonial education.[68]

Not all students faced such circumstances: they had a range of experiences at the school and responded to life away from home in different ways. Some enjoyed the classes, discipline, schedule, and work. Others quietly endured the impositions on their culture, while several resisted by running away. In the fall of 1914 Maymie Crozier, the daughter of the well-known Kate Crozier, ran away from school. Apparently, she left in the company of fellow students Olive Kehoe and Frances Jeff because they missed their families and disliked the treatment they received. She enjoyed her freedom from the school, but after several days at home officials brought her back. Records indicate that she received a punishment of extended work hours and limited time outside. Such punishments were light, considering that many children were chained to radiators, deprived of food, and locked in basement cellars.[69]

Ultimately, however, the school fell short of its assimilationist goals of totally separating the children from their families and stripping them of their culture. Numerous Hualapai families chose to live near the school or on its grounds so they could protect their children, and they brought their children home with them during holiday breaks. And despite pronunciations by Indian Bureau officials and "Friends of the Indian" that the school detribal-ized its students, the children and their families redefined the institution to meet many of their needs. They did not wholly accept the content of the curriculum or the overt attempts at proselytization. Parents saw the school as a source of food, shelter, and clothing when they could not provide for their own children due to their tenuous economic conditions. Students who learned English did not necessarily lose their ability to speak Hualapai, and students who proved adept with a sewing machine, for instance, did not nec-essarily forget basket weaving. Moreover, they used the skills they learned in agriculture, ranching, and other fields to build a reservation economy when they became active adults in tribal affairs. Finally, by demanding a school closer to their homes and thus redefining it in relation to the community, Hualapais influenced the nature and scope of the Americanization process.[70]

During the early reservation era Hualapais faced important decisions about their economic, cultural, social, and political future. Dispossessed from much of their aboriginal land, they faced a colonial geography of new laws and boundaries policed by bureaucratic dictates and state power. Tribal members worked for wages within the capitalist economy, but they manipulated the system to maintain kinship ties and mobility across the landscape. They incorporated new technologies such as the railroad into their lives, just as they rejected or assimilated foreign religious beliefs into their worldviews. Bands fractured under the weight of disease and the prerogatives of the mar-ketplace, but other bands merged and coalesced under a nascent Hualapai national identity.

Thus, Hualapais confronted colonization with a range of responses. In addition to working in regional industries, living in and around cities, and seeking allotments, Hualapais increasingly protested the meaning of the colonial spaces carved out of their homelands. As the federal government tried to contain bands within the confines of the reservation, many chose to live beyond the gaze of the state, even as other bands tried to push ranchers off their reservation. Individual allotments and the maintenance of camps even as the settler society constructed towns that excluded Hualapais as racialized noncitizens underlined Hualapais' persistent claims to the land and territory of their ancestors. As Hualapais adjusted to these monumental shifts, their leaders became increasingly vocal about demands to live on the reservation, evict non-Indians, and build a viable future. These struggles for self-determination and Indian rights were profound expressions of resistance to colonization, but they also revealed the deep ties Hualapais had to the places they called home.

# 4

# The Politics of Native Resistance, 1915–1941

Nothing was said about the railroad owning half of it.[1]

Fred Mahone had grown tired of seeing white ranchers running cattle on his reservation. A member of the Mahone Mountain band and nephew of Indian scout Jim Mahone, Fred served in World War I, walked across France, and pursued a college education. When he returned to Hualapai country in 1919 from his years abroad, Mahone was angered by ten thousand non-Indian-owned cattle on the reservation. Stubborn and loquacious, Mahone voiced concerns expressed by many Hualapais about their economic, political, and legal status in northwestern Arizona. Mahone wrote the commissioner about the "dictatorial" superintendent who controlled the reservation. He told the commissioner he wanted "freedom from 'restrictions or wardships' under which Indians exist" and demanded cancellation of all leases on the reservation. He wanted to "be as Americans are, free to develop our resources, as a community and to hold our reservation land for future generations." In a single letter Mahone combined Indigenous sovereignty with a unique brand of Americanism.[2]

Not all Hualapais possessed Mahone's rhetorical flair or his uncanny persistence when it came to matters of justice or fairness. Mahone did, however, give voice to a growing Indigenous nationalism that tied the common grievances of Pai bands to the abuses of the Indian Bureau, as epitomized in its failure to protect the Hualapais from ranchers and the Santa Fe Railway. Mahone's nationalism emerged from a hybrid political culture situated at the historical cusp of "traditional" and "modern" discourses that symbolized the colonial conditions for Hualapais and Indians across the West in the early twentieth century: land allotment, second-class citizenship, reservation tensions, boarding schools, and religious discrimination. Overt and covert forms of resistance to colonialism emerged within this matrix of cultural change and sociopolitical transformation as Indigenous band structures and political nationalism coalesced and defined Native strategies of survival. Such transformations are evident with the Hualapais because a decentralized social structure that privileged band autonomy and occasional cooperation in time of crisis had begun to shift toward centralization in large part due to Pais' reactions to modernity.

Mahone's forceful talk about Indians and tribes, rather than his specific band or family, indicates a changing notion of what it meant to be Hualapai in the early twentieth century. Pai bands did not suddenly create a hierarchical or concentrated form of leadership after La Paz, and nationhood does not necessarily require sociopolitical centralization, but as individuals increasingly defended rights common to all Pais, the construct of a Hualapai nation became prevalent in their discourse as the frequency of discourse about band identities declined. But because this process involved varied reactions to external pressures from the colonial world in which Hualapais lived, not all Pais identified with Hualapainess as it existed in the early twentieth century. Designations of land into private, state, and federal status barred Pai bands from traditional territories, while the creation of the Hualapai reservation reoriented them to a new space carved out specifically for the collective Pai people. Land policy, boarding schools, and wage labor caused some individuals to distinguish themselves from other bands and in essence reject Hualapai nationalism. The Big Sandy Pais and the band that was increasingly referred to as the Havasupais did not easily—if at all—coalesce around nascent Hualapai nationalism. These groups passively resisted "being Hualapai" and moving to the reservation, which they interpreted as the spatial expression of this national identity. Thus, as the trope "Hualapai" became ingrained in the cultural landscape of northwestern Arizona, not all Pais accepted it.[3]

These external changes pressured Pais and pushed them in different directions. While some Pais pulled back from interaction with Anglos and their institutions, some in the generations following La Paz and predating the Great Depression expressed their tremendous dissatisfaction with a system of colonial rule. The Indian Bureau tried to control life on the reservation, and this angered many Hualapais who believed that their "traditional" ways deserved respect. Simultaneously, leaders tried to incorporate many of the "new ways" into their political and economic lives. Hualapais such as Fred

Mahone embraced American institutions and practices on the reservation if Hualapais themselves could control them. But the Indian Bureau was not willing to concede power to Hualapais, even on their own lands. The reservation may have represented a "Native space" that afforded protection from non-Native civilian racism, but it simultaneously brought the Pais into the colonial gaze of the Indian Bureau. On the other hand, off-reservation bands maintained unique identities through connections to their aboriginal territories, but the nonreservation lands were also marked by socioeconomic dislocation, labor exploitation, and racial segregation. These contending discourses of "Native space," colonialism, and the geographies of capitalism simultaneously worked against and in support of nationalist leaders such as Mahone who flattened out band differences in favor of "Hualapai" national interests on the reservation.[4] The tensions between and sometimes overlapping interests in anticolonial resistance and decentralization of Pai identity presented a political dilemma for Mahone's nationalism because his general focus on the reservation inherently marginalized Pais who refused to live there. The historical negotiation of these uneven power relations provided evidence that the Hualapais refused to accept domination, but it also revealed the limits of Indigenous rights and nationalism.[5]

## Hualapai Nationalism and American Colonialism

The push to "open" reservations drove much of the policy changes impacting Native people in the early twentieth century. Couched in terms of progress and assimilation, policies such as allotment emanated from the demands of local and national political and economic interests that saw reservations as obstacles to growth in the West. In some cases the Indian agents allowed non-Indian ranchers and miners access to reservations, while locals wanted to incorporate reservations into the public domain or buy the land as private property. But more than their material impact, the policies promised to obliterate Native spaces and absorb Native people into the American mainstream.

Thus, activities such as ranching became arenas for contestation over sovereignty, assimilation, and Hualapai nationalism because they allowed Hualapais some economic independence and symbolized their separate political status.[6] This push to create a Hualapai cattle industry was a tangible attempt to make the reservation economically viable to Pai bands, but superintendents obstructed their efforts. As the local representatives of American colonial rule, superintendents used revenue from the cattle industry to grow the same reservation bureaucracy created to control and assimilate the tribe. Various forms of corruption began as far back as the

1850s, when the reservation system emerged in California, and it blossomed in the 1860s under President Grant with Indian Rings, groups of corrupt Indian Office agents, government contractors, and local businessmen that preyed on tribal weakness and thrived on federal largesse. Indeed, by 1931 the Truxton Canyon Agency bureaucracy had swelled to 37 people for fewer than 450 Hualapais, or roughly one employee for every twelve individuals.[7]

These difficulties notwithstanding, Hualapais increased their tribal herd and family holdings. By 1923 families held roughly three thousand cattle, the tribe claimed two thousand, and one thousand horses roamed the reservation. Superintendent William Light noted that the "cattle herds are increasing very rapidly" and predicted that within a few years they would utilize the entire reservation. He even went so far as to say that "the reservation will maintain a herd of from twelve to fifteen thousand head of cattle." Families such as the Mahones, Beechers, Majentys, and Fieldings expanded their stock, and by 1927 the tribal herd numbered nearly seventy-five hundred head. Fees for the five thousand non-Indian cattle on the eastern side raised $10,000, and the superintendent said that cattle sales brought in $95,000 for 1927.[8]

The following years brought new challenges, with drought in 1928 and 1929 leaving the cattle dehydrated and the rangeland parched. Poor irrigation led the stock manager to begin a reduction program in 1928 that killed hundreds of cattle. Pine Springs band stockmen on the central-northern section of the reservation felt the brunt of the reduction program, and Hualapai ranchers in the Trout Creek District to the south almost lost their entire herd. When reduction ended, Indian Bureau employees cut the number of cattle grazing on the reservation to six thousand, roughly 20 percent of peak numbers.[9] In contrast, non-Indian ranchers who had used the range continued to enjoy unfettered access to springs. According to Superintendent Light, Henry Caufman and the Sanford Cattle Company paid $15,000 in fees during the 1920s, while Caufman held one thousand head and Sanford owned six thousand. The sons of Charles Spencer ran cattle in Pine Springs and leased land to Jim Parker on the west end of the reservation. Sam Crozier, William Grounds, and others "owned large herds of cattle" around Pine Springs and Milkweed Springs, according to Fred Mahone, while the Duncan Cattle Company ran "many thousand head" on the range.[10]

Situated in a colonial context of unequal power relations and contending views of Indian culture, the ranching industry represented more than a source of income. It was a site where Native ranchers and tribal leaders contested wardship by enacting their own agendas to gain control over a viable industry. Ranching families added to their herds and gained profit and prestige in the process. Yet paternalistic Indian Bureau officials and Anglo farmers worked as self-designated reformers and exemplars of ethnic uplift seeking control over Native resources for the betterment of Native pupils. Underneath this rhetoric of improvement and civilization was a system that exploited the original inhabitants of the land while controlling the resources they needed to survive.

A milder version of the conflicts over ranching evolved in the regional mining industry, which emerged in the 1860s as prospects of silver, copper, and gold enticed people to migrate to northwestern Arizona. Mining became central to the region's economic stability, and Indians became intertwined with the industry, both protesting its intrusion into their land and depending on it for labor.[11] Mining interests also played a role in the campaign to open and allot the Hualapai reservation. Convinced it contained minerals, advocates throughout Mohave County petitioned the Department of the Interior to open the reservation in the 1880s and 1890s, and in the early 1900s the Department of the Interior reported deposits of gold, lead, copper, and silver in Pai lands.[12]

Although Hualapais defeated campaigns to open the reservation to unfettered mining, the industry introduced them to Arizona Congressman Carl T. Hayden, an ardent advocate for the exploitation of Indian lands. After he supported bills proposing mining on reservations, Hayden gained the support of the industry in Arizona. Lamenting the "loss" for the state, since reservations "locked up" a fourth of its land, he stoked interest in access to minerals on Indian holdings. In a 1917 letter to a constituent, Hayden confirmed his interest in opening tribal lands: "I heartily agree with what you have to say about the Indian policy of the Government. You can be sure that I shall overlook no opportunity to reform it. Over one fourth of the area of our State is included within the Indian Reservations, the resources of which must be developed if Arizona is to make the progress which we all believe to be possible." An Anglo supporter from Hackberry agreed: "I do not like to trouble you but I think if the government would open up the Wallapai reserve in Arizona they could get a lot of copper there." After Congress debated various bills, it passed a coal lands act to "open" lands in 1917 and another pro-mining bill in 1919, both of which Hayden supported.[13]

And yet, as Hayden and his peers promoted this land grab, Hualapais became more organized and politicized over issues such as cattle leases, mining, and access to water. Their activism incorporated demands for material resources necessary for survival with discourse about self-determination and sovereignty over Hualapai life. In 1913, for instance, Hualapai scout

Jim Mahone wrote a letter to federal officials expressing his worries about permits limiting his ability to cut wood. "I wish to call attention to the fact that I received a permit from Los Angeles to cut wood and after I received it, a letter not to. Now I don't know what to do," wrote Mahone. He wanted to "hunt to get a little meat" and cut wood to stay warm, but the regulations angered him. Mahone was born before Anglos immigrated to the region, so following rules created by outsiders troubled him. Continuing in his petition, he said: "I don't know how I am going to live this winter. The documents I enclose show the good service I have done to the government and I feel that I am not being treated right. Kindly let me know what you are going to do for me and return these papers enclosed." Mahone's letter implied that the government had a responsibility to protect his interests because he fought against the Apaches, but it also hinted at his rights *as a Hualapai* to hunt and use his own land as he saw fit.[14]

Sparked by similar abuses, Bob Schrum, Fred Mahone, Jim Fielding, and Philip Quasula (see fig. 4.1) initiated an unrelenting attack on the administration of the reservation. They and other members created pre–Indian Reorganization Act (IRA) political alliances under shifting names and varied constituencies with a common goal of representing Hualapai interests to the federal government. They were ephemeral organizations that coalesced under mutual concerns about external threats rather than internal disputes. They lacked force, relied on persuasion, and gained legitimacy if the members possessed the traditional characteristics of Pai leadership and at the same time could solve modern problems. Not surprisingly, Fred Mahone had a hand in most of the groups. In 1918 Mahone created the Redmen Self Dependent of America to promote self-government for the tribe, control grazing rights, and oversee boarding school education for children.[15] A related organization known as the Hualapai Welfare Committee and pre-IRA Tribal Council similarly funneled collective grievances about grazing policies, health care, education, water, and the railroad to federal officials. In 1919 this group requested control over the tribal herd. Following this pattern of organic leadership, in 1925 Hualapais in Kingman created a Welfare Committee with a speaker and a chairman to address group rights off the reservation. The committee also met with Kingman leaders about education, wage labor, and the status of Hualapai camps outside town. These political bodies sharpened Hualapais' leadership skills and concentrated band identity into nationalist institutions that represented individuals and families.[16]

The experiences that Jim Fielding, Philip Quasula, and Fred Mahone acquired in the Welfare Committee and early Tribal Council helped Hualapais with struggles for land and water rights in ensuing decades. Such a

FIGURE 4.1. Philip Quasula, circa 1910. Photographer unknown, #98-6501, Arizona State Library and Department of Public Records, Phoenix, Arizona.

contentious issue emerged in the Peach Springs water case, which began percolating in 1914 after the tribal cattle industry began on the reservation. Although non-Indians had used the springs for several years, Hualapais' request for access to Peach Springs, which is roughly four miles north of the town and train depot by the same name, sparked decades of legal battles and political shell games.[17] When Hualapais demanded the return of the springs, the railway said it had "improved" the springs, which it argued lay within the odd section of land it held under the 1866 federal grant, after extending the railway through the reservation. But before the General Land Office had accurately mapped the alternating sections, the railway had begun in the 1880s to pipe water from the springs to its station. When Mahone pressed the issue, Superintendent Shell admitted to the commissioner of Indian Affairs: "There is no record in this office that I can find showing what right the railroad Company has to this water." After inquiring about the springs and status of the land, the Department of the Interior conceded that its failure to survey the reservation prohibited resolution of many ownership issues.[18]

The confusion over title to the springs ballooned into an impressive legal dispute with overtones of ethnocentrism and Manifest Destiny. J. A. Christie, the regional superintendent of the Santa Fe Railway, wrote to Charles Shell in 1914 to assure him that the railway owned the springs and the odd section of land surrounding it. No one questioned the railway's use of it, said Christie, since the tracks entered the reservation in January 1883. In the 1866 grant, the Atlantic and Pacific Railroad, the predecessor of the Santa Fe, supposedly held the odd-numbered sections of land on both sides of the track, and the line of the road was determined through Arizona in March 1872 across "vacant, unreserved, non-mineral public lands," eleven years before President Arthur created the reservation. The railway used these "facts" to prove its claim to the springs. Shell did not help the Hualapais with his ambivalence, admitting that the "rights to water in this country are vague" but not supporting a survey to clarify ownership. Part of his reluctance stemmed from the fear that a survey of the reservation would reveal that Anglo and Hualapai ranchers owed fees retroactively for grazing cattle on the odd section of Santa Fe land and thus provide the Santa Fe with ammunition to indict Hualapai ranchers who had used its land. This, of course, ignored the fact that Shell should not have allowed the ranching to proceed in the first place, but that was another matter. In several threatening letters to Hualapai leaders Shell implied that if the group pursued its claim, the railway could win a judgment for a third of the reservation.[19]

Hualapais ignored the threats and pressed for ownership of the springs by attacking the validity of the original deed and in particular the argument that the railway purchased the springs in 1882 from two non-Indians named Crozier and Decker. Light could not find a deed from Crozier or Decker signing over the springs to the company, nor could he find evidence of their ownership in the county courthouse. And in one of his many letters to Assistant Commissioner Merritt he again wavered: "The spring had borne the name of Peach Spring for many years prior to the construction of the Railroad. Indians had lived there for a very long time before the railroad was built, and had planted peach trees there, and given it the name, Peach Springs."[20] He noted that the springs' 100,000 gallons per day provided water to the cattle on the reservation, and he believed that "we are paying this money for our own water." He even argued that the railway "has used the water belonging to the Indians for almost forty years, without having paid them a cent for the privilege." And yet he concluded a 1923 letter to the commissioner with lingering suspicions that the railway might possess deeds to the springs.[21]

As Assistant Commissioner Merritt and Superintendent Light failed to protect Hualapai water and land rights, Fred Mahone emerged as the most vocal critic of the colonial abuses of the Indian Bureau. Mahone, neither a "progressive" nor a "traditional" in the popular sense, was loved and criticized by his own people (see fig. 4.2).[22] Mahone was from the Mahone Mountain band, went to boarding school in Valentine, and attended Chilocco Indian School in Oklahoma until he enlisted in the army in 1917. During his service he attained the rank of sergeant and served with the Allied Expeditionary Force in France. Upon his discharge in 1919 he attended Valparaiso University for a few years. Like that of other Indian veterans, his perception of the surrounding society and its relationship with his tribe had been changed by his service. He had proven he could survive and succeed in the Anglo world, so when he returned to the reservation in 1920, Mahone was intent on reforming the relationship between the Indian Bureau and his people.[23]

These experiences in the war and in varied sociopolitical and cultural contexts convinced Fred Mahone that the stalemate with the railway and the Indian Bureau required the assistance of groups outside of Mohave County. While stationed in Riverside, California, Mahone met members of the Mission Indian Federation (MIF), an organization that sprang from the grievances of tribal communities in southern California that opposed allotment and appropriation of water rights. With Anglo founders such as Jonathan Tibbet and a Native constituency led by Adam Castillo, the federation became one of the most influential groups in California and the Southwest.[24] Mahone tapped into its support to build political alliances between Hualapai leaders and the MIF and in the process politicized tribal members in northwestern Arizona because he demonstrated that the challenges facing Hualapais were nearly universal among other Indian nations. Moreover, he explicitly connected the actions of the Indian Bureau to the poverty and dependency of the Hualapais and then offered tribal members a coherent plan to improve their condition by attacking the Indian Bureau. Moreover, he gained Hualapai collaborators by introducing them to members of the MIF. Mahone even managed to convince skeptics such as Kate Crozier and

FIGURE 4.2. Fred Mahone in the late 1930s. Courtesy of
Camille Nighthorse.

Richard McGee to attend MIF meetings in 1921. These alliances angered
non-Indians, especially Commissioner Charles Burke, who thought it "abso-
lutely necessary that the Government enter into the prosecution of these
[groups] vigorously and with a determination to bring about [their] undoing
and elimination." In an effort to stoke anti-Indian resentment in Mohave
County, Burke and his colleagues tried linking these Indigenous movements
with communism in an especially ironic instance of "Red-baiting."[25]

   Filled with political energy after his meetings with the MIF and backed
by some local Hualapai leaders, Mahone established an organization dedicated to "Human Rights and Home Rule." The "American Wallapai and Supai

Indian Association began in 1921 with the central aim of restoring Indian land and rights" and opposing the "rules and regulations" imposed "like slaves" upon them by the Indian Bureau. Mahone added that the renamed Walapai Indian Association had "the right to bring any matter before the state and Federal Court to justify any wrongful causes amongst the Wallapai Indians and others." The proclamations of Mahone and the association to protect "the Indians' right of prior occupancy of the lands and waters" not just of the reservation but of nearly all northwestern Arizona attracted several prominent Hualapais.[26] Jim Fielding, Kate Crozier, Philip Quasula, and Richard McGee were outspoken opponents of policies on the reservation. McGee, who accompanied Mahone to several MIF meetings, especially angered Superintendent Light, who in 1921 referred to him as a "parasite and an imposter." Light thought that Fielding, Crozier, Quasula, and the other "ringleaders of reservation discontent" were "full of self conceit and imaginary knowledge" for denouncing the government and "biting the hand that has fed them." Light claimed that "these fellows are never seen at work. They are beggars, parasites, ne'er-do-wells, and live upon the industry of better men and women." Light's irritation toward the group would only grow, but it demonstrated the efficacy of their nationalist agenda.[27]

Many members of the Walapai Indian Association posed an especially difficult dilemma for Light and the Indian Bureau because to denounce them was to inherently admit that the boarding schools failed to produce compliant citizens. The paradigm constructed by bureaucrats and reformers should have made these individuals into models of "civilization" and Americanness, yet the boarding school graduates turned their modern educations against the Indian Bureau to defend indigenous land rights and self-determination. This "betrayal" of the boarding school system was one of the greatest ironies of colonial education: Indigenous subjects used the colonizer's education against the colonizer. And yet the graduates of the school—along with elders who did not attend these institutions—did more than seek concessions from the nation-state: they transformed the Western rhetoric of rights and justice into a Hualapai-centered view of modernity. Neither fully rejecting their own pasts nor totally accepting the project of assimilation, these Hualapais wanted modern rights and liberties in their own homeland of origin stories and traditional landscapes. This brand of nationalism, which fused aboriginal occupancy with demands for self-determination within the Native space of the reservation, was a powerful argument that galvanized Pai bands and angered superintendents such as Light.[28]

And Light was especially angry. In a report to the commissioner he intoned that "these educated Indians are the worst elements of the tribe," referring to Mahone, Havatone, and the rest. Roger Havatone had especially roused the ire of Light as one of the "worst of the pack." But more than that, Havatone was a friend of Fred Mahone and a graduate of the very same Valentine boarding school that Light oversaw. Havatone even sounded like his mentor Mahone: "We are not free people. We are prisoners. . . . [W]e were here first befor[e] any whites came to this country." Building on the belief that their aboriginal occupancy gave them the moral authority to demand attention to their grievances, he sardonically asked, "Who was that person discovered American first and Meet Indians on that country? [H]e did not brought any Indians along with him to this country from other countries across the ocean."[29] Thus, history served as leverage to have their claims heard.

The Walapai Indian Association came at a propitious moment of transition in the political culture of the Pai bands. In the 1910s and 1920s the decentralized structure of the bands still limited efforts by individuals such as Mahone and Fielding to channel people and resources toward a specific goal benefiting the collective interests of the bands. This was rooted in pre-conquest leadership ideals that valued headmen with particular skills such as oratorical ability, good judgment, persuasion, fairness, and some success in defense of the band. Bands and families rarely engaged in prolonged battles, and individuals had difficulty mobilizing people for an extended period of time. Elders helped resolve conflicts, oversaw reconciliations, and devised consensus "punishments." Sometimes they had the offending individuals and their families move away. Pai leaders also made decisions within a sociocultural, historical, and religious context that was common to band members. They followed specific laws and traditions that Pais understood, and remnants of these expectations and legal codes still defined good leadership. But consensus building and band consent stood in competition with the ability of Hualapais to understand and manipulate new legal and political systems shaped by colonialism and sources of power far beyond the control of headmen.[30] Thus, to some extent, the meaning of leadership among the Pais changed as the world around them required some new skills and attributes.

This did not mean that Mahone and his allies were restrained by traditional political culture, nor did it imply that Pai leadership traits were inflexible. Rather, Pai identity allowed for innovation and creativity in the political realm despite the onslaught of change initiated in the 1860s. By the early twentieth century Pais had redefined leadership characteristics such as good judgment, oratory, and generosity in relation to new conflicts and situations. The content and meaning of leadership expanded from one's ability to resolve conflicts between band members to a broader set of skills such as one's dexterity with the English language and knowledge of the American political system. This cultural continuity and adaptive ingenuity rested in individuals such as Mahone, Havatone, Quasula, and Fielding, who knew the "new ways" yet drew cultural legitimacy from their band lineages and relationships with key elders. Steve Leve Leve, son of band leader Leve Leve, supported Mahone, who also relied on Jim Fielding and Kate Crozier. Younger leaders and "new nationalists" such as Mahone and Havatone repeatedly called upon support from Crozier, Jim Mahone, Hualapai Charley, and others in an effort to tie their political leadership to the cultural authority of "traditional" elders.[31] Indeed, unorthodox Pai leaders such as Mahone required the moral authority of individuals born before and during the La Paz era because he had characteristics rarely associated with Pai leaders: he was short-tempered, vain, and authoritative. Having his uncle, an Indian scout from the 1870s, behind him helped Mahone because he needed individuals familiar with the cultural cues and symbols traditional to Pais.[32]

The anticolonial resistance of Mahone and his associates reflects the observations of ethnohistorian Loretta Fowler, who notes that during the early twentieth century the Arapahoe Tribal Business Council worked as an "intermediary between the tribe, Old Chiefs, and the Indian Bureau." Similarly, institutions created by Fred Mahone and others in the 1920s and early 1930s sought to mediate between collective Hualapai interests and the invasive behaviors of non-Indians. They also operated within a specific historical moment and position of inequality that resulted in what Fowler terms "encapsulation." Referring to the Arapaho, "Within a few generations after their first contact with whites," she argues, their "political system was encapsulated, that is, partly regulated by and subordinated to the national political system while at the same time remaining somewhat independent." Hualapais' attempts to create pre-IRA political organizations that represented the interests of all bands and in turn strengthened a Hualapai identity echo Fowler's notion.[33]

Mahone and his group demonstrated their brand of political nationalism when they contacted a federal investigator named John A. Atwater to uncover the corrupt practices of the superintendent. Atwater arrived in Hualapai country in 1922 to hear the protests of tribal members to remove Light from the agency. For nearly four days Hualapais told Atwater about the mismanagement of funds, physical abuse, unregulated grazing of cattle, and other grievances.[34] The comments of Jim Fielding, a "Chief of the Hualapais," are illustrative. Speaking to Atwater, Fielding said: "We have done everything to comply with the rules. We have sent most of our children to be educated. This is the Government's wish, not ours. Some of the boys have been sent away to school, they have discovered many things are wrong. These things should be adjusted." Fielding implied that the superintendent obstructed graduates when they tried to improve conditions on the reservation. He continued: "The Agent does not seem to care whether we live or not." Fielding added that he wanted the superintendent to take the money the agency received from grazing fees and use it to build homes on the reservation rather than place it in the U.S. Treasury. "You saw today the manner of our living," Fielding continued. "The houses we have built have been erected by us and the sweat of our brows. We ask the Government to do all in its power for the benefit of the Indians." Willing to compromise, Fielding wanted the government to help the Hualapais help themselves.[35]

Other Hualapais echoed his complaints. Fred Mahone told Atwater: "We want to be independent. . . . There is no reason whatever, we the Walapai Indian tribe are to be restricted or government ward[s]." Mahone wanted to enjoy the "social equality, political equality, the common wealth and welfare" that all other Americans possessed. He believed that the tribe could conduct its own affairs and "produce and maintain and manage various resources as mining, lumbering, agriculturing, live-stock growing, manufacturing, [and] other enterprises." He also reminded Atwater of the obligations to "keep and maintain the Executive Order signed and issued by our late Hon. President Chester A. Arthur on January 4, 1883."[36] Butch Clark added that Light disregarded their needs and used "cruel" measures to enforce his rules. Clark wanted Light to help with his cattle, inquire about his daughter's education, and "find out anything that I want to know," but Light reprimanded him for interfering with Light's administration. Indian Beecher talked about working for the Caufman and Sanford ranching outfits, but he argued that they had no rights on the reservation. "The land in the Pine Springs country where I live is very suitable for farming, ranching, or anything that the Indians desire to do. We want no white people to use this land anymore."[37]

Atwater surely failed to see the events on the reservation as an anticolonial movement of resistance, believing instead that Mahone had seduced Hualapais with "utopian dreams for his people." Rather than listen to the grievances about the terrible conditions on the reservation, Atwater chastised Mahone, Fielding, Quasula, and others for working with the Mission Indian Federation. Atwater claimed the MIF forced Mahone and Fielding to make demands on the superintendent and interfere with Indian Bureau administration. Atwater even called Mahone a "dupe" of an individual named E. W. Myers, who had become involved with the conflict over land and water rights on the reservation.[38] Atwater's comments about Mahone and his cohort were exaggerations, and even though Myers fled the state in 1922 due to embezzlement charges, Atwater ignored the conditions that compelled the tribe to trust a man under investigation by the state of Arizona. Rather than investigate the causes of Hualapais' willingness to work with a felon, Atwater blamed the discontent on "outside agitators." Light followed his lead and thought that "transient miners . . . I.W.W.'s, socialists and communists" were influencing the leaders, whom he referred to as "the most insolent and ugly spirited Indians I have ever met in the Service."[39]

Despite the dismissive tone of Atwater and the excoriation from Light, Fred Mahone continued pressuring the government. He received negative responses to letters he sent to Commissioner Charles Burke in 1923, so Mahone gathered signatures protesting problems with grazing, leasing, and water. In his own letter Mahone stated that "for forty years, 1883 to 1923, our government collected thousands of dollars per year from lease holders upon the Wallapai Indian Reservation and such sums are held in the U.S. Treasury at Washington D.C. to be released to all Wallapai Indians in equal shares." Mahone clearly expressed his views on the reservation situation: "We want the use of these reserve funds for the purpose of developing the reservation in approved businesslike enterprises, employing our own people under a competent manager [and] we want freedom from the 'restrictions or wardships' under which Indians exist. We want all reservation land leases cancelled and leasees removed in our favor so that we may occupy the grazing land and use the waters upon it."[40] Mahone then offered his definition of self-determination: "We want to be as Americans are, free to develop our resources, as a community, and to hold as community property, our reservation land for . . . future generations. No separate allotments do we desire, but urge that the Executive Order of January 4, 1883 be enforced."[41]

Steve Leve Leve joined Mahone and Fielding with their plans to transfer power of attorney to the aforementioned Myers and an associate named Everett Dufour. Dufour, who lived in Washington, D.C., on John Marshall Way, promoted the idea even as Commissioner Burke warned him about meddling in Indian Bureau jurisdiction. Burke then contacted Arizona Senator Carl Hayden about the situation with the Santa Fe Railway, Mahone, Myers, the MIF, and the movement against the Indian Bureau. In a surprising display of unanimity, nearly one hundred Hualapai men signed papers giving Myers and Dufour power of attorney. This alarmed Hayden enough to inform Burke about the petition and correspondence with Mahone expressing their opposition to claims by the Santa Fe Railway that it had a right to reservation lands. Hayden was especially concerned about the problems Mahone could cause for the railway, which Hayden strongly supported. In his response to Hayden, Light denied Mahone's charges in a fifteen-page rebuttal in which he referred to Fred Mahone as "actually crazy" and Jim Fielding as "worthless" and "indolent."[42]

By the mid-1920s Hualapais, the Santa Fe Railway, cattle ranchers, the Indian Bureau, and state officials held radically different views of the situation in northwestern Arizona. The railway continued to press its claim to Peach Springs and the odd sections of grazing land, which totaled roughly 350,000 acres.[43] The Indian Bureau reiterated that Hualapais had to accept their fate and assimilate into the mainstream. In contrast, Hualapais viewed the debate as a struggle over homelands that could materially and culturally sustain them. As evidence of this, ninety-seven male members signed or gave their thumbprint to another letter expressing their "desire to make this tract our everlasting home for ourselves and our future generations."[44] In 1927 Bob Schrum followed up with his own letter to the commissioner, protesting decades of colonization. "We are much disturbed about our land leased to cattlemen," Schrum wrote, adding that "we want to use our reservation from now on." He knew leasing kept the tribe off the reservation, and he addressed assumptions that Hualapais did not want to live there. "There are Indians who wish to establish a home. But the agent objected, that we must stay out of the land that leased to cattlemen. Why?"[45]

The struggles of the 1920s revealed how Hualapais viewed their political situation and place in history. Hualapais grasped the foundations of the executive order creating their reservation and reminded officials about their service against the Apaches and in World War I. They employed discourse about citizenship, Americanism, and contributions to Arizona to support their right to self-determination. Much of their dissent rested on a sense that their historical struggles gave them a "charter," or right, to demand attention to their grievances. Citing their relationship with the government and their aboriginal claims to the land, leaders reminded officials that they wanted to decide their future on their terms.[46] This confluence of history, resistance, and political adaptation marked a turning point in Native leadership across the West, where numerous communities incorporated elements of American democracy and Indigenous nationalism to create hybrid political responses to modernity.[47]

## The Hualapais versus the Santa Fe Railway

The hybrid political entities that members of the Blackfeet, Arapahos, and Paiutes created in the early twentieth century gained political currency and cultural legitimacy when they faced an invasive foe threatening tribal resources. As alluded to previously, the dispute over ownership of Peach

Springs and the confusion over even and odd sections of land became a full-blown battle between the Hualapais and the railway during the 1930s. Raising questions about aboriginal occupancy and the validity of federal railroad grants, the dispute tied up decisions about land use and residency because Hualapais thought the government might transfer large portions of the reservation to the corporation. Few people wanted to move to the reservation if the railway was going to receive a third of the good grazing land and most springs. This possibility contributed to the high numbers of tribal members living across northwestern Arizona in towns such as Kingman, Seligman, Truxton, and Hackberry. At the same time, the struggle facilitated Hualapai nationalism by uniting bands to cooperate against a common threat. This deepened the sense that "being Hualapai" transcended band identities and separated them from non-Hualapais as well. The challenge to their land base underlined not only their sovereignty but their *peoplehood* by sharpening a nationalist agenda defined by defense of "tradition" mixed with discourse on progress and a desire to maintain a distinct homeland.[48]

The growing legal dispute of the 1920s and 1930s was part of a complex situation regarding ownership of land and water on the reservation. As stated previously, the Atlantic and Pacific Railway, predecessor to the Atchison, Topeka and Santa Fe Railway, also known by its shortened title, the Santa Fe Railway, received a large grant of land in the 1860s. After several failed attempts to lay the tracks, the railway crossed into the reservation one month after President Arthur signed the executive order. In ensuing years the railway built a train depot and began piping up water from Peach Springs. Unbeknownst to the tribe, legislation in 1904 enabled the railway to trade acreage on the reservation for land on the public domain, but this failed because of inaccurate surveys and ranchers who refused concessions to the company. In 1910 the Santa Fe offered to pay for a new survey to determine its holdings on the reservation, but the General Land Office refused because it feared establishing ownership for the company. The GLO then started its own survey, which stalled during the war, and in 1918 Congress prohibited the "creation" of new reservations by "taking" land from the public domain without three-fourths congressional approval.[49] Thus, the interested parties could not point to a decent survey nearly four decades after the creation of the reservation.

As Hualapai political pressure increased after the war, the Santa Fe continued pressing its claim to odd sections. In 1919 the railway offered $30,000 to survey the land. Commissioner Cato Sells opposed it, but the Department of the Interior supported the railway's claim because it feared a lawsuit against the government. The Department of the Interior estimated that the survey would give the railway 335,736 acres and the Hualapais 462,213 acres plus 150,000 acres in the canyons. A congressional act in 1925 only complicated things by proposing to split the reservation in half and give the eastern section to the Santa Fe and the western section to the Hualapais.[50]

Stunned at their exclusion from congressional debates and negotiations between the Santa Fe Railway and the Indian Office, Hualapais contacted the Indian Rights Association, following a strategy that they had developed with the Mission Indian Federation to seek outside assistance with their campaigns for justice. The IRA began in the late nineteenth century as an assimilationist organization, but by the 1920s it supported self-determination and seemed well suited to help the Hualapais against the Santa Fe. Representatives agreed with the Hualapais that the railway neither owned nor could claim the land, and the IRA argued that the company had forfeited its rights to the lands because it failed to immediately lay tracks after the 1866 grant. The group also noted that because Congress had not expressly extinguished aboriginal title, Hualapais still retained rights to all the land.[51]

This alliance of Indigenous nationalists and Anglo reform groups brought the conflict with the Santa Fe into the bright light of Indian affairs and congressional politics. In 1925 Hualapais wrote an appeal to the commissioner, and in the following year the group visited Arizona Governor George Hunt asking him to give state land to the railway in exchange for land on the reservation. Jim Fielding, Fred Mahone, Bob Schrum, Frank Wilder, and others were accompanied by Homer O. Davidson, chair of the Welfare Committee of the Mohave Tribe and member of the Mission Indian Federation. Both the letter from 1925 and the meeting with the governor in 1926 expressed similar sentiments. Hualapais had a right to the reservation because they never forfeited land, they helped the military fight the Apaches, Chester A. Arthur set aside the land in good faith, and the tribe had been trying to govern themselves for forty years. Moreover, the Indian Office mismanaged their land, sold their springs, and tolerated ranchers on their reservation.[52]

As tensions rose, Hualapai leaders continued pressuring the Indian Bureau with new tactics, organizations, and allies. During the winter of 1927 Philip Quasula, Bob Schrum, and Jim Fielding met with a surprising sympathizer: ex-superintendent William Light, who, for obscure reasons, now championed Hualapai land rights and supported their collaboration with the Indian Rights Association. Light even helped his old nemesis, Fred Mahone, compile oral histories in a case for aboriginal occupancy. Bolstered by tribal support and the data collected by Light, Mahone created the "Executive Committee of the Walapai Tribe" to press their demands.[53] Their work yielded some results, with a 1928 Justice Department investigation into the ownership of Peach Springs and the odd sections of land. Hearing about the Justice Department attack upon the Hualapais, William Light wrote to the assistant U.S. attorney in Phoenix who oversaw the investigation to argue: "The Walapai Indians have occupied and used the land and waters lying within the present boundaries of their reservation, from a time so far in the past that it antedates the records and history of the White man." In this astounding defense of Hualapai land rights, Light continued, "Evidence of their undisputed occupancy, use and ownership of this territory is contained in their family and tribal records, traditions, and legends; unwritten, but faithfully transmitted from parent and leader, to offspring and follower."[54]

This was an impressive statement for a former member of the Indian Office and a superintendent who was constantly at odds with the tribe. Echoing many of Fred Mahone's arguments, Light asserted that non-Indians acknowledged Hualapai occupancy in the early 1800s and that the U.S. military recognized their presence in the area before the 1866 grant to the Santa Fe. He also reminded the investigator that Hualapais had no knowledge of the grant and were fighting for their lives against the U.S. military for much of the 1860s. Moreover, relocation to La Paz and appropriation of tribal lands by non-Indians prohibited Hualapais from using the region that became the reservation. Light said that the Hualapais never would have forfeited their land had they known about the grant. In his letter Light included testimony from elder members of the Peach Springs band (Nora Schrum, Jane Huya, Jim Smith, and Mike Sue) as well as several white settlers who witnessed the arrival of the railroad and could testify that Hualapais lived on the lands claimed by the Santa Fe. Light concluded this unusual defense of tribal rights by predicting they would win the case.[55]

As what would later be known as the "Hualapai Land Case" grew in complexity, Native and non-Native participants became increasingly worried about the state of Indigenous lands and communities. Between the creation of the Pueblo Indian Lands Board in 1922 and the 1928 publication of Lewis Merriam's *The Problem of Indian Administration*, a small contingent of attorneys and activists caught wind of the conflict between the Santa Fe and the Hualapais.[56] The Board of Indian Commissioners and the Indian Rights Association had already been assisting the tribe in a letter-writing campaign to the U.S. Senate. This pressure resulted in a meeting of the U.S. Senate Committee on Indian Affairs in Valentine to determine the implications of the conflict for Indian law. The tension, then, was palpable in May 1930, when members of Congress and representatives from the state of Arizona and the Department of the Interior met in Valentine to clarify the ownership of nearly a third of the reservation.[57]

The group gathered in the boarding school auditorium to begin what must have been a frustrating experience for the tribe. Several dozen Hualapais sat behind Kate Crozier and Bob Schrum, son of Chief Schrum, as the two answered questions from Special Commissioner H. J. Hagerman, District Supervisor C. E. Farris, and Truxton Superintendent D. H. Watson. Hagerman opened the meeting by arguing that Hualapais did not need the land because they failed to utilize it with cattle provided by the Indian Bureau. It was a familiar argument, this time offered by a bureaucrat with a long history of exploiting Native people. An appointee of the disgraced Department of the Interior Secretary Albert Fall, Hagerman had helped divest the Navajos of oil, minerals, and gas resources, and he attacked New Mexico Indians through the Pueblo Indian Lands Board. Undeterred by Hagerman's anti-Indian pedigree, Bob Schrum challenged him on the issue of occupancy: "We once had this whole country to ourselves, but were put on a small reservation by the Government, and the Railroad is now after this reservation. We lived here before the white men came into this country, therefore it is ours." Farris responded: "What we would like to see is all the men and women of the Walapai Tribe say, 'We are going to work and do something.'" The exchange typified the divergent concerns of the tribe and the Indian Bureau: Hualapais focused on rights and identity, while the Indian Bureau stressed work and industry.[58]

The 1930 meeting also revealed important developments among Hualapai leaders and between the Hualapai and the non-Indian community in Mohave County. Despite the consensus in opposition to the railway, the alliance between Mahone and "traditional" leaders such as Jim Fielding had begun to weaken. Though their exchange is difficult to document, Fielding and Homer O. Davidson, chairman of the Mohave Committee (a political organization comprised of Mohave Indians) and supporter of the Hualapais, began disagreeing on strategies for addressing the land issue. They appeared less frequently at meetings, and their names did not appear together as often on petitions. The split between Davidson and Fielding weakened the relationship between Fielding and Mahone. At least one scholar interested in the court case against the Santa Fe Railway has argued that Mahone's leadership style and access to non-Indians threatened the typical paths to authority within Pai society. His bluntness may have irritated others.[59]

Despite the political tensions manifested at the meeting, Hualapai elders continued pressing their claims. Jim Mahone and Kate Crozier noted that they were both military pensioners and had fought for Generals Nelson Miles and George Crook as well as Colonels Wilcox and Price. Both attested that General Miles had brought them to his headquarters in Fort Whipple along with other scouts, where Miles informed them that he wanted the "Wallapais to return to the portion of Arizona which is now the Wallapai Indian Reservation and there to live in peace with their fellow men," according to Crozier. Mahone added that Miles said that "this section of country was their reservation and that he wanted them to fence it, and that if white men came within the reservation to conduct mining operations, they should report to the authorities so that the white people could be arrested and removed. That if the white men put their cattle inside the Indian reservation, they would report the same to the authorities so that the cattle could be confiscated and the white men arrested." Mahone and Crozier were adamant that the discussions leading up to the executive order and the order itself, along with their service for the military as well as their traditional connections to the area, formed their claim to the land. Crozier agreed that "the reservation belonged to the Wallapai Indian tribe and was given to them as their own home and in recognition of their services to the government. . . . The tribe agreed with General Miles that they would do as he said, and returned to their reservation and have ever since claimed to own the same, both in virtue of their agreement with general Miles and under the President's order of 1883."[60]

The politicking and general state of unrest across northwestern Arizona only continued. In 1931 Fred Mahone wrote an appeal on letterhead provided by the Swaskagame American Legion Post in Kingman to President Herbert Hoover. His letter and petition, signed by members of the Legion, thanked S. M. Brosius of the Indian Rights Association; ex-superintendent Light; and John Collier, future commissioner of Indian Affairs, who recently had begun assisting the tribe. Mahone's letter contained six provisions covering land and water issues as well as criticism of the system of leasing land to Anglo ranchers. True to form, he made grandiloquent statements in defense of his people: "All rights, privileges, and profits that have already accrued to the reservation in respect to any portion of the Colorado River, or may hereafter accrue, shall inviolably be secure to the Walapai Tribe," and he ended with a desire to "confirm and preserve the Walapai's moral right to the land" based on "the fact that their present home was a part of their ancient habitation which was guaranteed to them by the terms of the Treaty of Guadalupe Hidalgo in 1848."[61]

The government responded with another series of discussions during the summer that failed to address the concerns of the tribe. In 1931 the Senate Committee on Indian Affairs again met to discuss the land dispute, with Assistant Commissioner of Indian Affairs J. Henry Scattergood and senators Burton K. Wheeler and Carl Hayden presiding. The committee first heard

Fred Mahone, who went to the heart of the matter: "To begin with, this land belongs to the Walapai Indians in Arizona. . . . I protested against the leasing of the land or appraisal of this land because this land as our reservation itself was set aside by the United States Army officials in the early days." Wheeler asked for evidence. Mahone replied by bringing in Jim Mahone, who lived through La Paz and fought for the military against the Apaches. Jim Mahone claimed that President Arthur established the reservation as a reward for the services provided by Hualapai scouts and to protect the tribe, because "there were a lot of people all over the world, just like a bunch of worms, and . . . they [were] coming to crowd out the Indians."[62] Although the content of such comments drove home their argument, the style and pattern of the Hualapai leadership revealed an important set of cultural characteristics: the boarding school generation opened up the testimony, directly confronted the issues, and then introduced elders to verify and legitimize their claims. Fred Mahone followed this pattern later in the day, when he addressed the issue of occupancy and then introduced Chief Schrum. Through an interpreter Schrum argued: "We are people who have lived in this country far back. It is way back. [I am] one of the descendants from the early chief. [My] father was chief." He too opposed dividing the reservation because it would "prevent us from going into civilization." He said the descendants of the old chiefs agreed that the tribe deserved the land. Other members of the younger generation followed the same pattern. In addition, many of the speakers were relatives of prominent leaders from the nineteenth century. Philip Quasula was the grandson of a prominent headman, as was Jim Fielding, a descendant of Suwim Fielding, and Butch Clark, a relative of Hualapai Charley.[63]

This pattern was surely lost on the government representatives, who, after dismissing the Hualapais' claims, returned to the alleged failure of the tribal cattle business. Charles McGee, one of the few successful Hualapai cattlemen, described the challenges facing the tribe. McGee lived off the reservation in Trout Creek until he and his family moved onto the reservation. They relocated to Pine Springs and built a small farm for their cattle, but Superintendent Light informed them that they had to leave, since whites leased the land. After McGee spent months looking for a plot that white ranchers did not lease, he found land below Peach Springs Wash where he and his father could graze 135 head of cattle.[64] Assistant Commissioner Scattergood commended McGee on his efforts and asked why he protested. McGee told him that he personally owned sixty head but "could not make a living off that bunch of cattle," especially since non-Indian ranchers and the railway monopolized the springs. Scattergood told him that he could lease water from them, but McGee retorted that the springs belonged to the Hualapais. Inaccessible springs, a degraded range, and various regulations severely crippled the efforts of Hualapai cattlemen. McGee told Scattergood: "You know that. It is the same way with a lot of these younger fellows. To support ourselves we have to have more range and more cattle. This is the point I want to get at, and I think that is what the rest of these younger fellows would say." Scattergood and Hayden remained confident that McGee had enough land, but the agency stockman brought a smile to McGee's face when he told the officials that a family needed 200 to 250 head of cattle to make a living.[65]

Despite the testimony of dozens of Hualapais, the Senate committee nonetheless denied the tribe access to the whole reservation. Echoing the logic Hualapais heard for decades, the committee argued that the tribe's dwindling numbers did not merit the entire land base. Besides, the committee could not find anyone who agreed to swap land in the region, even if the railway wanted to. The committee's explanation revealed its flawed reasoning, since the conflict with the railroad and the uncertainty it created made Hualapais reluctant to live on the reservation. The committee solved little and added another confusing variable into the equation.[66]

In late 1931, after several meetings between the Senate committee and the Hualapais, the entire dispute took another surprising turn. In the midst of innumerable petitions and several fruitless confrontations with federal officials, Hualapais took their case to court. Thus, when the U.S. District Court for the District of Arizona, in ruling on the case filed by the Indian Rights Association, supported the tribe's claim to the springs, the Hualapais were as surprised as the railway and their opponents in the Senate. Supporting the tribe's claim that it held absolute title to the land around the springs, the court ruled that the final survey placed the springs on the even section of the reservation rather than the odd-numbered section claimed by the railway. The court qualified the ruling by affirming the Santa Fe's right to take water as long as it furnished a "reasonable quantity" to the tribe for livestock and domestic uses. The court based its ambivalent ruling on the argument that Hualapais had a right to the springs and the section surrounding it, but the improvements made by the railway gave it use rights. Essentially, the tribe "owned" the springs, but the Santa Fe Railway retained the right to "use" the water.[67]

The ruling left the Hualapais so unsatisfied that they began another lawsuit, but this time they caught the attention of Senator Carl Hayden, who brought the entire debate to a halt in 1932. He commissioned a full investigation into Hualapai history with an eye toward land and occupancy.

Combing eight decades of archival records, he wanted to prove that the Santa Fe owned the odd sections on the reservation and that Peach Springs was within an odd section. An advocate of industrialization and a skeptic of tribal rights, Hayden thought the federal land grant gave the railway superior rights to the land in question. He also thought that the Hualapais were a "dying race," to quote the senator.[68] Such racialized views informed Hayden's hope that the nearly four hundred–page report would vindicate his position. Surprisingly, it did not. In fact, the results stunned observers. Known by its shortened title, the *Walapai Papers* proved continuous recognition of the Hualapais from the U.S.–Mexico War to the present and negated the Santa Fe's claims. With this seemingly incontrovertible evidence provided by an arch-opponent of tribal rights, Hualapais thought they could win the case.[69]

Even though the government documents contained in the *Walapai Papers* directly contradicted the railway and Senator Hayden, it did not settle the dispute, and the case again went to the courts. In 1937 Commissioner John Collier returned to assist, joining the Indian Rights Association and a Phoenix lawyer named Bennett Marks and his son Royal in their defense of the land claim. Collier and Marks convinced Felix Cohen, Arthur Lazarus, and Abe Barber—all giants of Indian law—to join the escalating case. According to Christian McMillen, whose insightful *Making Indian Law* analyzes the land claim, they believed that the case not only addressed Hualapai rights but spoke to the validity of federal railroad land grants and emerging legal theories about aboriginal occupancy and the significance of oral testimony in courts. Hoping to appeal the ruling, the tribe and its legal team mounted another suit. In *United States of America for the Wallapai Tribe v. The Atchison, Topeka, Santa Fe Railway Company*, the plaintiffs argued that occupancy of the land predated the 1866 grant and that U.S. recognition of the Hualapais as aboriginal owners went back to 1850. These two arguments as well as subsidiary points regarding the use of oral histories as evidence promised to launch the case into the annals of Indian law.[70]

Despite the acumen of the legal team, numerous Hualapai witnesses, and a mountain of evidence supporting the Hualapais, the U.S. Court for the District of Arizona ruled in favor of the Santa Fe. It asserted that the tribe lacked a right to the land because the legislation creating the railroad gave it a right to the odd-numbered sections on both sides of its tracks. This was a narrow interpretation of the case, since the points made by the plaintiff surpassed the specific question of who owned odd or even sections. The Hualapais through their lawyers staked a claim to all traditional lands and based their argument on broader legal principles of aboriginal land rights and the "provability" of oral testimony in court. Thus, it was no surprise that the tribe appealed the district court ruling and took the case to the Ninth District Court of Appeals on 30 August 1940. The appellate court upheld the lower court's ruling and echoed its argument by returning to the narrow question of who owned the even and odd sections of land.[71]

The Hualapais had come too far to accept this negative ruling, especially considering the notoriety the case had gained in the world of Indian law and Indian affairs. With the resolve that had supported them for decades, Hualapais took the case to the Supreme Court in 1941, where Chief Justice William O. Douglas wrote the majority opinion reversing the lower court's ruling. In a monumental decision the Supreme Court recognized Hualapais' right to the land within the external boundaries of the 1883 executive order reservation.[72] The Court argued that Hualapais enjoyed aboriginal occupancy of the land long before the arrival of non-Indians, thus supporting the claims the tribe had been making for decades. In a ruling that would eventually shape Indian law, influence the "birth" of the field of ethnohistory, and provide the juridical ammunition for aboriginal land claims across the globe, the High Court noted that the federal government did not notify the tribe of the land grant in 1866, and, even if it had, the tribe and the military had been engaged in a conflict. This fact limited the ability of the tribe to agree to any transfer of land. After the war's end, the removal to La Paz further compromised the Hualapais' ability to protest the entrance of the railroad into their territory. The Court made the important observation that the tribe had not voluntarily ceded its land through a treaty or other official action, thus the federal government could not take its land. Finally, Douglas argued that only Congress had the right to abolish Indian title, which it never expressly did when it granted land to the railway. This particular appropriation of tribal land resulted in an unconstitutional taking that the executive branch had recognized as Hualapai territory.[73]

Since the tribe did, however, accept the boundaries outlined by the president in the 1883 executive order, it had implicitly forfeited its legal claim to land outside the reservation. The tribe would eventually press this, but the Supreme Court ruling marked a crucial turning point in Hualapai history. The court case was the culmination of several decades of uncompromising activism that drew upon Hualapai traditions that leaders such as Mahone, Fielding, Quasula, and others reshaped to fit the demands of a complicated world. These leaders knew that they had to solicit support from sympathetic outsiders such as the MIF, the Indian Rights Association, and lawyers like Marks, Cohen, and Barber, without whom they could not have mastered the arcane legal world, which seemed to work against them. Indeed, the court case stood as another benchmark in their history—much like the Hualapai Wars and the La Paz ordeal—because it demonstrated the fundamental tenacity of an Indigenous community that refused to accept the dictates of the dominant society. It was a profound victory that preserved Hualapai land, galvanized tribal leadership, and demonstrated precisely how a small tribe could win against tremendous odds.

The land claims case was also the culmination of several undercurrents within Hualapai political culture and social identity. With political organizations that blended tradition and modernity into a language of Hualapai nationalism, new leaders fought against corrupt superintendents, ethnocentric politicians, and powerful corporate entities such as the Santa Fe Railway. Their efforts strained some relationships between band members and Pai individuals, but their pragmatic unity in the face of destructive colonial forces revealed a new political language that symbolized shifts in Native self-identification. Layering their identities as individuals, as family members, as bands, and as a political entity called the Hualapai nation, the People had carved out a new discursive space within the landscape of Indigenous-settler relations. They recognized the importance of tradition and decentralization, yet they also drew upon new skills, contexts, and situations to go beyond adaptation and survival. These leaders and the people they fought for wanted autonomy, self-determination, and the powers of other nations that were inherent to Hualapais' identity as a sovereign people. And although the 1941 court case failed to return the land outside the reservation, it served as a fitting victory to the Hualapais' struggle to control their reservation, a struggle that began the day after the reservation was created in 1883.

## 5

# Citizenship, Status, and the Discourse of National Belonging

That is the only place where we have living water.[1]

In March 1918 Philip Quasula, a costrategist in the campaigns against corruption in the Indian Bureau, wrote a letter to the commissioner of Indian Affairs expressing his concern about the citizenship of tribal members, especially those considering war service. He had experienced problems mediating between men who wanted to fight in the war, those who avoided the draft, and men who were generally confused about their citizenship status. Quasula wanted to tell them whether they could or should register for the draft, but he also had confronted problems with the local draft board rejecting Hualapai volunteers. Superintendent Charles Shell told him that Hualapais had to "accept the matter the same as whites" since they were "similar to white people," and though Quasula was dubious about the advice, he told them to register. Not surprisingly, the head of the Mohave County registration board said that "citizen Indians" had to register and not necessarily fight, while "non-citizen Indians" could not join the war effort. Quasula remained confused about the status of his fellow Hualapais, especially because he did not want them to break the law. He also feared the impact of the war on the Hualapais, since they had "fallen into starvation, and [were] falling back into our old style." He needed the men to remain at home, not leave to fight a "bloody war" that he did not understand.[2]

The debate over citizenship and identity revealed competing discourses on status and belonging within the American and Hualapai nations. Such concerns became exceptionally important during the early twentieth century, as Congress unilaterally passed the Indian Citizenship Act of 1924 in an attempt to clarify the patchwork of regulations governing Native status and membership within or outside the American body politic. In addition to treaties and executive agreements, the 1887 Allotment Act, and myriad state and territorial laws, Hualapais confronted a confusing tangle of discourses that racialized Indigenous peoples as noncitizen subjects or as subservient others within the modern American nation-state. Indigenous peoples faced different definitions of their status in relationship to the federal, state, territorial, and county governments. They claimed status within their own tribal nations as a form of citizenship that non-Indians typically referred to as "tribal membership." Indian people thus inhabited several categories of citizenship, wardship, and membership within different political bodies.

These discourses of belonging and "nonbelonging" pervaded the political culture of Indigenous affairs, from the platform of the Society for American Indians, the assimilationist policies of the Bureau of Indian Affairs, and local debates among Native and non-Native peoples in places such as Peach Springs and Kingman. Did Hualapais belong in or to the tribe, the state of Arizona, or the national American citizenry? Did they have access to resources available to American citizens, and if not, why not? What was it about their Indian identity that prohibited them from being citizens of the United States, and, conversely, why didn't the government equate membership within the Hualapai nation with citizens of other nations? Or were Hualapais and other Native people "dual citizens"? Such debates bedeviled Native people during the late nineteenth and early twentieth centuries. Belonging and acceptance informed negotiations about blood quantum, tribal membership, private property ownership, boarding school education, wartime service, and access to New Deal programs because these political and social realities and policies exhibited the hegemonic notions of race, culture, and identity as defined by the dominant settler society and its institutions.

Indigenous peoples offered their own definitions of being and belonging, which created a fluid and contested border between colonial and anticolonial discourses of space, nation, status, and citizenship. Hualapais argued for their rights as members of an Indigenous nation, and they demanded equal treatment from non-Indian institutions as members of the larger U.S. citizenry. This chapter analyzes the narratives of military service, citizenship, education, and New Deal programs through the analytical lenses of "being and belonging" to contending nationalities. The contending nationalities in question are the somewhat halting but undeniable construction of a Hualapai national identity out of multiple band and family identities and the related processes of defining membership, drawing the boundaries of Native space, resolving the contradictions of boarding school education, adapting to wage labor, and building a Hualapai government and the colonial policies of assimilation and territorial incorporation that began in the mid-nineteenth century with wars against Pais and continued in education, racialized citizenship, and New Deal programs that sought to incorporate Indigenous lands and bodies into the American nation-state.

Though it may be tempting to paint these trajectories as divergent, discourses of belonging were indeterminate and even mutually reinforcing. As Hualapais battled the Santa Fe Railway in court, they sought a form of "dual citizenship," for instance, as they tried to carve out a sovereign space at the borders of the American and Hualapai political landscapes. Their acceptance of boarding school educations and work offered by New Deal programs as well as their implementation of a new IRA government tied them to the bureaucracies that oppressed them and yet provided them with resources and experiences that they used to construct a Hualapai national identity. Thus, the historical moment known as the interwar years was much more than many scholars have argued: the 1920s and 1930s were pivotal for Hualapais as they struggled for a sense of belonging within two national discourses.

## War Service, Obligation, and the Citizen/Noncitizen Question

The outbreak of World War I forced many Hualapais to confront questions of citizenship and status within the American nation-state for the first time. Because their reservation escaped allotment, Hualapais typically were not burdened by competency commissions and the racist blood quantum associated with the fracturing of Native lands. And although blood quantum and citizenship bedeviled Hualapais seeking land off the reservation on the public domain or admission of their children in public schools, Hualapais did not confront these issues as frequently as other Native people. War service, however, did raise concern among the Hualapais regarding citizenship, status, and the meanings of obligation and belonging to their own nation and the greater United States.[3] So when Congress established conscription in 1917, many Hualapais did not understand the war or their legal status and eligibility for service. Some ignored or resisted, others volunteered, but most waited to see what happened next. Philip Quasula, for example, resisted service, but Fred Mahone and Sam Swaskagame did not (see fig. 5.1).[4]

Individuals such as Quasula sought clarification of their obligations to fight in a war for a country that did not consider them citizens. Quasula's

FIGURE 5.1. Sam Swaskagame in France, 1918. Photographer unknown, #3663, Mohave County Museum of History and Arts, Kingman, Arizona.

inquiries led to a letter from Indian Commissioner Cato Sells, who distributed a circular stating that all Indian men between the ages of eighteen and forty-five had to register for the draft. In 1917 Superintendent Shell compiled a list of eligible Hualapai men, but most refused to register, since they did not know if they were citizens. Citing a lack of birth certificates, Shell utilized the annual reservation census to compile a list of fifty eligible men and used the date of the census, 30 June, for their birthdate. He estimated their age by extrapolating backward from this arbitrary date. In lieu of state-sanctioned documentation of Hualapais' births, Shell used the colonial census to fix Hualapais within a dominant notion of citizenship and belonging within the American nation-state to the end of serving that same bureaucracy as soldiers in an imperial war. This tactic failed to appease local draft boards in their refusal to register Hualapai men, whom they categorized as racialized noncitizen wards of the federal government. Some Hualapais thus expressed confusion about being an Indian and an American, with at least one noting that he should not go to war if he could not vote or send his children to public schools.[5]

While they aired their concerns about bureaucratic regulations, legal status, and cultural identity, Shell and some Hualapais wondered more broadly about the meanings of citizenship for Indigenous peoples at the metaphorical border between the American nation-state and Indigenous peoplehood. Philip Quasula, speaking with Shell and Sells, wanted to know if a Hualapai could be a U.S. citizen if he or she lived on the reservation and spoke English, or if that person had to break his or her ties with the tribe and leave the reservation to be a citizen. If Hualapais off the reservation were not citizens, what were they? What rights and obligations did they have? If they were not citizens and lacked rights, why should they follow Anglo laws? Conversely, when they lived on the reservation, they were "citizens" of the Hualapai nation, yet they had difficulties dealing directly with the federal government. His questions uncovered how Native identity and citizenship within the American nation were bound by the competing territorialities of Native space and its zero-sum incorporation into the U.S. body politic. In this spatial regime Native reservations were refuges for Indigenous peoples where their status may have been clear but where they were also targets of colonialism and racial transformation. Conversely, if Hualapais lived beyond the borders of the reservation, they inhabited a liminal space where they were racialized others at the bottom of the sociocultural hierarchy of America. Thus, their relationship with the pressing issue of the draft exposed a thicket of contradictory discourses. Even Commissioner Sells could not help Quasula with his inquiries: "All I can say to you at this time," noted Sells, "is that the Indian citizen is liable to the draft and the non-citizen Indian is entitled to exemption there from. Your Superintendent who knows the facts in each case is in the best position to advise each one as to his political status."[6] Shell, of course, did not know the facts.

Even as the debate over war, citizenship, and status continued, few Hualapais registered and fought for the Allied cause. J. S. Withers, the Mohave County clerk, informed Superintendent Shell that a few Hualapais seeking registration were "not considered citizens," but the registration board sent the new superintendent, Charles Wagner, a list of Hualapais eligible for service: George Wakayuta, George Mathayava, Pedro Peirce, Dick Grover, Frosty Querta, Will Hunter, and Pete Imus. They lived in Kingman, Chloride, and Ash Fork, spoke English well, and were relatively healthy, according to Withers, in apparent acknowledgment of their fitness for American citizenship and an implicit and racialized rejection of their "non-Indianness." Withers interpreted their English-language use and choice to live off the reservation as an indication of their denial of tribal membership, further revealing the popular belief in the dichotomies between being Hualapai and belonging to the American mainstream.[7]

As these discourses of national belonging continued, the war came to an end, leaving many of the questions unresolved. It did, however, create a symbolic legacy in the minds of non-Indians grappling with the place of Hualapais in the local racial imagination. Sam Swaskagame was a Hualapai who served in France for the Allied Expeditionary Force and died there after the war ended. When local non-Indians learned of his efforts, he became a regional hero and a symbol of popular perceptions of Indians during the war. The *Mohave County Miner* ran articles recounting and often embellishing his exploits in France, employing stereotypes of the "noble savage" and "good Indian," seeking acceptance by white America to explain his experiences and thus inserting him into the metanarrative of Americanization. A "keen sense of sight" and a "warrior's skill at the hunt" were but a few of his alleged characteristics as an Indian in war. In the spring of 1920 French prime minister Raymond Poincaré sent an engraved sheepskin to Sam Swaskagame's family and thanked them for their son's "secret service on the Marne." As evidence of this symbolic consumption of the "good Indian" in search of belonging in America, the local American Legion renamed its post after Swaskagame to demonstrate that "these boys have a place in the memory of the white residents of this country." When his body was returned, locals organized a parade and funeral and flew the flags at half-mast.[8] Swaskagame became a symbol used by whites to "tame" the Indian by incorporating him into the local history while simultaneously denying contemporary rights and sovereignty to the relatives and fellow Hualapais who knew and remembered him. As was increasingly popular among colleges and high schools across America, Anglos could embrace Indians as icons and mascots after death or conquest, extol their alleged natural abilities in the guise of "honor," and yet ignore their contemporary claims to sovereignty.[9]

Coming on the heels of the war, indeed sparked by the claims of veterans and non-Indian reform groups, the 1924 Indian Citizenship Act bestowed citizenship upon all Native people in the United States, but it nonetheless failed to resolve many questions of status and belonging that existed before it became law. Through allotment or service in war, nearly two-thirds of American Indians already were citizens, but most if not all Hualapais lacked this form of incorporation into the American political system.[10] Life after the act did not lead to equality in American society. Echoing Jim Crow laws in the South, non-Natives supported politicians who were rabidly anti-Indian. Western states passed laws prohibiting Indians from voting, staying out at night, attending public schools, holding office, and receiving legal representation in court. In clear violation of the Fifteenth Amendment, Native peoples in Arizona could not vote in most elections. The racial ideologies that pervaded the early twentieth century were predicated on the assumption that nonwhite peoples were incapable of fully participating in democratic institutions. These beliefs were increasingly rooted in language that used biological rather than cultural arguments about the inferiority of people of color. Institutions such as schools, courtrooms, and governments solidified this inferior treatment. Hualapais had few chances to practice their now constitutionally protected rights to vote. In Arizona court cases such as *Porter v. Hall* in the late 1920s challenged discrimination, but it was not until 1948 that Native activists won a court case overturning racist prohibitions on their right to vote in Arizona and New Mexico.[11]

## Native, Public, or Private: The Ambiguities of Hualapai Space

The confusion surrounding the legal status of Hualapais was exacerbated by their residency patterns across northwestern Arizona. Out of roughly 450 tribal members under the jurisdiction of the Truxton Canyon Agency, less than half lived permanently on a reservation that covered one million acres. By one account, 150 of them lived in Kingman.[12] These residency patterns had perplexed non-Indians ever since they entered the region in the nineteenth century, but the tendency of Hualapais to remain off-reservation resulted from their desire to maintain connections with their aboriginal cultural landscape, their need for wage labor jobs in regional industries, and the control of reservation resources by non-Indian cattle ranchers and the railway. This combination of structural limitations and Hualapai choice indicated the competing discourses of place, belonging, and territoriality that defined Hualapai life in the early twentieth century.

Malcolm McDowell, the secretary for the Board of Indian Commissioners, expressed the popular non-Indian confusion about Hualapai social geography when he visited the region in 1923. McDowell came to the reservation because Fred Mahone asked him to reprimand Superintendent Light, but McDowell was more surprised at the Hualapais' residency patterns, noting that the "Walapai are practically non-reservation Indians: they live on lands of white men without paying rent—they are squatters." McDowell thought that the 125 Hualapais living in four colonies around Kingman were "a part of the population of the town," and he continued: "So here is a reservation covering more than 1,100 square miles . . . with less than a quarter of the Indian owners living on it; the situation here is so unusual that I am puzzled as to what ought to be done to solve a really perplexing problem."[13] Although McDowell correctly described the geography of the Hualapais' reservation, his analysis of their situation was inaccurate.

Beyond the structural limitations impeding Hualapais' migration to the reservation, some Hualapais simply did not want to live there, and those who did not would have found irony in McDowell's assessment of them as "squatters" on the public domain. They also might have been amused to learn they had "changed from reservation to town Indians." But in reality, groups such as the Hualapai Mountain band had lived in the area before non-Indians established the city of Kingman, and they benefited from greater work opportunities while evading the gaze of the Indian Office.[14] But living off the reservation did not insulate them from the plans of Anglo citizens and reform groups. McDowell met with city leaders and Superintendent Light to discuss purchasing land for Hualapais in "Indian Town" and then building permanent homes with running water. McDowell thought this would have worked because the Hualapais were an important "source of common labor to [the] white citizens who do not wish to drive the Indians away," and the Chamber of Commerce thought the "quaint and harmless" Hualapais could sell baskets to tourists at the Santa Fe station.[15]

A contrasting plan involved removing the camps and "planting" families in Peach Springs on the reservation. One Kingman City Council member supported the idea, but McDowell cautioned that "the practicability of planting a colony of Indians on the reservation depends, in my opinion, upon the ownership of Peach Springs." McDowell admitted this would be difficult because "every alternate section of land in the reservation is owned by the Santa Fe Railroad." If the courts, Congress, and Interior resolved the dispute in favor of the tribe, which they eventually did, he believed the superintendent could "move all the Walapai back to the reservation in a town on the railroad where the present village of Peach Springs is located, a town with decent homes, a sewer system and piped water."[16] McDowell thought that they could lease water from the railway and begin dry farming on the reservation, but Light told McDowell that he was not "excited over the prospect of getting the Indians to become dry farmers." After discussion of the logistics, tempered by paternalistic views of the tribe, McDowell agreed, "I doubt if these town bred, town raised people would at all be happy living in remote places, far distant from railroads, automobile tourists and grocery stores." Like Light, McDowell was confused by Hualapais living in the camps, and he ignored a sense of place that led Hualapais to use the railroad, and eventually automobiles, to visit friends around the region.[17]

Other plans emerged in the late 1920s to alter space through colonial policies of relocation, incorporation, and the erasure of Hualapai historical geography. In 1927 the Indian Office ordered superintendents to survey tribal living conditions and institute homeownership campaigns for Indian communities across the West. Assistant Commissioner Merritt urged agents to organize the campaigns "with the central idea of trying to get the Indians to actually desire better homes" because, he argued, "you will find that if that desire is once awakened they will find ways and means of gratifying it, and better homes will actually result." He cautioned agents not to expect "every one to respond to the first effort" but rather to "carefully select a very few because they in some way seem to offer the best chance of success." He thought that once a few tribal members accepted the homes, the example would become "contagious." To document this homeownership process, he requested "before and after" photographs capturing the "individual progress" of the "Indian who is contemplating improvements."[18] Such plans for transformation—essentially a form of cultural genocide—marked the larger assault upon the identities of Native people.

But the investigations and plans to move, change, or rearrange Hualapais only continued. Earl Henderson from the Board of Indian Commissioners visited in 1928 to check up on the geography of Hualapai space. He noted the poor treatment the Hualapais received from whites and felt that "Indian Town" was an untenable situation that bred disdain among the Anglos and frustration among the Hualapais. And yet the idea of planting them on the reservation was implausible: "It seemed useless to force these people on their barren reservation," he argued, especially if the Indian Office refused to pursue the tribe's claim to the various springs on their land. Henderson reiterated that it was "incumbent upon the Indian Bureau [Office] to arrange some colony system for them near the towns where they can make a livelihood." He opined that "land could be purchased very cheaply" and the Hualapais placed in "small houses of a few rooms" with running water.[19]

In addition to demanding the full use of their reservation and the right to live freely in Kingman, a few tribal members requested allotments on Indigenous spaces redefined as "public domain." Following earlier patterns, most of these requests were for allotments in the Big Sandy area, southeast of Kingman, by the band of the same name. In 1928 a Hualapai woman named "Mrs. Mu-Ke-Che" applied for an allotment on land she had lived on for half a century. Superintendent Frank Mann said that she remained there after her husband, an Indian scout in the 1870s, died, so Commissioner Charles Burke approved the request because, reflecting the racialized and paternalistic tone of the era, "she is of the class of Indians for whose benefit the laws referred to were enacted." This meant that she spoke English, had adopted the "habits of civilized life," and had severed ties with the tribe; thus, she was "less Indian."[20] But not all applications were this clear. In 1929 Indian McGee received an allotment of 160 acres in the Big Sandy area, but he struggled to obtain additional land. In a 1935 letter from Commissioner John Collier to the new superintendent, Guy Hobgood, bureaucracy reared its ugly head and obstructed new claims. Collier told Hobgood he denied McGee's claim because, "as Mr. McGee has already received a public domain allotment under . . . the act of February 8, 1887, he would not be entitled, as an Indian, to make a stock-raising homestead entry under the Indian Homestead Act of July 4, 1884." Collier added: "He would, however, be entitled to file a stock raising homestead as a citizen. We cannot, therefore, furnish a certificate showing that he is entitled to file as an Indian." Making legalistic and symbolic distinctions between Indian identity and status as a citizen trapped Hualapais in a limbo of countervailing definitions and racist assumptions that "Indianness" precluded the ability to handle private property. Again, was McGee an Indian or a citizen or both?[21]

Other examples bear out the complexity of Indians filing for land off the reservation. On 8 May 1934 Dewey Mahone wrote a letter to the commissioner of Indian Affairs complaining about conflicts between Hualapais and Anglos on the Big Sandy. "I want to say a few words. I use[d] to own a ranch or land at the head of Big Sandy on the old settlement of Walapai Indians. Which they call Walapai Indian Reservation. . . . When the rent [was] due I came back to the ranch and found out that George Davis was gone nobody was there." George Davis was an Anglo who had agreed to watch Mahone's land while he visited the reservation to check on his cattle. Davis evidently struck a deal with another Anglo, giving him land Mahone had prepared for farming. After several trips between his land and the reservation, Mahone realized that Shell had failed to submit a patent request for him. Moreover, Shell told him that anyone could evict him from the land if they were citizens, that is, white. Frustrated, Mahone wrote to Commissioner Collier that "Mr. Shell did not listen to me or anything what I was trying to tell him. I told him I don't want to sell the place. I said, 'I want to keep the place.' He was after me hard he was telling me that somebody will take the ranch [a]way from me." Mahone wanted to give the land to two family members, Alice and Sterling, but "Mr. Shell forced me to sign this land sale. Therefore I believe Mr. Shell has wronged me and [my] family, in our properties."[22]

The new superintendent, Guy Hobgood, concluded that little could be done. Hobgood wrote to Commissioner Collier to confirm that Mahone lived on the land and was recognized by many people as the occupant. Hobgood said that confusion arose when George Davis made a payment to purchase land from Mahone when Mahone only intended to rent it out. Davis used this payment to support his alleged right to sell the land to a third party, which he did. Thus, Mahone lost the land. Moreover, Collier agreed with Hobgood that Mahone failed to live there "permanently" and thus had ruined his claim due to an "uncivilized" form of migratory land tenure. Mahone ultimately lost the land he had lived on, "improved," and planned to pass on to his family.[23]

The families that lived off the reservation continued to pose problems for the Indian Office, and they raised the ire of whites in the county because they refused to follow a system of private property and racialized citizenship that prohibited Hualapais from being landowners and members of the Hualapai nation simultaneously. Subverting the boundaries of Native and non-Native space as well as public, private, and Native territories, Hualapais carved out their own sense of belonging in the colonial landscape. They wanted to hold private property like white people, use the "public domain" to graze their cattle, and remain Hualapai at the same time. In response to these objectives, Superintendent Charles Shell said the Hualapais living off the reservation "consider themselves more or less outside the supervision of the Superintendent" and were "insolent, arrogant and more or less insubordinate." In general, Shell said that they "work for white ranchmen and for the railroad company but they are inconsistent in their work, easily take offence, and are easily affronted, after working a few weeks at the most, they wish to lay off, take a rest."[24] Whites were equally agitated by Hualapais' resistance to the reorganization of their aboriginal landscapes. Leaders in Kingman barred Hualapai children from public schools even though their parents contributed to the local economy, and politicians argued that Hualapais squatting on public land failed to pay taxes, so they did not deserve a public education. Hualapais were also barred from entering the one hospital in town without an Anglo accompanying them. Commenting on the tensions between whites and Hualapais, Malcolm McDowell noted that "the white people of this section . . . regard the Walapai as an inferior race."[25] These conflicts over land use, the meaning of space, and definitions of belonging continued to characterize interracial dynamics for much of the twentieth century.

## Boarding School Narratives of Displacement and Belonging

Struggling between their own agendas to reclaim aboriginal territory, live on the reservation, and adapt to modernity as well as confront the racialized constructs of citizenship and private property, Hualapais continued to face a system of colonial education. As noted previously, Hualapai leaders struck a bargain with the Indian Bureau to send their children to school if the government built a boarding school within Hualapai territory. Considering the distances that many children traveled across the country, situating such a colonial institution within the heart of Pai territory represented a literal and symbolic compromise between the cultural alienation that accompanied federal education and the adaptive incorporation of that same institution into the Hualapai national identity. The Valentine Indian School became an important school in the Indian Bureau's campaign to transform Native children in the Southwest, but its location within Hualapai land enabled parents to watch and protect their children from the extremes of cultural transformation.[26]

By the mid-1920s the school boasted an annual average of 225 students from the Navajo, Hopi, Hualapai, Havasupai, and O'odham reservations.[27] Over the course of its three-decade existence more than five thousand children passed through its doors.[28] Though they had diverse narratives within the school, students sought a sense of belonging in the midst of teachers and administrators who sought to erase the children's identities as Native people. In response, children became lonely, depressed, or angry, while others simply left the school. Some were abused, but they resisted. Many met children from other tribes for the first time. Others worked for the school and received wages and practical experiences that helped them after graduation. Jane Honga is one example. The daughter of Indian Kuni and Lucy Parker, Honga was born in 1908 near Clay Springs, on the west end of the reservation. Before marrying Jacob Honga, Jane went to school at Valentine until she finished the eighth grade. In her midteens she became an assistant matron for the school and watched over other children, many of whom she counted as cousins.[29]

Honga's ability to mediate between administrators and Hualapai children improved the quality of life for youth within the school and led to complex narratives of personal loss and resistance. One such narrative comes from Mazzie Wescogame Powskey, who entered the school in the mid-1930s. "When I attended school down there they didn't want [us] to speak Hualapai and so they punished us . . . and they cut my hair all off." Despite such cultural violence, Mazzie had fond memories: "When I went to school there, I think they made our dresses. I remember those big large gray bloomers that we used to put cheese or other foods [in], 'cause it was tight around the leg. The elastic was tight. Sometimes we would get caught by the cook."[30] Beth Wauneka, who was born in Chloride, remembered their clothing, chores, and classes: "We wore striped blue and white [uniforms] and the dark blue and white dresses. It looks like pillow stitching. Real tough material and we wore black stocking[s] and black bloomers and black shoes and gray sweaters for winter." Wauneka recalled the gendered nature of chores: "We [girls] had to scrub the floors and scrub the ceilings, work in the toilet room and we had to work in the wash room. We had to make our beds and we had [other duties]," many of which the boys were not required to do.[31]

Other students painted a similarly complex portrait. According to Jeannie Jackson, "We got up early. When I first got down there in 1930–1931 we used to have to drill like military. We'd all meet outside and we'd march and we had to do all that and we had to get in line to go to eat and we had to get in line to go to school. It was kinda strict. We couldn't be late and we had to be there right on time or else we'd get punished."[32] Lydia Beecher added that the girls had to wait until the matrons inspected their rooms before they could eat, and after classes they mopped and swept floors, washed windows, and picked up trash. During the weekends the older girls cleaned the teachers' living quarters.[33]

Social gatherings, celebrations, sports, and other events helped students cope with isolation from their families. These gatherings had an important place in the memories of Mrs. Wauneka: "In [those] years they used to have a big band there. There was Nannie playing piano, McKinley Willatouse—he used to be the drummer, and George Fisher he played the trumpet and they really had a nice band to dance to." She added, "At that time the man didn't choose us. We'd run across the floor and choose our own partner."[34] Emmett Bender also remembered social gatherings and dances. Bender was born in 1924 and first attended the school when he was six years old. He recalled some of the older students going to Kingman for movie shows, but he noted that most of the students participated in dances and plays at the school. Many Hualapais knew the traditional dances, but Bender remembered when modern dances became more popular, and the students performed them in tandem with the older dances. He especially enjoyed an elderly Hopi woman who occasionally visited the students.[35]

Jeannie Jackson said that the classes she took at Truxton mirrored those offered at other schools but that the plays in the auditorium made the school unique. "Somehow it seems like it was better down there, cause we used to have, ah, plays. We'd go to the auditorium and someone would tell us stories and we'd put on operas for the whole community and everybody would take part in the operas. Everything would be so nice, we had movies and a lot of recreational activities like baseball teams, basketball teams, and anything you could think of."[36] Willie Powskey remembered the carnival held at the end of the school year. During the semester students learned in workshops how to make tables, belts, clothing, and other objects, which they often sold to guests at the carnival. He remembered: "There were a lot of people that came to the carnival, like white people. [They] always bought our things [we] made during the year."[37]

Language became a crucial area of conflict because it clearly marked cultural identity. Instructors used physical and psychological punishment to stop the children from speaking their Native language, and they rewarded children for speaking English. These forms of oppression paralleled the techniques and goals applied to European immigrant children in public schools, but Indian language policy had a uniquely pernicious tone.[38] Beth Wauneka confirmed that teachers disciplined children for using Hualapai, recalling that "we used to get punished all the time 'cause I always called for my older sister around the campus" in Hualapai. Willie Powskey remembered when "a big white lady by the name of Mrs. Davis . . . would slap your mouth, pull your ears, and pull your hair" when he spoke Hualapai.[39] Grace Suminimo, a member of the Big Sandy band, clearly remembered: "We were not to speak Indian . . . if we did we were punished. That is why I speak English today." Suminimo recalled that students who spoke Hualapai had to stand against a wall in front of the other students during lunch. Benedict and Lydia Beecher both noted being disciplined for speaking Hualapai: "We had to be very quiet and you was not supposed to speak Hualapai. If you did you would be whipped with a ruler," recalled Benedict.[40]

In the midst of the struggles students rebelled and retained their traditions. They stole food from the cafeteria, something Jeannie Jackson saw students do every now and then. "I remember we were always hungry and we didn't know what to do, so before we come out of the dining room we tried to sneak out sandwiches or apples or oranges, and they'd search us at the door." Humor characterized students' search for food and adventure. Jackson recalled a time when "some of the girls would roll up peanut butter in a ball and hide it in their bloomers, and they caught on to that and punished them."[41] Jackson also recalled: "Sometimes in the night we'd dance Hualapai Circle Dances. Somebody would sing and that was fun, 'cause it was our tradition. Sometimes on the weekends, Saturdays, we'd steal apples, pears, or whatever they had and we'd go up in the hills and had a feast up there." Jackson's responses revealed how students subverted the goals of the school administrators while they tried making their life in the school bearable.[42]

Listening to Hualapai memories of boarding school education opens a window into the simultaneous experiences of personal loss, collective resistance, and remaking colonial space within the context of Indigenous landscapes. Narratives of covert language use, the persistence of traditional dances, and the innovative ways in which Native youth used modernity to navigate the federal education highlight the contending trajectories of incorporation into the American culture and maintenance of Hualapai identity. As boarding schools tried to Americanize Hualapai youth and prepare them for manual labor, Native people "Indigenized" the very same hallways and classrooms that they inhabited as colonial subjects. Refusing to act as passive vessels of racial dogmatisms, Hualapais used the colonizer's tools to build their own conceptualization of what it means to be a nation and in the process found a sense of belonging in the midst of assaults on their language, culture, and identity.

## The Political Economy of Hualapai Nation Building

As Hualapai youth battled with teachers and administrators in the schools, their parents confronted the economic, political, and sociospatial impacts of the Great Depression and Indian New Deal. Although the Great Depression rearranged the economic structure of northwestern Arizona more generally, it profoundly transformed the racial geography of Hualapai lands by causing an exodus of Anglos from the reservation. As ranchers went bankrupt and pulled cattle off the range, Hualapais moved to the reservation in unprecedented numbers and in the process transformed it into a Native space.[43] Into this reclaimed space moved Hualapai families, leaders, and the formal governmental structures of the modern Hualapai nation. That these transformations became possible during a global crisis in capitalism and that the Hualapai government contained elements of liberal state building should not detract from their significance for Hualapai national identity.

As the nation's economy spiraled downward, President Roosevelt's Indian New Deal brought significant changes to American Indian communities. The Indian New Deal resulted from the efforts of Roosevelt's commissioner of Indian Affairs, John Collier, and secretary of the Interior, Harold Ickes. An indefatigable social reformer from New York, Collier gained exposure to Indian affairs in the 1920s while in Taos Pueblo visiting Mabel Dodge Luhan and her husband, Antonio Luhan. Collier thought Puebloan culture contained a perfect balance of individualism and community solidarity that could teach other Americans about a better way to live. Rather than assimilate American Indians into mainstream culture, Collier believed they had valuable traditions that deserved respect. He also believed Indian communities had a right to govern themselves.[44]

This mixture of romanticism and pragmatism led Collier to launch an array of reforms to reorient the Bureau of Indian Affairs. Collier convinced Roosevelt to abolish the Board of Indian Commissioners, pass the Johnson O'Malley Act to modernize Indian education, and implement the Indian Emergency Conservation Work (IECW) and the Indian Division of the Civilian Conservation Corps (CCC-ID) to provide relief work for Native communities.[45] These programs marked a turning point for Arizona's more than 44,000 American Indians. According to the 1930 census, Native people constituted 10 percent of the state population, and reservations accounted for more than a quarter of the land.[46] The roughly forty-three programs targeting Arizona and New Mexico focused on resource protection and development, infrastructure, and recreation. By September 1933 the IECW employed more than four thousand Indians in projects on the Hualapai, San Carlos, Fort Apache, and other reservations. When it expired in 1942, nearly half of the 41,362 men in Arizona working with the CCC-ID had been Indians.[47]

The IECW and CCC-ID were important programs because they helped preserve natural resources, but they also provided Native men with important sources of income. The work camps brought men together across family and band divisions and instilled in them a common national identity, much like the boarding school experiences.[48] CCC-ID crews worked on horse and automobile trails, fencing projects, and cattle guards on the reservation. They also improved existing springs, built or renovated reservoirs, dug wells, and developed water tanks as well as check dams to conserve water and reduce runoff in arroyos.[49] Erosion control projects headed by Philip Quasula improved the health of the range and gave them a sense of ownership in the reservation, while Suwim Fielding's crew built a road to facilitate the transportation of goods and livestock. Howard Whatoname, a twenty-eight-year-old Hualapai from Kingman, began IECW employment

FIGURE 5.2. Hualapais working on a CCC-ID crew. Photographer unknown, Records of the Bureau of Indian Affairs, Central Classified Files, 1907–1953, Truxton Canyon Agency, Box 2, Folder 58813, RG 75, NARA, Washington, D.C.

in 1933 and "adapted himself to the work and proved to be a good sub-foreman," according to Supervisor Bixby. Mike Matuthanya and Rupert Parker also oversaw crews that thinned the forests to reduce the threat of fires (see fig. 5.2).[50]

These multigenerational sites brought band members together in a set of experiences that reinstilled a sense of national commonality. Youth such as Reed Watahomigie, Woodrow Hunter, Roy Sinyella, Eldon Cooney, Bill Imus, and Edward Hamidreck worked with their fathers and uncles in the camps during the summer of 1935 and returned to school in the fall.[51] More generally, the programs had an important and lasting impact on Hualapai families. In July 1936 the Emergency Conservation Work payroll listed nearly sixty Hualapais, many of them women. Superintendent Hobgood enlisted several females such as Jane Honga to work as a camp matron in the IECW. She cooked for a dozen men, kept the camp in order, and assisted with a variety of "quite strenuous" work. This labor typically supported several family members of a single worker: Dave, Emma, and Hamilton Grounds; Freddie, Norman, and Pete Imus; Teddy, George, and Pete Walker; and other families had members working on conservation programs. Many of the workers also had money sent to elderly, sick, or unemployed relatives.[52]

As these programs facilitated the ongoing cultural adaptation of the community to American institutions, they provided a forum for Hualapais to articulate changes in their individual and collective identities. During a conversation in May 1936 between Jim Fielding and Robert Marshall, the regional director of forestry, Fielding announced that his people wanted to develop their resources "like the rest of Americans." Fielding told him, "When you go back to Washington, tell the Commissioner you have found a tribe of Indians who want to go ahead, who want to build homes, who know they can't live anymore by the old ways and who want just a little help to start in the new ways." He told Marshall that "we have a good range and we want to use it so that it is a better range and not a worse range. We want to move our cattle around the way you tell us we should, we don't want the white men to come on with their cattle and eat the grass we need." Fielding saw potential on the reservation if the Hualapais had the freedom to run their own affairs.[53]

Fielding's desire to prohibit Anglos from running cattle on the reservation was part of an evolving nationalism that also targeted non-Hualapai Indians. During a council meeting in 1937 many tribal members said that they did not want people from other tribes working on IECW projects on the reservation. Hualapai rancher Charles McGee thought that they could complete more work if the IECW favored Hualapais. He did not like letting Navajos, Apaches, Paiutes, and others "take Hualapai jobs." Soil Conservation Agent V. D. Smith replied that the intent of the projects was to develop reservations and employ Indians, not to "choose favorites," and if the Hualapais wanted to exclude others, the government would end the projects.[54] McGee was not deterred, and he elaborated on the situation of his people: "At the present [time] we have many Hualapai return students" with skills such as carpentry, but he said they were "handicapped from furthering [their] educational knowledge" by the employment of non-Hualapais in the work programs. Talking as much to the young Hualapais as to Smith, McGee said: "Your government had spent a lot of time and money just for you to learn that trade and keep it up" rather than waste their skills when they returned to the reservation. McGee characterized the IECW projects as "another schooling . . . where you can be retrained so that you can be able to get out [into] the public affairs and [receive] a highly paying job for your own good."[55]

McGee offered a nationalist defense of boarding school graduates returning to a reservation that lacked employment opportunities. McGee saw the IECW as a perfect solution for graduates to continue training, make money, and build a future for themselves and the people, but employing non-Hualapais in the jobs seemed like an obstacle to this "advancement." Speaking to his fellow Hualapais, McGee said: "Today your chance has been limited. Your chance has been crowded out by other tribes who comes in and got their hands on the best jobs and trades just because they are [a] little whiter than you Hualapais." The racialized nationalism separated the Hualapais from "others" in Arizona who he implied were less Native than the Hualapais due to what McGee believed to be their lighter skin tone. "If the Hualapai Indian[s] work alone here they can be easily encouraged," argued McGee. The speech must have resonated with council member Dave Grounds, who supported McGee's motion to remove non-Hualapais from the reservation. Indeed, the Tribal Council agreed to a resolution protecting Hualapai jobs from nonmembers.[56]

As Hualapais such as McGee and Grounds tried to monitor the federal jobs, the reservation became the preeminent geographical space for the Hualapais. McGee's protectionism coincided with the activism of Fred Mahone, both of which overlapped the emigration of Anglo ranchers from the reservation. Indeed, the twin developments of a national Hualapai identity superimposed on band structures and the concentration of that identity on the reservation required innovations in political leadership that could defend the collective interests of all Hualapais. These innovations built upon the efforts of early-twentieth-century organizations such as the Welfare Committee and the Tribal Council that was in place before the passage of the Indian Reorganization Act, both of which epitomized the tensions between centralized political authority and decentralized band structures. Yet these hybrid institutions did not have consistent cultural support from band members who remained spread out across Arizona and who made decisions about their lives by consulting members of their family, not an institution like a council.

The events of the 1930s would do much to change but not resolve the tensions between traditional decentralization and modern centralization under the guise of a reservation-based formal government. Broad changes in federal Indian policy spurred new discussions among the Hualapais about leadership and political culture in the late 1930s. These changes came in the form of a key component of Collier's New Deal: the Indian Reorganization Act, which initially contained a wide array of political, economic, social, and cultural reforms, one of which targeted Native government. The original plan from Collier was changed by Senator Burton Wheeler from Montana and Representative Edgar Howard of Nebraska, who opposed the stipulations regarding Indian courts, among other things. The resulting Wheeler-Howard Act, or the Indian Reorganization Act of 1934, supported tribal governments and constitutions with limited self-governing powers. It also ended land allotment, increased funds for Indian education, and established credit for Indian corporations.[57] Collier took the weakened legislation into Indian country to argue for its adoption by tribal leaders. Designed to facilitate interaction with the dominant American political and financial institutions, the IRA did not always mesh with traditional or even evolving Indigenous governments. IRA constitutions offered hierarchies that consolidated power in the hands of a strong executive branch of government and sometimes but not always contained a weak legislative and judicial branch that endorsed the accumulation of power in the hands of business or tribal councils. As an example of neocolonialism, the federal government linked its support and acknowledgment of self-determination to acceptance of the constitutions.[58]

If Indian people were ambivalent about these policies, they were suspicious about the voting process. As representatives learned about the legislation, they discussed reorganization and held elections on adoption or rejection. This process differed from the procedures of many tribes, since the federal officials stressed majority rule and individual voting rights rather than compromise and consensus.[59] Having 51 percent approval and 49 percent disapproval may have passed muster in American elections, but it failed to reflect the traditions of most Native people. One aspect of the voting process was especially problematic: the official procedure of counting no-shows as votes *for* the government rather than not counting them at all. Some eligible voters did not vote on the constitutions because they could not reach the polling station or they had no knowledge of the proposition. Some tribal members expressed their opposition to the process by refusing to participate in what they believed was a foreign political framework that did not merit their attention. This procedural colonialism resulted in constitutions and governments supported by a minority of people who actively participated in the voting process and said yes to the new constitutions.[60]

This colonial dynamic emerged when the Hualapais first learned of and discussed the IRA in 1934. Tribal members met in Peach Springs to listen to Superintendent Hobgood and officials from the Indian Bureau promote the constitution. They also listened to the main political body on the reservation, the Walapai Livestock and Protection Association. Hobgood noted that "after considerable discussion" Hualapais "decided that, while they did not care to criticize the bill, they would still like to have more time to consider it before formally approving all of its contents." According to Hobgood, Hualapais were "very anxious to talk this matter over" with Collier, but Mathew K. Sniffen, secretary of the Indian Rights Association, would suffice.[61]

Hualapais episodically discussed the legislation for nearly four years, until they went to the polls in 1938. After the votes were counted, sixty-two members actively supported it, thirty-four actively rejected it, and the remaining individuals did not vote. That meant that only ninety-six people out of the potential two hundred actually voted. Conversely, more than half of the eligible people did not even vote, for whatever reason, while 138 either rejected it or did not vote. But the Indian Bureau added up the yes votes and the nonvotes and came to the conclusion that 166 people out of 200 voted for the constitution. Such discrepancies between the alleged support for and the real numbers actually voting failed to provide a mandate for change, but the Indian Bureau would implement the new government even if it brought the constitution into tribal life shrouded in suspicion.[62]

A considerable body of scholarship has debated the strengths and weaknesses of the Indian Reorganization Act. Some criticize the act for forcing tribes to approve boilerplate governments that distorted or destroyed traditional forms of governance, while others hail the act because it consolidated the power of tribal governments and facilitated self-determination. And still other scholars see the legislation as an open-ended struggle between neocolonial co-optation and Native resistance. Seen from this angle, rather than a hegemonic tool for controlling Native People, the governments were products of contestation that haltingly enabled communities to gain control of their resources. The governments emerged within a context of inequality, but Native people transformed them to their goals and objectives while recognizing their inherent structural limitations.[63]

Although the Hualapais changed their constitution several times, the structure of the government that emerged in 1938 was a mixture of standard elements seen across the country and variations to accommodate Hualapai political culture. The constitution stipulated that eligible adults would elect a nine-member Tribal Council, which in turn would vote for a chairman and vice chairman from their ranks. As evidence of the spatial and political nationalism of the new system, all council members had to live on the reservation, while the hereditary chief served as a tenth council member "selected by the sub-chiefs of the various recognized bands."[64] In contrast to the political nationalism of the council, its power over tribal members contradicted Hualapais' decentralized political traditions. No one really knew how the community would react to this new government. The constitution gave the council broad jurisdiction over tribal lands, resources, and funds as well as the ability to regulate hunting, fishing, and traders on tribal land. It also allowed the council to represent the tribe in state and national affairs. In addition, the council could establish the Tribal Court.[65]

Questions of cultural legitimacy, political independence, and liberal colonialism overshadowed early discussions among council members. The two most obvious manifestations of colonial management were the presence of the superintendent at council meetings and the ultimate authority of the secretary of the Interior to negate council decisions. Conversely, the participation of older leaders such as pre-IRA chairman Charles McGee, who repeatedly spoke to Congress and ultimately presided over the writing of the constitution, provided some legitimacy to the new government.[66] The first group of council members oversaw the implementation of the IRA constitution, and although they were not elected by the Hualapai people, they could claim a legitimate leadership role through their actions and ancestry. The interim chairman was Philip Quasula, the grandson of Chief Wauba Yuma; and Jacob Honga's family had a prominent status among the people. The other members of this transitional council began work in January 1939, only a month after the secretary of the Interior approved their constitution. They were Bruce Hunter, Dewey Mahone, Grant Tapija, Suwim Fielding, Bill Andrews, Charles McGee, and Sherman Whatoname, each of whom claimed relations to elder leaders.[67]

In July 1939 Hualapais held their first official public election to bring in a new council. The outgoing chairman, Philip Quasula, speaking in Hualapai during the last council meeting before the election, reviewed the council's work over the previous five months. His speech seemed especially important because it marked the first transition in power under the new constitution. Quasula reminded the tribe about the importance of running an efficient government, since some tribal members did not support it. Other outgoing council members gave short speeches about their work and encouraged the community to cooperate with the council. After the votes came in, eligible Hualapais elected Indian Honga, Carl Imus, Francis Clarke, Roger Havatone, Adam Majenty, and several others to the council. The veteran leader Charles McGee became chairman, and Grant Tapija moved into the position of vice chairman. Suwim Fielding continued as hereditary chief. All except Tapija, the vice president, and Francis Clarke were "full-blood" Hualapais, but every council member spoke the language fluently.[68]

The Tribal Council hoped to address many of the problems that had plagued it during the previous administration. Cattle ranching and a few remaining Anglo ranchers with unpaid leases were the first targets.[69] In 1938 and 1939 the council restructured the Walapai Livestock and Protection Association to allow any family with livestock to vote in elections and choose the association board. The association managed the tribal herd and the revolving cattle fund so that members could purchase cattle from the tribe. By 1946 7,800 tribally owned cattle grazed the reservation.[70] The council next turned to a law and order code, solicited applications for the Tribal Court, hired several judges, and addressed marital disputes, theft, disorderly conduct, public drunkenness, gambling, and other misdemeanors.[71]

As the council and the court struggled to gain stability, community members expressed concern about the new government. During a meeting in 1941 the new chairman, Grant Tapija, lamented: "We have since last year had two or three of our members who quit the council and none have been elected to fill their place." Several Hualapais had complained about the inattentiveness of the government and the high turnover rates of council members. "Last year we had very faithful members. This year some of us are backslipping in our duties and that is why we are together this afternoon."[72] During this free-for-all meeting the council and Indian Bureau talked about a list of important issues. Carl Amis, speaking for Kate Crozier, said Crozier wanted Virgil or Bob Schrum to replace Suwim Fielding, who stepped down as hereditary chief. After community members aired grievances about the lack of jobs, problems with housing, and the presence of unlicensed traders, the meeting closed with promises to bring jobs to the reservation, stabilize the range, end the lawsuit with the Santa Fe Railway, and improve the day school: no small agenda for such a young council.[73]

The interwar era was a complex historical moment for the Hualapais. They reorganized themselves to cope with shifting historical forces in ways that seemingly ignored tradition when in fact much of Hualapai culture provided familiarity to new structures and conditions. Band identities still formed the basis of identity, though they became incorporated into a larger Hualapai national consciousness. Political developments carried this same mixture of change and continuity that integrated new processes into familiar contexts in the early twentieth century. Hualapais' confrontations with competing discourses over belonging to an Indigenous nation and a colonizing nation-state exposed contradictions in their status and territoriality. They were racialized as noncitizen subjects incapable of holding private property, but they filed for allotments on the public domain. They tried crafting a refuge on the reservation as a global crisis in capitalism caused the emigration of Anglo ranchers but contended with the colonial gaze of the Indian Bureau. And although acceptance of government labor programs and the imposition of a foreign constitution tied the people to the liberal state just as closely as it strained Hualapais' attempts to create an identity that respected families and bands, the Hualapai nation had firmly rooted itself in the social, political, and cultural landscape of northwestern Arizona.

# 6

# The Hualapai Nation in Postwar America

On 1 May 1942 tribal members filled the Valentine Indian School auditorium to hear the good news. As they did during the moments before the beginning of plays and talent shows held regularly at the old school, the crowd buzzed in anticipation for the meeting to begin. They fell silent as Chairman Grant Tapija read the Supreme Court ruling recognizing the tribe's right to "all lands relinquished by the Santa Fe Railroad Company, within the exterior boundaries of the Hualapai Reservation, as defined by the Executive Order January 4, 1883." Those in the audience who understood the case absorbed the words of a decision that ended five decades of conflict. Hualapais had defended their rights to the land, and they could be proud of the "favorable and final disposition of the Hualapai Land Case."[1]

The Supreme Court ruling in 1941 ended the arduous legal battle and seemed to assure future generations of a home on the reservation, which was increasingly becoming the locus of Hualapai national identity. Families moved there as Anglo ranchers, whose cattle businesses had gone bankrupt during the Great Depression, abandoned the reservation. The resulting migration to Hualapai land that began in the 1930s and continued after the postwar years ran against the national trends toward urbanization, relocation, and new policies of termination. But the security represented by the land case and the growing settlement of the reservation gave way to national and global events that threatened institutions the tribe had recently constructed.

Western powers, shaken by the unprecedented destruction of World War II, saw their global empires crumble under the weight of decolonization and the cold war. Nationalisms, including Indigenous nationalism, competed and overlapped with liberalism, capitalism, and Communism as Native peoples carved out a place for themselves on a global landscape fraught with ideological debates and countervailing loyalties. And yet, even as some Western powers lost control over peoples they sought to oppress, Indigenous nations like the Hualapais and others throughout the United States experienced renewed attacks on their aboriginal lands and status as semi-independent nations in the form of termination and relocation.

Within this global context of decolonization the Hualapai Tribal Council faced growing demands from a community undergoing rapid growth and demographic change. Termination legislation, migration to the reservation, poverty, water disputes, and other challenges raised questions of cultural legitimacy for the council because it was the only institution able to protect community resources and advocate for all members. Band affiliations remained important, but a new political culture based on a semidemocratic constitutional template sometimes undermined band affiliations and obstructed political behavior based on bands or traditional headmen. Individualized voting in secret ballots corroded culturally rooted processes of consensus and debate. And although families replaced bands as the sociopolitical interest groups or "political action committees," the creation of a reservation-based neocolonial government with all of the related bureaucratic structures and institutional apparatuses alienated many Hualapais who felt that the Tribal Council served its own interests and the interests of the most powerful families rather than the concerns of the Hualapais as a people. These critiques notwithstanding, the Hualapai Tribal Council entered the postwar era as the central institution poised to protect the Hualapai nation.

## The Politics of Neocolonial Government

In the years after Hualapais won the court case against the Santa Fe Railway, life on the reservation changed considerably. The 1938 reservation census counted 459 people, the 1945 census counted 519, and by 1954 the population had grown to more than 700 people. These individuals and families lived a precarious economic life that was dependent upon the new government and its ability to protect reservation resources, procure federal employment programs, and initiate and successfully manage reservation-based industries such as cattle ranching, forestry, tourism, and, in some cases, mining. Most of the families in the postwar years relied on a mixture of wage labor, government employment, and subsistence in the form of family gardens and small-scale cattle holdings. Of eighty-seven Hualapai men interviewed during a federal survey of the reservation, thirty-one relied on federal jobs, ten were self-employed, twelve worked for private companies, six worked for the Hualapai government, and twenty said they were unemployed. Sixty reported owning cattle on the reservation. Out of seventy-two women interviewed, fifty-four reported housework as their main occupation, seven worked for the federal government, two said they made baskets for a living, and the rest claimed they were unemployed. Average incomes ranged from $10 to $1,260 per year.[2]

These numbers suggest a community under economic strain. Part of this situation stemmed from the conditions in northwestern Arizona following the Great Depression. The collapse of the cattle industry forced many ranchers to sell their herds, which meant fewer jobs for Hualapai cowboys. A few Hualapai-run operations also went bankrupt. And as the federal government trimmed New Deal programs on the reservation, there was a growing community that lacked jobs. This economic vacuum forced Hualapais to turn to the Tribal Council for employment, housing, and education, making its decisions about development more important. In turn, the council's ability to provide jobs and spark development profoundly affected the morale of the community and the legitimacy of the council itself.[3]

Postwar pressures on the council followed a trend in the political culture of the Hualapai community dating back to the early twentieth century, when Jim Fielding, Fred Mahone, and others created organizations that superseded traditional band and hereditary leaders. This suspicion of centralized leadership resulted in the reluctant support for and sometimes opposition to the IRA government and the council that emerged from it in 1938. And yet the migration of Hualapais to the reservation precipitated an economic crisis that only compounded an ongoing suspicion of the centralized, hierarchical, and, to some degree, foreign Hualapai Tribal Council. Bands and individuals not familiar with the pre-IRA institutions championed by Mahone valued the "traditional" political culture characterized by decentralization and the ability to speak Hualapai; thus, they were concerned about a council that some people felt moved "too fast" or "acted white." Moreover, families and bands retained many of their alliances and were concerned about a system that repeatedly elected council members from a few families such as the Mahones and Quasulas. On the other hand, band ties weakened, as did some of the older political characteristics, as the new government relied on majority rule and individual votes rather than consensus.[4]

This is not to say that Hualapais could not adapt; they did. But the new form of representation guaranteed people a voice in electing leaders to a government that possessed limited control over forces shaping the reservation. This contradiction reveals another intrusion of colonialism into

Hualapai political culture: not only was the form and process of creating the IRA government dubious, it failed to give local leaders the full ability to manage their own economy as an emerging nation. Rather, it bred suspicion and confusion among the people, allowed the superintendent to remain as gatekeeper, and enabled the commissioner of Indian Affairs and the secretary of the Interior to veto council resolutions. Hampered at the local level and subject to the control of Washington, D.C., the Tribal Council had the near impossible goal of providing for a growing community that did not always understand the limited powers of the Hualapai government.[5]

As chairman in the early 1940s, Grant Tapija realized that the institution lacked credibility with people in the community, especially the "traditionals," born as far back as the 1870s. He nonetheless believed that Hualapais had to embrace the new constitution to help the tribe succeed. And yet he lamented the limited powers and financial problems facing the council. He also believed that the legitimacy of the council required it to change the political culture of the reservation. He believed the council represented people who were uninformed about important aspects of the new government.[6] For instance, tribal members directly elected council members, who elected the chair and vice chair. Many people did not understand this, and they were angered by what they perceived to be their lack of control over the two highest positions in government. Moreover, few people knew they had a right to petition, initiate referendums, or recall a member of the council. Tapija thought that people would support the council if they knew more of their rights, participated in the process, and understood the power of the federal government over council decisions. Charles McGee said that he had not "spoken with anyone who thought that we ought not let the Tribe choose the council." In response, Mr. Marmon, an Indian Bureau supervisor of elections, reiterated: "The general intent [of the constitution] was that the people would be the ones to nominate the members on the floor, which we felt would not be a very large group yet would represent the people." In time, the tribe would have "more representation for the different family groups or bands" and change the constitution to allow popular election of the highest posts.[7]

Yet the structure of the new government was difficult for Hualapais to adjust to, since traditional forms of leadership depended on familiar face-to-face relationships, and the new political regime required different bands to vote on unfamiliar candidates. As more Hualapais moved to the reservation from across Pai territory, they tried to work their way into a political system that had been shaped by leaders who had been willing to engage the federal government and participate in the council. Newcomers had a difficult time acquiring council seats dominated by a few families within a few bands to gain control of the entire government. They had never known some of the leaders who would now make decisions impacting their own lives. This does not mean that a Hualapai oligarchy emerged after World War II, nor does it mean that voters felt permanently alienated. The common experiences of boarding school, military service, the Santa Fe Railway case, wage labor, and the more general defense of Hualapai lands and rights broke down many band and family divisions and paved the way for a stronger Hualapai national identity. But in the political realm, where individuals voted for a council that oversaw band members who may not have been represented in it, the centralization of power concerned many people.

Working at the margins of Indigenous sovereignty and American colonial rule, postwar Tribal Councils continued facing crises in political and cultural legitimacy. Whether or not the community elected a Honga, Beecher, Quasula, Fielding, Parker, Mahone, or Tapija, the council consistently struggled to increase its sociocultural currency.[8] It tried to support traditional ceremonies, defer to elders, use the language in meetings, avoid confrontation, and even seek consensus despite its contradiction with representative government. Furthermore, the council sought legitimacy by creating jobs, providing health and social services, enforcing reservation laws, and representing the Hualapais to the federal government.[9] By proving its worth to the community, the council hoped to gain its acceptance.

In response to concerns about the power of the council, the Hualapais held a special election that resulted in the revision of the constitution and charter in 1955.[10] Under the guidance of Chairman Rupert Parker, the revisions granted the Tribal Council expanded powers to negotiate timber, cattle, and mining leases, "engage in any business that will further the economic well-being of the members of the tribe," and implement contracts with "any person, association, or corporation, with any municipality or any county, or with the United States or the State of Arizona" for public services.[11] The charter stipulated that the Hualapais would manage their own internal affairs and negotiate directly with the federal government. The council could grant water and mineral rights, collect taxes, enact laws, establish tribal courts and law enforcement, appoint guardians for minors, settle civil disputes, and remove nonmembers from the reservation. Revisions also addressed the rights of tribal members. Members "shall be accorded equal political rights and equal opportunities to participate in the economic resources and activities of the tribe" and guaranteed the "freedom of conscience, speech, association, and assembly."[12]

Three changes were particularly noteworthy. Registered voters would directly elect the chairman and vice chairman, a decision that emanated from the concerns community members expressed about the legitimacy of the IRA government. In addition, the new constitution revised membership to include "any child of one-fourth degree or more of Hualapai Indian blood who is born to a resident member after the date this Constitution is approved." This was one of the few times that blood quantum had been mentioned in the twentieth century. Previously, it entered Hualapai political discourse when members sought allotments off the reservation and when the IRA government was implemented in 1938. But the rearticulation of blood quantum as the main qualification for membership within the Hualapai nation demonstrated how deeply American racial ideologies had worked their way into Indigenous governmental institutions. Like other Indian nations across the United States, Hualapais chose the fiction of blood rather than parental lineage or "national citizenship" as the key indicator of membership. This set the Hualapais on a dangerous path because they would have to constantly reassess the fraction of blood necessary for membership within the nation. Sometime in the future Hualapais would have to evict people who did not meet the one-fourth requirement and thus alienate friends and family.[13]

But, most surprisingly, the new constitution ended the system of including a hereditary chief on the Tribal Council. The reasons for this are unclear. Previous hereditary leaders expressed some disillusionment with the government because it equated them with regular council members rather than as spiritual and political leaders, so several of them had resigned from the council. On the other hand, having a solitary "hereditary chief" did not reflect the traditional patterns of leadership among Pai bands, which had never recognized a singular leader with oversight over all bands. Thus, as more bands moved to the reservation after the war, they may not have recognized the authority of a "chief" from a band they were not members of. While the expansion of council powers may have placed the Hualapais on firmer ground in relation to the federal government, the institutionalization of blood quantum and the elimination of the hereditary chief from the council were difficult decisions that still elicit surprise and dismay among Hualapais today.[14]

## Maintaining Peoplehood in the Termination Era

The constitutional revisions of the 1950s revealed the desires of Hualapai leaders searching for greater sovereignty over the reservation lands and people.[15] These changes emanated from local concerns about the cultural legitimacy of the Hualapai government and the external refusal of the United States to treat the Hualapais as an Indigenous nation. Negotiating these local, national, and, to some extent, global economic and ideological shifts began when the federal government implemented a new program to dismantle Native self-determination and the sovereign integrity of Indigenous political territorial space. Commonly known as termination, the period from 1945 to the early 1960s saw Congress try to liquidate reservations and incorporate them into the surrounding states and counties. The goal of termination legislation was an end to Indigenous control of their resources and the "government-to-government" relationship with federal authorities.[16]

Congress offered several arguments for this agenda. Fear of economic depression led Congress to reduce spending for social programs, while narrow definitions of Americanism made cultural diversity seem dangerous during the cold war. Political conservatives believed reservations were Communist enclaves where individual will and freedom suffocated, and liberals compared reservations with the segregated South and argued that Indians should "integrate" and enjoy a growing postwar society. Finally, corporations wanted resources that were allegedly "wasted" on reservations. This mixture of politics, economics, and ideology fueled sentiment to open reservations, "free" the Indians, and integrate them into society.[17] This ideological context led Congress, the Department of the Interior, and the Bureau of Indian Affairs to initiate a series of surveys on Indian reservations. Assistant Commissioner for Indian Affairs William Zimmerman cataloged the natural resources, population, land base, financial health, and alleged "acculturation" of each tribe to facilitate decisions about the future status of Indian nations. Zimmerman did not intend for partisans to use the list to dissolve reservations, but Congress and Interior placed Indian reservations in one of three categories of "preparedness" for termination.[18] Of the three categories, the first group lost trust relations immediately, the second had to wait up to ten years, and the third would wait an indefinite period until federal authorities deemed it viable. Congress placed Indian nations into these categories based on acculturation, economic viability, views on termination, and the opinion of the state the reservation was located in.[19]

When the "termination bill," HR 108, passed in 1953, Native people across the United States prepared to defend their lands. Congress immediately targeted the Klamaths of Oregon, the Menominees of Wisconsin, the Salish-Kootenais of Montana, the Hupas of California, the Osages of Oklahoma, and several others. The passage of Public Law 280 in the same year allowed California, Nebraska, Minnesota, Oregon, and Wisconsin to assume civil and criminal jurisdiction over tribal lands. Iowa, Washington, and Alaska followed suit, but some states with large Indian populations, such as Arizona, refused the responsibility. In addition to PL 280, the BIA transferred some programs from the Indian Health Service to the Public Health

Service (PHS) in 1955, and Public Laws 815 and 874 provided money for the construction and operation of new public schools on reservations.[20]

Native leaders across the United States opposed the legislation and the sentiment fueling it. In 1944 Hualapai leader Leo Andrews wanted his people to join the National Congress of American Indians (NCAI), which held its first meeting that year in Denver. Fred Mahone attended the gathering and reported back to the council that the NCAI represented all nations in the United States.[21] When Hualapais joined, they entered into a multinational organization that served as a clearinghouse of information and conduit between Native nations and the federal government.[22] Although its initial years lacked focus, in 1946 the NCAI became involved in the Indian Claims Commission and in 1948 supported Indian voting rights in Arizona and New Mexico. By 1950 it was the preeminent critic of termination legislation.[23]

Participation in the NCAI was related to the tense relationships between Indian communities and the state of Arizona, which began preparing for the withdrawal of federal services to reservations. The Arizona Commission on Indian Affairs (ACIA) and the Inter-Tribal Council of Arizona (ITCA) emerged as leading organizations at the nexus of Native-state politics. The Hualapai Tribal Council was very active in this process, hoping to protect reservations by adopting resolutions in 1952 that requested "the House of Representatives of Arizona to favorably pass HB 68 to create a State Commission of Indian Affairs." The council hoped the legislature would create the organization so that "Indians in the state of Arizona, as well as the state officials, [could] sit down and seriously consider and study conditions among the Indians residing within the state," which it did in 1953.[24] Hualapais sent Charles McGee and Wilson Honga to meet with Governor Howard Pyle "for the purpose of activating the Arizona State Commission of Indian Affairs" in 1954. But when the state decided not to assume jurisdiction, the ACIA lost much of its original focus. And yet many tribal governments continued to send representatives to discuss Indian policy. The ACIA sponsored annual "Indian Town Halls" where tribal leaders discussed contemporary issues with state officials. In the 1960s the ACIA began reservation surveys that generated data on education, natural resources, health, economic status, and law and order, but they did not directly impact policies. Lack of funding and a dubious mandate kept the ACIA from becoming a useful institution to resolve disputes or increase tribal-state communication.[25]

The Inter-Tribal Council of Arizona, unlike the ACIA, was established in 1952 by Native people "to provide a united voice for tribal governments located in the State of Arizona to address common issues or concerns," and it had a more productive life. In 1953 Chairman Leo Andrews attended an

Inter-Tribal Council meeting in Phoenix to adopt a constitution and bylaws for the organization. As the ITCA gained influence it worked with the NCAI on issues facing tribes throughout the United States. In 1955 Chairman Rupert Parker attended an institute sponsored by the NCAI and ITCA in Phoenix to acquaint Indian leaders with laws regarding health, education, and crime on reservations. In ensuing years the ITCA improved tribal relations with the state as it helped Arizona Native leaders share information and resources.[26]

Hualapai leaders tried to link the efforts of tribes in Arizona with a nationwide movement to oppose termination. In 1955 Rupert Parker went to Santa Fe for a conference held by the New Mexico Association of Indian Affairs to instruct Native leaders about termination. When he returned to debrief the council he relayed how "it was brought out that the various tribes should be planning for the future and that their planning would come from the reservations," not the federal government. To support cooperation across the Southwest, the council created a committee composed of Rupert Parker, Sterling Mahone, and Raymond Havatone to monitor termination issues. The three remained in contact with leaders on other reservations to share strategies to prevent the dismantling of their semisovereign status.[27]

Hualapais watched termination closely and registered their complaints in Washington. After reading proposed termination bills in 1949, the council argued that the bills were "misleading in that they are labeled 'competency' bill and 'emancipation' bill, wherein truth and fact they do not truly emancipate the Indian." Writing to the commissioner of Indian Affairs, the council argued that the bills "tend to further confuse the issues, and subject certain Indians to the possibility of losing their homes and lands . . . granted to Indians by Treaties or Acts of Congress." The council wanted "an opportunity to be heard on this question before the bills are hastily passed."[28] Termination touched them in other ways, as congressional cutbacks led to the consolidation of agencies and reduction of services. When Sterling Mahone heard a plan in 1951 to consolidate the Truxton Canyon Agency with the Colorado River Agency, he became concerned about the council's ability to improve life on the reservation. In one council meeting he told Superintendent Thomas Dodge that "the problems of the Hualapai Reservation are entirely different and have nothing in common with the Colorado River Reservation." Dodge relayed Mahone's concerns to Phoenix Area Director Ralph Gelvin, but Gelvin supported the changes.[29] To quiet the protests, Gelvin said: "I see nothing in this consolidation that will take away any of the services to the Hualapai Indians," especially health care and law enforcement. Gelvin noted the national context: "Your consolidation is only one of many such consolidations throughout the entire Indian

FIGURE 6.1. Hualapai Tribal Council members and Judge E. E. Wishon, mid-1950s. Back row from left: Suwim Fielding, Judge E. E. Wishon, Sterling Mahone, Willie MacGee; front row from left: Taft Clark, Sherman Whatoname. Photographer unknown, #6417, Mohave Museum of History and Arts, Kingman, Arizona.

country. These consolidations have been made necessary by appropriation limitations and personnel ceilings that have been imposed upon the Bureau of Indian Affairs by the Congress." He added: "The Commissioner of Indian Affairs has repeatedly stated to us in the field that he wants us to handle these adjustments and consolidations in such a manner that they will have a minimum effect upon the Indian people, and that is what we have conscientiously tried to do." These comments did little to reduce the concerns of the council regarding its ability to protect the community.[30]

In 1953 Sterling Mahone wrote a letter opposing termination to Congressman A. L. Miller of the House Committee on Interior and Insular Affairs (see fig. 6.1). The letter was only one of many actions taken by Mahone, who had learned about tribal politics and activism from the iconoclastic Fred Mahone. The younger Mahone was born on the Big Sandy in 1915, attended boarding school in Truxton and Phoenix, served in World War II, and became involved in tribal politics, a trajectory similar to Fred's. In contrast, Sterling's moderate style allowed him to become chair of the tribe for many years.[31] In November 1954 he and other council members discussed termination and Public Law 280. Representing the council, Mahone told Royal Marks, Leon Grant, director of the Phoenix Indian Center, and officials from the ACIA that termination "would be detrimental to the interests of the Hualapai Tribe and other tribes in Arizona."[32]

Unlike the Alabama-Coushattas, Menominees, and Klamaths, the Hualapais escaped termination. Several factors explain this. Though the tribe had natural resources, it suffered from financial instability, isolation, and poverty. The council, through individuals such as Sterling Mahone, opposed withdrawal and admitted the need for assistance from the BIA. The state of Arizona expressed little interest in assuming responsibility for the reservation. The county already lacked adequate law and order services, and gaining jurisdiction on the reservation did not appeal to it. Industries that expressed interest in the reservation had difficulties exploiting the mineral and timber resources. The range needed work, and the high plateaus lacked sufficient water to make them profitable. These converging factors saved the Hualapais from termination.[33]

The tribe did not totally avoid the fallout from termination, which threatened tribes in additional ways. In addition to HR 108 and PL 280, the federal government created the Indian Claims Commission (ICC) in 1946 to settle debts and lawsuits against the federal government and to clarify land disputes due to treaty violations and breaches of trust. The ICC began as an extension of Congress but quickly became a quasi-independent institution that ruled on approximately 370 claims and awarded nearly $900 million by the time Congress ended it in 1978. The ICC mandated contradictory objectives: reimburse tribes for massive financial losses, atone for moral injustices, and clear the books of any debts so that Congress could cut its ties with Indian people. Ironically, hearing land claims admitted guilt and reinforced the moral position of tribes.[34]

Hualapais voiced their opinions on the ICC once they heard about it. In 1944 the Tribal Council sent Fred Mahone to Washington, D.C., as a representative to "the Indian Convention on land claims," and in 1945 the council sent a letter to President Harry Truman urging him to support the Claims Commission Bill and, using a popular phrase of the day, "give Indians their day in court" (see fig. 6.2). Initially, the tribe thought the ICC only intended to compensate tribes for land loss, and they did not realize that the ICC ultimately sought the termination of government-to-government relations.[35] Nonetheless, in 1950 the Hualapais officially embarked on the long

FIGURE 6.2. Fred Mahone (bottom row, third from right) at a meeting of the National Congress of American Indians, Washington, D.C., 1944. Courtesy of Camille Nighthorse.

process of proving their aboriginal occupancy to the ICC. While gathering evidence, the tribe combined legal research in archives with archaeological excavations, geographical surveys, interviews, and conversations with adjacent tribes. Sterling Mahone, the main representative on ICC matters, met with local tribes to determine their views on the territory of Pai bands. In this process tribal members stressed the importance of the midstream and center of their boundary on the Colorado River, since there had been debate about whether or not the reservation ended at the high-water mark or the "spine" of the river. If the tribe could prove that its aboriginal lands extended into the center, it could strengthen its legal claim to the river.[36]

When the Hualapais presented to the ICC in 1957, they employed several experts to argue their case on the premise of aboriginal occupancy. The council hired Robert C. Euler from the Museum of Northern Arizona and Henry F. Dobyns to conduct archaeological investigations. They had hired Arthur Lazarus, Jr., to replace Felix Cohen, who had passed away in 1953. They also had the commitment of Royal Marks. This group, joined by Grant Tapija, Sr., Fred Mahone, Carl Amis, and other individuals over the next decade, won an ambiguous victory in 1960 when Royal Marks announced that Congress was in the process of appropriating the money. Meanwhile, the tribe devised an economic development plan, received approval from the commissioner, and then submitted that plan to Congress and the ICC. The ICC received the tribe's plan in 1967 but told the tribe to present it to the community and conduct a census of all enrolled members to ensure that dispersal of the funds went to real people.[37]

Conducting a census and discussing the plan with the community opened up a whole new set of complications. Edna Bender oversaw the census and had difficulty tracking down Hualapais in cities, other states, and Mormon families. She gathered hundreds of signatures, verified them with previous rolls and birth certificates, and then submitted a list of names to the council in 1967. On 4 May 1968 the council called a general meeting for members to listen to the settlement and vote on its provisions. The tribe discussed the offer and voted in secret ballots. Chairman Parker read the offer and began the long process of deciding how to use and distribute the money.[38] In 1969 the tribe sent the plan to Congress, but Calvin Brice, a BIA official, said Congress rejected it because it lacked a clearer statement describing who received per-capita payments how the council would invest the money, oversee funds reserved for minors, and distribute checks. John T. Kozakes, also from the BIA, said the money provided the tribe with an "opportunity to remedy the problems that they are now facing up against," but he agreed with concerns expressed by Congress.[39]

Hoping to resolve the new set of problems, in 1970 the council created an ICC committee comprised of Superintendent Charles Pitrat, Kozakes, Indian Development District of Arizona (IDDA) Director William McPhee, and Hualapais Ben Beecher and Dallas Quasula. Determining what percentage of nearly $3 million would go directly into the hands of Hualapai citizens as compensation for three-quarters of their ancestral homelands was a contentious issue. Rupert Parker quit as chairman, ostensibly angered at the ICC committee and the proposed use of funds.[40] In June the tribe submitted its plan to the commissioner and Congress, and President Nixon signed the judgment funds.[41] Errors in the tribal census held up distribution. Parents had switched the enrollment of their children from tribes not receiving ICC funds in an effort to provide them with a larger sum of money. Undocumented members appeared on the reservation when they heard about per-capita distributions, so it took awhile to confirm their enrollment.[42] These difficulties led to the election of Lena Bravo as the "per-capita secretary" to deal with the census and distribution of funds. Superintendent Pitrat then announced in 1972 that members would receive a per-capita check for $642.55, and the council would place $1 million into a trust fund to help with development. The remaining funds went toward attorneys' fees and general reservation projects.[43]

Like PL 280, HR 108, and the ICC, the relocation program strained Hualapai families and the Tribal Council right when they were adjusting their government to better serve reservation residents. For nearly two decades the policies associated with termination sought to relocate Indians to cities such as Chicago, Detroit, Los Angeles, San Francisco, and Cleveland.[44] From 1940 through the '60s more than 120,000 American Indians participated in the official relocation programs, which reflected the belief that reservations were prisons that segregated Indians from America. Couched in terms of liberal integration and conservative budget cutting, relocation was the velvet glove covering the iron fist of termination because it promised poverty-stricken reservation residents a chance at a new life in the city while the federal government liquidated their reservations. The appointment of Dillon S. Meyer, the past director of the War Relocation Authority and Japanese American internment, as commissioner of Indian Affairs, clearly revealed the spirit of the program.[45]

Hualapais who "volunteered" for the program joined other Arizona Indians in Phoenix, which served as a transfer station before the relocation association sent them outside the state.[46] Although most Hualapais who volunteered for the program relocated in the 1960s, a few left earlier. In 1955, "hoping to find opportunity knocking at their door," Mr. and Mrs. Leo Powskey moved their family to Chicago all the way from Peach Springs. After a string of frustrating experiences, including redlined housing districts, inability to find employment due to the exclusionary practices of unions, and general anti-Indian sentiment, the Powskeys returned to the reservation. The Powskeys' experience was not necessarily indicative of all Hualapais who moved to urban areas in the 1960s and 1970s. Most "urban Hualapais" lived in Kingman, but others lived in Phoenix, Tucson, and Flagstaff and even Los Angeles, Denver, and Kansas City.[47] Margaret Havatone was the first Hualapai to complete the Adult Vocational Training Program in 1960. Margaret entered Lamson Business College in Phoenix, graduated in 1961, and relocated to San Francisco, where she worked as the finance manager for a furniture company. Like the Powskeys, she returned home in the 1970s and became a council member.[48]

Other Hualapais followed a similar path in search of employment and new experiences. Timothy Hunter worked as a barber, Ronald Susanyatame worked as a welder, and Veronica Havatone became a stenographer in Phoenix. *Gum-U: The Hualapai Newsletter* recounted the story of Lucinda June Honga and Cleophus Parker and their journey across America. Parker moved to Phoenix, where she enrolled in classes to become a dental hygienist. When she completed her training, she made the trek across the desert to San Francisco.

Lucinda Honga also went to Phoenix, sought training in cosmetology, and upon completion of her classes went east to Cleveland. It would not have been a stretch to say that Lucinda was the only Hualapai in Ohio. Austin Wilder and Cecil Benn went to Denver and to Dallas, respectively, as mechanics.[49]

Urbanization—whether or not it was voluntary—raised important issues of identity. Although numerous Hualapais had lived in towns off the reservation long before relocation policies, the Hualapai government nonetheless had to determine their political status, right to vote in elections, and access to resources and BIA funds typically available to reservation residents. In 1955 the council discussed the status of children born in cities and informed the parents that the newborns were not officially enrolled. The parents had one year to enroll their children, otherwise they could lose their official status as a Hualapai.[50] Life in cities also contributed to the frequency of multitribal relationships. As intermarriage raised the issue of affiliation, the Hualapai Tribal Council noted how a few tribal members accepted the last names of people from other tribes. When Hualapai women married such men, the council wanted to know if they changed affiliation or if they planned to return to the reservation. If they did the latter, the council warned them that the husband lacked the rights of the wife.[51]

The relatively low rate of Hualapai participation in the relocation program did not mean that Hualapais avoided urban areas. Hualapais had lived in towns and small cities such as Kingman long before World War II. Established in the 1870s, Kingman and its five thousand Anglos had mixed relations with Hualapais. Discrimination, segregated housing, inadequate social services, police harassment, and poverty characterized Hualapais' experiences. Indian Town residents had survived for decades with temporary labor, work on the railway, and subsistence hunting and gardening, but in 1949 the Kingman City Council, Indian Town leaders, and the Hualapai Tribal Council confronted each other over the status of Indian Town.[52] Royal Marks said that if the colony moved a quarter mile west, off railway land, the railway and the city could pipe it water. The council tended to agree with that advice. Indian Town leader Sherman Whatoname fired back at the city government and the Tribal Council for not respecting town residents' right to live unmolested, since his people had claimed the land as their aboriginal territory long before the incorporation of the city. Whatoname refused assistance from the council as adamantly as he refused the requests by the city to relocate. In response, the council said the matter was up to the individuals in question and absolved itself of responsibility.[53]

Part of the troubles facing the colony stemmed from actions of the Santa Fe Railway, even though many Hualapais relied on it for employment. As one of the largest employers in the region, the railroad complained to the city and Tribal Council about Indian Town Hualapais diverting water from its facilities and living on land it allegedly owned. Shifting his support to the Kingman Hualapais, Marks informed railway officials that "some action would be taken in determining the status of Indians living in Kingman," reiterating the residents' refusal to move. Whatoname defended the right of the community to live on the disputed acreage, and he even raised the memory of the railway's lost court case. Whatoname used the tribe's historic victory as a reminder that even a small Indian colony could not be intimidated. Fortunately, during a special meeting in 1950 the council opposed the Santa Fe's lawsuit against the Kingman Hualapais for allegedly trespassing on railway lands. The council granted five hundred dollars for attorney fees to assist Taft Clark, a Hualapai, and Louis Wallace, Jr., of Kingman to represent the colony. Tribal members in Kingman refused to move, and the railway decided against litigation.[54]

Other issues caused friction between Hualapais and Kingman officials. In 1953 the council met with Leo Bellieu, a criminal investigator for the BIA, the Kingman City Council, and the chief of police. They discussed the legal status of Hualapais in Kingman and whether or not Hualapais had trespassed on private property or stolen various objects from local whites. They appointed Bill Andrews, Wilson Honga, and Sterling Mahone to formulate "a definite plan" to help tribal members in Kingman when the city refused to assist them. In 1955 Royal Marks relayed the concerns about discrimination in housing, employment, and education in Kingman to Mohave County officials. The council wanted to investigate the mistreatment of "drunk Indians" who complained of harassment, warrantless arrests, lack of representation in court, and unreasonable time in jail.[55] Council members stated that Hualapais were citizens of the United States and thus deserved the protection of the U.S. Constitution.[56] When Ben Beecher traveled to Kingman in 1966, he visited tribal members in jail to investigate a survey made by tribal policeman Ernie Smith about harassment toward Hualapais.[57]

Despite the presence of Hualapais in Kingman, Phoenix, or Cleveland, the reservation remained the locus of Hualapai national identity. Beginning with the first major migration of Hualapais to the reservation in the 1930s, by the 1960s the administrative space began to more closely resemble a community. While some Hualapais lived in rural areas such as Pine Springs, most tribal members moved to Peach Springs, where the school, churches, tribal administration, several gas stations, a motor lodge, and community building and sports center were located. In the process, housing arose as a matter of concern for the tribe. Houses on the reservation consisted of brick homes with windows, insulation, and indoor plumbing; wickiups or hogans; and older houses made from scrap materials. The council established a Housing and Development Program under the auspices of the Hualapai Housing Authority in 1963 to assist tribal members with loans and construction. In 1966 the Housing Authority submitted an application to the Economic Development Administration for federal assistance for houses. Within a few years the Hualapai Housing Authority had fifty new homes planned.[58]

The tribe completed the first phase of housing, and this encouraged more people to move to the reservation, making housing more important. Hualapai Housing Director Lydia Beecher worked with federal agencies to acquire funds for another round of construction. During her time at the Authority, she coordinated workers from the reservation and Operation Mainstream, a federally funded program, to build homes for tribal members. Foreseeing considerable sums flowing into tribal accounts from the Indian Claims Commission decision, in 1970 Beecher requested $150,000 from the council to assist with home construction. She and other Housing Authority members drafted the Peach Springs Housing Plan to map a system for providing homes to tribal members.[59] The Department of Housing and Urban Development (HUD), the Public Health Service (PHS), the BIA, and other federal agencies told the council that it ought to build the third phase of homes several miles away from the town of Peach Springs. Citing concerns about overuse of the present water system, the agencies thought that the community should be split in half, with the new homes built at the western end of the reservation. The council and the Housing Authority disagreed: "This is not a satisfactory answer taking into consideration the cohesiveness of the community and the political stability of the tribe." Yet by the early 1980s Peach Springs consisted of three housing sections: the first division southeast of the railroad tracks near the gym, jail, and old Tribal Court offices; another northwest of the railroad, where the present administration building and school are located; and another section southwest on Buck and Doe Road.[60]

By the 1980s, a half-century after most people began moving to the reservation, several tribal institutions and locations served as central hubs of community activity. The Peach Springs Elementary School brought tribal members together with meetings, regular sports events, and the common concern about the welfare of the children. The community and council were concerned about Hualapai youth, who needed a recreation and community center where tribal members could also join together for speeches, ceremonies, powwows, and other occasions. The tribe expressed an interest in a community center in the 1950s, but the project faced financial obstacles.[61] Hualapai youth and non-Indian volunteers built a small center, but tribal members pressed for a larger building. In 1965 the council received a petition for a community hall, in 1966 the council applied to a grant funded by the Indian Community Action Program, and in 1967 it appropriated $15,000 from general funds for a multipurpose building. A grant from the Economic Development Association helped the council complete the building in 1969.[62]

Great Society programs assisted Hualapai youth who were interested in improving the community. Though they faced challenges such as alcohol, cultural alienation, and limited job opportunities, Hualapai youth—many of whom would become tribal leaders in the following decade—made important contributions to the reservation community. Chairman George Rocha reported on the summer programs under the auspices of the Neighborhood Youth Corps (NYC), a project growing out of the Community Action Programs of the Johnson years.[63] Claudia Mapatis, Margaret Vaughn, Ina Jackson, and Cyrus Watuema all participated in the program. In 1969 the National Indian Youth Council (NIYC) cooperated with the Hualapai Project Mainstream to devise community projects that trained youth for employment opportunities, and in 1970 the tribe began a Youth Camp Project for leadership and survival skills.[64]

Although these programs helped youth develop leadership skills, Hualapai children faced numerous challenges growing up. In particular, structural poverty on the reservation made it extremely difficult to feed and educate tribal youth. Broken homes due in large part to alcoholism and unwanted pregnancies resulted in homeless children or children who lacked stable environments. Most parents struggled to provide for their children, and many needed support from tribal, state, and federal sources. In 1970 the Tribal Council approved a plan by Paul Moffat, the social worker for the tribe, to contract with the BIA for a children's home. In 1973 the council discussed funding for a day-care center to help parents balance work and family. One major breakthrough came with the passage of the Indian Child Welfare Act of 1978, which stipulated that tribal members could adopt abandoned children first if they lacked a viable relative.[65]

As the tribe struggled with quality of life on the reservation, it dealt with two sensitive issues: alcoholism and religion. Whether it had deleterious effects on Indian populations due to biology or whether socioeconomic factors played a larger role, alcohol caused tremendous problems for Hualapais in the twentieth century even though it had been barred from the reservation.[66] To learn more about the causes and treatments of alcoholism, in 1969 the council sent tribal members to Tucson to attend the Southwestern School of Alcohol Problems. Leo Powskey returned and reported that most people refused to attend alcoholism programs even if they wanted to quit.

Powskey drafted a resolution for a program that resolved some of the issues keeping tribal members from seeking help.[67]

This initial effort evolved into the Hualapai Alcoholics Anonymous under the auspices of the tribe's Community Education Program. Treatment consisted of group meetings based loosely on the twelve-step process popularized by the national Alcoholics Anonymous program. According to Leo Powskey and his codirector, Sylvia Bender, people attending the meetings said they drank due to depression, alienation, and unemployment. Most people understood the devastation alcoholism caused, but they still had difficulty quitting. In 1969 the Tribal Council asked a member to resign his position due to his addiction. This particular incident was not the first time the council had problems with alcoholic members, but the leadership believed it had to make an example of this individual.[68]

In the 1970s the tribe expanded the Hualapai Alcoholics Anonymous, and in 1974 the council created the Hualapai Alcohol and Drug Abuse Prevention Program (HADAPP). Partially the brainchild of Ben Beecher, the HADAPP worked with community members, the federal government, the council, and universities conducting research on alcoholism. Beecher appeared qualified since he had a background in social work with an emphasis on drug abuse and alcoholism. Beecher worked for the program for years, but he himself struggled with drinking. By the end of the decade alcoholism had become pervasive, according to Carrie Bender, a concerned tribal member. She argued that lack of finances, education, employment, and other social factors caused the abuse of alcohol, even as members tried ending its prevalence in the community.[69]

In an era associated with assaults on tribal land, Hualapais asserted their right to live on the reservation and build institutions for the community. The Tribal Council gained legitimacy when a generation before doubts about its validity threatened to make it impotent. Familiar leaders like Rupert Parker, Sterling Mahone, Grant Tapija, Ben Beecher, Fred Mahone, and Adam Majenty charted a course in opposition to forces that jeopardized their sovereignty. Working with the NCAI, the ITCA and the ACIA demonstrated that tribal leaders had the vision and ability to link local problems with national issues and then seek solutions to both. But these leaders did more than simply react to threats and shifts in policy. Their determination to hold on to the land, demand a voice in politics, and cooperate on crucial community issues symbolized core values and tribal traditions. Though not always unified, the Hualapai nation overcame numerous pressures and changes during the postwar years as they began to fulfill the unprecedented demands for Native self-determination in the twentieth century.

# Local Realities in an Era of
# Self-Determination

When the national media reported on the protests of American Indians during the 1960s and 1970s, many Americans seemed shocked that Native people still existed. The fish-ins across the Pacific Northwest, the occupation of the Bureau of Indian Affairs building, the standoff at Wounded Knee, and the Trail of Broken Treaties stunned a nation that had grown up with pop culture "Indians" in movie westerns and TV programs such as *The Lone Ranger*. Activists such as Dennis Banks and Russell Means and organizations such as the American Indian Movement (AIM) may have shattered stereotypes with their demands for treaty rights and sovereignty, but the "new" issues championed by these iconoclasts had actually occupied people on reservations for over a century. The demonstrations of AIM captivated the public and helped shift Indian policy, but the daily struggles of community leaders on reservations made the promises of self-determination possible. When Hualapai educator Lucille Watahomigie watched AIM members occupy the Bureau of Indian Affairs building in Washington, D.C., she "cheered for AIM but did not participate." As a "reservation Indian" she agreed that the movements and legislation of the 1960s and 1970s marked the "beginning of empowering people" across the country, but real sovereignty took root at the local level, where Native leaders and community members built institutions and made social changes that impacted the lives of everyday people.[1]

Indian activism during this tumultuous era should not have surprised anyone. In the midst of post–World War II decolonization and multiple movements for rights and equality, the activism of national organizations such as AIM built upon the efforts of the multitribal National Congress of American Indians and the older Society of American Indians and the

Mission Indian Federation. Groups such as AIM defended Indigenous people from land loss, racism, and cultural genocide, but they lacked deep ties to reservation communities, where the real work of sovereignty played out. This political and economic responsibility fell into the hands of Native governments and the communities they represented, where the prevailing concerns about sovereignty and nationhood evolved.[2] Reservation-based leaders demanded adherence to Native land and cultural rights even as the realities of postwar colonialism limited their ability to control their resources. Termination legislation attacked Indigenous territorial sovereignty and presented relocation as a salve to reservation poverty, while the Indian Claims Commission furthered the goal of liquidating Native lands. It was within this context of prolonged and coordinated attacks on the Indigenous land base that other struggles should be understood.[3] Movements toward global Indigenous decolonization that took aim at colonial political rule, extraction of resources, and manipulation of local government mirrored the local struggles of the Hualapais as they chafed under federal regulations, institutional racism, structural poverty, and environmental degradation. The Hualapais' fight against these oppressions is a testament to their political tenacity and their ability to define sovereignty as they perceived it.

## "White Man Talks with Forked Tongue": The Limits of Tribal Sovereignty

The Hualapai Tribal Council expanded the tribal government to meet the needs of a growing reservation population after World War II. It established departments for law and order, health, education, and outdoor recreation, adding to the preexisting Livestock Association, the ICC Committee, and the Natural Resources Committee.[4] These entities helped the council become accountable to the people as it increasingly served as a broker between citizens of the reservation and non-Indian institutions and the economic and political forces reshaping the region. George Rocha, tribal chairman in the mid-1960s, commented on the relationship between Hualapai citizens and their government: "Planning together, working together, settling our differences in a constructive way, cooperating with various agencies, supporting our leaders, eventually will lead to improving and effective work of our tribal leaders in our operation of Tribal Self-Government."[5] Rocha was optimistic about a process that was complicated, especially for Hualapais moving to the reservation and adjusting to the unique legal, cultural, political, and racial boundaries around them.

This tribal nation-building project was an unpredictable endeavor because of the impact of national and state economic, political, and demographic factors, on the one hand, and tensions between families and the Hualapai government, on the other. Part of the problem rested in tribal members' continued suspicion of the government. Rocha acknowledged these divisions in his updates published in the tribal newsletter.[6] He tried persuading people to attend meetings of the council, listen to debates, and contribute to discussions about the future of the tribe. "I wish more of you folks would attend our council meetings," where tribal members would receive "first hand information and knowledge of the way the elected governing body of the Hualapai Tribe is doing in promoting matters and issues that would be beneficial to the Tribe."[7]

For citizens of an Indigenous nation and members of a reservation community as well as workers in a growing bureaucracy, Hualapai life continued to evolve and change. The new bureaucracy provided tribal members with needed income, but employees adjusted slowly to the dictates of rigid nine-to-five work schedules. Many people missed work, appeared late, forgot to turn in time cards, had financial problems, and missed deadlines. Moreover, many struggled with alcoholism or family conflicts.[8] Some people resided off the reservation and drove considerable distances to work. Community members needed relatives or friends to watch their children when they did not leave them alone at home. Many Hualapais had a high school education or less, which limited their career options. Housing and the basic challenges of life without running water or electricity hampered economic development. All of this interacted cyclically and reflected the dire conditions for people on the reservation (see fig. 7.1).[9]

Yet there were many positive developments. One was the growing impact of women in Hualapai government. This trend reflected both the value of women in Hualapai culture and shifting American gender roles in the 1960s. Because Hualapai leadership rested less on gender and more on qualities such as oratorical ability, ability to resolve conflicts, good judgment, and kinship ties, women could gain access to council positions on these bases. But the encroachment of non-Indian patriarchy initially limited women's employment to secretarial, "feminine" positions. This changed in the late 1950s as Lydia Beecher, Evelyn Hamidreck, and Lena Bravo worked in nonclerical, administrative positions.[10] By 1965 four women had run for council: Lydia Beecher, Edna Mae Bender, Juliet Querta, and Lena Bravo, with Beecher and Bender receiving the highest votes and serving three-year terms. In 1968 tribal members elected Bender again, bringing her to six consecutive years on the council, as long as any male. In 1970 Evelyn Smith

FIGURE 7.1. Camille Nighthorse and her grandmother Nellie Mahone in Peach Springs, 1964. Courtesy of Camille Nighthorse.

won a position, and in 1971 Lena Bravo returned for a second term and then became the vice chair, the first woman to do so.[11]

Across the country Native women joined organizations and political forums to protect the rights of women, children, and tribal nations. They encountered oppression as women and within the larger society as Native people. Often men, regardless of race, tried to force them to choose their allegiances. Women encountered such questions about their allegiances as women and as Indigenous people.[12] The 1976 Arizona Indian Women's Conference revealed these ongoing trends, with Melinda Powskey, Jean Fielding, and Jeannie Irwin meeting women across the state to discuss Native, state, and national politics. The conference highlighted bias in tribal and state government, discrimination in education, gendered violence, and poverty. The leaders of the meeting agreed to bring their concerns to the state level and to plan additional gatherings in the future.[13]

Hualapai women worked on various levels to improve the quality of life for their people on and off the reservation. Women served on the Hualapai Tribal Court, and in the elections for chief judge in 1963 two out of three of the applicants were women: Irene Walema and Shirley Nelson.[14] Walema moved into the position for two years but resigned due to illness. The council replaced her with Linda Querta, while Juliet Querta became associate judge.[15] These and other women on the court relayed to the council their concerns about lack of adequate resources, inoperable phone lines, subpar housing, and creeping efforts of the federal government to infringe upon the right of the court to rule on cases across the reservation. Senate bills in 1965 provoked the council to express its opposition to efforts that did not "allow for the preservation of tribal sovereignty and the adequate maintenance of law and order on the Hualapai Reservation as well as the extension of constitutional rights to tribal members." The council, with guidance from Querta, drafted responses criticizing legislation that would "grant any person convicted of a crime by the Hualapai Tribal Court, who has been 'deprived of a constitutional right,' the right of appeal to the U.S. District Court having jurisdiction over the reservation." Both institutions believed that Hualapais deserved control over their legal system.[16]

This desire to maintain control over their court system was part and parcel of Hualapais' struggles for self-determination. They did not, for instance, object to the U.S. Constitution. They favored legislation that would "authorize the Attorney General to receive and investigate complaints by Indians alleging that they have been deprived of their constitutional rights," which were "available to all persons." More precisely, the council balked at regulations imposed on the tribe "without the consent of the Hualapai Tribal Council," and it wanted to control the legal system on the reservation.[17] This desire coincided with congressional discussion of an Indian Civil Rights Act. Although many scholars have argued that the ICRA of 1968 undermined sovereignty because it imposed the individualism of U.S. civil rights law onto the legal systems that tribes wanted to devise on their own, the council passed a resolution announcing that it would seek assistance to enforce the 1968 Indian Civil Rights Act to "effectively handle criminal justice on Indian reservations."[18]

At the same time, the council took the advice of the court and allowed tribal members to act as their own legal counsel during litigation. This signified Hualapais' commitment to solving their own problems, but when the resolution reached the commissioner's desk, he rejected it on the grounds that the tribe had to rely on "real attorneys." The council overturned the veto and held firm to its original decision.[19] Rupert Parker informed Superintendent

Pitrat that judges found the legal references of the lawyers confusing, and attorneys ignored the cultural realities of the reservation. Parker remained worried about the confusion brewing in the court and wondered about the future of justice on the reservation. On the other hand, the council had difficulty hiring appellate judges, since qualified Hualapais were related to the people filing appeals. The council noted: "There are no local members willing to act as Judges," since so many people were "related by marriage or blood."[20] In 1969 Chairman Sterling Mahone expressed an "urgent need" to overhaul the court.[21]

The tribe slowly improved its relations with the state of Arizona, unlike the problems with the court system. Tribal member Leo Powskey attended Arizona Commission on Indian Affairs meetings in the mid-1960s, while Louise Benson and Sterling Mahone received seats on the ACIA board in 1974. In 1966 Charles Gritzner met the Tribal Council and listened to concerns expressed by the tribe about its relationship to the state. A more effective organization, the ITCA provided tribes with a forum to debate issues, exchange ideas, and learn about their similarities. George Rocha supported the solidarity that underpinned the ITCA at a meeting he attended in Sells during November 1966. After talking with representatives from tribes across Arizona and hearing their dilemmas, he concluded: "Most of the problems of the Indians are identical, and because of this, they need to cooperate on these common concerns." Hualapais' commitment to the ITCA was so strong that they spared one of their most important leaders, Sterling Mahone, to serve as president of the organization in 1975.[22]

This range of developments from local to national marked an era, according to many scholars, of heightened self-determination. The confluence of a generation returning from World War II with heightened democratic aspirations, the context of civil rights activity, a backlash against termination, congressional legislation weakening the BIA, and the global landscape of decolonization seemed to open political spaces for Indigenous governments to gain control over their human and natural resources. Rupert Parker, a frequent chairman for the tribe, noted in 1967, before the passage of self-determination legislation: "Through the years, our government has initiated programs they feel is good for the advancement of the American Indians. Today, more than ever before, our Tribal Councils are trying to plan and work for the future of their tribes." His tone suggested the optimism of the era, but tribal governments remained tangled in a web of poverty and unemployment, hostility from states, alcoholism, bureaucratic apathy, and anti-Indian racism. The tribal nations that seemingly gained power during the 1960s and 1970s by building upon the gains of previous generations ran up against the limits of sovereignty in a nation-state that treated them like colonial subjects. That individuals such as Rupert Parker believed in self-determination was more a testament to the tenacity of Native leaders rather than the cultural or political inclusiveness of non-Indians.[23]

Some tribal leaders disagreed with or tempered the assessments offered by Parker. Wilfred Whatoname served as chairman in the 1970s, and he had more sobering views of political developments at the reservation, state, and federal levels. Writing in the *Hualapai Times*, Whatoname urged members to "come out and elect Tribal members to hold office" because "it is your right under the Hualapai Tribal Constitution." Whatoname was concerned by the lack of participation in politics when the state and national governments passed laws that impacted Hualapai members. Whatoname pointed to recent efforts by the state to pass legislation that would force Hualapais to pay state taxes on property and various transactions on the reservation. Noting that the "state has endeavored to infringe on our sovereignty," he believed that by "uniting with other tribes," they would defeat the measure.[24] Reflecting the contradictions of rhetoric about sovereignty and ongoing dependency on federally funded programs, Whatoname was "very critical of the U.S. Government" for its obstruction of tribal initiatives. He noted that the government "can help all the foreign countries with billions of dollars, while we, the Hualapai Tribe, are continually held back with just enough to maintain our people with a minimum of health care and education." One year earlier, in 1975, Congress had passed PL 23-638, also known as the Native American Self-Determination and Education Assistant Act, but Whatoname felt that the act had done little for tribes. "I have learned . . . that not everyone can be trusted, like the saying 'Whiteman talks with a forked tongue.' I have experienced this just the past year." Coming on the heels of Nixon's ostensibly enlightened Indian policy and America's venture in Southeast Asia, Whatoname's criticisms were poignant.[25]

Whatoname and other Hualapai leaders were especially concerned about their dependency on federal programs for economic development. Whatoname noted the contradictory position of accepting federal aid for housing, health care, and education while simultaneously railing against Congress for limiting Native sovereignty. But he also pointed out that support of Native people rested on a historical legacy of land theft and colonial rule. Thus, while the federal government had an obligation to atone for past economic, political, and cultural sins, Indigenous people opposed the bureaucratic and regulatory chains that restrained their governments. This, essentially, was the tightrope that Hualapais walked in the 1960s and 1970s, an era best associated with President Lyndon Johnson's Great Society.

President Johnson wanted to end hunger and poverty in America, expand economic opportunities for Americans, and increase the participation of communities in their own political and economic futures. Medicare provided health insurance for elderly citizens, Medicaid targeted the poor and unemployed, and the Elementary and Secondary Education Act assisted underfunded schools.[26] The centerpiece of his "War on Poverty" was the Economic Opportunity Act of 1964, which created the Office of Economic Opportunity (OEO) to direct antipoverty programs. The OEO, through the Community Action Programs, increased participation in planning and management of institutions in the community. Job Corps, VISTA, Upward Bound, and Head Start suddenly became household names symbolizing the prosperity and, ironically, the poverty of America. Funded at more than $3 billion, the War on Poverty programs helped communities across the country.[27]

Reservations gained considerable attention during the Johnson administration, and Hualapais made numerous efforts to capitalize on the programs. In 1962 the council submitted its first application to the federal Area Development Program (ADP), and in 1965 the council appointed the Overall Economic Development Program Committee (OEDPC) to seek funds for feasibility studies to improve infrastructure, sanitation, and water facilities. The OEDPC in 1966 promoted long-term leases with corporations for development, something committee member George Rocha had supported for years.[28] Efforts at planned reservation development faced bureaucratic and financial obstacles. The council and the OEDPC investigated designating the reservation a "depressed EDA area" under Public Law 89-136 to qualify for greater federal assistance. In 1966 the Economic Development Administration informed the tribe that the federal legislation favored private communities, not tribes on federal land, so the OEDPC decided to seek grants from HUD.[29] But when the tribe applied for loans, the credit officer of a bank that maintained some Hualapai accounts said that the community lacked training in many industries. Its distance from a sizeable population and market for products manufactured by the tribe also hurt its chances for a loan. The reservation lacked a source of water and dependable energy, and inadequate administrative structures and lack of capital hindered tribal development as well.[30]

To solve some of these problems, in 1967 the tribe joined the Indian Development District of Arizona (IDDA), a group comprised of tribes exchanging data on reservations. The IDDA conducted surveys to determine valuable resources and provided a forum for leaders to discuss ways to pressure the state legislature.[31] Rupert Parker represented the tribe and became the assistant director for the Northwest Planning Area, a subdepartment of the IDDA. He increased Hualapais' influence in the organization and in 1969 completed a report entitled "Economic Development District: Overall Economic Development Program—Hualapai Tribe" that cataloged the resources of the reservation.[32]

These movements toward economic development and increased control over tribal resources led to a growing bureaucracy that in turn created unforeseen liabilities. Grants from HUD, the Department of Health, Education, and Welfare (HEW), the Department of Agriculture, and the Department of the Interior had special stipulations for the use of funds that surprised leaders. The grants were short-term allocations of money that required specially trained grant writers and managers to oversee them. Many salaried positions demanded a college education, so the Hualapais increasingly relied on outsiders to administer grants and direct programs. The Indian Manpower Program of the Comprehensive Employment Training Act (CETA) of 1973 prohibited hiring relatives, and this created problems for smaller communities such as the Hualapais because many people were related. In one meeting Royal Marks commented that "having only about 700 people residing in Peach Springs, it is next to impossible to comply with this nepotism regulation and still carry out the intent of the program." Lucille Watahomigie agreed, recalling how her cousins were banned from Tribal Work Employment Programs (TWEP) because a relative ran the workshops.[33]

These federal programs were helpful, but they did not fundamentally change the Hualapai economy. The traditional industry of cattle ranching went into decline in the 1970s due to poor range conditions, economic competition, and the rise of other programs on the reservation, but it did not disappear. The Hualapai Livestock Protection Association faced financial losses, and the tribal herd stood on similar ground. Both faced industry-wide consolidation and technological advancements that made large companies more profitable. Yet the two associations continued to deal with the dilemmas as best they could. In 1968 the council requested federal assistance due to a series of storms that froze the ground and killed cattle.[34] In 1969 William Beck, the BIA range conservationist, informed the tribe that its range had deteriorated considerably, and Jim McDougal, a Mohave County extension agent, told the tribe to overhaul the cattle program. He claimed that it would take five years to get the herd fully profitable again. During Robert Jackson's ten years as tribal cattle manager, he repeatedly declared that the herd was in a "state of emergency" that required assistance from the federal government.[35]

The other major reservation industries fared no better. The timber industry had a less significant impact on the economy, and after several large sales between 1951 and 1962 the tribe did not generate much revenue from forestry. The cuts during the 1950s brought nearly $1 million to the community and supported the tribe while it negotiated with the ICC, but this was a short-term source of revenue. These cuts gave Hualapais experience with forestry, but BIA workers approached the industry cautiously because they did not want to clear-cut sites that might be profitable in the future. Treating the forest as a harvestable crop, the BIA argued that the tribe should wait several decades before it began another round of cutting.[36] With few new sales on the horizon, the BIA and tribe focused on fire suppression, erosion control, management of invasive plants, and prescribed burns in the woodlands. This caused some difficulties when elder Hualapais protested that the BIA destroyed culturally important plants they used in ceremonies.[37]

Mining, perhaps the most controversial of the older industries, failed to provide revenue, although it did generate heated discussion as the council thought about uranium extraction. During the early stages of the cold war the Atomic Energy Commission approached the tribe about uranium deposits, and in the 1950s it conducted exploratory surveys on the land. This attempt elicited strong opposition from community members, as did several other overtures during the 1960s. So when a corporation from Colorado approached the tribe in the early 1970s, the tribe had some experience with the subject. According to Lucille Watahomigie, the council entertained the offer because tribal revenues had recently plummeted, but the council rejected the deal.[38]

As cattle ranching, mining, and timber waned in economic significance, the council expanded its interest in tourism. Tourism and other service industries could provide employment and avoid the environmental impact of mining, timber cutting, and ranching. Yet recreation and tourism suffered from seasonal interest and economic downturns that made long-term planning difficult. In the 1960s the council also worked with the BIA to develop Quartermaster Canyon as a resort and campground. If campers survived the rough road from Route 66 to what would become Grand Canyon West, they could enjoy breathtaking views of the canyon and river.[39] The council established the Hualapai Wildlife and Recreation Department in 1970 to give permits, deal with hunters and fishermen, and devise regulations for tourists. In addition, rafting was gaining popularity, and more people were braving the waters of the Colorado River. The Hualapai reservation was perfectly situated for rafters because it was one of the few places in the Grand Canyon with road access to the river.[40]

Rafting on the river opened up new possibilities and new problems. In particular, it fueled a dispute with the Grand Canyon National Park over boundary rights, cultural identity, and tribal sovereignty. Hualapais claimed that the executive order of 1883 placed their boundary at the center, or spine, of the river and thus gave them jurisdiction not only over the Diamond Creek Beach but nearly half of the river. Controlling this portion of the river signified control over their cultural identity and economic future. In contrast, the Grand Canyon National Park wanted to regulate rafting on the river, especially within the boundaries of the park, which the park claimed went to the high-water mark of the river. This not only differed from the Hualapais' view that their boundary went to the spine of the river, but the park's version of the boundary would have taken important tribal properties such as Diamond Creek.

Though initially sparked by disagreements over river rafters and tourists, the location of the boundary would be a source of conflict between the Grand Canyon National Park and the tribe for decades. In 1970 Sterling Mahone addressed park officials, the superintendent, law enforcement, and tribal members about "the special problem of river runners that do business through the reservation." Mahone cited the boundary disputes and added that "river runners have come in and out of the Hualapai reservation without a proper permit obtained from our office." The Hualapais had to maintain the road and the campgrounds, which seemed unfair when they lacked power over the rafters.[41]

The Hualapais tried to solve one aspect of their dilemma by directly participating in the river-rafting industry. In 1973 the council received a grant from the Indian Development District of Arizona to train river runners, and they hired two guides named Breck O'Neill and Peter Resnich to run the operation. The outfitters remained under the jurisdiction of the Hualapai Wildlife and Recreation Department and took people from Diamond Creek down the river to Pearce's Ferry. A helicopter or bus would then return rafters to Peach Springs.[42] Difficulties with O'Neill and Resnich resulted in the tribe terminating the contract and starting its own tribal business in 1977. The move made Hualapais the only Indian nation with its own river-rafting endeavor, but lack of capital and opposition from the Grand Canyon National Park and other rafting businesses hampered the tribe's ability to make a profit.[43]

By the late 1970s the Hualapai economy faced perplexing dilemmas. The council and numerous new departments improved the educational status of community members and tried to transfer that success into job training and equitable hiring practices. The Tribal Council devised development plans and hired a tribal manager and planner to coordinate the web of financial, administrative, and construction programs on the reservation. New housing projects and modern sanitation improved the quality of life for people on the reservation. Moreover, the Hualapai River Runners, the Wildlife and Recreation Department, and other endeavors indicated a brighter future for the economy. Yet the one million–acre reservation still lacked water, the cattle industry declined, and the timber projects had to recover from clear-cutting.

Reflecting back on these and other changes, Inez Manakaja, the tribal treasurer and assistant employment director for the tribe during the 1960s and 1970s, seemed philosophical about many of the problems her people faced. Manakaja was born during the Great Depression in Valentine, Arizona, fifteen miles from the reservation and spent the early years of her life struggling against tuberculosis in a Phoenix sanatorium. Her parents, Grant Tapija, Sr., and Emma Grover, moved her to the reservation in the late 1940s, like many Hualapai families. Manakaja went to school in Seligman, and after her graduation in 1954 she went on to Haskell Institute to complete a degree in business administration. She returned to Peach Springs after graduation, and Chairman Jacob Honga hired her in 1959 to work as the tribal treasurer.[44]

Manakaja was a perfect example of a woman who held an important leadership role and a community member with a keen sense of the political and economic situation of the tribe. Married to a Hualapai rancher named Dudley Manakaja, she was an asset to the tribe for decades. Noting that she could "write a book" about her experiences under half a dozen chairmen, Manakaja witnessed the growth in tribal business accounts from "3 to 30." She felt that the most important achievements of the tribe were the doll factory, Head Start, and the preservation of more than one million acres of "beautiful land." She believed that the constitution was an "important set of rules to live by" and warned tribal leaders to "be good to your employees, talk to them, [and] tell them you appreciate what they do. Those of you who sit in the seat of authority be honest, rule and lead your people in the right way, be truthful with them. Remember they're the people that put you in there." Speaking directly to council members, she said, "Do not hold your position and authority as a weapon over the heads of those whom you disagree with." Her comments about the tribal political economy were important reflections upon economic hardship, while she optimistically believed Hualapais could overcome obstacles and fight for what they believed in.[45]

## A Hundred Miles on the River and Not an Ounce of Water

Looming behind the reality noted by Manakaja, Whatoname, and other Hualapai leaders was the perennial battle for water in the West. Water for crops, industry, and municipal and domestic use as well as the power it could generate was of fundamental importance for a poverty-stricken nation like the Hualapai. Inadequate water hindered economic development, and after the war most homes on the reservation lacked basic utilities such as running water, indoor plumbing, and decent sanitation. Nearly every effort to develop the reservation and improve life for the people returned to the never-ending search for water, which observers thought would have been easily solved. With one hundred miles of the reservation's northern boundary running along the Colorado River, the tribe should not have had difficulty finding water, and yet it did. Fred Mahone had complained about the tribe's lack of access to the river when he met with Inspector John Atwater in the 1920s and when he spoke during ICC hearings in the 1950s. Other tribal leaders also expressed frustration about their inability to use water from the Colorado River. But the lack of water was a perplexing situation that intertwined the tribe with a larger set of issues, as western states and the federal government carved up the Colorado River in the early twentieth century.

Several pre–World War II events set the stage for the tribe's alienation from the river. First, the executive order creating the reservation placed its northern border on and along the river without clarifying what it precisely meant. This paved the way for disagreement over whether or not the boundary went to the center of the river or to the low- or high-water mark of the river. This ambiguity would, arguably, have favored the Hualapais in terms of Indian law, but the importance of the Colorado River for regional water use, ensuing water compacts, and the power of the Grand Canyon National Park seemed to outweigh Indian interests. Second, the expansion of the Grand Canyon National Park adjacent to the Hualapai reservation created a powerful political counterbalance to Hualapais' claims that their boundary went to the center of the river. Indeed, the park had always opposed Hualapais' claims to the river, as it had direct lines of communication with the Department of the Interior and the office of the president. The park made repeated claims that the interests of the states and the general public, which relied on the river, vastly outweighed the needs of the Hualapais. Third, the signing of the 1922 Colorado River Compact, which apportioned water in the lower Colorado River basin, excluded Hualapais and denied them participation in the negotiations. Indeed, few Hualapais even lived on the reservation, and even fewer could have known about the meeting between the states. Although post–World War II events further blocked Hualapais from the river, these three events structured the history of bureaucratic colonialism, technocratic exclusion, regional politics, and western demographic growth, which merged to alienate Hualapais from the river of their origins.[46]

As this narrative of environmental contestation evolved, Hualapais made numerous efforts to find water for the community. Following earlier demands for springs on the reservation, in 1939 the tribe requested funds from the BIA for a water system in Peach Springs, and in 1942 the Tribal Council wanted to expand Frazier's Well for distribution of water across the reservation. Due to high costs, in 1943 the council authorized Superintendent Crow to investigate alternatives. Crow told them to ask the Santa Fe Railway to sell them water from Peach Springs, which the railway had retained the use of in the 1941 court case.[47] The tribe protested this injustice, noting that "a consent decree was entered in the case of *USA v. Santa Fe*, adjudicating water rights to the springs in favor of the said railway company; and thus a valuable tribal asset was taken away from the Hualapai tribe without its consent and without any compensation."[48] Surprisingly, the railway offered to sell the springs, but the BIA opposed the deal due to the cost of maintenance and repairs. The council argued that "the Government is morally and legally responsible for the protection and conservation of the tribal rights and properties of the Hualapai Tribe" and should support its plan to assume control over the water system. The transfer of the springs to the Hualapais would "repair the great damage inflicted on the Tribe by the court decree rendered in the case against the Santa Fe."[49]

Superintendent Thomas Dodge, a Navajo employee of the BIA, expressed optimism that the railway would transfer the springs. In a letter to the commissioner, Dodge wrote that "operating the spring for the tribe was the humane thing to do for the welfare of the Hualapai people living in Peach Springs," since "some things only the government can do and this is one of them, not because of profit motive but rather because human decency and welfare requires it." With the BIA tentatively supporting it, the council began a search for a manager to operate the project.[50] A 1954 study by the Stanford Research Institute determined that the tribe could handle the costs and manage the logistics of a water system. Royal Marks said that the Santa Fe presented him with a preliminary draft to turn the Peach Springs water facility over to the tribe, but the BIA stalled the process. By the end of the decade the system had become lodged in an administrative maze despite the efforts of Royal Marks and Senator Carl Hayden, who supported the tribe's claim because he hoped access to the springs would keep the tribe from demanding water from the river.[51] Yet the tribe limped along for several years, searching for a stable source of water.

This dire situation was the local context for a monumental battle over water that would dominate the political and natural landscape of the American West in the twentieth century. As far as the Hualapais were concerned, their participation in this larger drama began at least in 1883, when their reservation used the river as a northern boundary, and later in 1914, when

Phoenix politicians and developers began to eye the reservation as a good place for a dam. In 1914 an engineer named J. B. Girand of Phoenix proposed to "construct dams in the Colorado River on the Walapai Reservation for power purposes." Superintendent William Light claimed Girand's site was "the most desirable and valuable power site outside the boundaries of National Parks or Monuments" and noted that "at no other point on the river can the water be so easily and economically controlled during the construction of the dam." Neither Girand nor the Federal Power Commission (FPC) consulted the tribe about the dam. In 1925 the FPC permitted Girand to survey a dam site on the river near Diamond Creek on the reservation. Following plans outlined in the 1922 Colorado River Compact and with support from the Department of the Interior, Girand's survey initiated more than half a century of turmoil for the tribe.[52]

Using Girand's survey after the completion of the Hoover Dam in 1935, engineers and the federal government returned to the Hualapai reservation as a site for future dams. These plans coalesced around an early version of the Central Arizona Project (CAP): a series of canals, dams, and reservoirs to control the Colorado River and provide irrigation and hydroelectric power for central Arizona.[53] The Bureau of Reclamation promoted the project in the 1940s with proposed dams at Bridge and Marble canyons on the Colorado River. The potential Bridge Canyon Dam sat several miles south of where Diamond Creek emptied into the river, while Marble Canyon Dam sat adjacent to the Navajo reservation. Though both projects would flood reservation land, no agency contacted the tribes for their permission or support.[54] In 1944 Arizona Senator Carl Hayden urged the Bureau of Reclamation to produce a CAP inventory, including the Bridge Canyon Dam, which would generate 750,000 kilowatts of power per year, rise nearly 800 feet, and cost $325 million. Profits from the sale of energy would offset the costs of the CAP, and the reservoir behind the Bridge Canyon Dam would remain "relatively small." This "relatively small" reservoir promised to flood more than twenty thousand acres of the reservation.[55]

The Hualapais protested their exclusion from discussions about the project more than they did the proposed flooding of the reservation. As Hualapais learned of the plans hatched by engineers and politicians far from Peach Springs, they sent letters and petitions, spanning decades, that demanded greater participation in the planning of the project. As early as 1939 the Tribal Council had passed a resolution, stating: "Be it established that the Federal Government shall consider the rights of the Walapai Tribe and that the Tribe shall share a portion of any water that may become available because of the construction of the dam, and also the tribe shall receive a share of the power that may be produced."[56] When Secretary of the Interior Earl Krug confirmed plans for the Central Arizona Project in 1948 and a Senate committee supported a CAP bill estimated at $708 million, Hualapais again went on the offensive: "In the event said Bridge Canyon Dam Project should be constructed and operated, the lands and rights of the Hualapai Tribe would be materially affected, and unless said lands and rights of the tribe are protected, the tribe and its members will be severely damaged." The council wrote to Arizona congressmen and asked them to include Native rights in the CAP bill.[57]

The council continued pressing for the tribe's rights to water and the benefits of the dam even after Arizona and California began a massive lawsuit in 1952 over how to allocate the Colorado River. The council critiqued bills in 1955 that would "deprive the Hualapai Indians of their rights without giving them the opportunity to negotiate for fair compensation" or "judicial hearings as to the value of the lands that may be taken" from them. The council argued that the recent phase of litigation reverted back "to the undemocratic methods that were dropped many years ago."[58] It even allowed members of the National Park Service to enter the reservation and visit the site of a potential recreation area behind the dam. While community members expressed concern about tourists, they admitted the need for jobs and would "approve the creation of a recreational area along the Colorado River within the Hualapai Reservation under certain conditions and stipulations."[59]

The council, under the advice of Royal Marks, ignored the pending court case and began talks in 1957 with the Arizona Power Authority (APA) about a deal to construct the dam. Marks told the council that the APA, created to promote the state's share of energy from Hoover Dam, requested permission to survey the site. The APA argued that the dam would provide power, irrigation, and flood control and would conserve wildlife. In 1958 the tribe requested that the secretary of the Interior meet with the FPC before granting licenses for dams on the reservation. During an October meeting that year with state and national representatives and the APA, Vice Chairman Bill Andrews officially supported a permit. The council and the APA began what seemed to be a fruitful relationship.[60]

Tribal leaders saw the battle between California and Arizona as an opportunity to discuss the rights of all tribes on the Colorado River rather than as a stumbling block to their own development plans. In 1956 the council requested the "Justice Department, Commissioner of Indian Affairs, Secretary of the Interior, and the Attorney General of the United States to vigorously protect the water rights of the Indians of the lower basin of the Colorado River and other water rights of the Indians of the United States."

The council also authorized then-chairman Rupert Parker to consult with "other Tribes of the State of Arizona to cooperate and employ special counsel to advise the Tribes of Arizona on the pending case of *Arizona v. California.*" Several tribal chairmen worked with the Inter-Tribal Council of Arizona to petition for Arizona tribes before the Supreme Court in regard to *Arizona v. California.*[61] The following year the secretary of the Interior invited Hualapai council members to Washington, D.C., to view the evidence accumulated for the case. Council members implored the secretary to consider the fact that "much water runs from the reservation down into the Colorado River," so the Hualapais argued that their tributaries should have guaranteed them an allocation of water.[62]

Hualapais' advocacy for the dam raises important questions about Native responses to federal reclamation projects during the termination era. Indian nations typically opposed large-scale federal projects like dams because they flooded aboriginal lands and violated their sovereignty. The Three Affiliated Tribes of the Arikira, Mandan, and Hidatsa on the Fort Berthold Reservation in North Dakota protested the Garrison Dam on the Missouri River. The Bonneville, Grand Coulee, and The Dalles dams on the Columbia River ruined Indian fisheries and flooded the lands of Native people in the Northwest. The immense Pick-Sloan Plan on the Missouri River obliterated hunting and agricultural lands on nearly half a dozen reservations in the upper Midwest. Other projects, such as the Kinzua Dam in New York and reclamation efforts in the Florida Everglades, brought the Western pastime to the East and displaced numerous Indian communities. Yet Hualapais still supported the dam in the midst of a termination climate that allowed unilateral decision making in regard to Indian land. And it was the latter point that irritated them most. Self-determination meant the Hualapais had the right to decide what they would do with their lands even if that included flooding a portion of their reservation.[63]

By the early 1960s the council had demonstrated considerable agility negotiating competing state and national interests even if their support for the dam was a surprising expression of self-determination. Yet, reflecting back on their history with the proposed dam, in 1960 the council stated that "litigation of such magnitude never was within the contemplation" of the tribe. As they grasped the scope and potential of the dam, Hualapai leaders tried to balance the damage to the reservation with potential benefits a dam would bring. "Under proper circumstances," the council argued, "the construction of the so called Bridge Canyon Dam and Power Project can result in wonderful benefits to the Hualapai Tribe, providing greatly increased income, employment, and other social and economic opportunities."

Superintendent Wesley T. Bobo noted the "very good working relationship between the Tribe and APA" and even encouraged the council to demand a larger block of power, since it was "the most valuable item of compensation," representing "a golden opportunity for the Hualapai Tribe."[64]

Hualapais apparently lost this "golden opportunity" as the Supreme Court handed down its ruling on *Arizona v. California*. The 1963 ruling ended a decade of litigation by granting Arizona 2.8 million acre-feet of Colorado River water per year. The ruling provided reservations on the lower Colorado River with an annual total of one million acre-feet, but it did not include the Hualapais in its statement. The decision cleared one set of legal hurdles for the CAP (how much water each state would receive), but it also ushered in another era of debate over the location of the dam and continued frustration for the Hualapais. *Arizona v. California* did not terminate the construction of a dam, nor did it prohibit a dam on the Hualapai reservation per se. But one aspect of the ruling would come to haunt and trouble the Hualapais: the Court cited a 1955 opinion from the solicitor general stating that the tribe lacked "practicably irrigable acreage" on its reservation; thus, it could not reasonably use water from the river even if it had legal rights to the water. The Court also argued that the tribe's failure to file an official lawsuit with the lower Colorado River tribes excluded it from making claims on the Court.[65]

These two most recent developments compounded the previous obstacles facing tribal use of the river. The alleged vagueness of the executive order, the claim of the Grand Canyon National Park that its boundary extended to the high-water mark of the river, and the exclusionary implications of the 1922 Colorado River Compact had set the groundwork for the post–World War II turning points. The solicitor general's ruling on practicably irrigable acreage and the Hualapais failure to join the lower Colorado River tribes in a court case were additional insults to Hualapai sovereignty and self-determination. Hualapais were highly aggressive in their search for water and their demands to use the river, so it seemed odd that the solicitor general would conclude that their absence from the multitribal lawsuit indicated their lack of interest in the water. Moreover, not only did the shockwaves emanating from the 1963 *Arizona v. California* court case narrow Hualapais' legal access to the river, but the scope and breadth of the case drove home the magnitude of conflicts over water in the West. The case convinced even the most passive citizens of the affected states that this resource—and the laws and policies regulating it—was of profound interest for the future of the region. All of these events towered over Hualapais' demands for water.

And yet Hualapai leaders continued pursuing the project. To a great extent they had no other choice when it came to providing a foundation for development. "The key to the whole problem is water," noted Herb Voigt, the general planner for the tribe. Voigt was looking backward as much as he was evaluating the conditions facing the tribe in 1976, years after the lawsuit between Arizona and California. "There simply is not enough water; there are other industry plans, [but] there is everything else but water." Lack of water held up development, limited the construction of water works and sanitation systems, stunted the construction of government buildings, and hamstrung tribal efforts to attract businesses.[66]

Voigt was not the only observer of the Southwest's most obvious characteristic of aridity. Nor was he the only one who tried to engineer his way out of the limitations imposed by the region's lack of water. Voigt had repeatedly argued that the federal government could pipe water up from the river to the plateau of the reservation if it had enough energy to power the pumps. He, like other Americans in the postwar era, had a love affair with the idea that science and technology, implemented by the Bureau of Reclamation and the Army Corps of Engineers, could solve the "problems" created by nature, especially in the West, where rivers like the Colorado ran like rare diamonds through the parched desert. The notion that massive pipelines could redirect rivers and that hydroelectric dams strategically placed along the Colorado River could irrigate farms in California and Arizona and provide energy to Phoenix and Los Angeles had reached the level of gospel for boosters and politicians across the region. And Hualapais, or at least the council, were not immune to this belief.[67]

Nor were they deterred by the moratorium on projects between Glen Canyon and Hoover dams. In late 1963 Royal Marks advised the Tribal Council to write letters demanding recognition of the tribe's water rights and for participation in the water deals following *Arizona v. California*. The council reminded engineers about the geologic soundness of the proposed location of the dam and emphasized its willingness to assist with the planning, construction, and maintenance of the facility.[68] Council members met with the Arizona Power Authority, sympathetic engineers, and others interested in the project. In 1965 the council sent George Rocha, Delbert Havatone, Douglas Mapatis, and Willie Walker with Royal Marks and Arthur Lazarus to Washington, D.C., to appear before the House Interior Committee on Lower Colorado River Basin Issues. George Rocha explained that the Hualapais had been "denied the benefits from this major resource on the Reservation for the past twenty years due to the fact it had been reserved by the State of Arizona and the United States."[69] Rocha spoke for the council regarding new limits to construction on the river, saying that it was "for the best interest of the Hualapai Tribe to resist such a moratorium so that it may proceed with an application before the Federal Power Commission."[70]

The construction moratorium that followed *Arizona v. California* highlighted a larger array of impositions that contradicted the spirit of the self-determination era and revealed the limitations of federal commitments to Native autonomy when they were in conflict with agribusiness and economic interests in Los Angeles, Las Vegas, and Phoenix. "As in the previous bills introduced," noted a council resolution, "the property rights of the Hualapai Indians are not protected." The council claimed that the ruling reflected a deep pattern of dispossession of Native land and water rights by federal agencies, ranging from the Bureau of Reclamation to the National Park Service: "Valuable tribal lands have been lost by Indian Tribes in the past when said lands were seized for public use without the opportunity for prior negotiations by the Tribes." Moreover, the council criticized politicians who wanted to integrate Indians into American society but failed to support their efforts at development. "If prominent officials in public life," observed one member, wanted to "bring the American Indians into the main stream of American society . . . the Hualapai Tribe as well as the other tribes in Arizona should not be forced like Indian Tribes have in recent years to petition Congress for gratuities *after* the damage is done." Such comments indicated Hualapais' awareness of the limits of federal bureaucracies such as the Department of the Interior and the National Park Service to Native self-determination.[71]

Council members persisted with their advocacy of the Bridge Canyon Dam, but the prospects for construction dwindled after *Arizona v. California*. In 1967 George Rocha, Rupert Parker, Benedict Beecher, and Dallas Quasula went to Washington again and testified on behalf of the project.[72] The council admitted that "the only remaining major resource belonging to the Hualapai Tribe on the Hualapai Reservation is the dam site at Bridge Canyon . . . and the prospects appear very dim at this time."[73] This statement was prescient, as Congress passed legislation in 1968 permanently barring all dams and hydroelectric projects within the Grand Canyon and boundaries of the national park.

The Colorado River Basin Project Act of 1968 placed a moratorium on all dams and projects between the Glen Canyon and Hoover dams, with particular mention of the Bridge Canyon Dam, which Hualapais had rechristened the Hualapai Dam. It also stipulated that the Central Arizona Project would begin at Parker Dam, roughly 150 miles south of the reservation. Parker Dam became the starting point for CAP, which was an engineering marvel that would transport 1.2 million acre-feet of water through pumps and canals to a dizzying array of farms, businesses, and human-made lakes in central Arizona. Total cost for the project upon completion in the early 1990s surpassed $5 billion.[74]

This apparent deathblow to the tribe's hopes did not stop Sterling Mahone from "one more try at Hualapai Dam," because it would bring "economic independence" and "self-determination" to the Hualapais.[75] During much of the early 1970s the council worked with the Hualapai Dam Commission and garnered support from the Arizona Association of Counties and other entities that had previously promoted the project.[76] Mahone, Quasula, and others continued to travel to Washington to advocate for the dam and, more broadly, to inform Congress of their situation. After years of fruitless lobbying, one council member seemed prepared to concede defeat, but not without one final demand from Congress: "in-lieu monies [$40 million] as compensation for revenues denied the Hualapai Tribe due to Congressional action preventing construction of Hualapai Dam." It was one last effort to extract resources from a government that denied Hualapais the water they needed to survive in the modern West.[77]

The Colorado River Basin Project Act served as a bellwether of larger shifts in federal resource management and environmental awareness, all of which ended the dam. By the late 1960s and early 1970s many Americans had become concerned about the impact of pollution, economic growth, and poorly planned development on the environment. President Nixon made some overtures to the demands of this nascent environmental movement in the establishment of the Environmental Protection Agency, which built upon previous legislation strengthening regulation of air and water contamination. Moreover, President Carter came into office with a skeptical view of large federal water projects in the American West, and he attempted to pull funding from endeavors such as the Hualapai Dam. Carter's pragmatic conservationism raised the ire of many westerners and concerned Hualapai leaders who had worked hard with interest groups to pursue the project.[78] Carter was caught, however, between his dislike of western dams and policies promoted to increase renewable energy use such as hydropower when the country faced an international oil crisis. It seemed like an awkward time to oppose hydroelectric dams when the United States lacked fuel and oil for domestic consumption and development. Yet it was this odd combination of environmental sentiment against dams, a renewed and reactionary interest in fossil fuels, and an international political economy shaped by the cold war that worked against the Hualapai Dam.

The failure of Bridge Canyon Dam threatened to sap the political will of many Hualapai leaders who hoped it would bring the tribe out of poverty and solve their structural problems with development. But not all Hualapais pinned their hopes—or fears—on the construction of the dam. They saw other problems on the horizon that posed much more enduring obstacles than the death of a dam. The Grand Canyon National Park, a seemingly benign bureaucracy with a relatively positive image, emerged during the dam controversy as an increasingly influential foe of Indian tribes in the Southwest. Hualapais' long-term relationship would touch upon some of the most complicated and technical legal disputes of the tribe's history. The park and the tribe disagreed over economic development and natural resource management, but new disputes promised to stretch the patience of both parties. The relationship with the National Park Service resurrected a near-century-old series of questions about the boundaries of the reservation and the tribe's ability to control its future economy and cultural history.[79]

The friction emerging in the 1970s had its roots in a history of land conflicts and disputes over jurisdiction between Indian nations and the bureaucracies managing the natural resources in America. Beginning in the late nineteenth century and growing in the early twentieth century, many Americans voiced their concerns about the exploitation of natural resources in the American West. Concern for "wilderness" entered the national consciousness as individuals such as Gifford Pinchot and John Muir personified the dominant environmental philosophies of "conservation" and "preservation," respectively. Pinchot and Muir lived in a rapidly changing America where the so-called frontier had closed and booming population growth, partly from immigration, had changed the ethnic landscape of the country. Fearing that industrialization threatened the nation, reformers believed that preservation of "natural spaces" in national parks would limit environmental exploitation and protect the cultural symbols of American identity while providing citizens with pristine places to renew their spirits and improve their collective well-being in the midst of rapid population growth and urbanization.[80]

The national park system originated in the 1860s, but the push to designate the Grand Canyon as a national park began not with Muir or Pinchot but with John Wesley Powell's expedition down the Colorado River. A one-armed Civil War veteran, ethnographer, and advocate of the U.S. Geological Survey, Powell led expeditions down the Colorado River in 1869 and 1872. His exploits and observations, along with the writings of Henry Thoreau and the pragmatism of Gifford Pinchot, contributed to the decision of President Theodore Roosevelt to establish the Grand Canyon National Monument in 1908. For the next eight years Congress, the Department of the Interior, the state of Arizona, and local ranching, mining, and timber interests fought over the boundaries and meaning of the monument. In 1916 Congress established the National Park Service under the direction of Stephen T. Mather, who pushed in 1919 for President Woodrow Wilson to bring the Grand Canyon into the national park system. He did, and the new park encompassed 645,000 acres and hugged 56 miles of the Colorado River in Arizona.[81]

Although it is difficult to determine if the Hualapais knew about the designation of the Grand Canyon as a national park, the post–World War II rise in environmentalism and the growing concern about development on the Colorado River surely introduced them to the National Park Service and one of its frequent defenders, the Sierra Club. And it must have been a surprise when the Sierra Club, led by David Brower, questioned the motives of the tribe for supporting the Bridge Canyon Dam in the 1950s and 1960s. After several rounds of debate via national newspapers and periodicals, the Hualapais eventually invited Brower to the reservation for a trip down the river to see the artifacts and paintings on the canyon walls. They hoped such an excursion would demonstrate their history along the river and convince the club that their prior occupancy gave them the moral right to use the canyon for their survival. The Sierra Club remained convinced of its mission to stop all economic activity within the Grand Canyon, especially after passage of the 1968 legislation ended dam building within the canyon. Indeed, the Hualapais could convince neither the Sierra Club nor the National Park Service of their claims to the region. These differences only escalated as the park sought to expand its territory along the reservation.[82]

As they had done previously, the Hualapais defended their boundaries and access to the Colorado River when the park gained support for a new round of expansion to the west along the northern reservation border. When Sterling Mahone learned of the proposed expansion, he contacted Senators Paul Fanin, Henry Jackson, and Barry Goldwater as well as Representative Morris Udall and Secretary of the Interior Stewart Udall, "respectfully request[ing] the Congress of the United States not to enact any legislation which provides for the extension of the boundaries of the GCNP." Mahone claimed that any enlargement of the park following the high-water mark of the southern bank of the Colorado River as its boundary would be "detrimental to the best interests of the Hualapai Tribe," since "the lands and waters which would be encompassed in the extension of the National Park would take away from the Hualapai Tribe one of its most vital resources."[83] Tying the expansion to larger issues concerning the Hualapais, in a 1972 resolution to Secretary of the Interior Rogers Morton, the council stated: "We have many problems concerning land and boundaries which are of vital interest and concern to us" and expressed its intent to "bring about some possible solutions of our many complex land and water cases."[84]

The National Park Service generally ignored these claims and inflamed an already tense situation with new boundaries that the Hualapais felt encroached onto their land. Differences over the boundary led to jurisdictional confusion and, as far as the tribe was concerned, numerous instances of trespassing onto Hualapai land. During a meeting in 1975 the council listened to Robert Euler, then working with the National Park Service as a liaison to Indian tribes, confirm that park employees used the beach at Diamond Creek without tribal approval because park employees thought the boundary of the park extended up to the high-water mark of the river. This boundary would have given the National Park Service control of one of the most important pieces of riverfront along the entire northern border. The Hualapai Wildlife and Recreation Department reported that park employees asserted they could "do what they wanted to in the area." The department also told the council about private river parties that said the park allowed them to exit the river at Diamond Creek and camp there without a permit. Sterling Mahone replied that anyone using Diamond Creek had to pay, "regardless of who they were," and "if they don't want to pay, they can just bypass our area."[85] Royal Marks said that the Grand Canyon National Park risked a lawsuit and affirmed that the "executive order dated in 1883 establish[ing] the Hualapai Reservation [was] very definite that the reservation boundary is along the Colorado River and in fact extends to the middle of the Colorado River." He added, "The GCNPS has no jurisdiction the minute they step off that river." During an October meeting with park employees, Marks and the head of the tribe's Wildlife and Recreation Department argued that if the Hualapais had oversight to charge rafters entering the reservation, it could have collected $16,000 already.[86]

The debates over the high-water mark of the river and jurisdiction over tourists revealed larger issues of sovereignty and identity. Tribal leaders protested that the boundary promoted by the National Park Service at the high-water mark of the river, even if supported by a recent solicitor general's opinion, contradicted their origin stories and the original executive order creating the reservation. Council members Wendell Havatone and Sterling Mahone even traveled to Washington to meet with Senator Goldwater and BIA representatives to dispute the recent opinion. But more than that, council members placed the Park Service debate within the century-long process of administrative dispossession and estrangement from the Colorado River.[87] After numerous meetings in Washington regarding problems with the river boundary, Hualapai leaders drafted a resolution and letter to the BIA and the Department of the Interior demanding answers to several important questions. They wanted to know why, for instance, they lacked access to the river under the Winters Doctrine and how they had been excluded from the Colorado River Compact of 1922, but, more than anything else, the council wanted to obtain water, water rights, and acknowledgment of their boundary at the center of the river.[88]

Chairman Earl Havatone followed up with a letter to Superintendent Curtis Nordwal. Referring to a 1977 council discussion of the Lake Mead National Recreation Area, the Grand Canyon National Park, and tribal jurisdiction on the river, Havatone reminded Nordwal: "The Hualapais believe that their boundary is the center of the river. Attorneys have said that it might be the edge of the river. Now the Park Service map refers to the Wilderness Area boundary as being the south bank of the river with references to a high water line. They also show the Park boundary encroaching onto the reservation. This is an outright falsehood on the map."[89] A joint resolution with the Havasupais restated: "The interests of the Hualapai and Havasupai Tribes in their tribal lands and rights have been infringed upon in past years by the National Park Service acting in excess of its proper authority." The resolution demanded that the National Park Service, Interior, and Congress include the tribes in future discussions about the river. Despite the steady stream of similar resolutions and the numerous visits from Hualapai representatives, federal bureaucrats in Washington continued to ignore Hualapais' claims to the water in general and the boundary of the river in particular. If the government acknowledged that the spine of the river was the legitimate tribal boundary, it would have thrown the entire fate of the Colorado River, allocation of water, and jurisdiction along the Hualapai northern border into question. The Havasupais won a favorable increase to their reservation within the Grand Canyon, while the Hualapais continued to struggle with the hostile Grand Canyon National Park, which ignored the efforts of the tribe to gain control over its land and resources. Even in the twenty-first century, the Hualapais and the national park remain deadlocked in disagreement over boundaries and jurisdiction on the river, as Hualapai water rights seem to have been sacrificed by the federal government for the sake of regional development and water compacts negotiated without the input of the tribe holding the longest boundary along the river.[90]

The struggles over land, water, boundaries, and the Hualapai economy revealed deeper patterns and problems at the core of Hualapai nationhood. First, history pervaded discussions between the tribe and non-Indian bureaus and organizations. Tribal members noted that their historic presence in the region gave them cultural, legal, and moral rights to the landscape of northwestern Arizona. In particular, the tribe claimed that the Colorado River constituted a central place in Hualapai identity: it was their place of origin, it watered their gardens, and it constituted a geographic boundary and marker for their identity. Colorado River references fill tribal history, and Hualapais stressed the center, or spine, of the river as the boundary of their lands, illustrating how Hualapais had blended their historical connection to the river with "modern" legal discourse and discussions of hydroelectric power, development, and tourism.

These debates revealed that Hualapai nationhood stood on a fault line between sovereignty and neocolonial dependency upon the federal government. Native-initiated businesses improved the economic conditions of residents, but the federal War on Poverty programs that frequently served as a safety net for people on the reservation also tethered Hualapai government and control over local resources to federal approval and limitations. The gains made by the Tribal Council (the Santa Fe Railway case, money from the Indian Claims Commission, and a growing reservation community) were tempered by high unemployment rates and inadequate infrastructure. Hualapais participated in local, regional, and national movements for self-determination, but they had to appeal to the secretary of the Interior for assistance with projects like the Hualapai Dam. This problematic situation reflected the delicate balance of autonomy and dependency characterizing Indian nations in the United States during the so-called era of self-determination. Though they fought for control over their lives and resources, many of their efforts were thwarted by new legal restrictions, institutional racism, and a ballooning bureaucracy associated with federal programs that the community depended upon. And yet nearly one hundred years after Pai leaders demanded the creation of the reservation, the Hualapai nation was fully engaged with the difficult and complex project of decolonizing its government, adapting to a postindustrial economy, and policing its spatial and cultural homelands in northwestern Arizona.

# Contemporary Reservation Affairs

The recent history of the Hualapais might best be symbolized by the image of the Hualapai River Runners navigating the Colorado River. The pilots of the boats know the twists and turns, the canyon walls, and the rapids of a river they've interacted with for years. They know how to safely ferry their guests down the river, but there is always the potential for unexpected snags, poor weather, and difficult currents. The Hualapai nation, like the River Runners, had tremendous experience navigating the political and economic waters of the twentieth-century American West, but unexpected events always kept them on edge. Strong and intelligent leaders fought for rights they believed were inherent to their status as an Indian nation: the right to control life on the reservation, maintain their culture, develop their resources, and educate their children. But no amount of skill and experience could negate the powerful forces of a postmodern, postindustrial world. Nearly every bend in the river of the twentieth century brought new problems that cumulatively threatened to render the tribal government unable to protect and provide for community members.

Hualapais crafted responses that reflected their economic desperation and principled judgment rooted in the desire to protect the sovereign status of their land and people. And assaults on Hualapai sovereignty increased in the late twentieth century even as termination and relocation policies died in the face of Native opposition. But the new infringements upon Native land and cultural rights came in less perceptible institutional forms that masked their origins and made the long-term implications more difficult to assess and thus counteract. A moderately sympathetic legal system failed to provide reliable protection for Native sovereignty as tribal governments made moderate progress toward self-determination. The devolution of power from the federal level to the states sparked numerous new disputes between Indian nations and state and county governments. Tribes became more vocal about protecting sacred sites and cultural patrimony, but tribal customs and traditions were challenged by popular culture, alcoholism, and demographic change. Institutional racism, environmental pollution, and structural poverty forced many tribes to build casinos and move into the gaming industry even as those moves provoked a backlash and required them to sign compacts with states that reduced tribal sovereignty. Many of these challenges emanated from broad changes in American political culture and deep shifts in the national and international economy that Hualapais could not always protect themselves from. A post–civil rights backlash merged with deindustrialization to undermine some of the economic development programs of previous eras. Anti-Indian agendas promulgated by politicians such as Washington Senator Slade Gorton epitomized a general right-wing suspicion of Native sovereignty that was tied to broader attacks on affirmative action, Great Society programs, alternative energy, and minimum wage standards, most of which benefited Native communities. And yet Hualapais navigated these waters guided by the belief that sovereignty—though community members disagreed on its scope and meaning—should structure interactions with non-Indians.

## The Hualapais in National Context

One of the most significant themes of the tribe's recent history has been the chasm between the expectations and realities of the years after self-determination legislation passed in the 1970s. When Congress passed the Indian Self-Determination and Education Assistance Act in 1975, many governments believed they would gain greater control over their economies. The act stipulated that tribes could create and manage new programs and contract directly with the secretary of the Interior, the Department of Health and Human Services, and non-Indian service providers rather than work through the Bureau of Indian Affairs. Government agencies were supposed to assist tribes with new and preexisting programs they could "take over" and, in the process, free themselves from the federal government. However, a wrinkle in these plans quickly emerged: most tribes chose contracts for a set number of years and thus remained connected to the federal government. As these contracts did not generally solve structural problems, tribal governments had to reapply for support at the end of the contract cycle. While engagement with the federal government offered tribes a chance to pressure it to uphold its trust responsibility, it also made tribes subject to control by secretaries of the Interior, who retained considerable leverage over contracts, finances, and operation of the programs.[1]

Acting as sovereigns and at the same time retaining the support of the federal government was a difficult balancing act for Native peoples in the wake of self-determination legislation. And many Native leaders commented on the shortcomings of the 1975 law: Navajo Nation President Peter MacDonald protested that the post-1975 process of contracting with non-Native businesses and federal agencies was not self-determination because the BIA retained power. The governor of Gila River echoed MacDonald, saying, "Some tribal members are concerned about termination; but some are reluctant to contract because they are not sure the funding will continue when the contract expires." The National Tribal Council Association president thought the BIA used contracts to "bully" tribes into accepting smaller budgets for their programs and, in the process, threaten the withdrawal of funds for challenging the BIA.[2] Indeed, many of the programs raised employment on reservations without fundamentally strengthening the economic and political institutions of Native governance.

Native scholar M. Annette Jaimes argues more forcefully that unemployment and social problems grew in the late 1970s and early 1980s as many Great Society programs disappeared. She believes that the self-determination legislation failed to truly help tribes control their economies. Critiquing the Kennedy and Johnson administrations, Jaimes observed that "the actual results [of "self-determination" legislation] led to more bureaucracy, institutionalization and more usurpation of Indian control that actually led to more sophisticated forms of assimilation, compared to termination and relocation." In associating self-determination with greater control over federal monies and programs, the policies offered a neocolonial model that perpetuated assimilation and limited sovereignty.[3]

These shifts in policy have shaped the history of relations between tribal governments and the federal system. David Wilkins argues that a deep-seated ambivalence has structured relationships between tribal governments and the United States, with treaties, executive orders, and rulings such as the *Winters* case acknowledging tribal rights, while decisions such as *Lonewolf v. Hitchcock*, the Dawes Allotment Act, and the termination era signify anti-Indian tendencies and the plenary power of the state.[4] In the late twentieth century the BIA has waned in power, but other bureaucracies with new interests, regulations, and political characteristics filled the void. Native economies remained hamstrung by legal bonds that shackled leaders and made it nearly impossible to use reservation resources. Coupled with the new regulatory expectations of federal programs, the near-constant struggle to write and submit grants, a reliance on outsiders with technical degrees, and rapid shifts in the national and global economy, few communities have made much progress toward controlling their own economies.[5]

These structural problems worsened with the rise of Ronald Reagan, who won the 1980 election on anti-Communism and small government slogans and proceeded to cut $1 billion from the $3.5 billion BIA budget. This era of privatization and "new federalism" devolved power from the federal to state governments and gave them greater influence over reservations. The policy shifts avoided terms like *termination*, but the demands of capital and interest groups seeking to privatize reservation and public lands gained political access to Congress and the president. Secretary of the Interior James Watt appeased alleged "Sagebrush Rebels" and "wise use" advocates to help launch a new attack on tribal communal land bases and the resources beneath them. In 1988 President Reagan signed into law PL 100-472 (HR 1223), which contained amendments to Title I of PL 93-638 and included a new section creating a block program for nearly two dozen tribes. This was supposed to serve as a model for relations between the federal and Native governments by increasing tribal latitude in creating and managing programs and the funds used for them. This might have worked had the larger economic and political winds of the era not stalled reservation development. Reagan's Indian policy epitomized a paradox for tribes as it declared support for self-determination while facilitating the exploitation of Native resources as it slashed the federal programs that helped tribes move toward self-sufficiency.[6]

Presidents after Reagan altered the tone of his policies without fundamentally strengthening government-to-government relationships. George H. W. Bush, according to Wilkins, was "devoted to reducing tribal reliance on federal financial support and increasing tribal dependence on the private sector and individual entrepreneurship." These policies assumed that Indian nations worked on a level playing field without federal regulations and with the internal technical capacity to address contradictory state, federal, and local laws, when most did not. Indian governments did not easily adapt to entrepreneurialism when it required large amounts of capital and collateral for loans. This laissez-faire approach symbolized neoliberal policies that claimed that deregulation and the market would modernize underdeveloped communities, when in fact the ideology brought rampant exploitation, environmental pollution, low wages, poor work conditions, and resource export strategies that actually impoverished the people the policies were supposed to help. These neoliberal programs failed to change the structures and institutions that caused the poverty, and they transferred local wealth and talent beyond reservation borders. Reliance on outside capital and technical expertise with little accountability and dedication to local populations left Native governments wondering what went wrong. Ironically, the privatization policies paved the way for Indian gaming and casinos.[7]

President Clinton did the most to reverse the privatization trend and used his presidency—if only symbolically—to support economic development, bolster social and educational programs, and increase political powers for the tribes without challenging their jurisdiction. In 1998 he articulated his vision of the trust relationship and commitment to Native sovereignty, but his use of the domestic-dependent nations paradigm was problematic because it implied the limited nature of self-government. According to Robert Williams, the use of Chief Justice John Marshall's jurispathic rhetoric contributed to the unequal power relations between tribes and the federal government and perpetuated the underpinnings of neocolonialism.[8] Clinton's rhetoric was no match for a conservative Congress, led by Newt Gingrich, that in 1994 launched an array of bills, spearheaded by Washington Senator Slade Gorton, to tax Indian gaming profits, terminate sovereign immunity, and reduce court funding and Native economic development grants from Congress. Such actions hindered whatever efforts President Clinton made to strengthen tribal governments and economies.[9]

Even the courts were not as clearly aligned in support of Native governments as has been historically suggested. Legal scholar Charles Wilkinson argues that "during the 1970s and 1980s the tribal position lost out in some important cases. The [Supreme] Court, for example, upheld broad state court jurisdiction to hear Indian water rights cases; permitted some state taxation within Indian country; ruled that some reservation boundaries had been implicitly diminished during the allotment era; and allowed national forest road building that infringed on tribal ceremonies at sacred sites."[10] The 1968 Indian Civil Rights Act was the first piece of legislation to extend the provisions of the U.S. Bill of Rights onto reservations, but, according to Wilkins, "The ICRA was a major intrusion of U.S. constitutional law upon the independence of tribes." In 1972 the arrival of William Rehnquist to the U.S. Supreme Court signaled a shift away from trust responsibility and against sovereignty. "By the mid-1970s the tribal jurisdiction over non-Indians [on reservations] had become a white-hot emotional issue," observes Wilkins. The 1978 Oliphant case severely reduced—if not ended—tribal jurisdiction over non-Indians. Since then, the additions of Antonin Scalia and Clarence Thomas and, most recently, John Roberts and Samuel Alito to the Supreme Court affirmed the shift away from Native self-determination.[11]

These trends exacerbated dwindling grant money, greater acceptance of "being Indian," and a boom in casino dollars to make Indigenous identity a highly contested commodity. Although Native peoples had their own systems of determining membership, conquest and the imposition of new legal and racial classifications distorted many of these pre-1492 processes. Scientific racism, social Darwinism, the legacy of American slavery, and the invasion of the West brought new forms of social coding that placed people in racial hierarchies. Native people in the late nineteenth century grappled with the powerful trope of blood quantum combined with the use of force and congressional legislation. Initially employed as a tool to statistically and administratively erase Native identities, the use of blood quantum in allotment and determination of "competency" became a problematic concept that divided Native communities.[12]

Blood quantum was not a divisive issue for the Hualapai until the post–World War II era, when members began debating how to use money from the Indian Claims Commission. Although the IRA constitution had pegged tribal membership at one-quarter blood quantum, few Hualapais failed that test. A generation later, the ICC required that the Hualapais conduct a census to count members who had enough "Hualapai blood" to receive a per-capita check, and Great Society programs and federal grants demanded proof of blood quantum. As federal programs dwindled in the 1980s, the Hualapais started relying on blood quantum rather than civil citizenship to determine who received money, resources, and services. Native governments made enrollment requirements stricter to reduce the numbers of people eligible for funds, but this simply increased the importance of blood quantum as the main factor determining tribal enrollment and access to those funds.[13]

As Native American studies scholars Circe Sturm and Eva Marie Garroutte have observed, American racial ideology had begun filtering into Native communities by the mid-nineteenth century.[14] By the late nineteenth century it was common to use terms such as *mixed-blood* and *half-breed* to refer to people of multiple ancestries and then create hierarchies within Native communities based on the alleged characteristics of those individuals. Mixed-bloods supposedly exhibited "progressive" traits and acceptance of mainstream American trends while simultaneously lacking "traditional" knowledge. Conversely, full-bloods were more skeptical of Anglo institutions and held firm to older beliefs and customs. The federal government capitalized on the pervasiveness of these terms and used blood quantum to determine membership within a Native community. It implemented tribal census rolls and guestimated whether or not the people it counted were full- or half-blood. It then stipulated that tribal members had to have a particular percentage of "blood" in them to remain within the community and to receive rations and other resources. By the early twentieth century many Indian nations had adopted blood quantum to define their membership rather than use citizenship, cultural identity, kinship, and other traits.[15]

One of the many implications this trend has had is the growth in the number of children with multitribal ancestries who do not qualify for membership anywhere. Or, in the case of Hualapais with parents from wealthier tribes, youth changed enrollment to places such as Fort McDowell, Gila River, and Yavapai Prescott after the 1994 Hualapai casino failed. Hoping to clarify such confusion, the BIA in 2000 established regulations on the documentation requirements and standards necessary for Indians to receive a Certificate of Degree of Indian Blood Card, which the government now uses to determine whether individuals qualify for federal services. The BIA uses one-fourth as the minimum for programs it controls, but tribes set their own requirements.[16] Hualapai council meetings have included discussion about changing the blood quantum requirements from one-fourth to one-eighth, especially as money flows in from tourism.[17]

## Culture, Race, and Environment in Regional Development

This was the political and economic context for Native sovereignty in the Southwest. As governments exerted authority over their reservation resources, they confronted exploitation of Indigenous landscapes, cultural properties, and religious sites. The nexus of cultural identity, race, and environment in regional development exposed this especially complicated era of colonialism. Although Hualapais lost control over their traditional landscape outside of the reservation, they nonetheless opposed mining, road construction, suburban sprawl, and pollution across northwestern Arizona.

Two large projects beginning after World War II on the Navajo and Hopi reservations created ecological problems across the Southwest. Coal from the Black Mesa Mine on lands jointly claimed by the Navajos and the Hopis went north to the Navajo Generating Station at Page, Arizona, which generates electricity for adjacent states. The second project owned by Peabody Coal mined millions of tons of coal and sent it through a slurry pipeline across northern Arizona to Laughlin, Nevada. The 275-mile pipeline, which runs a few miles south of the Hualapai reservation, pumped water from an aquifer underneath much of the Navajo and Hopi lands. At the Mohave Generating Station in Laughlin, the coal is used for electricity for southern California, Las Vegas, and Arizona, with some of the power lines crossing back over the Hualapai reservation. The impact of five deep wells pulling roughly 2,310 gallons of water per minute from the aquifer has had a tremendous impact on the environment and people of the Four

Corners region. One estimate has the wells pulling 3,600 acre-feet per year and upward of a quarter of a million acre-feet since the early 1970s. Towns fifty miles away reported drops in their wells, and Hopis are convinced that their crops have suffered irreparable harm.[18]

As Native governments, environmental organizations, and some cities protested pollution, in 1990 Congress ordered the Environmental Protection Agency to reduce the haze above parks and wilderness areas in Arizona and across the West. In 1995 tribes in the region attended a summit dedicated to reducing regional pollution by working with the Environmental Protection Agency. Clay Bravo from the Hualapai Natural Resources Department attended the summit and expressed his concern that future generations would not have the ability to experience the views that he had known since his childhood.[19] An agreement between western states and Indian nations sought a reduction in sulfur dioxide from power plants within five years and nearly 50 percent by 2040 in order to reverse an estimated 30 percent decline in visibility.[20]

Many tribal members felt that the reductions in pollution over national parks would fail because of a proposal to construct a large bridge to bypass the road going across Hoover Dam, less than two hours southwest of the reservation. In the 1990s state and federal officials began to worry about the dam's structural integrity, especially as traffic spurred by growing trade and development caused a spike in the number of vehicles using it. When tribes protested their exclusion from the planning for the bypass, Congress amended the National Historic Preservation Act in 1999 to establish a framework for federal agencies to talk with American Indians impacted by construction. In response, more than a dozen tribes met with federal officials to discuss the Hoover Dam Bypass Project. The bypass at Sugarloaf Mountain 1,500 feet downstream from Hoover Dam included roughly 4 miles of roadway on either side of the river, required a 1,900-foot-tall bridge, and was estimated at $200 million.[21]

This commercial corridor was extremely important because it contained the burial grounds and traditional cultural properties of Mohave, Chemehuevi, Hualapai, and other Native peoples. Conflicts like this between tribes trying to protect sacred sites from corporations and states developing the land became more complex when Indian nations had new sources of judicial and legislative leverage to employ. In 1990 President George Bush signed into law the Native American Graves Protection and Repatriation Act, known as NAGPRA, to create a mechanism for handling human remains, burial sites, and objects of cultural patrimony on federal lands. NAGPRA stipulated that all museums, libraries, and institutions receiving federal funds had to conduct inventories of their human remains and cultural artifacts. It also contained a process for protecting Native remains and cultural properties on federal lands and in projects receiving federal dollars.[22] In response to these and other demands, the Hualapais created the Department of Cultural Resources in 1994 as the entity responsible for working with federal, state, and local agencies regarding the cultural dimensions of tribal resources. First headed by Monza Honga, the department worked with the Bureau of Indian Affairs, the National Park Service, the state land department, and other entities to protect tribal cultural properties. Honga and ensuing directors were also responsible for working with elders to collect oral histories about the Hualapai landscape.[23]

With the Department of Cultural Resources playing an important role in regional development, the Hualapais added their voice to Native opposition against the Hoover Dam bypass. Larry Eddy from the Colorado River Indian Tribes said the bypass would destroy traditional medicine areas for the Mohave, while Juanita Kinlichinia from the Southern Paiutes said: "The talks are not going to help us. They do everything to us natives and we're the last ones to know about it. They've really done us in." Loretta Jackson, the new director for the Hualapai Department of Cultural Resources, agreed: "They always seem to steamroll over tribes to get their certain projects done and really don't listen to what Native Americans have to say." When the new bypass site is completed, it will foster development and growth because Highway 98, which crosses the bypass, is a North American Free Trade route linking much of the American West to Canada and Mexico. Tribal members may not have known that the superhighway promising to destroy cultural sites and burial grounds was part of the neoliberal policies of NAFTA, three nation-states, and multinational corporations. Thus, the Hualapai tribe, eight hours' drive from the U.S.–Mexico border, was feeling the direct impact of globalization.[24]

The bypass promises to increase regional urban sprawl, contribute to pollution, and damage Hualapai sacred sites. Throughout Arizona new homes have used landscaping rocks mined from quarries and mountainsides on land containing Hualapai burial grounds and sacred sites. Several quarries had sprung up in the 1990s along Route 66 to mine flagstone and rock for homes in southern California and Arizona. Tribal Vice Chairman Edgar Walema worried about the irreparable harm it would cause: "You can never replace the beauty of that environment. From the Indian point of view, it's terrible what they're doing."[25] The tribe was especially concerned about mining in Crozier Canyon, a few miles from the reservation. Loretta Jackson said that Crozier Canyon, known in Hualapai as Gwal jil wy: a by, was an important site in the tribe's cultural geography. "If the mountain is not there anymore," said Jackson, "we lose a bit of our history." Landowner Fred Grigg, who approved the mining on his property, told *High Country News*: "If I can't do with my own property what I'd like to do with it . . . why should I pay taxes on it year after year?" Jackson was not impressed. When Grigg said that his family had lived there for generations, Jackson pointed out that "they couldn't have been there if the Hualapai had not been forced out."[26]

When Jackson became director of the Department of Cultural Resources, she routinely pressured state and federal officials to end mining on tribal sacred sites. Hualapais traditionally cremated the dead and placed their remains in unmarked graves with many of their possessions. This was a traditional practice that also protected them from growing numbers of grave robbers and anthropologists in the early twentieth century. Much later, as people moved to the region, the lack of markings made it more difficult for non-Indians to see them and report the discovery to officials. Hoping to protect burial sites with recent legislation, the tribe in 2002 asked for a moratorium on mining at traditional Pai sites. State law stipulated that individuals had to report human remains and burial grounds to the Museum of Northern Arizona to begin an inventory and prepare the relocation of the materials. Private property was beyond the scope of NAGPRA legislation, so convincing citizens such as Fred Grigg to follow this protocol was extremely difficult for the tribe and state officials.[27]

While the tribe tried to extinguish numerous fires in the form of the Hoover Dam bypass, unauthorized archaeological projects, and pervasive rock mining, the eastern fringes of the Hualapai cultural landscape entered the national spotlight when owners of the Arizona Snowbowl, a premier skiing destination, sought to expand operations in the San Francisco Peaks. In the 1980s Norm Johnson, a Flagstaff businessman and the owner of the Snowbowl, tried to expand his skiing operation by building larger slopes and clear-cutting trees, but environmentalists and nearby Native communities sued him under the recently passed American Indian Religious Freedom Act. Though Johnson won the case in the U.S. Supreme Court, an environmental impact statement and mounting legal bills forced him to sell his business. The impact statement limited the boundaries of the ski area and designated the Coconino National Forest, where the Snowbowl was located, as wilderness, ostensibly protecting it from development. Despite these obstacles, businessman Eric Borowsky purchased the old Johnson outfit in 1992 and proposed expanding the Snowbowl within its legal boundaries. His announcement triggered another round of opposition from environmentalists and Indian nations.[28]

Tribes that same year protested against the expansion of a pumice mine on the San Francisco Peaks not far from the location of the skiing site. Havasupais, Navajos, Hopis, Apaches, and Yavapais resented the destruction of the sacred space of the peaks. The Hopis believed the San Francisco Peaks were the home of their *katsinam*, spiritual beings who embodied religious deities and the Hopi creator. The mine would produce thousands of tons of pumice for use in stone-washed jeans and lightweight concrete. However, the Forest Service placed a moratorium on mining and designated the peaks a Traditional Cultural Property because of the claims of tribes that the mountains were sacred and integral to their religious beliefs.[29] These protests continued for years as representatives from tribes, including the Hualapais, held meetings across the Southwest. The Forest Service considered a ban on mining in a 74,000-acre area, even though the White Vulcan Mine had already been mining for years.[30] In 2000 federal officials negotiated a deal to pay Tufflite, Inc., the owner of the White Vulcan Mine, $1 million to stop gouging the mountain. Interior Secretary Bruce Babbitt said of the situation: "The mine is on land which is sacred to 13 Native American tribes and the operation of this mine has scarred the San Francisco Peaks."[31]

Before the ink dried on the agreement to close the White Vulcan Mine, the dispute over the Snowbowl in the San Francisco Peaks reemerged. In March 2002 the Flagstaff City Council approved a plan to pump 1.5 million gallons of treated wastewater to the Snowbowl ski area to use as snow. Native activists referred to the plan as "environmental racism to native peoples."[32] After tense debate, in 2004 the Forest Service supported the decision of the Flagstaff City Council to sell some of its wastewater to the Snowbowl. A Havasupai official told the city council: "We as indigenous people will not tolerate further desecration of our peaks," and Hopi representatives said that artificial snow would keep the *katsinam* from granting rain. Other tribes said the wastewater would harm sacred sites and medicinal herbs.[33] In February 2007 the Ninth District Court ruled in favor of the tribes on the basis of religious freedom, but by 2008 those gains had been reversed in appeals by the owners of the Snowbowl. Hualapais opposed what they considered the desecration of the sacred peaks, and they joined several lawsuits against the Snowbowl and the city of Flagstaff.[34]

## A Postindustrial Indigenous Economy

This was the national and regional context for Hualapais at the turn of the millennium. The contradictions of self-determination, shifting federal policies, limited resources, neocolonialism, and blood quantum in a postindustrial economy structured Hualapai nationalism and struggles for autonomy. As the tribe confronted regional development, the central goal of building a viable economy on the reservation continued to occupy the Hualapai government. But eight years after the 1975 American Indian Education and Self-Determination Act, the economy looked bleak. In the early 1980s unemployment rates hit 70 percent, with 20 percent of employed reservation residents working in mining and agriculture, 10 percent in construction, 14 percent in retail and service industries, and 45 percent in tribal government or the BIA. The remaining found temporary work or drove to an off-reservation town. The reservation population grew at a faster rate than the general population of the state. According to census data, the 1980 population was 988. By 1983 it had reached 1,100, an 11 percent growth in three years.[35]

These and other indicators revealed a community at a crossroads. Self-determination legislation and Great Society programs helped tribal economies, but budget cuts in the 1980s threatened whatever gains Hualapais had made. The Hualapai Dam died in the 1970s, but uranium mining reemerged as a possible, yet controversial, option for development. Interstate 40 bypassed Route 66 and reduced tourist traffic, but river rafting gained in popularity. And as the Peach Springs Elementary School began by using computers to help teach children to speak Hualapai, many families continued the century-long tradition of running cattle on the range. Other examples abound of a tribe poised on the edge of desperation and hope, fighting to build a foundation on which they could create a stable economy and healthy community and bring jobs to the reservation.

Wendell Havatone, an assistant tribal administrator in the 1980s, commented on the problems facing the economy. He didn't like having the tribe and the BIA as the largest employers, but government positions were slightly less susceptible to swings in the economy. Havatone knew that tribal members suffered, especially the younger adults who returned from school. He echoed the comments of Hualapai leaders nearly fifty years ago in his observations that youth returning to the reservation could not find employment and had to "do whatever they can to survive." Others echoed the urgency in Havatone's voice. Tribal planner Herb Voigt, who warned about the lack of water on the reservation, believed that tourism was the tribe's last option for economic development. This delicate balance of providing employment and protecting the land elicited numerous perspectives and opinions in the 1980s. Louise Benson, a prominent leader and frequent member of the council, cautiously agreed with Voigt. However, she tempered the need for development with concern for the environment. "Our land is really valuable to us," said Benson as the tribe collectively discussed ways to grow the economy in the 1980s.[36]

The tribe urgently needed new solutions because few of the old industries persisted. Many of them such as ranching had been interwoven with Hualapai culture since tribal members worked as cowboys in the 1870s. Ranching provided Hualapais with financial support, served as a marker of status, connected them to the land, and anchored family and community values. Yet ranching fell on hard times in the 1980s due to declining consumption and stiff competition from large corporations. Only a few families continued the tradition. Lena Bravo recalled working with the family herd when she was a child in the 1930s. She laughed at the memories it provoked: "I always had all kinds of close calls, cattle run over you, they kick you, they knock you down." Her father, Charles McGee, was one of the most successful ranchers in the community. Before his death Charles was inducted into the National Cowboy Hall of Fame. His father, "Cap" McGee, began ranching off the reservation in the Chino Valley area around 1900. In 1926 he moved to the reservation and helped establish ranching on tribal lands. Following in her grandfather's footsteps, in the early 1980s Lena owned 125 head of stock and ran them from the window of her truck while her children followed on horses.[37]

Leonard Majenty also ran several hundred head in the 1990s, when many Hualapais had given up on their cattle. Leonard recalled his youth, working with his father on their land in the Big Sandy: "From sun up to sun down, working in the fields was hard. At times I would be very tired, but my father was always pushing me to finish the day's work. I wanted to give up, but as I look back, today I am very proud of my father and grandfather for what they taught me." He brought that same determination with him when he and his wife, Corrine, moved to the reservation in the 1950s. They raised several children and eventually grandchildren, all of whom helped with the cattle. Majenty said fondly: "My children [are] my greatest help in ranching," and he made sure that each of his children and grandchildren learned the business and acquired an interest in ranching. Since they were small "they all had their own cattle," Majenty boasted. By 1996 he had four great-granddaughters and a great-grandson named Kaleb who he hoped would one day take over his ranching operation.[38]

Like the decisions to begin a cattle business in the 1910s, nearly every discussion about development and cultural identity since the 1975 American Indian Self-Determination and Education Assistance Act caused debate in the community. After the failed Hualapai Dam and as the cattle business declined, the tribe looked for other large-scale development projects like oil, gas, mineral, and uranium exploration. They contracted with Houston-based Caasa International Corporation to conduct surveys for natural gas on the eastern end of the reservation, and although several firms visited the reservation, little oil or gas drilling occurred. After nearly forty years of tentative interest in oil and gas exploration, in 1983 the tribe joined the Council of Energy Resource Tribes, a coalition of Indian nations with nonrenewable resources, to learn more about managing and marketing those resources.[39]

The 1970s oil crisis and the economic downturn of the early 1980s heightened the demands for domestic sources of fuel as well as alternate forms of energy such as wind and solar power. But the political influence of nuclear and coal groups drowned out these cleaner sources of energy. Working from a position of political weakness and socioeconomic desperation, in the early 1980s Hualapais entertained offers from Energy Fuels Corporation of Colorado to again explore for uranium on the reservation. Tribes across the West faced similar situations. Roughly one-third of the low sulphur coal, one-fifth of the country's reserves of oil and natural gas, and over half of the nation's uranium sat underneath reservations during the 1980s. When faced with few options, deep poverty, and a cold war arms race that spurred exploration for coal and uranium, tribes with these resources had little choice but to gouge the earth and create massive open pit mines.[40]

The thirty-year history of uranium corporations hounding Hualapais for the right to explore on their reservation taught the community about the potential problems caused by mining, and many people opposed it because of the recent "dangers that have been linked to uranium mining on the Navajo reservation," according to tribal leader Earl Havatone. But the economic situation left leaders with few options. As Havatone saw it, economic development and sovereignty were linked: "One basic Hualapai Tribal objective is that self-determination is not possible without economic self-sufficiency."[41] Like Havatone, Edgar Walema, a veteran of the Vietnam War and chairman in 1984, understood the situation facing the tribal economy. Walema reacted by making a controversial decision to support uranium exploration and mining on the reservation. Sylvia Querta, a young council member in the mid-1980s, also thought mining would help her people. Those were "desperate times," she recalled in an interview in 1989. She worried about the environmental risks involved but hoped that the jobs and revenue would help alleviate rising suicide rates, spousal abuse, emotional depression, and alcoholism caused in large part by the precarious economic conditions and the related decline of social services.[42]

When the council voted in support of the mining deal in 1985, the community reacted by trying to recall Walema and Querta, the two most visible individuals supporting exploration. Walema survived the attempt, but Querta lost by one vote, an indication of deep divisions in the tribe. Yet the council turned around and rejected the recall because the petitioners had not supplied enough absentee ballots for off-reservation voters. According to *Arizona Republic* reports, the effort "had been started by traditionalist tribal members unhappy with the more progressive economic development plans of Walema and Querta."[43] Although the newspaper probably distorted reservation politics, throughout the twentieth century many tribal members felt that some leaders moved too fast with development. Several families in Peach Springs believed the council's support for mining contradicted traditional Hualapai reverence for the land and instead reflected short-term economic gains despite long-term environmental damage.

The negative reaction to the uranium deal caused the council to reject the contract in 1985 even as it agreed to open new exploratory bids the following year. Community disputes, contracting differences, new elections, and other factors delayed bids until 1988. In the meantime unemployment skyrocketed, alcoholism and domestic abuse persisted, and juvenile delinquency rose. Edgar Walema was philosophical despite the problems: "When I think about it, it's pretty amazing that we're still alive." He did not want to hurt anyone, but he saw few options. "We complain about all our problems, and we sure got 'em, but we're still alive. We're trying to take the next step—to live, not just to be alive."[44] His thoughts were echoed by Carrie Bender, a mother of three who was elected in 1988 to lead the tribe. "Uranium would bring revenues to our little tribe. It would mean employment when we have hardly any. We have to do something," she intoned as the issue came up again in 1989. A graduate of Northern Arizona University, Bender understood the risks: "Everything in life is a risk. I've seen a lot of sorrow, misery, pain—we all have." That December the council voted 7 to 2 to allow the Denver-based Energy Fuels Corporation to begin drilling.[45]

Hualapais hesitantly followed through with the permits until a new group of council members changed course in the early 1990s and canceled many of the agreements. The new council oversaw a watershed moment on 14 February 1991, when Hualapais approved a newly revised constitution in order to "maintain [the] culture, language and the inherent sovereign rights and powers of an Indian tribe," according to its text.[46] With this constitution as its mandate, the council prohibited uranium mining on the reservation. The council also created a semiautonomous tribal corporation to expand new industries such as tourism, while timber, ranching, and mining became less viable.[47] According to Hualapai Judge Joseph T. Flies Away, this council was trying to listen to the voices of the people by rejecting an economy based on extractive industries and simultaneously building a government more responsive to tribal members.[48] Refocusing on tourism, however, raised concerns within the community. Lucille Watahomigie said she did not want any more Anglos or tourists on Hualapai land, while others felt that the Hualapai Dam had not been fully explored. According to the *Arizona Republic*, Louise Benson said: "The dam has been a lifetime project of the Hualapai people. At a time when the dam could become a reality, we no longer have the . . . support." Council member Wilfred Whatoname echoed her frustration with Governor Bruce Babbitt's opposition to the dam and the larger economic situation that neocolonial policies had created on the reservation: "People here said you've done it to us again, 'You've sold us down the river.'" Benson added, "In lieu of the dam, we get tourism, which will tear down our land. . . . we respect our reservation . . . [because] our land is our sustenance."[49] Such sentiments reflected the frustration of many Hualapais who had tired of the limits imposed upon them by the federal government.

The late 1980s and early 1990s were a transitional era, as the Hualapai Dam was clearly dead, uranium mining was out of the question, and tribal members reconsidered the possibility of developing tourism on the western end of the reservation. Into this atmosphere came yet another Tribal Council, this time with plans for Grand Canyon West, forty miles from Peach Springs, on the edge of the Grand Canyon. Spearheaded by Edgar Walema, in 1987 the tribe began operating Grand Canyon West as a tourist destination with a picnic area, restaurant, and tours along the rim. Some members remained concerned that the development harmed sacred ground once inhabited by the Grass Springs band. For instance, Lucille Watahomigie was concerned about tourism because it might bring in an endless stream of outsiders who would disrupt their lives. "Two hundred years ago," she asserted, "the white man took all our land from Needles, California to Wikiup to Flagstaff. I don't like to see white men on our roads, in our canyons or on our river. It upsets me that this has come about."[50]

Despite some disapproval within the community, the small resort at Grand Canyon West was a central component of economic development by the mid-1990s. The tribe could capitalize on the tourists going to the Grand Canyon National Park and Las Vegas because the reservation was conveniently situated between the two destinations. The increased traffic to the national park made visiting it a long-drawn-out ordeal that involved honking horns, thousands of visitors, lumbering recreational vehicles, and, of all things, smog. In contrast, Grand Canyon West offered stunning views of the canyon unencumbered by gridlock or guard rails. Hualapais like Edgar Walema served as businessmen and cultural interpreters to the thousands making the trip from Los Angeles, Las Vegas, or New York. "The canyon is the beginning of our people. This is our stronghold. When the white man came and sent the cavalry after us, the cavalry couldn't get to us because we were in the canyon." Others thought tourism was a source of income and pride. Blake Watahomigie moved from the construction industry to a job as a tour guide for Grand Canyon West. At twenty-eight years old, Watahomigie thought it was "so great to be out here. It's so beautiful, people are amazed."[51]

The tribe sought to capitalize on its small endeavor at Grand Canyon West by taking a difficult leap into the world of casino gambling. In 1987 the U.S. Supreme Court ruled in favor of the Cabazon Band of Mission Indians in California and their assertion that they had a right to gamble on their reservation. Congress immediately tried to narrow the implications of the ruling by passing the Indian Gaming Regulatory Act in 1988 to legalize only certain forms of gambling on tribal land. By the early 1990s tribes across the country had negotiated gaming compacts with states. In Arizona casinos cropped up in Gila River, Fort McDowell, Ak-Chin, and the Salt River Pima Maricopa Indian Community as gaming promised new opportunities for tribes that lacked other sources of revenue.[52] Following their lead, in 1994 the Hualapai Tribal Council entered into a compact with Arizona to purchase fifty slot machines and place them at Grand Canyon West. According to Hualapai Judge Joseph T. Flies Away, gambling had a history on the reservation in the form of small gatherings of septuagenarian women in the 1970s playing poker, but high-stakes gaming raised a different set of questions. Tribal Gaming Commissioner Earl Havatone hoped to make it a "prosperous venture for the reservation and its members," but the Hualapais closed the casino in 1995. According to council member Waylon Honga, "The revenues just weren't meeting expenses. It was because of the locale and market." The failed effort left the tribe $1 million in debt.[53]

Qualities such as solitude and breathtaking vistas that made Grand Canyon West an attractive tourist destination were the main factors that doomed the casino. According to Louise Benson, "People weren't coming to a casino. They were coming to see the Grand Canyon." Alex Cabillo, the director of the Hualalai Public Works Department, agreed: "There were high hopes for that casino, but the reality of it was that we were too isolated." The Hualapais were one of only two tribes statewide to shut down their casino since legislation in 1988 opened the door for the gaming boom. Since then, national revenues have surpassed $20 billion per year. The Mohaves saw their employment rates grow from 27 percent to 74 percent between 1991 and 1997. Fort McDowell, Gila River, and the Yavapai-Prescott have also done well, but a fraction of tribes have made the lion's share of this revenue.

"Everybody thinks that tribes are getting rich from gaming and very few of them are," said Benson.[54]

Despite the failed casino, tourism on the Hualapai reservation has continued to grow in the twenty-first century. But the attacks on the World Trade Center in 2001 caused a drop in profits for Native nations that relied on vacationers. Unemployment rates for the most financially sound communities had spiked but rebounded by late 2002. Such swings in the economy were nothing new, according to Rory Majenty, the director for tourism. Speaking at a conference on tourism, Majenty noted that "as Indian people, we've always been in the tourism business. We now need to market it, control it, and present it." Majenty understood that tourism was a "balancing act for us to coordinate," but he believed that it was better than mining.[55]

In addition to the return of tourism, the tribe began receiving checks from the casino profits of other tribes in Arizona. In 2002 most gaming tribes in Arizona signed new compacts with Governor Jane Hull after they won a battle with non-Indian racetracks challenging the constitutionality of the gaming compact process. After the legislature refused the request of the non-Indian racetrack groups to vote on the new compact, the issue went to the voters in a ballot initiative. A narrow majority supported Proposition 202, which increased the number of slot machines that tribes could operate in exchange for a guaranteed transfer of 8 percent of gaming revenues to the state. The new compact also contained a novel stipulation allowing nongaming tribes to lease their gambling rights to gaming tribes in return for a share of revenues.[56] The Hualapais received the first annual check in 2004, which supplemented programs for health, education, and social services.[57]

Perhaps the most controversial decision of the tribe in recent years has caught the scorn, praise, and amazement of people from around the world. Rooted in a long history of using the Grand Canyon and Colorado River as a source of cultural identity and a basis for the tribal economy, Hualapai leaders embarked on an audacious project in 2004. The tribe began the construction of the seventy-foot-long horseshoe-shaped Hualapai Skywalk, which juts out over the edge of the cliffs at Grand Canyon West. For months the plan was the source of confusion and exaggeration as news outlets from around the globe picked up on the story of a small tribe in Arizona building an engineering marvel on one of the natural wonders of the world. Allegations that the tribe desecrated the landscape competed with arguments about the dire economic situation of a tribal government that had been in debt for the entire twentieth century. Facts slowly replaced fiction: the Hualapais contracted with a Chinese American business man, David Jin, who had made millions in the tourist industry. Jin owned a bus company that took Las

Vegas tourists to the reservation and the Grand Canyon. He realized that the location of Grand Canyon West was perfect for a daring project. Upon receiving support from the Tribal Council, Jin supplied the capital for what has become a modern engineering marvel and a consistent source of debate.[58]

Although council members and chairpersons such as Charlie Vaughn and Louise Benson played prominent roles in the project, one person quickly moved to the forefront: Sheri Yellowhawk, former chief executive officer of Grand Canyon West. Yellowhawk, a recurring council member and mother of five, has received withering criticism and voluminous praise for the plan. She supported the project because "tourism is our only means of self-sufficiency, of our people coming out of poverty and social problems." Speaking to one of the many reporters who have contacted her, Yellowhawk noted that the Skywalk, which sits four thousand feet above the canyon floor, can withstand sustained winds in excess of one hundred miles per hour and survive a magnitude eight earthquake. Money from the project would contribute to tribal government, road maintenance, and educational, health, and cultural programs. Yellowhawk understands her critics, but she remains firm on the need for bold measures: "There really is not anything else for funding but tourism and this way we don't have to rely on gaming."[59] Robert Bravo, a tribal member and manager at Grand Canyon West, echoed Yellowhawk: "This will feed our tribe. This will support our children."[60]

Not all tribal members agreed with the project. Clay Bravo, the assistant director for tribal natural resources, understood the need for employment, but he was concerned that the project lacked comprehensive planning. "There needs to be a balance between economic development and protection of natural resources," and this project did not seem to meet that standard. Joe Powskey, a tribal member who designed the official logo of the tribe and guides tourists at Grand Canyon West, hoped that leaders considered how the Skywalk would impact the natural and cultural beauty of the area. He wanted the area to remain pristine, but he understood that the airstrip, concession store, and helipad constituted a project that would possibly alleviate tribal poverty and unemployment. Other members worried that the Skywalk would harm sacred sites and cultural properties, but Yellowhawk reiterated that a small fraction of the designated zone would actually have permanent structures built on it.[61]

The criticisms from community members hit hard, and people were understandably worried about the land and culture. But it was the non-Indian accusations that seemed to draw the ire of the strong-willed woman who had raised a family, served on the Tribal Council, and recently begun pursuing a doctorate. In response to the comments of Robert Arnberger, past superintendent of the Grand Canyon National Park, Yellowhawk said: "You look at the park side, they have 4.5 million people a year—it's Disneyland in itself. They have too many cars and can't resolve their transportation issues. We're looking at their problems and trying to resolve them up front. We've gone through two and a half years of going back and forth with cultural assessment and biological assessments and community input. We have to find a means to self-sustain ourselves. The money is dwindling."[62]

The criticism against the Skywalk from the Grand Canyon National Park was nothing new. In fact, the tribe was still arguing with the park over the number of river rafters coming down the Colorado River. Tied up with the dispute over the location of the boundary between the reservation and the park, the tribe had little success convincing the park that it had a right to decide the number of boats it could send on a daily basis down the river. These differences were rooted in more than a century of conflict over the boundary of the reservation: the center or high-water mark of the river. But the rapidly growing numbers of rafters and helicopter rides as well as regional development led to growing pressure on the National Park Service by environmentalists to regulate usage of the Grand Canyon corridor. These factors increased the long-standing tendency of the Park Service to assert itself on lands claimed by Indian nations, but Native people were adamant in opposition. During a 1996 meeting of the National Congress of American Indians, Richard Boland of the Tibisha Shoshones told delegates in Phoenix: "We want the world to hear the real story of how the National Park Service views Indians. When most people think of the Park Service they think of the happy, smiling ranger wearing a Smokey the Bear hat. . . . We have a different story to tell."[63] Hualapais at the meeting may have agreed, because the twenty-first century has brought increased friction between the tribe and its neighbor.

Hoping to coordinate analyses of the problems facing the river, Grand Canyon Park Superintendent Rob Arnberger wanted to reevaluate the process for scheduling river runners through the Grand Canyon. Private outfitters wanted to increase the number of runs, while environmental groups wanted a "wilderness declaration" for the river. Hualapai leaders hoped to double the number of trips from Diamond Creek.[64] These agendas revealed the unresolved differences over boundaries, jurisdiction, and traffic on the river. Confusion persisted until a lawsuit filed by private boaters and commercial outfitters forced the hand of the park. In reaction to a court ruling, between 2002 and 2004 a series of public meetings revealed diverse views regarding the future of human activity on the river. The Sierra Club, Long Rivers, and others demanded a reduction in rafting and air traffic over the canyon, while the Hualapais said they had a right to increase the number of daily rafting trips. Chairman Charlie Vaughn noted: "From our perspective there's a question of whether or not they have the jurisdiction to impose this on the tribe," referring to the 2004 Colorado River Management Plan. Vaughn and others in the tribe believed it was their right to use the river due to their boundary extending to the center of the river. "The Park Service is using [the river management plan] to throttle our tribal economic development," Vaughn said. The new superintendent of the park, Joe Alston, responded to claims about the boundary with incredulity: "Our simple answer to this is it doesn't really matter where the Hualapai boundary is, Congress established where the Grand Canyon is—and it is the south side of the river." Guidelines released in 2006 reducing the number of passengers the Hualapais could take on rafting trips from a proposed 1,800 to 600 per day did not sit well with the tribe and failed to address the issue of the reservation's northern boundary.[65]

## "The Key to the Whole Problem": Hualapais and Water

The long shadow of aridity still looms over issues surrounding tourism, boundaries, and development. The lack of water on the high desert plains of the Hualapai landscape has served as a structural barrier to all forms of activity. For nearly three quarters of a century, the tribe attempted to solve this dilemma by trying to use the Colorado River by constructing a dam that would produce energy, by pumping water up the slope of the canyon, and as a vehicle for entertaining tourists. And at nearly every moment in that history the Grand Canyon National Park, Congress, and environmental groups blocked the tribe with catastrophic vigor.

The history of exclusion from the river was an especially bitter pill to swallow because communities hundreds of miles away from the Colorado River received its water. After Congress approved the Central Arizona Project in 1968, it argued with Arizona and the Department of the Interior over funding and engineering plans. The Colorado River Basin Project Act limited dams between Glen Canyon and Hoover dams, but it opened the door for construction and upgrades to begin in 1973 farther to the south on infrastructure and canals at Lake Havasu and Parker Dam. This construction was part of the CAP, which persisted for nearly twenty years while Hualapais demanded water from the river in the form of a pumping system or a smaller version of the dam proposed decades ago. Indeed, Congress even considered revisiting the dam during a 1981 legislative session because the cost of fuel and dependence on foreign oil made hydroelectric dams attractive, but the proposal died in the face of environmental concern and engineering costs. Moreover, incoming data on accumulation of silt and the impact of cold water on ecosystems below Glen Canyon confirmed the notion that additional dams would damage the river.[66]

As the Hualapais demanded water and the Bureau of Reclamation worked on the All-American Canal between Lake Havasu and Phoenix, policy experts and scientists expressed concerns that Arizona farmers could not afford the real cost of the imported water.[67] This concern became reality as the financial burden associated with providing "wet water" to fields rose astronomically. Because legislation paving the way for CAP stipulated that groundwater use had to decrease as CAP water increased, municipalities and agricultural users had to shift from well water to CAP water, which was being sold in part to pay for the construction of CAP itself. Essentially, farmers could not use CAP water and groundwater at the same time. The cost of CAP water, however, was more than the cost of water from the aquifer. Shifting to CAP water was especially expensive because farmers needed new infrastructure to connect their farms to the CAP canals. These factors caused many farmers to refuse CAP water. Combined with the declining profits of agriculture and the aging population engaged in the industry, the allocation of the Colorado River for farmers seemed shortsighted. After the Bureau of Reclamation completed all canals associated with CAP in 1992, the dearth in demand for CAP water produced a financial crisis for the state of Arizona. This worked in tandem with competition from farms in California to cause agricultural contractors in Arizona to declare bankruptcy. After several feasibility studies, the state of Arizona in 1995 admitted that Congress needed to negotiate short-term leases with farmers to subsidize CAP water. These federal subsidies further escalated the cost of the project, which was approaching $5 billion.[68]

Cities in central Arizona jumped on the chance to capture CAP water left over from low agricultural demand. But there was a catch: Central Valley cities had to keep growing to ensure their share of the river. This combination of guaranteed water and undeveloped desert created a powerful incentive for suburban sprawl, because if cities stopped growing, they lost their allocation of water and would have to limit themselves to what they really needed. The "use it or lose it" maxim negated incentives for long-term planning, and the subsidies contradicted the western ideology of independence. In the midst of it all Hualapais received neither the measured sovereignty they hoped for nor the water they needed.[69]

The paradox of Hualapais' exclusion from Colorado River water dated back to the early twentieth century, but the 1963 *Arizona v. California* ruling and the 1968 legislation that made CAP possible were recent manifestations of their plight. In the legislation Indian tribes would receive 310,000 acre-feet of water per year, but in the 1970s it was not clear how the state and federal government would deliver this water to tribes on the Gila River, in Ak-Chin, and elsewhere. In response, Native governments began filing lawsuits for failing to provide them with water. As these debates entered the 1980s, the water that the CAP legislation reserved for Indian tribes became especially valuable. With promises that they would be the first to receive CAP water, some tribes settled out of court, but others continued until the federal and state governments promised them 453,000 acre-feet per year of CAP water.[70]

Hualapais stood outside these developments and watched as a resource they claimed went to communities that had little or no ties to the river.[71] Arizona and the federal government tried solving the problems of farmers, provided water to growing cities, facilitated suburban sprawl, and met their promises to many tribes in the state, but Hualapais received nothing. In light of these insults and in the middle of a drought, Chairman Charlie Vaughn began talk of a lawsuit against the federal government for failing in its trust responsibilities to reserve water for the tribe. Rumors of a lawsuit against the federal government for water rights and against the National Park Service over the boundary issue had stirred the tribe for years. Hualapai leaders were never satisfied with their inability to procure water after the 1968 legislation and the death of the Hualapai Dam in the 1970s. Nor did they agree with the argument that the boundary as articulated in the 1883 executive order precluded access to the river or later claims that the reservation lacked irrigable acreage.[72]

The tribe did not begrudge the Quechans, Mohaves, Cocopas, Cheme-huevis, or the people of the Colorado River Indian Tribes for wringing water from the state and federal governments, but Hualapais wanted water as well. The Chemehuevis had been partially relocated after Lake Havasu, the reservoir behind Parker Dam, flooded sections of their reservation in the 1930s. Their history with the river was indisputable, as was their con-temporary dependence on it for irrigation and tourism.[73] Likewise, news that the U.S. Supreme Court allowed the Quechans to pursue their claim to water did not surprise the Hualapais.[74] And they could empathize with the sentiments of Cocopa leader Onesimo Gonzales, who, after years of protesting half a century of declining water levels, said: "Our river is gone." Gonzales was lamenting the damage done to his Mexican village, which sits at the Colorado River Delta, where one of the most tightly managed rivers in the world ends in a trickle far from the ocean it emptied into for millen-nia. Thriving estuaries once home to fish, birds, and other wildlife were on the verge of extinction as the river described by Aldo Leopold in 1922 as "everywhere and nowhere, for it could not decide which of a hundred green lagoons offered the most pleasant and least speedy path to the gulf," was polluted by 70,000 tons of fertilizer and 100,000 gallons of insecticide.[75]

Leaders like Vaughn and Benson were frustrated by non-Indian institutions telling the Hualapais that they could not have water from the river when Arizona, California, Nevada, and the Department of the Interior were arguing over who would receive surplus CAP water. The preceding years of confusion were especially galling to them. For instance, Arizona had surplus CAP water in the 1990s even when California used more than its allocation of 4.4 million acre-feet. In 2000 the Department of the Interior oversaw an agreement that reduced California's usage and, in turn, reserved more water for Arizona, but Hualapais saw none of the surplus.[76] Worse, a potential deal in 2003 would have renegotiated the 2000 agreement and allowed Nevada and California to again draw Arizona's surplus water from the Colorado River. In another ironic twist of events, in 2004 federal officials began ordering Arizona to implement water conservation measures to ensure a century's supply of CAP water for Phoenix and Tucson, while at the same time the CAP board guaranteed 1.25 million acre-feet of its allotment to Nevada.[77] These were the contradictions pushing Charlie Vaughn toward a lawsuit.

One of the most bittersweet moments for the tribe came in late 2004, when a U.S. Senate committee institutionalized several preexisting plans to give a considerable amount of the state's "unused" surface water to several tribes. In addition to the guarantees of the 1980s, the Gila River Water Plan encompassed nearly half of the water flowing through the CAP canals. The plan included money for infrastructure, canals, and pipelines to transport the water from the main stem to farms and other target areas on reservations.[78] The contradictions of supplying Nevada with CAP water, preparing for drought in Arizona, supporting non-Hualapai Native water needs, responding to the state's threatening lawsuits in 2005, and confronting the specter of a huge development project that promised 150,000 homes in Mohave County's Golden Valley an hour and a half west of the reservation proved too much for Hualapais to ignore.[79] In late 2005 and throughout 2006 tribal leaders began the long and arduous process of preparing for lawsuits against the National Park Service for control over their share of the river and against the state and federal governments for failing to secure water from the Colorado River, which runs along 108 miles of the reservation boundary.

As the court cases for access to Colorado River water attest, Hualapais have been in the center of some of the most volatile political and economic debates of recent years. But the leaders and institutions of the Hualapai nation were only the support structures that helped but did not totally define the community itself. In the twenty-first century the reservation was an increasingly stable place even though insufficient infrastructure, legal problems, and environmental debates made life difficult. In the 1990s Hualapais held more festivals, celebrations, and events to commemorate and educate the people about important issues. Today an Annual Sobriety Festival discusses alcoholism and teaches families the social and economic consequences of the disease. The Festival of the Pais celebrates regional tribal culture by bringing Hualapais, Havasupais, and Yavapais together to dance, sing, share stories, and sell baskets and crafts. An annual Youth Pow-wow attracts competitive dancers from across North America and connects the tribe with a new national tradition that combines competition, honor, and friendship. And finally, the La Paz Run symbolizes the people's escape from internment on the Colorado River Indian Reservation.

These commemorative events and festivals demonstrate that the collective memory of the tribe has not died and the contemporary vitality of the community has not waned in the face of increasingly complex political and economic challenges of life within a postindustrial nation-state. Growing numbers of tribal youth attend college and, most impressively, return to northwestern Arizona to work with the tribe. They bring important skills to the ongoing struggles over economic development, wildlife management, tourism, health, and education. Youth attend colleges as far away and diverse as Dartmouth, Yale, Stanford, and Haskell Indian Nations University, or they commute to Flagstaff and Phoenix. Walking around the reservation, one continues to hear the Hualapai language spoken not just among elders but by a generation educated under the auspices of the programs implemented in the Peach Springs Elementary School. Growing numbers of Hualapais work for the Grand Canyon Resort Corporation. These and other efforts demonstrate that nearly two centuries of colonization have not ended in the disappearance of the Hualapai people. Their perseverance is a testament to their deeply held beliefs, ties to the land, and powerful sense of themselves as an enduring people.

# Conclusion

## History and the Hualapai Nation

When the Hualapai Tribal Council heard the proposal for this project in 1999, they wanted to discuss Hualapai history. They knew their own past, but they wanted to know what I had read in books or learned on the reservation. This past, we all agreed, formed an important story that Natives and non-Natives could learn from. Hualapai struggles for the land were powerful examples of cultural persistence that could motivate other oppressed peoples to fight for justice, and their legal battle against the Santa Fe Railway illustrated how a small nation could be victorious against a multi-million-dollar corporation that claimed Indigenous land. Their history of wage labor, respecting female leaders, and struggling for water rights stood as powerful examples of resilience. After discussing these and other issues for two hours, they supported my proposal to write about their history.[1]

I mention this moment in the research and writing process to high-light how this book has never been a solitary or dispassionate exercise. The proposal to the council and more than a decade visiting the reservation are crucial to balancing power relationships at the root of scholarly inquiry into Indigenous pasts. Presenting the proposal to the council acknowledged that the Hualapais have a right to comment on what outsiders write about them, especially when many of the primary sources in this book were produced within a colonial context and placed in the National Archives and made available to the public without their permission. It also was necessary to talk with them to avoid revealing sacred sites, sensitive religious practices, and valuable cultural properties. Finally, the meeting with the council, like conversations with community members, demonstrated my respect for a people who have endured a century of colonial research into their history and culture.[2]

Reciprocity and cooperation are part of an important shift in research methodologies and the relationships between Indigenous peoples and academics. As argued by Linda Tuhiwai Smith in *Decolonizing Methodologies: Research and Indigenous Peoples*, scholars can no longer ignore the people whose cultures they have mined for profit. Something of a conspiracy has been perpetuated by those who claim that research can be conducted into the pasts of Indigenous peoples without recognizing the ways that the academy has facilitated the colonization of Indigenous peoples. Scholars historically have supplied the intellectual support for congressional legislation and popular stereotypes held by non-Indigenous Americans that have resulted in catastrophic losses for Native peoples. Many scholars have hid behind the veils of objectivity and academic freedom to avoid responsibility for the implications of work that has portrayed Native people as savage, antimodern relics of the past.[3]

Writing a history of a people who have survived ethnic cleansing, racism, and oppression has been emotionally charged and professionally rewarding. No amount of reading fully drives home the reality of standing in the middle of a one-room house inhabited by ten family members. Listening to elders talk about stories handed down from their great-grandparents brought me into conversation with people born in the 1800s. Their views and the views of many other Hualapais reshaped the interpretations and premises of this book. Innumerable conversations revealed how community members live in a social space that is populated by the ghosts of history and the ruins of the past. Just as the stories about the escape from La Paz or the achievements of World War II veterans structure Hualapai nationalism, their exclusion from the Colorado River, lack of arable soil, and unemployment as well as the ubiquity of alcoholism and diabetes are direct functions of historical processes that have alienated them from their land and resources. In ways that are good and bad, the inseparability of the Hualapais' past from their present casts a long shadow over the reservation.

This participant-observation methodology has improved the book, and it has also raised important questions about authorship. Talking with people about their family history, participating in local activities, and simply sitting in the living room of a tribal member, for instance, are a few of the most memorable experiences of this project. I had the honor to meet with the Tribal Council dozens of times. We talked about the tribal constitution and what it means for the nation, debated blood quantum as a basis for tribal membership, and discussed the deep-rooted problems plaguing their economy. I worked for the tribe on different projects, wrote grants, taught research methods to teenagers, discussed the book with the Hualapai

History Review Board, ate lunch with elders, and took tribal members to the National Archives to find information on tribal institutions. This level of participation yielded important yet difficult questions. There were times when family and personal differences pulled the project in competing directions. Several individuals noted mistakes about historical events, perceived imbalances and biases, and raised concerns about how outsiders would view their community. They offered hard and important suggestions that improved the book. Somewhere between my own archival research, interviews with and input from Hualapais, and numerous outside reviewers, the narrative that has emerged is both mine and theirs.

An additional challenge of this book involved addressing the different fields that have engaged Indigenous histories and cultures. This book draws upon Native American studies, Indian history, ethnohistory, postcolonial and subaltern studies, and the literature on colonialism and imperialism to provide an analytical narrative focusing on the history of one Indigenous nation. It has not offered a definitive or comprehensive interpretation, nor can it resolve the questions raised by decolonial research. Yet through the use of interviews, participation in local activities, attempts at creating an equitable politics of representation, and transparent discussion of the publication process, it strives for an ethical practice of scholarship.[4]

The concerns with colonialism, postcolonialism, decolonization, and subaltern studies in particular have been raised and addressed by a number of authors. Many scholars have interpreted the post-1776 history of the United States as a postcolonial history, but they have problematized the notion that it lacked colonial inequalities and exploitation. They grapple with the chronological and philosophical meanings of the term *postcolonial* and argue that the United States has not moved beyond a colonial relationship with its internal subjects. Rather than accepting a liberal or neoliberal view of the American nation-state, they argue that it is a colonial power that has subjugated nonwhite peoples and relegated their land and labor to marginality. "Neocolonial" seems a more apt description of the structural inequalities within the United States. Indeed, Indigenous nations as colonized subjects have as much in common with the postcolonial struggles of people in India, Africa, and Southeast Asia as they do with the African American and Mexican American populations in the United States. This unique status as "nations within a nation" demands more critical forms of inquiry than are typically offered by ethnohistory or American Indian history.[5]

Interpreting Hualapai history as an ongoing confrontation with state power provides a different vantage point for understanding the internal and external dynamics of Hualapai community.[6] Juridical rulings created a political and discursive field within which Hualapai struggles for liberation were radically restrained. Contradictory trajectories epitomized by the *Winters* and *Lonewolf* decisions of the early twentieth century denied the legitimacy of Hualapai history, epistemology, and sense of place within a legal system that ignored the "language" of Hualapai worldviews. But when Hualapais employed the colonizers' lexicon of law and science, the courts trapped them in a pre- if not antimodern existence by delegitimizing their claims to the land and the evidence they marshaled to support those claims. In relation to the colonial regime they nearly became, to use a powerful image, like insects trapped in amber: denied the right to represent their history and unable to shape their future.[7]

Native American studies scholars recognize how colonization continued through the twentieth century via institutions such as the courts and educational systems. Rooting their work in the land and epistemologies of Native peoples, they offer trenchant analyses of colonialism, racism, and exploitation and remind us of the humanity of the communities we represent in texts that are often never read by those same individuals. They keep us from forgetting that our scholarship contributes to a larger world where the seemingly innocent process of writing has consequences.[8]

These intellectual shifts are related to larger movements respecting the integrity of Indigenous populations as nations and peoples with the inherent right to define themselves and govern their lands. Indigenous self-definition for the Hualapais extends back into a past that shapes and structures what must be conceived of as an Indigenous nation or people in the present. This definition of the nation goes beyond the constitution and bylaws of the Indian Reorganization Act, the government bureaucracy, and the elected council. By Hualapai nation I mean the convergence of historical, discursive, performative, spatial, administrative, and political elements that constitute both the idea and reality of a modern Hualapai peoplehood.[9]

This national identity constitutes the shifting relationships between leaders, the tribal government, and the community, the language of Hualapai cultural identity, common historical memories, and the symbolic and real boundaries distinguishing them from surrounding populations. This nationhood is rooted in a preconquest world when Northeastern Pais differentiated themselves from others *and* acknowledged band autonomy, not following one centralized leader. Pai bands were independent, but they followed common rules for marriage and land use, spoke variations of one language, and shared social structures, kin networks, cultural practices, environmental niches, and so on. In contrast, as non-Indians invaded their lands, the federal government labeled the Pais as "Hualapais," set aside a reservation for them, and made resources and recognition contingent upon acceptance of that administrative identity. Thus, the notion of being Hualapai rather than belonging solely to a band deepened. Some people rejected the notion, while others embraced it and fleshed it out with the creation of political institutions, government bureaucracies, legal codes, and internally recognizable cultural cues and behaviors. Band differences and family rivalries persisted but within common experiences and solutions to community problems, bringing people together. External threats to their land, sovereignty, and language left a new tribal government with no choice but to protect people who were relatives and fellow citizens. In short, the Hualapai nation today could not have evolved historically as it did without a preexisting sense of common peoplehood.[10]

The inseparable processes of colonialism and Indigenous resistance transformed the Northeastern Pai from a decentralized people into a politicized and increasingly centralized nation characterized by networks of families, cross-band relationships, and mutually shared perspectives on the historical changes around them. The Hualapai nation was a product of modern forces and pressures deeply rooted in the values, traditions, and structures of the preconquest era. Contributing to this sense of nationhood was a powerful narrative of Hualapai history that sometimes dominated the stories that the bands told of themselves. Historical consciousness is an important ingredient to national identity. All nations tell stories about themselves even if they use a language of essentialism that is less than "accurate." Sometimes they employ stories that simplify the past and deny the existence of historical contingency, indeterminacy, and multiple perspectives. Nations use narratives to explain who they are, demarcate their boundaries, and then define who is inside or outside the history of their nation so they can claim political legitimacy and silence controversy. The historical project of becoming national is simultaneously situational, performative, prescriptive, and culturally functional. In this sense the nation requires a narrative that explains and validates its existence even if it does not acknowledge that it and its history are constructed.[11]

As the Hualapai nation developed over the twentieth century its members created a "metanarrative" that weaves in and out of this book as both a cause and a consequence of sociopolitical and cultural change. This narrative held the Hualapais together as a collective even as it silenced the complex stories of bands and families. This general history states that the Hualapais, or the People, emerged from Spirit Mountain and lived on the Colorado River until one of several events caused them to leave their place of origin. Hualapais and the ancestors of the Mohaves, Navajos, Hopis, and others migrated across the region and established themselves in specific places across the Colorado Plateau. Bands lived amid a six million–acre landscape and exploited a diverse range of topographical features and flora and fauna. Their worlds were turned upside down as the secondary impact of the Spanish introduced guns, horses, diseases, and Christianity. Afterward, Americans in the 1850s brought violence that culminated in the Hualapai Wars of the 1860s, followed by the Long Walk and escape from La Paz. Finally, the Hualapais demanded a reservation on the Colorado River, thus bringing them into the "modern" era.[12]

Although elders today recount histories of their families and bands, the vast majority of Hualapais embrace this general narrative, especially when in conversation with non-Indian individuals and institutions. It accompanies official Hualapai materials and exemplifies the seamlessness of many national histories. The narrative ties diverse bands of people into a unified entity called the Hualapais, which some project into the past as if the name had always existed. It explains the connections between bands, highlights their survival in the face of aggression, and places Hualapais on their present reservation. Its ultimate conclusion in the creation of the Hualapais as a people makes it a presentist rendering that explains the connections between history and the contemporary era.

There is nothing wrong with this version of Hualapai history. It serves the purpose of bringing Hualapais together on a particular level of tribal collective imagination. It does not fully negate or replace various personal, family, or band histories that frequently merge into the Hualapai metanarrative. Individuals may talk about bands and families and then at some point in the conversation shift to Hualapai to explain who they were and are, lacking any apparent tension in the transition. However, when pressed to elaborate or when in intra-"tribal" contexts, especially when one family offers a story that contradicts another, the multiplicity of narratives reemerges. This metanarrative, then, serves a political and historical purpose of binding the people together on one level without fully erasing subsidiary histories.[13]

As a metanarrative and cultural mnemonic device it requires important events and themes to make it comprehensible while remaining flexible enough for Hualapais to incorporate new ideas into the storyline. Events such as the Hualapai Wars, the Long Walk to La Paz, and the escape a year later, however, stand as foundational historical pivot points for both the Hualapai people and their notion of what history means. The pre–Hualapai Wars era barely qualifies as "history" in the common usage of the word: that category is primarily reserved for the period beginning in the early 1860s and going up to the creation of the reservation. The time before the Hualapai Wars is typically referred to as "a long time ago" or "before whites came" or simply "before La Paz." The Pai past becomes "history" at the precise moment when racial violence and Anglo invasion disturbed the Indigenous landscape, an ironic point, considering the epistemological violence done to Native people by the Western notion of history itself. Post-1883 issues such as boarding school, military service, ranching, and the battle with the Santa Fe Railway are integrated into the narrative, though in a less powerful way than La Paz.[14]

This historical memory does cultural work by influencing the choices of individuals within a community that constructed a political and cultural entity understandable as the Hualapai nation.[15] This general narrative of Hualapai history has played a powerful role in setting a basis for how Hualapais think about who they are as a people and a nation, even though the unity expressed in the metanarrative did not always exist for much of the twentieth century. Some of the most important events of their history include pre–Indian Reorganization Act leadership, which revealed differences between various leaders and bands. Off-reservation communities offered diverse responses to colonialism and strained the ability of the Hualapai leadership to present a united front to BIA officials and Arizona politicians. Both challenged the narrative that tied Hualapai historical identity to the reservation. Yet their decentralized responses were common to bands that saw themselves as independent from others, even when nationalist leaders such as Fred Mahone advocated for "all Hualapais." In addition, cultural schisms, changing gender roles, and bands that refused to move to the reservation strained the cohesive power of the metanarrative of Hualapai history.

And yet Hualapai history, despite the metanarrative, mirrors the multilayered processes of reconstructing a history of the Hualapai nation. Both are ongoing dialogues open to interpretation and critique. Just as it is nearly impossible to separate the metanarrative as a construct from subsidiary band and family histories, it is difficult to isolate a moment when the Hualapai became a nation. Neither the narrative reconstruction of Hualapai pasts nor the construction of a nation is a linear process built upon consensus. At various points in the Hualapai past there have been moments of agreement and unity punctuated by dissonance and acrimony in the narrative sense and their existence as a nation in various "presents." In part due to decentralized origins and band identities, it has been difficult to draw clear borders around the Hualapai nation and illuminate one common history. Consequently, I would argue that Hualapais engaged their past as they built their future and used history in complex and surprising ways in the process of self-definition and interaction with non-Indians. They employed it while confronting skeptical institutions such as the Indian Claims Commission, the Supreme Court, and the National Park Service. Some tribal leaders pointed to the band histories and identities to argue against centralized government and in defense of remaining in territories associated with particular bands rather than moving to the reservation. Thus, Hualapai national history has performed work that has been crucial to the land, culture, and identity of the People.

This discussion of history as it relates to Hualapai nationalism echoes to some extent the debates on nationalism in general. In solidifying myths, creating new ones, and explaining how the present relates to various pasts, national memory shapes contemporary identities and binds society into an "imagined community." This model seems useful for the bands of Hualapais, since they inhabited six million acres of land and may have rarely interacted with each other. Imagined national communities are constructs that explain how diverse and isolated peoples reacted to centralizing forces and modern political boundaries and disruptions in their traditional cultures and ways of living. And yet Benedict Anderson's concept has been critiqued by Indigenous peoples because it creates a dichotomy between the notion of a nation and kin-based peoples living in the modern era.[16] Indigenous peoples constitute nations in ways that European and American scholars have ignored: kin networks and familial relationships cut across time and space, while political institutions, legal systems, and formal bureaucracies closely associated with modern nation-states coinhabit Indigenous spaces. Indigenous peoples and nations emphasize family and band identities while incorporating characteristics of the modern nation-states in the form of large budgets with the power to tax, control land, determine and police membership, enforce codes and laws, and regulate myriad activities and behaviors within a legal space known as the reservation.[17] Indigenous languages, knowledge, sense of place, and spirituality also alter most definitions of national identity and nationalism.

This seems to be one of the most important points of this book: Hualapais and their history have remained a crucial part of the cultural landscapes and Indigenous geographies of the American Southwest. They reshaped traditional identities within a modern context and held onto a history that reflected their band identities, national adaptations, and dynamic interaction with settler communities colonizing their land. Considering the trauma that has befallen the community, it continues to persevere and flourish. Political leaders are recalled and reelected a few years later. The language suffered due to boarding school, but students learn it in their classes, and people speak it on the reservation. Poverty persists, but the community adapts and finds new ways to survive—see the Grand Canyon Skywalk, for instance. Popular culture and the Internet compete with Hualapai ceremonials, but reggae music and basketball have enabled the youth to create social bonds, strengthen their sense of self-esteem, and find new ways of "being Hualapai." Despite social and health problems, Hualapais seek solutions to their own problems in ways that borrow from the surrounding world and yet are tailored to the realities and needs of the people.

The collision between non-Indians and the Pai people created a history of conflict and cooperation that can teach us much about colonialism, violence, cultural arrogance, and community resistance. Numerous Hualapais have sacrificed for their families and children in an attempt to bring them a life free of the uncertainty and want that they experienced, while they simultaneously have tried to impart to them the traditions and values of their ancestors. Somewhere between this continuum of pain and possibility exists an optimism born of the need to believe that the future, though shaped by the past, is not shackled by its mistakes. With this respect for the past and hope for the future, the history of the Hualapai people should serve as a cautionary tale about conquest and colonialism as they are masked in the American imagination, but it should also remind us that the voices and stories of Hualapais are a testament to the strength of the oppressed to endure and create for themselves a more just and fulfilling world.

# Notes

## Introduction

1. Author's notes, 16–20 March 2001, Peach Springs, Arizona.
2. Stelp, "Hualapais Remembering 'Trail of Tears,'" *Kingman Daily Miner*, 28 May 1998, Box 31-A, Mohave County Museum of History and Arts.
3. Ibid.
4. Nunpa, "Dakota Commemorative March," 216.
5. Kaplan, *The Anarchy of Empire*; Jacobson, *Barbarian Virtues*; Silva, *Aloha Betrayed*.
6. Edmunds, "Native Americans, New Voices"; Hoxie and Iverson, *Indians in American History*; Deloria, "Historiography," 10.
7. Blackhawk, *Violence over the Land*; Ostler, *The Plains Sioux*, 2.
8. Ostler, *The Plains Sioux*, 3.
9. Denetdale, *Reclaiming Dine' History*, 6; Smith, *Conquest*.
10. Bruyneel, *The Third Space of Sovereignty*, xiii.
11. Wilson, *Remember This!*; Scott, *Weapons of the Weak*; Ostler, *The Plains Sioux*.
12. Foster, *Being Comanche*; Fowler, *Tribal Sovereignty*.
13. Deloria, "Historiography"; Smith, *Decolonizing Methodologies*.
14. Scott, *Domination and the Arts of Resistance*; Wolf, *Europe and the People without History*.
15. Smith, *Decolonizing Methodologies*.
16. See, among others, Prakash, "Subaltern Studies," 1477; Chakrabarty, "Radical Histories," 752; Cherniavsky, "Subaltern Studies," 87.
17. Alfred, *Peace, Power, Righteousness*; Fanon, *Wretched of the Earth*.
18. Wilson, *Remember This!* 13–14, quote from Wheeler on 13.
19. Trouillot, *Silencing the Past*.
20. Spivak, *A Critique of Postcolonial Reason*.
21. Smith, *Conquest*.
22. Prakash, "Subaltern Studies," 1475–90.
23. See Hoxie, *Parading through History*; Rosier, *Rebirth of the Blackfeet Nation*; and Iverson, *Dine*. Most "tribal" or "community" histories do not directly address

questions of national identity or nation building: Clemmer, *Roads in the Sky*; Perry, *Apache Reservation*; Hirst, *Havsuw 'Baaja*; Sando, *Nee Hemish*; Spicer, *The Yaquis*; Holt, *Beneath These Red Cliffs*; Young, *The Ute Indians of Colorado*.

24. The relevant literature is extensive, ranging from Hobsbawm, *Nations and Nationalism since 1780*, to Chatterjee, *The Nation and Its Fragments*.

25. Anderson, *Imagined Communities*, 5–7; Smith, *National Identities*, 9.

26. Eley and Grigor Suny, *Becoming National*; Levin, *Ethnicity and Aboriginality*.

27. Alfred and Corntassel, "Being Indigenous," 600.

28. Deloria and Lytle, *The Nations Within*; Hoxie, *Parading through History*; Rosier, *Rebirth of the Blackfeet Nation*; Saltman, *Land and Territoriality*, 217; Chatterjee, *The Nation and Its Fragments*.

29. Smith, *National Identities*, 34.

30. Fowler, *Tribal Sovereignty*, xvii.

## Chapter 1. From Origins to La Paz

1. Suwim Fielding, interview by Fannie Woodward, 10 July 1968, Peach Springs, Arizona, 8 (Doris Duke no. 464), American Indian History Project, Supported by Doris Duke, Western History Center, University of Utah, Salt Lake.

2. Hinton and Watahomigie, *Spirit Mountain*, 15. There are minor variations in the names of places, such as Madvil, Mativil, Matevil, and there are slightly different versions of the origin story.

3. Hinton and Watahomigie, *Spirit Mountain*, 26, 29, 39.

4. Ibid., 45, 47, 52.

5. Basso, *Wisdom Sits in Places*, 5; Wilson, "Grandmother to Granddaughter," 27–32; Ridington, *Trail to Heaven*; LaGrande, "Whose Voices Count?" 180.

6. Walker and Bufkin, *Historical Atlas of Arizona*, 5.

7. Ibid.

8. McGuire, "Walapai," 7.

9. Biolsi, *Indians and Anthropologists*; Mihesuah, *Repatriation Reader*; Thomas, *Skull Wars*; Dobyns and Euler, *Walapai People*, 5–6; Kroeber, *Walapai Ethnography*, 47; Martin, "Prehistory and Ethnohistory," 138; Manners, "Tribe and Tribal Boundaries," 7; Euler, "Walapai Culture History"; McGuire, "Walapai," 25–37.

10. Dobyns and Euler, *Walapai People*, 6–7, 25–26; Spicer, *Cycles of Conquest*.

11. Dobyns and Euler, *Walapai People*, 14.

12. Ibid., 19.

13. Hinton and Watahomigie, *Spirit Mountain*, 5; Dobyns and Euler, *Wauba Yuma's People*, 1.

14. Dobyns and Euler, *Wauba Yuma's People*, 3.

15. Ibid., 16–18, 20–23.

16. Ibid., 23.

17. For a fascinating debate over Pai sociopolitical structure see the exchange between Henry Dobyns and Robert Euler with Timothy Braatz in several volumes of the *American Indian Quarterly* (1999).

18. Dobyns, "The Walapai Country. Section 8. The Burro Creek Band"; Braatz, *Surviving Conquest*.

19. Dobyns, "The Walapai Country. Section 9. The Big Sandy Band."

20. Dobyns, "The Walapai Country. Section 10. The Whala Pa'a Band," 62.

21. Ibid., 10–12.

22. Dobyns and Euler, *Wauba Yuma's People*, 16.

23. Weber, *The Spanish Frontier*, 32.

24. Dobyns and Euler, *Walapai People*, 27; Spicer, *Cycles of Conquest*, 262; Wagoner, *Early Arizona*, 95; Braatz, *Surviving Conquest*; Crosby, *Ecological Imperialism*.

25. Sheridan, *Arizona*, 26; Weber, *The Spanish Frontier*, 48.

26. Sheridan, *Arizona*, 27; Weber, *The Spanish Frontier*, 32; Spicer, *Cycles of Conquest*, 262.

27. Sheridan, *Arizona*, 27; Weber, *The Spanish Frontier*, 66; Spicer, *Cycles of Conquest*, 263.

28. Sheridan, *Arizona*, 28; Weber, *The Spanish Frontier*, 66; Spicer, *Cycles of Conquest*, 263; Braatz, *Surviving Conquest*.

29. Braatz, *Surviving Conquest*; Spicer, *Cycles of Conquest*, 263.

30. Spicer, *Cycles of Conquest*, 266.

31. Garcés, *On the Trail of a Spanish Pioneer*, 325.

32. Braatz, *Surviving Conquest*; Spicer, *Cycles of Conquest*, 264.

33. Braatz, *Surviving Conquest*; Spicer, *Cycles of Conquest*, 266.

34. Braatz, *Surviving Conquest*, 165.

35. Brooks, *Captives and Cousins*.

36. Braatz, *Surviving Conquest*.

37. White, *It's Your Misfortune*, 37; Weber, *The Mexican Frontier*, 82.

38. White, *It's Your Misfortune*, 38; Weber, *The Mexican Frontier*, 83.

39. Wagoner, *Early Arizona*, 242–50.

40. White, *It's Your Misfortune*, 45; Weber, *The Mexican Frontier*, 86.

41. Goetzmann, *Exploration and Empire*; Calloway, *One Vast Winter Count*; Hurtado, *Indian Survival*.

42. Braatz, *Surviving Conquest*, 79; Dobyns and Euler, *Walapai People*, 31; Dobyns, "The Walapai Country. Section 3. The Truxton Canyon Band"; Casebier, *Camp Beale's Springs*, 18.

43. Ives, *Report: Colorado River*; Casebier, *Camp Beale's Springs*, 18.

44. Ives, *Report: Colorado River*, 97; Wagoner, *Early Arizona*, 323; Sheridan, *Arizona*.

45. Ives, *Report: Colorado River*, 101; Wagoner, *Early Arizona*, 323; Sheridan, *Arizona*.

46. Dobyns, "The Walapai Country. Section 10. The Whala Pa'a Band," 90; Casebier, *Camp Beale's Springs*, 19.

47. Dobyns, "The Walapai Country. Section 10. The Whala Pa'a Band," 92.

48. Casebier, *Camp Beale's Springs*, 20; Dobyns and Euler, *Walapai People*, 35; Wagoner, *Early Arizona*; Sheridan, *Arizona*.

49. Casebier, *Camp Beale's Springs*, 21.

50. White, *The Middle Ground*.

51. Dobyns, "The Walapai Country. Section 10. The Whala Pa'a Band," 28.

52. Dobyns, "The Walapai Country. Section 9. The Big Sandy Band," 24.

53. Extract from the Annual Report of the Commissioner of Indian Affairs, 1864, in U.S. Congress, Senate, *Walapai Papers*, 33, hereafter cited as *WP*; Braatz, *Surviving Conquest*, 87.

54. Contract between Walapai Indians and Mohave and Prescott Toll Road Company, 15 July 1865, *WP*, 34; Dobyns and Euler, *Wauba Yuma's People*, 27.

55. Sibley, *Geographies of Exclusion*; Harris, *Making Native Space*; Casebier, *Camp Beale's Springs*, 21.

56. Casebier, *Camp Beale's Springs*, 21; Dobyns and Euler, *Walapai People*, 36; Wagoner, *Early Arizona*, 253–55; Sheridan, *Arizona*; Report of George W. Leahy, Superintendent of Indian Affairs, Arizona Territory, 12 April 1866, La Paz, *WP*, 37; Report of George W. Leahy, Superintendent of Indian Affairs, to D. N. Cooley, Commissioner of Indian Affairs, Washington, D.C., in Letters Sent, vol. 3, RG 393, NARA, Washington, D.C.

57. Braatz, *Surviving Conquest*, 92.

58. Casebier, *Camp Beale's Springs*, 21; Dobyns and Euler, *Walapai People*, 38; Dobyns and Euler, "The Nine Lives of Schrum," 367.

59. Casebier, *Camp Beale's Springs*, 21; Dobyns and Euler, *Walapai People*, 36; Dobyns and Euler, "The Nine Lives of Schrum," 375.

60. Cited in Braatz, *Surviving Conquest*, 89.

61. Report from George Leahy on August 27, 1866, Relative to Fight at Skull Valley, to Office of Indian Affairs, Washington, D.C., Letters Sent, vol. 3, RG 393, NARA, Washington, D.C.

62. Ibid. The son of Wauba Yuma was Sookwanya, "chief of Yavapai Fighters sub-tribe" or several bands but not of Leve Leve's Hualapai Mountain band. Dobyns and Euler state: "The post-conquest aggrandizement of Leve Leve was a heavy blow to aboriginal Pai chieftainship patterns" because the military preferred to deal with Leve Leve as the "peace chief" (*Wauba Yuma's People*, 27).

63. Casebier, *Camp Beale's Springs*, 21; Dobyns and Euler, *Walapai People*, 39; Dobyns and Euler, "The Nine Lives of Schrum," 368.

64. Casebier, *Camp Beale's Springs*, 21; Dobyns and Euler, *Walapai People*, 40; Dobyns and Euler, "The Nine Lives of Schrum," 368.

65. Casebier, *Camp Beale's Springs*, 21; Dobyns and Euler, *Walapai People*, 40; Dobyns and Euler, "The Nine Lives of Schrum," 368.

66. Letter Press Books of William Redwood Price, Colonel, Eighth Cavalry, Commanding District of Upper Colorado, Camp Mohave, 16 June 1867, RG 393, NARA, Washington, D.C.

67. Ibid.

68. Price to Lt. Thomas T. Wright, A.A.A.G. Dist. Arizona, 20 January 1868; Letter Press Books, Wright to Maj. John P. Sherburne, Assistant Adjutant General, Department of California, 20 July 1867, RG 363, NARA, Washington, D.C.

69. Price to Maj. John P. Sherburne, 20 July 1867.

70. Price to Sherburne, 10 November 1867, Camp Willow Grove, Arizona Territory, NARA, Washington, D.C.

71. Price to Sherburne, 7 December 1867.

72. Price to Sherburne, 15 January 1868; Report from Captain S.B.M. Young, Eighth Cavalry, to Price, 20 January 1868; Price to Wright, 20 January 1868, RG 393, NARA, Washington, D.C.

73. Price to Sherburne, 9 January 1869.

74. Price to Sherburne, 21 April 1868; Casebier, *Camp Beale's Springs*, 23; Dobyns and Euler, *Walapai People*, 42; Dobyns and Euler, "The Nine Lives of Schrum," 369.

75. Dobyns and Euler, *Wauba Yuma's People*, 28.

76. Price to Sherburne, 25 September 1868.

77. Price to Capt. C. H. Lester, Commander of Camp Willow Grove, 7 October 1868.

78. Price to Sherburne, 14 November 1868.

79. Price to Sherburne, 17 December 1868.

80. Price to Sherburne, 13 February 1869.

81. Casebier, *Camp Beale's Springs*, 23; Dobyns and Euler, *Walapai People*, 44; Dobyns and Euler, "The Nine Lives of Schrum," 370.

82. Dobyns and Euler, *Walapai People*; Anderson, *The Indian Southwest*, 1580–1830.

83. Dobyns and Euler, *Walapai People*, 45; Dobyns and Euler, "The Nine Lives of Schrum," 370; Hirst, *I Am the Grand Canyon*.

84. Dobyns and Euler, *Walapai People*, 46; Dobyns and Euler, "The Nine Lives of Schrum," 370; Dunlay, *Wolves for the Blue Soldiers*.

85. Dobyns and Euler, "The Nine Lives of Schrum," 372; Utley, *The Indian Frontier*, 164.

86. Dobyns and Euler, *Walapai People*, 47; Dobyns and Euler, "The Nine Lives of Schrum," 371; Casebier, *Camp Beale's Springs*, 47; Utley, *The Indian Frontier*, 158; General George Crook to Assistant Adjutant General, Military Division of the Pacific, San Francisco, 22 July 1872, *WP*, 92.

87. Dobyns and Euler, *Walapai People*, 48; Dobyns and Euler, "The Nine Lives of Schrum," 372; Casebier, *Camp Beale's Springs*, 48.

88. Dobyns, "The Walapai Country. Section 8. The Burro Creek Band," 3.

89. Kate Crozier, interview by Henry F. Dobyns, 1953, in Indian Claims Commission, *The Hualapai Tribe of the Hualapai Reservation, Arizona, Petitioner v. The United States of America, Defendant*, Docket no. 90.

90. Dobyns and Euler, *Walapai People*, 51.

91. Records of the U.S. Court of Claims, Indian Depredation Case Records, Folder 6123, Box 485, HM 1997, RG 123, NARA, Washington, D.C.

92. Dobyns and Euler, *Walapai People*, 51; Dobyns and Euler, "The Nine Lives of Schrum," 372; Mrs. Tim McGee, interview by Clifford Purcell, spring 1967, page 7, Doris Duke Oral History Project, 59a–60b.

93. Dobyns, "The Walapai Country. Section 10. The Whala Pa'a Band," 31 July, 74.

94. Capt. Thomas Byrne, in Dobyns and Euler, *Walapai People*, 52.

95. Indian Honga, interview, 6 April 1943, Peach Springs, Arizona, and Felix Cohen to Judge Richard H. Hanna, 17 April 1943, Field Service, Office of Indian Affairs, Land Division, Box 48-A, Folder, "U.S. vs. Santa Fe Railway" RG 75, NARA, Washington, D.C.; Deposition of Indian Koara, 17 February 1900, Hackberry, Arizona, Box 486, RG 123, NARA, Washington, D.C.

96. Dobyns and Euler, *Walapai People*, 51; Dobyns and Euler, "The Nine Lives of Schrum," 372; Mrs. Tim McGee, interview, 7.

97. Dobyns, "The Walapai Country. Section 10. The Whala Pa'a Band," 29 May 1954, 4.

98. Dobyns and Euler, *Walapai People*, 54; Mrs. Tim McGee, interview, 6.

99. *WP*, 102.

100. Ibid., 103.

101. Ibid., 104.

102. Dobyns and Euler, *Walapai People*, 56.

## Chapter 2. The Colonization of Hualapai Space

1. Affidavit of Jane Huya, 19 November 1927; and Affidavit of Nora Schrum, 22 December 1927, both in Central Classified Files, Box 26, Folder 31229-23, Part 2 of 3, RG 75, NARA, Washington, D.C.

2. Kate Crozier, interview, 5 April 1943, Peach Springs, Arizona, and memorandum and documents from John Collier to Judge Richard S. Hanna, Box 48a, Folder "U.S. vs. Santa Fe Railway," RG 75, NARA, Washington, D.C.

3. Nora Schrum, interview, 5 April 1943, Peach Springs, Arizona, and John Collier to Judge Richard S. Hanna, Box 48a, Folder "U.S. vs. Santa Fe Railway," RG 75, NARA, Washington, D.C.

4. Queen Imus, interview, 12 April 1943, Peach Springs, Arizona, and John Collier to Judge Richard S. Hanna, Box 48a, Folder "U.S. vs. Santa Fe Railway," RG 75, NARA, Washington, D.C.

5. Dobyns, "The Walapai Country. Section 9. The Big Sandy Band," 9, 24.

6. Agent J. A. Tonner to Headquarters Department of Arizona, Prescott, telegraph, 21 April 1875, *WP*, 110.

7. Report of August V. Kautz, Colonel, Eighteenth Infantry, U.S. Army, Commanding Department of Arizona, 1875, 113, and Tonner to General Kautz, 7 May 1875, *WP*.

8. W. M. Eubank and S. Owens, Mineral Peak, Mohave County, Arizona, to Gen. August V. Kautz, Commanding Department of Arizona, and Colonel Morford, Acting Indian Agent at Colorado River Indian Reservation, 13 January 1877, *WP*, 115.

9. Sheridan, *Arizona*; Sibley, *Geographies of Exclusion*, v.

10. H. L. Haskell, First Lieutenant, Headquarters Department of Arizona,

Prescott, 20 August 1878, to the Assistant Adjutant General, Department of Arizona, *WP*, 118.

11. Malach, *Peach Springs*, 52.

12. Quote from Ben Wittick in ibid., 9.

13. Ibid., 13.

14. Ostler, *The Plains Sioux*.

15. Hine and Faragher, *The American West*.

16. Governor of Arizona A.P.K. Safford, Relative to the Hualapai, Territory of Arizona, Executive Department, 8 May 1875, *WP*, 105; Dobyns and Euler, "The Nine Lives of Schrum," 373.

17. *WP*, 120–50; Dobyns and Euler, *Walapai People*, 60–65.

18. Report of the Governor of Arizona, 1879, *WP*, 122–24; Wagoner, *Arizona Territory*, 164–67.

19. Capt. Thomas Byrne, Fort Mohave, Arizona Territory, to Assistant Adjutant General, Department of Arizona, Whipple Barracks, Prescott, Arizona, 12 November 1879, *WP*, 120.

20. H. L. Haskell to the Assistant Adjutant General, Department of Arizona, 20 August 1878, *WP*, 119; Report of the Governor of Arizona, 1879, 123; Lt. George Wilson to Whipple Barracks, Prescott, Arizona, 18 November 1879, *WP*, 124–26.

21. Superintendent Henry Mallory, Colorado River Indian Agency, 22 September 1879, Roll 24, RG 75, NARA, Washington, D.C.

22. Petition from Mohave County residents, Mineral Park, 8 September 1879, Roll 24, RG 75, NARA, Washington, D.C.

23. U.S. Representative John Campbell to Commissioner of Indian Affairs, 21 July 1880, Roll 26, RG 75, NARA, Washington, D.C.

24. McMillen, *Making Indian Law*; Asst. Adjutant General S. N. Benjamin to Maj. A. K. Arnold, Sixth Cavalry, Acting Asst. Adjutant General, 16 September 1881, and Statement of Jim Fielding Submitted by H. O. Davidson, 12 October 1928, both in Records Concerning *U.S. v. Santa Fe Pacific Railroad Company*, Box 2, Entry 824, RG 48, NARA, Washington, D.C.

25. Felix Cohen to Judge Richard H. Hanna, 17 April 1943, Field Service, Office of Indian Affairs, Land Division, Box 48a, Folder "U.S. vs. Santa Fe Railway," RG 75, NARA, Washington, D.C.

26. Jim Fielding, Philip Quasula, Pete Lambert, Chief Aniyarre Askit (Mohave), Sherman Ross (Mohave), 17 January 1928, to Secretary of the Interior Hubert S. Works, Central Classified Files, Box 26, Folder 31229-23, Part 2, RG 75, NARA, Washington, D.C.

27. Commissioner of Indian Affairs Hiram Price to the Secretary of the Interior, 22 July 1881, *WP*, 133.

28. Maj. Irvin McDowell to Headquarters Military Division of the Pacific and Department of California, 10 December 1879, *WP*, 129; Dobyns and Euler, *Walapai People*, 60–62; Price to Col. S. N. Benjamin, Assistant Adjutant General, Department of Arizona, 1 July 1881.

29. Dobyns and Euler, *Walapai People*, 60; Brig. Gen. O. B. Willcox, to Headquarters, Department of Arizona, Whipple Barracks, Prescott, 22 November 1879, *WP*, 128; Price to the Secretary of the Interior, 22 July 1881.

30. Herbert Welsh, "Visit to the Navajo, Pueblo, and Hualapai Indians," Corresponding Secretary, Indian Rights Association, 1885, *WP*, 148–49.

31. Affidavit of W. F. Grounds, Sr., 23 November 1927, Central Classified Files, Box 26, Folder 31229-23, RG 75, NARA, Washington, D.C.

32. Annual Report of Jonathan Biggs, United States Indian Agent, Colorado River Agency, for 1882, *WP*, 129; Report from the Commanding General, Department of Arizona, Relative to the Hualapai Indians, 1882, Brevet Maj. Gen. O. B. Willcox to Assistant Adjutant General, Presidio of California, 30 June 1882, *WP*, 139–40; Charles Spencer to Department Commander, Fort Whipple, September 20, 1882, and Charles Spencer to the Assistant Adjutant General, Department of Arizona, 14 November 1882, *WP*, 144–45.

33. Dobyns and Euler, *Wauba Yuma's People*, 89.

34. Ibid., 92.

35. Dobyns and Euler, "The Nine Lives of Schrum," 373.

36. Executive Order Creating Hualpai (Walapai) Indian Reservation, Executive Mansion, 4 January 1883, signed by President Chester A. Arthur, *WP*; Dobyns and Euler, *Walapai People*, 62.

37. Hoxie, *Parading through History*; Iverson, *Dine*; Crum, *Po'I Pentum Tammen Kimmappeh*.

38. Campbell, "The Lemhi Shoshoni," 539–78.

39. Hall, "The West and the Rest," 278.

40. Todorov, *The Conquest of America*; Said, *Orientalism*; Fisher, "They Mean to Be Indian Always," 468–92.

41. Kroeber, *Walapai Ethnography*, 47; Dobyns and Euler, *Walapai People*; Carson, "Ethnogeography," 769–88.

42. Allen, *Lost Geographies*, 10; Whatmore, *Hybrid Geographies*.

43. Jett, "The Navajo Homeland," 168–83.

44. Horsman, *Race and Manifest Destiny*.

45. Hoxie, *A Final Promise*.

46. McMillen, *Making Indian Law*.

47. Frazier, Margai, and Tettey-Fio, *Race and Place*.

48. McMillen, *Making Indian Law*.

49. Gen. George Crook, "Conditions of the Hualpai Indians," 24 March 1885, to Headquarters, Department of Arizona, Prescott, *WP*, 149.

50. Capt. F. E. Pierce, Fort Mohave, to the Assistant Adjutant General, Department of Arizona, Whipple Barracks, Prescott, 24 September 1884, *WP*, 160.

51. Carlson, *Indians, Bureaucrats*; McDonnell, *The Dispossession*.

52. Carlson, *Indians, Bureaucrats*, 90; Deloria, *American Indian Policy*.

53. Dobyns and Euler, *Walapai People*, 72; Henry P. Ewing, Superintendent and Special Disbursing Agent, Report of School at Truxton Canyon Agency,

Arizona, 30 July 1901, *WP*, 194–97; Oliver Gates, Report of Superintendent in Charge of Hualapai, Truxton, Arizona, 22 August 1905, *WP*, 201.

54. Commissioner of Indian Affairs to the Mohave County Board of Supervisors, H. S. Welton, Special U.S. Indian Agent, 23 January 1888, *WP*, 157.

55. Lt. G. M. Brayton, Whipple Barracks, to Assistant Adjutant General, Department of Arizona, Los Angeles, California, 8 June 1888, *WP*, 158.

56. Truxton Canyon Agency Fact Sheet, RG 75, NARA, Laguna Niguel.

57. Malach, *Reflections*, 14.

58. Henry P. Ewing, Industrial Teacher in Charge of the Hualapai and Havasupai Indians, Hualapai Indian Agency, Hackberry Arizona, July 1898, to the Commissioner of Indian Affairs, *WP*, 189.

*Chapter 3. Society and Culture in the Early Twentieth Century*

1. Jacobson, *Barbarian Virtues*; Bender, *A Nation among Nations*.

2. Knack and Littlefield, *Native Americans and Wage Labor*.

3. U.S. Bureau of the Census, Special Reports, *Occupations*, cxi; U.S. Bureau of the Census, Special Reports, *Supplementary Analysis*, 181.

4. Bauer, "Working for Identity," 206–38; Meeks, "The Tohono O'odham"; U.S. Department of the Interior, *Fifty-ninth Annual Report*; Merriam, *The Problem of Indian Administration*, 686.

5. Knack and Littlefield, *Native Americans and Wage Labor*.

6. *WP*, 140–42.

7. Ibid.; James, *In and around the Grand Canyon*, 173; Dobyns and Euler, "The Nine Lives of Schrum," 375; J. S. Schirm, President of the Grand Canyon Lime and Cement Company to Superintendent Oliver Gates, Truxton Canyon Agency, 13 September 1907, and C. F. Larrabee, Acting Commissioner of Indian Affairs to Superintendent Oliver Gates, Truxton Canyon Agency, 18 November 1907, Records of the Bureau of Indian Affairs, Box 32, Folder 71159-07, RG 75, NARA, Washington, D.C.

8. Fourth Annual Report on the Hualapai and Havasupai Indians, from Superintendent Henry P. Ewing, Hackberry, Arizona, to the Commissioner of Indian Affairs, 18 August 1899, Truxton Canyon Agency Files, Folder 1899–1900, Box 1, Letter Press Copy Books, RG 75, NARA, Laguna Niguel; Superintendent Charles Shell, Truxton Canyon Indian Agency, to J. W. Wood, Needles, California, 28 May 1910, Central Classified Files, Folder "Employment of Indians," Box 59, RG 75, NARA, Laguna Niguel.

9. June 1912, Annual Narrative and Statistical Reports, Roll 151, Truxton Canyon Agency, 1910–1931, RG 75, NARA, Washington, D.C.

10. Merriam, *The Problem of Indian Administration*, 690.

11. Bataille and Sands, *American Indian Women*; Klein and Ackerman, *Women and Power*; Perdue, *Cherokee Women*; Shoemaker, *Negotiators of Change*; Osburn, *Southern Ute Women*; O'Neill, *Working the Navajo Way*.

12. Raibmon, *Authentic Indians;* U.S. Bureau of the Census, Special Reports, *Occupations,* cxi.

13. Dobyns and Euler, *Walapai People,* 65; Merriam, *The Problem of Indian Administration,* 686; Malcolm McDowell, Member of the Board of Indian Commissioners, to the Truxton Canyon Agency, Arizona, 23 September 1923, Records of the Bureau of Indian Affairs, Box 7, Folder 81372-23, RG 75, NARA, Washington, D.C.

14. Jacobs, *Engendered Encounters;* Scharff, *Twenty Thousand Roads.*

15. Letter in Report to Commissioner of Indian Affairs from the Mohave County Board of Supervisors to H. S. Welton, Special Indian Agent, 23 January 1888, *WP,* 157; Iverson, *When Indians Became Cowboys;* Watahomigie et al., *Waksi,* 22.

16. Earl Y. Henderson, Assistant Secretary of the Board of Indian Commissioners, "Report on the Condition of the Hualapai Indians, Arizona," to the Commissioner of Indian Affairs, 1 February 1928, Records of the Bureau of Indian Affairs, Box 7, Folder 14531, Truxton Canyon Agency 150, 7, RG 75, NARA, Washington, D.C.; Dobyns and Euler, *Walapai People,* 74.

17. Truxton Canyon Superintendent Charles E. Shell to the Commissioner of Indian Affairs, Washington, D.C., 16 February 1914, Central Classified Files, Folder 900 Employment of Indians, Box 59, RG 75, NARA, Laguna Niguel; Dobyns and Euler, *Walapai People,* 75.

18. Lewis, *Neither Wolf nor Dog;* J. A. Gutches, District Forester, "General Report on Care and Protection of Timber within the Walapai Indian Reservation," 6 August 1910, Indian Service, Folder 65077-10, Truxton Canyon Agency 339, 33, Central Classified Files, RG 75, NARA, Washington, D.C.; Forty-sixth Annual Report of the Board of Indian Commissioners to the Secretary of the Interior, 30 June 1915, 25; White, *It's Your Misfortune;* Worster, *Rivers of Empire;* Pisani, *Reclaim a Divided West;* Iverson, *When Indians Became Cowboys,* 84.

19. Tom Susanyatame, Nelson, Arizona, to Commissioner of Indian Affairs, 23 November 1916, Records of the Bureau of Indian Affairs, Box 9, Folder 122174-16, Truxton Canyon Agency 155, RG 75, NARA, Washington, D.C.

20. Wagoner, *Arizona Territory,* 68; McMillen, *Making Indian Law;* Dobyns and Euler, *Walapai People,* 64; Bryant, *History;* McLuhan, *Dream Tracks.*

21. Cronon, *Nature's Metropolis.*

22. Bryant, *History;* McLuhan, *Dream Tracks,* 17–20; Dilworth, *Imagining Indians;* 116; Wagoner, *Arizona Territory,* 68, 205; Dobyns and Euler, *Walapai People,* 65.

23. Henry P. Ewing, Indian Agent, Hackberry, Arizona, to Gen. Arthur G. Wells, Superintendent, AT&SFRR, Los Angeles, 23 June 1899, Truxton Canyon Agency Files, Letter Press Copy Books, Box 1, Folder 1899–1900, RG 75, NARA, Laguna Niguel; Santa Fe Pacific Railroad Company to Henry P. Ewing, Indian Agent, Hackberry, 10 February 1900, Central Classified Files, Box 20, Folder 181, Transportation Requests, RG 75, NARA, Laguna Niguel.

24. Dobyns and Euler, *Walapai People*, 65; Sheridan, *Arizona*, 120; Peters, "Santa Fe Indian Camp," 33–70; U.S. Department of the Interior, Census Office, *Report on Indians Taxed*, 136.

25. Dobyns and Euler, *Walapai People*, 65–66; Sheridan, *Arizona*, 120.

26. Dobyns and Euler, *Walapai People*, 65.

27. Ibid., 66; Peters, "Santa Fe Indian Camp."

28. Vicenti Carpio, "Countering Colonization."

29. Miller, *Forgotten Tribes*.

30. Braatz, *Surviving Conquest*; Iverson, *Dine*.

31. Meeks, *Border Citizens*.

32. Crum, *Po'I Pentum Tammen Kimmappeh*.

33. Truxton Canyon Superintendent Charles Shell to George Wakayuta and other Kingman Indians, 8 December 1912, Central Classified Files, Box 13, Folder 100 Administration, 1897–1951, RG 75, NARA, Laguna Niguel.

34. *Mohave County Miner*, 1 September 1894, 29 December 1894, 1 July 1895, 8 July 1895, 16 July 1895; Ewing to Wells, 23 June 1899; Captain Schrum and Captain Leve Leve to Superintendent Enos Atkinson, Truxton Canyon Agency, 9 June 1910, and Atkinson to Schrum and Leve Leve, 16 June 1910, Central Classified Files, Box 4, Folder 47161-10, Truxton Canyon Agency 063, RG 75, NARA, Washington, D.C.

35. *Mohave County Miner*, 3 August 1893, 12 August 1893, 1 September 1893, 25 August 1894, 5 January 1895.

36. *Mohave County Miner*, 19 January 1895, 19 December 1896, 19 March 1898; Shell to Wakayuta and other Kingman Indians, 8 December 1912.

37. Dobyns and Euler, *Walapai People*.

38. Shell to Wakayuta and other Kingman Indians, 8 December 1912; George Wakayuta, Kingman, Arizona, to Superintendent Charles E. Shell, 10 December 1912, Truxton Canyon Indian School, Valentine, Arizona, Box 13, Folder 100 Administration, 1897–1953, RG 75, NARA, Washington, D.C.

39. Wakayuta to Shell, 10 December 1913.

40. Shell to Wakayuta and other Kingman Indians, 8 December 1912.

41. Testimony of George B. Davis in the Matter of the Application of Indian Grover, 1 November 1919; Testimony of Nama, or Indian Grover, in his Application for Allotment of Land, 28 September 1919; and Superintendent William Light to Commissioner of Indian Affairs, Regarding the Application of Indian Grover for allotment on lands outside the reservation, Valentine, Arizona, 13 November 1919, all in Records of the Bureau of Indian Affairs, Box 25, Folder 52970-17, Truxton Canyon Agency 308.2, RG 75, NARA, Washington, D.C.

42. Annual Report, 19 April 1910, Annual Narrative and Statistical Reports, Roll 151, Truxton Canyon Agency, 1910–1931, RG 75, NARA, Washington, D.C.

43. Ibid.

44. Correspondence between F. E. Clarke, Commissioner E. B. Merritt, and Superintendent Charles E. Shell, 3 March–28 March 1916, RG 75, NARA, Laguna Niguel.

45. Meyer, *White Earth Tragedy;* Sturm, *Blood Politics.*

46. Adams, *Education for Extinction.*

47. Malach, *Mohave County,* 34.

48. Dobyns and Euler, *The Ghost Dance,* 185.

49. Lomawaima, *They Called It Prairie Light;* Child, *Boarding School Seasons,* 7–8.

50. Dobyns and Euler, *The Walapai People,* 76; Henry P. Ewing, Industrial Teacher in Charge, Hualapai Agency, Hackberry, Arizona, 2 August 1896, and Report of the Field Matron for Hualapais, Henry P. Ewing, Hackberry, Arizona, *WP,* 180.

51. Fourth Annual Report on the Hualapai and Havasupai Indians, Henry P. Ewing, Hackberry, Arizona, to Commissioner of Indian Affairs, Washington, D.C., 18 August 1899, Truxton Canyon Agency Files, Box 1, Folder 1899–1900, RG 75, NARA, Laguna Niguel; Annual Report, Superintendent of Indian Schools, Bureau of Indian Affairs, 1900, *WP,* 191.

52. Individual Building Report, Truxton Canyon Agency, Department of the Interior, Bureau of Indian Affairs, n.d., Central Classified Files, Box 42, Folder 410, RG 75, NARA, Washington, D.C.

53. Shepherd, Ethnographic Report.

54. Ibid.

55. Superintendent Henry P. Ewing to Commissioner of Indian Affairs, Washington, D.C., 14 May 1899, and Superintendent Henry P. Ewing to Commissioner of Indian Affairs, Washington, D.C., 23 June 1899, Truxton Canyon Agency Files, Letter Press Copy Books, Box 1, Folder 1899–1900, RG 75, NARA, Laguna Niguel.

56. Iliff, *People of the Blue Water,* 4.

57. Ibid., 24.

58. Ibid., 59–74.

59. Gates, Report, 22 August 1905; Population Data on Indian Reservations, Lower Colorado River Basin, Compiled from the Annual Report of the Commissioner of Indian Affairs for the Years 1883 to 1956, Contained in Program Analysis Sent by John Artichoker, Jr., Area Director of the Bureau of Indian Affairs Area Office, Phoenix, Arizona, to the Library Division of the Arizona State University, 31 March 1976, in Government Documents, Arizona State University Library.

60. Gates, Report, 22 August 1905; Extract from the Annual Report of the Commissioner of Indian Affairs, 1916, *WP,* 202.

61. Superintendent Enos B. Atkinson to Commissioner of Indian Affairs, 15 December 1908, Central Classified Files, 1907–1941, Box 49, Folder 78148-08 852, RG 75, NARA, Laguna Niguel.

62. Superintendent Charles Shell to Phoenix Indian School, Central Classified Files, 1907–1941, Box 49, Folder 00-1911 825, RG 75, NARA, Laguna Niguel.

63. Superintendent to Kate Crozier, 21 January 1913, Truxton Canyon Indian School, Valentine, United States Indian Service, Department of the Interior, Superintendents' Correspondence, Box 2, RG 75, NARA, Laguna Niguel.

64. Inspection Re: Treatment of Pupils Report by L. F. Michael, Special Supervisor, Records of the Bureau of Indian Affairs, Truxton Canyon School, 18 February 1917, Inspection Division, Inspection Reports, 1917–1922, Central Classified Files, Box 70, Folder E-953, RG 75, NARA, Washington, D.C.

65. George Wakayuta to Superintendent Shell, 10 December 1913, Central Classified Files, 1897–1951, Box 13, Folder 100 Administration, RG 75, NARA, Laguna Niguel.

66. *Mohave County Miner.*

67. Correspondence between Superintendent Charles E. Shell and Mrs. Ovington Jewitt, Field Matron at the Sherman Institute, Riverside, California, 4 March 1915, Central Classified Files, 1897–1951, Box 50, Folder 800, RG 75, NARA, Laguna Niguel.

68. Ibid.

69. Superintendent Shell to Superintendent of Livestock Mather Willis, Peach Springs, Arizona, 6 October 1914, Central Classified Files, 1897–1951, Box 60, Folder 930 Stockraising, RG 75, NARA, Laguna Niguel.

70. Child, *Boarding School Seasons*, 7–8.

*Chapter 4. The Politics of Native Resistance*

1. Statement of unnamed Hualapai to M. K. Sniffen, Secretary of the Indian Rights Association, to Charles Rhoads, Commissioner of Indian Affairs, 7 August 1931, *WP*, 313.

2. Mahone to Albert B. Fall, Secretary of the Interior, 1 July 1921, Central Classified Files, Box 447, Part 1, Folder 34163-21-175—General Service, RG 75, NARA, Laguna Niguel.

3. Hirst, *I Am the Grand Canyon*, 65. The creation of the Havasupai reservation in 1880 contributed to the growing sense that Havasupais and "Hualapais" were different nations rather than different bands.

4. Knack, *Boundaries Between.*

5. Radding, *Wandering Peoples.*

6. Fixico, *The Invasion of Indian Country;* Knack and Littlefield, *Native Americans and Wage Labor,* 4; Hosmer, *American Indians in the Marketplace;* Hosmer and O'Neill, *Native Pathways;* White, *The Roots of Dependency.*

7. Dobyns and Euler, *Walapai People,* 79.

8. Superintendent William Light to the Commissioner of Indian Affairs, 29 June 1923, Records of the Bureau of Indian Affairs, Box 11, Folder 30310-23, Truxton Canyon Agency 174.1, RG 75, NARA, Washington, D.C.; U.S. Department of the Interior, *Fifty-ninth Annual Report.*

9. Dobyns and Euler, *Walapai People,* 76.

10. Light to the Commissioner of Indian Affairs, 29 June 1923; Fred Mahone, Jim Fielding, and "the Wallapai Indian Tribe," to the Commissioner of Indian Affairs, 23 April 1923, Records of the Bureau of Indian Affairs, Box 11, Folder 30310-23, Truxton Canyon Agency 174.1, RG 75, NARA, Washington, D.C.

11. Dobyns and Euler, *Walapai People*; Sheridan, *Arizona*; Wagoner, *Arizona Territory*.

12. Muller, "A Study of the Carl T. Hayden Papers," 20.

13. Ibid., 26; Ambler, *Breaking the Iron Bonds*, 44.

14. Jim Mahone to the Secretary of the Interior, 13 August 1913, Records of the Bureau of Indian Affairs, Central Classified Files, 1907–1939, Box 9, Folder 100802-13, Truxton Canyon Agency 15, PI-163-E-121, RG 75, NARA, Washington, D.C.; Scott, *Weapons of the Weak*.

15. McMillen, *Making Indian Law*, 13.

16. WP, 220, 251; Merriam, *The Problem of Indian Administration*, 698.

17. McMillen, *Making Indian Law*, 14.

18. Superintendent Charles Shell to the Commissioner of Indian Affairs, 14 June 1914, Records of the Bureau of Indian Affairs, Central Classified Files, Box 37, Folder 68188-14-371, Truxton Canyon Agency 371, RG 75, NARA, Washington, D.C.; McMillen, *Making Indian Law*, 15.

19. J. A. Christie, Superintendent of the Atchison, Topeka and Santa Fe Railway Company, Needles, California, to Superintendent Charles Shell, Truxton Canyon Agency, 14 October 1914; Assistant Commissioner of the General Land Office to Commissioner of Indian Affairs Cato Sells, 14 November 1914; and Superintendent Charles Shell to the Commissioner of Indian Affairs, 7 January 1915, all in Records of the Bureau of Indian Affairs, Central Classified Files, Box 37, Folder 68188-14-371, Truxton Canyon Agency 371, RG 75, NARA, Washington, D.C.

20. Assistant Commissioner E. B. Merritt to Superintendent Light, 29 December 1922; and William Light to Commissioner of Indian Affairs, 24 January 1923, in Records of the Bureau of Indian Affairs, Central Classified Files, Box 37, Folder 68188-14-371, Truxton Canyon Agency 371, RG 75, NARA, Washington, D.C.

21. Superintendent Light to Commissioner of Indian Affairs, 24 January 1923, Records of the Bureau of Indian Affairs, Central Classified Files, Box 37, Folder 68188-14-371, Truxton Canyon Agency 371, RG 75, NARA, Washington, D.C.

22. Lewis, "Reservation Leadership," 125–48; McMillen, *Making Indian Law*.

23. Atwater Report, 4–24 October 1922, Records of the Bureau of Indian Affairs, Central Classified Files, Box 9, Folder 79173-22, Truxton Canyon Agency 154, RG 75, NARA, Washington, D.C.; Britten, *American Indians in World War One*, 4.

24. Castillo, "Mission Indian Federation," 345–45; Castillo, "Twentieth Century Secular Movements," 713–17.

25. McMillen, *Making Indian Law*.

26. Statement of Fred Mahone, 28 June 1921; Mahone to Governor Campbell and State Highway Engineer Maddok, 21 June 1921; and Mahone to Albert B. Fall, Secretary of the Interior, 1 July 1921, all in Records of the Bureau of Indian Affairs, Central Classified Files, Box 447, Part 1, Folder 34163-21-175—General Service, RG 75, NARA, Washington, D.C.

27. Light, Annual Report, 20 June 1921, in Annual Narrative and Statistical Reports, Roll 151, RG 75, NARA, Washington, D.C.

28. Raibmon, *Authentic Indians*; McMillen, *Making Indian Law*.

29. Light, Annual Report, 20 June 1921.

30. Dobyns and Euler, *Wauba Yuma's People*.

31. Foster, *Being Comanche*; Radding, *Wandering Peoples*.

32. McMillen, *Making Indian Law*.

33. Fowler, *Arapahoe Politics*, 6, 134.

34. Atwater Report.

35. Jim Fielding, 16 October 1922, in ibid.

36. Fred Mahone in ibid.

37. Statement of Butch Clark and Indian Beecher in ibid.

38. Ibid.

39. Ibid.; Charles H. Burke, Commissioner of Indian Affairs to Fred Mahone, 23 November 1922, Records of the Bureau of Indian Affairs, Central Classified Files, Box 9, Folder 79173-22, Truxton Canyon Agency 154, RG 75, NARA, Washington, D.C.

40. Petition by the Wallapai Indian Tribe, Sheet #13, Written by Fred W. Mahone, 6 April 1923, Records of the Bureau of Indian Affairs, Central Classified Files, Box 4, Folder 30310-23, Truxton Canyon Agency 174.1, RG 75, NARA, Washington, D.C.

41. Ibid.

42. Superintendent Light to Commissioner Burke, 29 June 1923; Carl T. Hayden to Commissioner Burke, 13 April 1923; and "Power of Attorney" Petition from Steve Leve Leve, Jim Fielding, and Fred Mahone, signed by "The Members of the Wallapai Tribe of Indians," 23 April 1923, all in Records of the Bureau of Indian Affairs, Central Classified Files, Box 11, Folder 30310-23, Truxton Canyon Agency 174.1, RG 75, NARA, Washington, D.C.

43. Malcolm McDowell, Board of Indian Commissioners to Department of the Interior, 25 September 1923, Records of the Bureau of Indian Affairs, Central Classified Files, Box 7, Folder 81372-23, Truxton Canyon Agency 150, RG 75, NARA, Washington, D.C.

44. "Power of Attorney" Petition.

45. *WP*, 269.

46. Fowler, *Tribal Sovereignty*.

47. Rosier, *Rebirth of the Blackfeet Nation*; Knack, *Boundaries Between*.

48. Alfred and Corntassel, "Being Indigenous."

49. *WP*, 255–67.

50. American Indian Technical Services, Inc., "Hualapai Plateau," 57–58.

51. Extract from Annual Report of Commissioner Malcolm McDowell to the Board of Indian Commissioners, 1924, *WP*, 205; Extract from Annual Report of Assistant Secretary Earl Henderson to the Board of Directors of the Indian Rights Association, for the year ending 15 December 1925, Philadelphia, 16–17, *WP*, 208.

52. Arizona Governor George Hunt to Commissioner of Indian Affairs Charles H. Burke, 16 November 1926, Central Classified Files, Box 26, Folder 31229-23, Truxton Canyon Agency 313, Part 1 of 2, RG 75, NARA, Washington, D.C.

53. Bob Schrum, Philip Quasula, and Jim Fielding of the Walapai Tribe Committee to Hubert S. Works [sic], 17 January 1928, Central Classified Files, Box 26, Folder 31229-23, Truxton Canyon Agency 313, Part 2 of 2, RG 75, NARA, Washington, D.C.

54. William Light to B. E. Marks, Assistant U.S. Attorney, Phoenix, Arizona, *WP*, 209–18.

55. "Suit to Quiet Title to Water of Peach Springs, Transmits Affidavits and Depositions of Indians and Whites as to Occupancy, Use, and Ownership of Lands and Water, By Wallapai Indians on the Present Wallapai Reservation—Submits views on the Same," Superintendent William Light to Assistant U.S. Attorney B. E. Marks, Phoenix, 8 May 1928, *WP*, 210.

56. Hoxie, *A Final Promise*; Hertzberg, *The Search*; Philp, *John Collier's Crusade*.

57. *WP*, 226–27.

58. Ibid.

59. Petition from Mohave County Residents, 5 April 1930, Records of the Bureau of Indian Affairs, Central Classified Files, Box 26, Folder 31229-23, Part 2 of 3, Peach Springs, RG 75, NARA, Washington, D.C.

60. Affidavits of Jim Mahone and Kate Crozier, 18 August 1930, Central Classified Files, Box 26, Folder 31229-23, Part 2 of 3, Peach Springs, RG 75, NARA, Washington, D.C.

61. Fred Mahone to President Hoover, 28 January 1931, Records of the Bureau of Indian Affairs, Central Classified Files, 1907–1939, Box 27, Folder 31229-23, Truxton Canyon Agency 313, Part 3 of 3, RG 75, NARA, Washington, D.C.

62. U.S. Congress, Senate, Committee on Indian Affairs, Subcommittee, *Survey of Conditions*, 71st Cong., 3rd sess.; Hearings at Valentine, AZ., U.S. Senate, Subcommittee of Committee on Indian Affairs, Valentine, Ariz., Friday, 22 May 1931, *WP*, 240.

63. *WP*, 250–51.

64. Ibid.

65. Ibid., 275.

66. Ibid., 275, 282.

67. Ibid.

68. Hayden to Attorney General's Office, 21 March 1941, Box 649, Folder 17, Series 1, Subseries: Interior, Carl T. Hayden Papers, Arizona State University.

69. *WP,* 254.

70. Dobyns and Euler, *Walapai People,* 81; American Indian Technical Services, Inc., "Hualapai Plateau," 60; *The United States of America v. The Atchison, Topeka, Santa Fe Railway Company,* L-338–Prescott, 1931.

71. McMillen, *Making Indian Law.*

72. Ibid.

73. *The United States v. Santa Fe Pacific Railroad Company,* 314 U.S. 339, 345, 1941.

## Chapter 5. Citizenship, Status, and the Discourse of National Belonging

1. *WP,* 313.

2. Philip Quasula and Walapai Indians to the Commissioner of Indian Affairs, 11 March 1918, Records of the Bureau of Indian Affairs, Central Classified Files, Box 6, Folder 22609-18, Truxton Canyon Agency 125, RG 75, NARA, Laguna Niguel.

3. Britten, *American Indians in World War One.*

4. Dobyns and Euler, *Walapai People.*

5. Britten, *American Indians in World War One,* 52; Walapai Indians Eligible for Registration, 25 May 1917, Truxton Canyon Agency, Superintendent Charles Shell, Records of the Bureau of Indian Affairs, Central Classified Files, Box 44, Folder 610, RG 75, NARA, Laguna Niguel.

6. Bruyneel, *The Third Space of Sovereignty,* xxiii; Superintendent Charles Shell to Commissioner of Indian Affairs, 21 March 1918; Philip Quasula to Commissioner Cato Sells, 6 April 1918; and Commissioner Cato Sells to Philip Quasula, 17 April 1918, all in Records of the Bureau of Indian Affairs, Central Classified Files, Box 6, Folder 21885-18, Truxton Canyon Agency 124, RG 75, NARA, Laguna Niguel.

7. J. S. Withers, Chief Clerk of the Local Registration Board for Mohave County to Superintendent Charles Shell, 7 June 1918; and Withers to Superintendent Wagner, 21 September 1918, Records of the Bureau of Indian Affairs, Central Classified Files, Box 5, Folder World War I Service and Registration, RG 75, NARA, Laguna Niguel; Hawley, *The Great War.*

8. *Mohave County Miner,* 9 March 1920, 1; "Sam Swaskagame World War Hero Funeral Sunday," *Mohave County Miner,* 23 September 1921; "Wallapais to Hold Pow-wow," *Mohave County Miner,* 17 June 1921.

9. Deloria, *Playing Indian.*

10. Iverson, *We Are Still Here,* 64.

11. Ibid.; "Indians to Vote for the First Time This Year," *Mohave County Miner,* 18 July 1924, 1.

12. Crum, *Po'I Pentum Tammen Kimmappeh.*

13. Malcolm McDowell, Board of Indian Commissioners to the Commissioner of Indian Affairs, 25 September 1923, Records of the Bureau of Indian Affairs,

Central Classified Files, Box 7, Folder 81372-23, Truxton Canyon Agency 150, RG 75, NARA, Washington, D.C. (hereafter cited as McDowell Report).

14. Ibid., 8.

15. Ibid., 2; Light to Commissioner of Indian Affairs, 29 January 1924, Records of the Bureau of Indian Affairs, Central Classified Files, Box 7, Folder 81372-23, Truxton Canyon Agency 150, RG 75, NARA, Washington, D.C.

16. McDowell Report, 3.

17. Ibid., 10.

18. Assistant Commissioner E. B. Merritt to Superintendent Light, 21 March 1927, Records of the Bureau of Indian Affairs, Central Classified Files, Box 4, Folder 3433-23, Truxton Canyon Agency 101, RG 75, NARA, Washington, D.C.

19. Light to Commissioner of Indian Affairs, 29 January 1924, Folder 81372-23; and Earl Henderson, Assistant Secretary of the Board of Indian Commissioners, 1 February 1928, Folder 14531, both in Records of the Bureau of Indian Affairs, Central Classified Files, Box 7, Truxton Canyon Agency 150, RG 75, NARA, Washington, D.C.

20. Superintendent Frank T. Mann to Commissioner of Indian Affairs, 27 April 1928; and Commissioner Charles Burke to Superintendent Frank T. Mann, 18 May 1928, both in Records of the Bureau of Indian Affairs, Central Classified Files, 1907–1939, Box 29, Folder 31229-23, Truxton Canyon Agency 313, Part B6, to Folder 85306-36, Truxton Canyon Agency 320, RG 75, NARA, Washington, D.C.

21. Correspondence between Superintendent Guy Hobgood and Commissioner John Collier, Records of the Bureau of Indian Affairs, Central Classified Files, Box 29, Folder 24832-28, Truxton Canyon Agency 313, RG 75, NARA, Washington, D.C.

22. Mahone to Commissioner Collier, Records of the Bureau of Indian Affairs, Central Classified Files, 1907–1939, Box 29, Folder 30308-34, Truxton Canyon Agency 313, RG 75, NARA, Washington, D.C.

23. Hobgood to Collier, 20 June 1934; and Collier to Hobgood, 18 July 1934, Records of the Bureau of Indian Affairs, Central Classified Files, 1907–1939, Box 29, Folder 30308-34, Truxton Canyon Agency 313, RG 75, NARA, Washington, D.C.

24. Charles Shell to Commissioner, Records of the Bureau of Indian Affairs, Central Classified Files, Box 29, Folder 61237-28, Truxton Canyon Agency 313, RG 75, NARA, Laguna Niguel.

25. McDowell Report; 1921 Narrative Report from Superintendent Shell, and Light to Commissioner of Indian Affairs, 29 January 1924, Records of the Bureau of Indian Affairs, Central Classified Files, Box 7, Folder 81372-23, Truxton Canyon Agency 150, RG 75, NARA, Washington, D.C.

26. Annual Report of the Board of Indian Commissioners for 1924, Truxton Canyon Indian Agency, Arizona, Commissioner McDowell, Records of the Bureau of Indian Affairs, Central Classified Files, Box 7, Folder 81372-23, TC 150, RG 75, NARA, Washington, D.C.

27. Extract from the Annual Report of the Board of Indian Commissioners, 1928, Truxton Canyon Indian Agency, Arizona, *WP*, 208.

28. Citizens Committee Survey of Indian boarding Schools, for Superintendent Frank T. Mann, Truxton Canyon Indian School, Re: Circular no. 2546, to E. B. Merritt, Assistant Commissioner, Kingman, Arizona, 13 February 1929, *WP*, 222.

29. "Tribute to Jane Honga," *Hualapai Times* 1, no. 1 (1976), Museum of Northern Arizona, Flagstaff.

30. Mazzie Wescogame Powskey, interview, 9 April 1968.

31. Beth Wauneka, interview, 26 July 1999.

32. Charlotte Wellington and Jeannie Jackson, interview, 30 September 1999.

33. Benedict and Lydia Beecher, interview, 16 September 1999.

34. Beth Wauneka, interview, 26 July 1999.

35. Emmett Bender, interviews, 16 October 1999, 14 March 2001.

36. Wellington and Jackson interview.

37. Willie Powskey, interview, 13 August 1999.

38. Child, *Boarding School Seasons*; Lomawaima, *They Called It Prairie Light*.

39. Willie Powskey, interview, 13 August 1999.

40. Beecher interview; Grace Suminimo, interview, 3 November 1999.

41. Wellington and Jackson interview.

42. Ibid.

43. Luechtenberg, *Franklin D. Roosevelt and the New Deal*; Badger, *The New Deal*.

44. Philp, *John Collier's Crusade*.

45. Ibid.

46. Collins, *The New Deal in Arizona*, 240.

47. Ibid., 241–45.

48. Ibid., 242; Emergency Conservation Work Report, 1 November 1933, Hualapai Indian Reservation, Truxton Canyon Agency, Superintendent Guy Hobgood, and O. H. Schmocker, Camp Supervisor to Superintendent Hobgood, September 26, 1933, both in Records of the Bureau of Indian Affairs, Central Classified Files, Indian Emergency Conservation Work, Box 41, Folder 341-8, RG 75, NARA, Laguna Niguel.

49. Collins, *The New Deal in Arizona*, 256; *Indians at Work*, 1 September 1935, 48.

50. *Indians at Work*, 1 May 1935, 35; Collins, *The New Deal in Arizona*, 257; Leader Camp Enrollment Blank for Philip Quasula, signed by Superintendent Hobgood, n.d., and Leader Camp Enrollment Blank for Howard Whatoname, signed by Superintendent Hobgood, n.d., both in Records of the Bureau of Indian Affairs, Central Classified Files, Indian Emergency Conservation Work, Box 41, Folder 341-8, RG 75, NARA, Laguna Niguel; *Indians at Work*, 15 June 1935, 49, 15 October 1935, 1 May 1935.

51. Superintendent Guy Hobgood to Dr. Carl Skinner, Superintendent of Phoenix Indian School, 5 October 1935; Superintendent Guy Hobgood to Dell Shockley, Peach Springs IECW Project Manager, 21 September 1935;

and Kate W. Smith, School Social Worker, to Superintendent Guy Hobgood, 20 September 1935, all in Records of the Bureau of Indian Affairs, Central Classified Files, Indian Emergency Conservation Work, Box 41, Folder 341-8, RG 75, NARA, Laguna Niguel.

52. List of Employees on ECW Payroll, July 1936; and Superintendent Guy Hobgood to Representative Anson Smith, Kingman, 10 January 1934, both in Records of the Bureau of Indian Affairs, Central Classified Files, Indian Emergency Conservation Work, Box 41, Folder 341-8, RG 75, NARA, Laguna Niguel.

53. "A Hualapai Indian on Grazing," *Indians at Work*, 1 May 1936, 38.

54. Minutes, 1 March 1937, Hualapai Tribal Council Meeting, Peach Springs, Arizona, Records of the Bureau of Indian Affairs, Indian Service Records, Hualapai Tribal Minutes, Boxes 71–73, Row G3, RG 75, NARA, Laguna Niguel. Hereafter cited as Minutes plus the date.

55. Ibid.

56. Ibid.

57. Deloria and Lytle, *The Nations Within*, 267.

58. Ibid., 276; Biolsi, *Organizing the Lakota*.

59. Ibid., 279.

60. Ibid., 280.

61. Superintendent Guy Hobgood to Commissioner of Indian Affairs, 25 June 1934, Records of the Bureau of Indian Affairs, Central Classified Files, 1907–1939, Box 29, Folder 32244-34, Truxton Canyon Agency 13, RG 75, NARA, Washington, D.C.

62. Dobyns and Euler, *Walapai People*, 82.

63. Philp, *John Collier's Crusade*; Deloria and Lytle, *The Nations Within*; Rosier, *Rebirth of the Blackfeet Nation*.

64. U.S. Department of the Interior, Bureau of Indian Affairs, *Constitution and By-Laws*, 1–3.

65. Ibid., 3–4.

66. Dobyns and Euler, *Walapai People*, 82.

67. Ibid., 84; Minutes, 7 January 1939.

68. Minutes, 3 June 1939.

69. Minutes, 7 January 1939.

70. Dobyns and Euler, *Walapai People*, 86; Minutes, 7 January 1939.

71. Minutes, 2 November 1940.

72. Minutes, Special Meeting, 8 January 1941.

73. Ibid.

*Chapter 6. The Hualapai Nation in Postwar America*

1. Minutes, 24 March 1947.

2. Chevreaut, "Report Survey"; R. D. Holtz, Superintendent, 1 June 1941, Written by J. Howard Cheuvront, Frazier's Well Day School, Peach Springs, Arizona, Museum of Northern Arizona, Flagstaff.

3. Berman, "All We Needed Was Our Gardens," 133-55.

4. Iverson, *Dine*; Sturm, *Blood Politics*.

5. Biolsi, *Organizing the Lakota*; Biolsi, "Indian Self-Government," 26.

6. Dobyns and Euler, *Walapai People*, 84; Minutes, 8 January 1941.

7. Minutes, 8 January 1941.

8. Minutes, 4 June 1949, 20 June 1950, 2 June 1951.

9. Philp, *Indian Self-Rule*.

10. Dobyns and Euler, *Walapai People*, 88; Minutes, 7 August 1954.

11. U.S. Department of the Interior, Bureau of Indian Affairs, *Amended Corporate Charter*.

12. Ibid.

13. Sturm, *Blood Politics*; Garroutte, *Real Indians*.

14. Author's observations and informal conversations, 2002-9.

15. Iverson, "Building toward Self-Determination," 163-73.

16. Philp, *Termination Revisited*.

17. Fixico, *Termination and Relocation*; Iverson, *We Are Still Here*.

18. Fixico, *Termination and Relocation*.

19. Ibid.; Philp, *Termination Revisited*; Iverson, *We Are Still Here*; Peroff, *Menominee DRUMS*.

20. Metcalf, *Termination's Legacy*.

21. Minutes, 8 November 1944, 2 December 1944, 8 June 1946.

22. Cowger, *The National Congress of American Indians*.

23. Ibid.

24. Resolutions 7-52 and 8-52, in Minutes, 20 February 1952; see also Minutes, 7 February 1953; Liebow, "Urban Indian Institutions," 15.

25. Liebow, "Urban Indian Institutions," 17; Weaver, *Indians of Arizona*, 69; Minutes, 6 March 1954, 9 July 1955.

26. Inter-Tribal Council of Arizona, http://www.itcaonline.com/mission.html; Minutes, 8 September 1951, 4 April 1953, 6 May 1955.

27. Minutes, 6 November 1954, 5 February 1955.

28. Resolution 178, 9 July 1949, Records of the Bureau of Indian Affairs, Hualapai Tribal Resolutions, 1939–1991, Boxes 61–68, RG 75, NARA, Laguna Niguel. Hereafter cited as Resolution plus date.

29. Resolution 26-51, 13 October 1951; Phoenix Area Director Ralph Gelvin to Sterling Mahone, Hualapai Tribal Council President, 9 November 1951, Records of the Bureau of Indian Affairs, Hualapai Tribal Resolutions, 1951–1952, Box 61, RG 75, NARA, Laguna Niguel.

30. Gelvin to Mahone, 9 November 1951.

31. Minutes, 11 July 1953.

32. Resolution 16-54, 6 November.

33. Rupert Parker, "Editorial Update," *Hualapai News*, January–March 1956, 4; "Sterling Mahone Is Indian of the Year," *Hualapai Times* 1 (April 1976), Museum of Northern Arizona, Flagstaff.

34. Rosenthal, *Their Day in Court;* Iverson, *We Are Still Here,* 117.

35. Minutes, 5 February 1944, 17 August 1946.

36. Resolution 226, 10 November 1950.

37. Minutes, 1 October 1966, 7 January 1967, 27 January 1968.

38. Minutes, 4 May 1968.

39. Minutes, 18 February 1969; Resolution 23-65, 7 October 1965.

40. Minutes, 18 February 1969.

41. Minutes, 6 June 1970, 18 July 1970, 3 October 1970.

42. Minutes, 16 December 1970.

43. Minutes, 16 November 1974.

44. Townsend, *World War Two and the American Indian.*

45. Fixico, *Termination and Relocation,* 137; Fixico, *The Urban Indian Experience.*

46. Minutes, 6 April 1957.

47. Weibel-Orlando, *Indian Country, L.A.;* Vicenti Carpio, "Let Them Know We Still Exist"; Lobo and Peters, *American Indians.*

48. Fixico, *Termination and Relocation;* Clark, "Bury My Heart in Smog," 278–91; "Notes from the Relocation Office," *Gum-U: The Hualapai Newsletter,* November–December 1961, 2.

49. "Report on Relocatees," *Gum-U: The Hualapai Newsletter,* January–February 1962, 2; "Notes from the Relocation Office," *Gum-U: Hualapai News,* November 1964, 3.

50. Minutes, 6 August 1955.

51. Nagel, *American Indian Ethnic Renewal;* Minutes, 16 August 1955.

52. "Facts About Truxton Canon Subagency," Colorado River Agency, U.S. Department of the Interior, BIA n.d., Records of the Bureau of Indian Affairs, Central Classified Files, Box 7, Folder 040 Publicity (Agency Brochures, Fact Sheets), RG 75, NARA, Laguna Niguel.

53. Minutes, 5 March 1949.

54. Minutes, 2 April 1949, 9 November 1950.

55. Minutes, 5 March 1955.

56. "Tribal Updates," *Hualapai Newsletter,* November–January 1958, 4; Minutes, 1 August 1953, 2 April 1955, 10 September 1955, 9 July 1955.

57. "Neighborhood Youth Corps Interviews," *Gum-U: The Hualapai Newsletter,* September 1966, 12; Minutes, 7 May 1966.

58. Minutes, 7 December 1963, 23 June 1966, 27 August 1966, 7 February 1967.

59. Minutes, 2 August 1969, 6 December 1969, 7 February 1970, 6 April 1970.

60. Resolution 34-76, 1976.

61. Resolution 29-60, 1960.

62. Minutes, 6 February 1965, 1 October 1966, 10 June 1967, 12 July 1969; Resolution 13-67, 1967.

63. George Rocha, "Tribal Updates," *Gum-U: The Hualapai Newsletter,* July–September 1965, 1.

64. "National Youth Corps Interviews," *Gum-U: The Hualapai Newsletter*, September 1966, 12; Minutes, 27 August 1967, 15 November 1969, 20 June 1970.

65. Minutes, 8 August 1970, 5 May 1973; Resolution 6-80, 1980.

66. French, *Addictions and Native Americans*; Hamer and Steinbring, *Alcohol and Native Peoples*; Mancall, *Deadly Medicine*.

67. Minutes, 4 January 1969, 5 June 1969, 13 September 1969.

68. Minutes, 18 October 1969, 15 November 1969.

69. Hualapai Alcohol and Drug Abuse Prevention Program: Guidelines for Rehabilitation of Alcoholic Offenders Between LARC and Hualapai Tribal Court, 29 November 1974, Records of the Bureau of Indian Affairs, Hualapai Tribal Resolutions, 1974, Box 66, RG 75, NARA, Laguna Niguel; Minutes, 2 April 1979.

## Chapter 7. Local Realities in an Era of Self-Determination

1. Lucille Watahomigie, interview, 6 December 2001, in author's possession.

2. Wilkinson, *Blood Struggle*.

3. Ibid.

4. Minutes, 6 April 1963.

5. George Rocha, "Indian Self Government," *Hualapai News: Gum-U*, December 1964, 1.

6. Ibid.

7. George Rocha, "To the Tribe and Interested People," *Hualapai News: Gum-U*, December 1964, 1.

8. Minutes, 5 November 1966.

9. Minutes, 7 January 1967.

10. Minutes, 5 April 1969.

11. Minutes, 5 June 1965, 2 July 1968, 6 June 1970, 5 June 1971.

12. Angela Cavender Wilson, Andrea Smith, Jennifer Nez Denetdale, and Devon Mihesuah.

13. "Arizona Indian Women's Conference," *Gum-U: The Hualapai Times*, November 1976, 2.

14. Minutes, 24 April 1963.

15. Minutes, 26 January 1963, 9 February 1963.

16. Minutes, 3 April 1965.

17. Ibid.

18. Minutes, 5 August 1967; Resolution 10-69, 1969.

19. Minutes, 2 December 1967.

20. Minutes, 2 August 1969; Rupert Parker to Charles Pitrat, Superintendent, Truxton Canyon Agency, 4 December 1967, Records of the Bureau of Indian Affairs, Hualapai Tribal Resolutions, 1967, Box 64, RG 75, NARA, Laguna Niguel; Resolution 5-68, 1968.

21. Minutes, 2 August 1969, 7 March 1970.

22. Minutes, 5 November 1966, 4 January 1975.

23. Rupert Parker, "Tribal Operations," *Hualapai News: Gum-U*, May 1967, 3.

24. Watanome, "Tribal Members Urged to Participate," *Hualapai Times*, May 1976, 2; personal conversations with Wilfred Whatoname, 2002–7.

25. Watanome, "Tribal Members Urged to Participate."

26. Dalleck, *Flawed Giant*.

27. Patterson, *America's Struggle*; Castile, *To Show Heart*.

28. Minutes, 18 November 1965, 14 June 1966.

29. Minutes, 8 July 1966, 1 October 1966.

30. Minutes, 4 February 1967.

31. Minutes, 28 July 1967, 5 August 1967.

32. Minutes, 13 September 1969.

33. Minutes, 10 April 1976; Lucille Watahomigie, interview, 6 December 2001, in author's possession.

34. Minutes, 6 January 1968.

35. Minutes, 15 November 1969, 27 January 1970, 18 June 1971, 3 February 1979.

36. American Indian Technical Services, Inc., "Hualapai Plateau," 130.

37. Ibid.

38. Watahomigie interview, 6 December 2001.

39. Minutes, 13 July 1963, 1 May 1965, 6 January 1968.

40. Minutes, 7 March 1970.

41. Minutes, 25 April 1970, 3 October 1970; Rothman, *Devil's Bargains*.

42. Minutes, 12 April 1973, 22 February 1975.

43. Resolution 24-76, 1976; Minutes, 31 October 1978; letter to Mr. Thomas, National Park Service, in Minutes, 25 June 1979.

44. "Former Tribal Treasurer Appointed New Position," *Hualapai Times* 1, no. 10 (1977): 2.

45. Ibid.

46. Hundley, *Water and the West*.

47. Resolution 6, 10 May 1939; Minutes, 8 January 1942, 1 May 1943.

48. Resolution 15-51, 5 May 1951.

49. Ibid.

50. Superintendent Thomas Dodge to Commissioner of Indian Affairs, 15 May 1951, Records of the Bureau of Indian Affairs, Hualapai Tribal Resolutions, 1951–1952, Box 61, RG 75, NARA, Laguna Niguel; Minutes, 6 November 1954; Resolution 1-54, 6 February 1954.

51. Resolution 5-54, 5 March 1954; Minutes, 5 February 1955, 10 January 1957.

52. Superintendent Charles E. Shell to the Commissioner of Indian Affairs, 2 February 1914; and Superintendent William Light to the Commissioner of Indian Affairs, 26 May 1922, Records of the Bureau of Indian Affairs, Central Classified Files, 1907–1939, Box 33, Folder 20011-14, Truxton Canyon Agency 341, Box 1, RG 75, NARA, Washington, D.C.; Johnson, *The Central Arizona Project*, 19.

53. Worster, *Rivers of Empire.*

54. Pearson, "We Have Almost Forgotten," 299.

55. White, *It's Your Misfortune;* Worster, *Rivers of Empire;* Fradkin, *A River No More;* August, *Vision in the Desert,* 19–23.

56. Resolution 4, 6 May 1939.

57. Resolution 1-66, 8 March 1949.

58. Resolution 8-55, 5 February 1955.

59. Minutes, 4 October 1952; Resolution 47-55, 17 November 1955.

60. Minutes, 7 September 1957, 5 October 1957, 2 August 1958, 4 October 1958.

61. Minutes, 10 October 1953, 31 May 1956, 7 July 1956.

62. Parker, "Statement Concerning the Proposed Central Arizona and Colorado River Basin Projects," 21.

63. Iverson, *We Are Still Here,* 130–32; Lawson, *Dammed Indians;* White, *It's Your Misfortune.*

64. Resolution 14-60, 7 May 1960; Assistant Superintendent Wesley T. Bobo to F. M. Haverland, Area Director, 6 September 1960, Records of the Bureau of Indian Affairs, Hualapai Tribal Resolutions, 1960, Box 63, RG 75, NARA, Laguna Niguel.

65. Johnson, *The Central Arizona Project,* 21; Pearson, "We Have Almost Forgotten," 305; Iverson, *We Are Still Here,* 169.

66. Minutes, 29 June 1976.

67. Worster, *Rivers of Empire;* Fradkin, *A River No More.*

68. Minutes, 7 December 1963.

69. Worster, *Rivers of Empire,* 275; Minutes, 10 July 1965, 15 August 1965; Rocha, "Tribal Updates," 2.

70. Resolution 21-65, 1965.

71. Resolution 32-65, 1965.

72. Arthur Lazarus, Jr., to Chairman George Rocha, n.d., reprinted in *Hualapai News,* June–September 1965, 8.

73. Minutes, 1 April 1967; Resolution 28-67, 1967.

74. Worster, *Rivers of Empire,* 275; Sheridan, *Arizona,* 341–47.

75. Minutes, 12 June 1970; Resolution 33-75, 1975; Resolution 52-77, 1977.

76. "Hualapai Dam Commission," *Hualapai Times,* April 1976, 6, copy in Museum of Northern Arizona, Flagstaff; Resolution 33-75.

77. Resolution 18-79, 1979.

78. "Reevaluation of Water Projects," *Hualapai Times,* March–April 1977, 6.

79. Morehouse, *A Place Called Grand Canyon;* Hirst, *Havsuw 'Baaja;* Keller and Turek, *American Indians and National Parks.*

80. Hays, *Conservation.*

81. Worster, *A River Running West;* Morehouse, *A Place Called Grand Canyon,* 43–45.

82. Morehouse, *A Place Called Grand Canyon,* 45–50.

83. Minutes, 3 May 1969, 18 October 1969; Resolution 11-69, 1969.

84. Resolution 27-69, 1969; Minutes, 12 June 1970; Resolution 3-72, 1972.

85. Minutes, 2 August 1975.

86. Minutes, 2 August 1975, 6 September 1975, 4 October 1975.

87. Minutes, 13 March 1976, 12 November 1977; Resolution 41-76, 1976.

88. Resolution 64-77, 1977.

89. Chairman Earl Havatone to Superintendent Curtis Nordwall, 15 December 1977, Records of the Bureau of Indian Affairs, Hualapai Tribal Resolutions, 1977, Box 67, RG 75, NARA, Laguna Niguel.

90. Keller and Turek, *American Indians and National Parks*; Resolution 69-77, 1977.

## Chapter 8. Contemporary Reservation Affairs

1. Clarkin, *Federal Indian Policy*; Wilkinson, *Blood Struggle*; Jaimes, "The Hollow Icon," 34–44.

2. Wilkinson, *Blood Struggle*, 51; McClellan, "Implementation," 45–55.

3. Jaimes, "The Hollow Icon," 40.

4. Wilkins, *American Indian Politics*, 398.

5. Ibid., 9.

6. McClellan, "Implementation," 52; Wilkins, *American Indian Politics*, 90.

7. Wilkins, *American Indian Politics*, 84.

8. Williams, *Like a Loaded Weapon*, 89.

9. Wilkins, *American Indian Politics*, 79.

10. Wilkinson, *Blood Struggle*, 251.

11. Wilkins, *American Indian Politics*, 126.

12. Sturm, *Blood Politics*; Garroutte, *Real Indians*; Menchaca, *Recovering History*.

13. U.S. Department of the Interior, Bureau of Indian Affairs, *Constitution and By-Laws*.

14. Menchaca, *Recovering History*; Miller, *Forgotten Tribes*.

15. Sturm, *Blood Politics*; Garroutte, *Real Indians*.

16. Wilkins, *American Indian Politics*, 28.

17. Personal observation during Tribal Council meetings, 1997–2007.

18. Wilkinson, *Blood Struggle*, 309; Iverson, *Dine*, 243; "Black Mesa Environmental Impact Statement, Project Area Map," Office of Surface Mining, U.S. Department of the Interior, http://www.wrcc.osmre.gov/wr/BlackMesaEIS.htm.

19. "Tribes Discuss Fate of Grand Canyon Indian Country Today," *Tulsa World Oklahoma*, 26 December 1995.

20. Berny Morson, "Power Plants Targeted," *Rocky Mountain News*, 11 June 1996.

21. Joelle Babula, "Bypass Proposal Concerns Tribes," *Las Vegas Review Journal*, 8 May 2000.

22. Mihesuah, *Repatriation Reader*.

23. Conversations with directors of the Cultural Resource Center (Monza Honga, Loretta Jackson, and Greg Glascoe), 1997–2008.

24. Babula, "Bypass Proposal."

25. Matt Kelley, "Fight over Quarries Rocks Arizona," *Sunday Oregonian*, 13 September 1998.

26. Abbie Gripman, "Turning a Vista into a Mess," *High Country News*, 25 May 1998.

27. "Tribe Trying to Stop Mining to Inventory Ancient Burial Sites," Associated Press state and local wire, 18 September 2002; "BLM Ups Reward for Gravesite Desecration," Associated Press state and local wire, 21 April 2006.

28. Michael Kiefer, "Snow Clouds over the San Francisco Peaks," *Phoenix New Times*, 19 March 1998.

29. "Mine Expansion on Peaks Draws Indian Opposition," Associated Press state and local wire, 11 December 1998.

30. "Environmentalists Back Forest Service on Mining Withdrawal Proposal," Associated Press state and local wire, 1 April 1999.

31. Scott Thomsen, "Interior Department Strikes Deal to Close Mine on Sacred Mountain," Associated Press state and local wire, 20 August 2000.

32. "Critics Protest Using Treated Wastewater on Ski Slopes," Associated Press state and local wire, 20 March 2002.

33. "American Indian Advocates Oppose Snowmaking Plan," Associated Press state and local wire, 14 February 2004.

34. David Kravets, "Indians Say Arizona Ski Resort Desecrates Mountains," Associated Press state and local wire, 12 September 2006.

35. "Hualapai Indian Reservation: Arizona Community Profile," Hualapai Tribe and the Indian Services Program of the Office of Economic Planning and Development, with assistance from the Arizona Department of Economic Security, May 1984, Phoenix, Arizona Folder: Hualapai Reservation, 1968–Present, Box ACIA, Section D13, ACIA General Correspondence, 1965–Present, Arizona State Archives, Phoenix.

36. "Stormy Skies over Peach Springs," *Arizona Indian Monthly: The Voice of Arizona Indians* 3, no. 11 (1981), a Publication of the Indian Development District of Arizona, Arizona Historical Society, Tucson.

37. Ibid.

38. Laura Flood, "Leonard Majenty: Hualapai Cattleman," *Arizona Cattlelog*, July 1996, Arizona Historical Society, Tucson.

39. "Surveys Planned on Arizona Reservation," *Oil and Gas Journal*, 24 May 1982, 45.

40. Wilkinson, *Blood Struggle*, 482.

41. Delbert Havatone, "The Hualapai Reservation: Reservoir of Wealth and Jobs," *Mohave: Monthly Newspaper Supplement to the Kingman Daily Miner*, December 1983, Mohave County Museum of History and Arts.

42. Paul Rubin, "A Tribe on the Threshold: Haunted by Drugs, Alcohol and Unemployment, the Hualapai Indians Look for a Savior in Uranium," *New Times*, 20–26 December 1989; Sylvia Querta, interview.

43. "Hualapais Rule Election Recall Illegal," *Arizona Republic*, 22 May 1985, Hualapai General File, Box 3, ACIA Section, D13 ACIA Correspondence, Attorney General Records, 1960–1965, Arizona Department of Library, Archives and Public Records, Phoenix.

44. Rubin, "A Tribe on the Threshold."

45. Ibid.

46. U.S. Department of the Interior, Bureau of Indian Affairs, *Constitution and By-Laws*.

47. Steve Daniels, "Hualapai Tribe Rejects Plans to Boost Grand Canyon Tourism," *Arizona Republic*, 6 April 1980.

48. Judge Joseph T. Flies Away, interview, 1 September 2001, in author's possession.

49. Daniels, "Hualapai Tribe Rejects Plans."

50. Rubin, "A Tribe on the Threshold."

51. Matt Kelley, "Grand Canyon West Offers an Indian View of the Canyon," 26 September 1998, Associated Press state and local wire.

52. Mason, *Indian Gaming*.

53. William Quinn, "Hualapai Tribe's Casino Opening This January," *Kingman Daily Miner*, 12 December 1994, Box 31-A, Mohave County Museum of History and Arts; Judge Joseph Thomas Flies Away, interview, 10 September 2001; David Pace, "Most Indians Haven't Benefited from the 1990s Casino Boom," 1 September 2000, Associated Press state and local wire.

54. Pace, "Most Indians Haven't Benefited."

55. Sara Thorson, "Conference Aims to Diversify Tribal Tourism," Associated Press state and local wire, 3 August 2003.

56. "Tribe to Build Grand Canyon Skywalk," Associated Press state and local wire, 22 July 2004.

57. Personal observation during Tribal Council meetings, 2003–7.

58. Nick Christensen, "Road to Riches?" *Las Vegas Sun*, 6 November 2005.

59. St. Germain, *Spectrum*, Associated Press state and local wire, 8 February 2006; informal conversations, 2004–8.

60. Greg Lavine, "Engineering Marvel Could Be Tribe's Savior," *Salt Lake Tribune*, 2 January 2006; Robert Bravo, interview, 6 October 2008, in author's possession.

61. Lavine, "Engineering Marvel"; Joe Powskey, interview, 3 August 2008, in author's possession.

62. Julie Cart, "Tribe's Canyon Skywalk Opens One Deep Divide," *Los Angeles Times*, 11 February 2007.

63. Todd Wilkinson, "Native Americans Challenge Park Agency for Land Rights," *Christian Science Monitor*, 22 October 1996.

64. "Grand Canyon Chief Wants to Change River Runner System," Associated Press state and local wire, 18 March 2000.

65. Christopher Smith, "Park Service Struggles Anew with How to Run the river," *Salt Lake Tribune*, 23 June 2002; Bob Christie, "New Plan Should Allow

More People to Tour Grand Canyon by Boat," Associated Press state and local wire, 10 November 2005; Jennie Lay, "Colorado River Gets a Recreation Plan," *High Country News*, 23 January 2006.

66. William MacDougall, "Will Grand Canyon Turn into a Lake of Mud?" *U.S. News and World Report*, 28 September 1981.

67. Robert A. Young and William E. Martin, "The Economics of Arizona's Water Problem," *Arizona Review*, March 1967.

68. Haneman, "The Central Arizona Project."

69. Wiley and Gottlieb, *Empires in the Sun*; Haneman, "The Central Arizona Project," 6.

70. Haneman, "The Central Arizona Project," 9; "Tribes May Wind Up with a Majority Control of Colorado River Water," Associated Press state and local wire, 11 October 1999.

71. Burton, *American Indian Water Rights*, 40.

72. Carelli, "Court Sets Arguments in Colorado River Dispute," Associated Press state and local wire, 18 February 2000; McKinnon, "States Wrangle for Colorado River Share," Associated Press state and local wire, 15 December 2005.

73. Kelley, "Tribe at the Center of Water Dispute," Associated Press state and local wire, 17 October 1998.

74. Kelley, "Colorado River Ruling Gives Tribes a Rare Victory," Associated Press state and local wire, 19 June 2000.

75. Rosenblum, "Fighting over the Last Drops as Colorado River Reaches Its End," Associated Press state and local wire, 19 May 2001.

76. Snedeker, "Interior Secretary Announces Plans for Colorado River Water," Associated Press state and local wire, 14 December 2000.

77. "States That Use Colorado River Water Need Conservation Plan," Associated Press state and local wire, 30 April 2004; "CAP Board Endorses Colorado River Water Deal with Nevada," Associated Press state and local wire, 4 December 2004.

78. "Senate Committee Endorses CAP Water Plan for Indian Tribes," Associated Press state and local wire, 16 September 2004.

79. McKinnon, "Gambling on Water: Vegas Builder's Mohave County Plan Stirs Worries," *Arizona Republic*, 5 February 2006.

## Conclusion

1. Author's personal notes, meeting with Hualapai Tribal Council, 7 November 1999, Peach Springs, Arizona.

2. Smith, *Decolonizing Methodologies*.

3. Mihesuah, *Natives and Academics*.

4. Holm, Pearson, and Chavis, "Peoplehood," 9.

5. Prakash, "Subaltern Studies," 1475–90.

6. Scott, *Domination and the Arts of Resistance*.

7. Williams, *Like a Loaded Weapon*.

8. Alfred and Corntassel, "Being Indigenous," 597–614; Wilson, *Remember This!*; Denetdale, *Reclaiming Dine' History*; personal conversations with David Anthony Tayamee Clark.

9. Biolsi, "Imagined Geographies," 239–59.

10. Wilkins, *American Indian Politics*; Campbell, "The Lemhi Shoshoni," 540.

11. Eley and Grigor Suny, *Becoming National*.

12. Kramer, "Historical Narratives," 525–35.

13. Gooding, "Place, Race and Names," 1190.

14. Nunpa, "Dakota Commemorative March," 230.

15. Lone-Knapp, "Rez Talk," 638.

16. Anderson, *Imagined Communities*.

17. Forbes, "The Use of Racial and Ethnic Terms," 58.

# Bibliography

**National Archives and Records Administration (NARA)**

*Collections at the Main Branch, Washington, D.C.*

Record Group 48. Records Concerning *U.S. v. Santa Fe Pacific Railroad Company.*

Record Group 75. Annual Narrative and Statistical Reports from Field Jurisdictions of the Bureau of Indian Affairs, 1907–1938. Truxton Canyon Agency. Microfilm 1011. Rolls 150–52.

Record Group 75. Records of the Bureau of Indian Affairs. Central Classified Files, 1907–1953. Truxton Canyon Agency, Boxes 1–50. Letters Received by the Office of Indian Affairs, 1824—Arizona Superintendency, 1865–1880. T1014-Z10. Microfilm 234. Rolls 24–28.

Record Group 94. The Adjutant General's Office. Enlistment Papers: U.S. Indian Scouts. 91-W 765. Folders 436–80.

Record Group 123. Records of the U.S. Court of Claims. Indian Depredation Case Records. Case Files, 5 March 1891–17 March 1894, 21 September 1917. Folders 6118–23. Boxes 485, 486, 541.

Record Group 279. Records of the Indian Claims Commission. Closed Docket Files, 1947–1982. Docket 70. Boxes 843, 1231, 12,311. Entry 11 UD.

Record Group 393. Records of the U.S. Army Continental Commands. Part 5. Army Posts. Fort Mohave, Arizona. Letters Sent, September 1859–July 1890. Volumes 1–10.

*Collections at the Pacific Regional Branch, Laguna Niguel, California*
Record Group 75. Records of the Bureau of Indian Affairs
Central Classified Files, 1897–1951
Hualapai Tribal Minutes, 1937–1989
Hualapai Tribal Resolutions, 1939–1991
Letters Received, 1899–1913
Letters Sent, 1899–1913
Superintendents' Correspondence, 1912–1920
Truxton Canyon Agency Files

## Other Manuscript Collections

*Arizona Historical Foundation*
Ray Brandies Collection MSS 75
Barry Goldwater Papers
Indian Census Rolls Microfilm 595

*Arizona State Museum Archives, Tucson*
Sarah Tucker Jones Collection MS 183

*Arizona State University, Arizona Room, Tempe*
Bruce Babbitt Papers
Thomas Dodge Papers MSS 033
Charles Gritzner Collection MSS 044
Carl T. Hayden Papers MSS 033
Royal Marks Papers MSS 87

*Arizona State University, Labriola Center, Tempe*
Indians at Work. A News Sheet for Indians and the Indian Service. Native
    Americans and the New Deal: The Office Files of John Collier,
    1933–1945

*Hualapai Nation Department of Cultural Resources, Peach Springs,
Interviews*
Beecher, Benedict. 16 September 1999
Beecher, Lydia. 16 September 1999
Bender, Emmett. 16 October 1999
Jackson, Jeannie. 30 September 1999
Powskey, Willie. 13 August 1999
Suminimo, Grace. 3 November 1999

Wauneka, Beth. 26 July 1999
Wellington, Charlotte. 30 September 1999

*Hualapai Nation Peach Springs Public School, Peach Springs*
Rochelle Lieber Ethnographic Collection
Parker, Rupert. Interview. 25 June 1968
Prescott College Hualapai Oral Tradition Project

*Mohave County Museum of History and Arts, Special Collections,
Kingman, Arizona*
   **Doris Duke Oral History Project, Interviews**
   Anderson, Lillian. 24 September 1967
   Beecher, Frank. July 1968
   Fielding, Suwim. 10 April, 10 July 1968
   Honga, Jane. 30 April 1968
   McGee, Charles. 8 April 1968
   McGee, Mrs. Tim. Spring 1967
   Powskey, Loly. 13 April 1968
   Powskey, Mazzie Wescogame. 9 April 1968

*Museum of Northern Arizona, Katherine Bartlett Room, Flagstaff*
Crystal Jahr Collection MS-185

*Northern Arizona University, Special Collections, Flagstaff*
Florence Barker Collection MS 67.2
Alfred F. Whiting Personal Papers and Research Notes MS 90.42, Flag-
   staff City–Coconino County Public Library Oral History Project
   MS 76.20

*Prescott College, Special Collections, Prescott*
   **Prescott College Hualapai Oral Tradition Project, Interviews**
   Fielding, Suwim. 25 June 1968
   Honga, Jacob. 12 July 1968
   Honga, Jane. 11 July 1968
   Mahone, Fred. 24 June 1968
   Mahone, Nellie. 31 May 1968

*University of Arizona, Special Collections, Tucson*
John L. Riggs Collection AZ 251

## Interviews by the Author

Beecher, Benedict and Lydia. Peach Springs, Arizona. 16 September 1999
Bender, Emmett. Peach Springs, Arizona. 16 October 1999, 14 March 2001
Flies Away, Joseph Thomas. Peach Springs, Arizona. 10 October 2001
Powskey, Melinda. Peach Springs, Arizona. 6 December 2001
Querta, Sylvia. Peach Springs, Arizona. 7 December 2001
Suminimo, Grace. Peach Springs, Arizona. 3 November 1999
Watahomigie, Lucille. Peach Springs, Arizona. 6 December 2001
Watahomigie, Philbert. Peach Springs, Arizona. 6 December 2001
Yellowhawk, Sandra. Peach Springs, Arizona. 6 December 2001

## Newspapers

*Arizona Cattlelog* (Kingman)
*Arizona Indian* (Phoenix)
*Arizona Republic* (Phoenix)
*Christian Science Monitor*
*Gum-U: The Hualapai Newsletter* (*Hualapai Times, Hualapai News*) (Peach Springs)
*High Country News*
*Hualapai Times*
*Indian Arizona News* (Phoenix)
*Kingman Daily Miner* (Kingman)
*Las Vegas Review Journal*
*Los Angeles Times*
*Mohave County Miner* (Kingman)
*New Times* (Phoenix)
*Rocky Mountain News*
*Salt Lake Tribune*
*Sunday Oregonian* (Portland)

## Miscellaneous Unpublished Documents

American Indian Technical Services, Inc. "Hualapai Plateau: Forest, Wood-
    lands, and Range: A Forest History of the Hualapai Indian Reservation of
    Northwest Arizona." Bureau of Indian Affairs, Phoenix. Truxton Canyon
    Agency, Valentine, Arizona, 1987. In Peach Springs Elementary School,
    Peach Springs.
Arizona Department of Commerce. "Kingman-Mohave County: Arizona
    Industrial Profile." 1991. Vertical File. Mohave Community College,
    Kingman Branch, Kingman.

Bliss, Sam W. "Higher Education Needs on the Navajo, Hopi, Whiteriver Apache, and Hualapai Indian Reservations of Northern Arizona." 1980 Special Collections, Northern Arizona University, Flagstaff.

Boyer, David G. "Water Resources Development Study for the Hualapai Indian Tribe." Laboratory of Native Development Systems Analysis and Applied Technology, Office of Arid Land Studies, University of Arizona, Tucson. September 1978. Mohave Museum of History and Arts, Kingman.

Census of City of Kingman. "Basic Counts of Population and Housing, Mohave County, Arizona." 6 June 1995. Mohave County Community College, Kingman Branch.

Chevreaut, J. Howard. "Report Survey of the Hualapai Indian Tribe Preparatory to the Revision of the Curriculum of Instruction for the Hualapai Reservation Elementary Day Schools." Truxton Canyon Agency, 1941.

"Community Action Program of the Hualapai Tribe and the Community of Peach Springs, Arizona." Prepared by the Standing Committee for Community Action, 10 January 1965. Hualapai Department of Cultural Resources, Peach Springs.

Dajevskis, Peter. "Tribal Management Procedures of the Hualapai Reservation." University of Arizona and the Bureau of Ethnic Research, Tucson. May 1974.

Dobyns, Henry F. "Pine Springs Band Hualapai Habitat." Report Submitted to Marks and Marks, Phoenix, Arizona, 1 August 1956. Box 31-A. Mohave Museum of History and Arts, Kingman.

———. "The Walapai Country. Section 3. The Truxton Canyon Band." Report Submitted to Marks and Marks, Phoenix, Arizona, 9 August 1954. Box 31-A. Mohave Museum of History and Arts, Kingman.

———. "The Walapai Country. Section 8. The Burro Creek Band." Report Submitted to Marks and Marks, Phoenix, Arizona, 20 May 1954. Box 31-A. Mohave Museum of History and Arts, Kingman.

———. "The Walapai Country. Section 9. The Big Sandy Band." Report Submitted to Marks and Marks, Phoenix, Arizona, 24 May 1954. Box 31-A. Mohave Museum of History and Arts, Kingman.

———. "The Walapai Country. Section 10. The Whala Pa'a Band." Report Submitted to Marks and Marks, Phoenix, Arizona, 12 August 1955. Box 31-A. Mohave Museum of History and Arts, Kingman.

———. "The Walapai Country. Section 11. The Cerbat Mountain Band." Report Submitted to Marks and Marks, Phoenix, Arizona, 6 August 1955. Box 31-A. Mohave Museum of History and Arts, Kingman.

Dobyns, Henry F., and Robert Euler. "Aboriginal Socio-political Structure and the Ethnic Group Conflict of the Pai of Northwestern Arizona." 1960. Box 31-A. Mohave Museum of History and Arts, Kingman.

Haneman, W. M. "The Central Arizona Project." Working Paper no. 937. Department of Agricultural and Resource Economics and Policy, Division of Agricultural and Natural Resources, University of California at Berkeley, 2002.

Hualapai River Runners. "Adventure River Rafting." Peach Springs, Arizona. Brochure. November 1994. Box 31-A. Mohave Museum of History and Arts, Kingman.

Kipp, Henry W. "Indians in Agriculture: An Historical Sketch." Prepared for the Task Force of the American Indian Agricultural Council, U.S. Department of the Interior, Bureau of Indian Affairs. Washington, D.C.: Government Printing Office, 1989. Special Collections, Arizona State University, Tempe.

Muller, Sister Carol Ann. "A Study of the Carl T. Hayden Papers as They Reflect Indian Legislation of the 20th Century with Emphasis on the Hualapai Indians." Paper submitted to Dr. James Kearney, Arizona State University, 4 December 1972. Special Collections, Arizona State University, Tempe.

"Overall Economic Development Plan." Hualapai Redevelopment Area. Joint Project of the Bureau of Indian Affairs and the Hualapai Tribal Council. Peach Springs, Arizona, 1962.

Parker, Rupert. Chairman of the Hualapai Tribe. "Statement Concerning the Proposed Central Arizona and Colorado River Basin Projects before the Subcommittee on Water and Power Resources of the Senate Committee on Interior and Insular Affairs." 2 May 1967. Box 31-A. Mohave Museum of History and Arts, Kingman.

Shepherd, Jeffrey P. Ethnographic Report. On file at the Hualapai Department of Cultural Resources, Peach Springs, Arizona.

Sierra Club. Letter from Jeffrey Ingram, Southwest Representative, to Rupert Parker, Acting Hualapai Tribal Chairman. 10 March 1967. Albuquerque, New Mexico. Box 31-A. Mohave Museum of History and Arts, Kingman.

Udall, Stuart. Secretary of the Interior. Letter to George Rocha, Hualapai Tribal Chairman. 14 July 1966. Box 31-A. Mohave Museum of History and Arts, Kingman.

Woods, Charles H. *The United States of America, as Guardian of the Indians of the Tribe of Hualapai in the State of Arizona, plaintiff, v. Santa Fe Pacific Railroad*

*Company, a corporation, defendant.* Suit to quiet title and for accounting. Prescott Courier, Charles H. Woods, Joyce Cox, et al., 1938.

Zimmerman, William, Jr. "Establish Aboriginal Rights of Walapai Indians." Office of Indian Affairs. 15 March 1947. Museum of Northern Arizona, Kathleen Bartlett Reading Room, Flagstaff.

## Theses and Dissertations

Bateman, Paul. "Culture Change and Revival in Pai Basketry." Master's thesis, Northern Arizona University, Flagstaff, 1972.

Christy, Mary Rose. "American Urban Indians: A Political Enigma. A Case Study: The Relationship Between Urban Indians and Phoenix City Government." Master's thesis, Arizona State University, 1979.

Coult, Alan D. "Conflict and Stability in a Hualapai Community." Ph.D. diss., University of California at Berkeley, 1961.

Drake, Gordon. "A History of the Hualapai Indians and a Study of the Acculturation of Hualapai Indian Students Formerly Attending Indian Schools on the Reservation, and in the Public Schools of Seligman, Arizona, after a Trial Period of Three Years." Master's thesis, Arizona State College, Flagstaff, 1955. Special Collections, Cline Library, Northern Arizona University, Flagstaff.

Euler, Robert C. "Walapai Culture History." Ph.D. diss., University of New Mexico, 1958.

Hoikkala, Paivi Helena. "Native American Women and Community Work in Phoenix, 1965–1980." Ph.D. diss., Arizona State University, 1995.

Housley, Harold. "Route 66." Master's thesis, Arizona State University, 1996.

Liebow, Edward B. "A Sense of Place: Urban Indians and the History of Pan-Tribal Institutions in Phoenix, Arizona." Ph.D. diss., Arizona State University, 1984.

Manuel-Dupont, Sonia. "Analysis of English Language Usage of Hualapai Children in an Academic Setting." Ph.D. diss., University of Kansas, 1986.

Quintana, Penny Ann. "The Early Years of the Albuquerque Indian School, 1879–1928." Master's thesis, Arizona State University, 1992.

Vicenti Carpio, Myla. "Let Them Know We Still Exist: Indians in Albuquerque." Ph.D. diss., Arizona State University, 2001.

Warren, Stephen Andrew. "Shawnee Political Culture in the Reservation Era." Master's thesis, Arizona State University, 1994.

Weil-Moore, Tina. "From Reorganization to Relocation: Arizona Indians and World War Two." Master's thesis, Arizona State University, 1995.

## Federal Government Documents

*An Act to Provide for Exchange of Government and Privately Owned Lands in the Walapai Indian Reservation, Arizona. Statutes at Large* 43 (1923).

Hualapai Indian Reservation. 1969–1973. General Correspondence. Governor Williams. Arizona Indian Files. 1969–1973. Accession AA-74-9. Box 726.

From Hualapai Tribal Association, signed by Fred Mahone, July 28, 1934. Letter from Mahone to S. M. Brosius, Representative from the Indian Rights Association. Washington, D.C. September 30, 1933. Box 5A. G2 1-1.

*Indians and Arizona's Future: Opportunities, Issues, and Options.* Thirty-fourth Annual Town Hall. April 8–11, 1979. Arizona Academy, Sponsor of Arizona Town Hall. Tucson: University of Arizona, 1979.

Indian Claims Commission. *Examiner's Report on the Tribal Claim of Related Railroad Lands in Northwest Arizona* (together with transcript of final hearing and exhibits). Docket no. 91, exhibit no. 8. 1982.

————. *The Hualapai Tribe of the Hualapai Reservation, Arizona, Petitioner v. The United States of America, Defendant.* Docket no. 90. Decided: November 19, 1962. 11 Indian Claims Commission 447. Box 31-A. Mohave Museum of History and Arts, Kingman.

————. *The Hualapai Tribe of the Hualapai Reservation, Arizona, Petitioner v. The United States of America, Defendant.* Docket no. 122. Deposition of William F. Grounds. Kingman, Arizona, 21 July 1967. Box 31-A. Mohave Museum of History and Arts, Kingman.

Ives, Lt. Joseph C. *Report: Colorado River of the West Explored, 1857 and 1858.* Under the Direction of the Office of Explorations and Surveys. A. A. Humphreys, Topographical Engineer in Charge, by Order of the Secretary of War. Washington, D.C.: Government Printing Office, 1861.

Letter from Henry Ewing, Hualapai Indian Agency. U.S. Department of the Interior. Re: Census of Hualapai and Havasupai Indians. June 27, 1998. Governor McCord, 1898. In Governors Hughes, McCord, Kibbey, Sloan, and Hunt. 1895–1932. Box 1.

U.S. Bureau of the Census. *Fourteenth Census of the United States Taken in the Year 1920.* Vol. 3, *Population. Composition and Characteristics of the Population by States.* Sam L. Rogers, Director. Washington, D.C.: Government Printing Office, 1922.

————. *Special Reports. Occupations.* Twelfth Census, 1900. S.N.D. North, Director. Washington, D.C.: Government Printing Office, 1904. Special Collections, Arizona State University, Tempe.

————. Special Reports. *Supplementary Analysis and Derivative Tables.* S.N.D. North, Director. Washington, D.C.: Government Printing Office, 1906. Special Collections, Arizona State University, Tempe.

U.S. Congress. Senate. *Walapai Papers: Historical Reports, Documents, and Extracts from Publications Relating to the Walapai Indians of Arizona.* 74th Cong., 2nd sess. Document no. 273. Washington, D.C.: Government Printing Office, 1936.

U.S. Congress. Senate. Committee on Indian Affairs. Subcommittee. *Survey of Conditions of the Indians of the United States.* 70th Cong., 2nd sess. Washington, D.C.: Government Printing Office, 1929. Special Collections, Arizona State University, Tempe.

————. *Survey of Conditions of the Indians of the United States.* 71st Cong., 3rd sess. Washington, D.C.: Government Printing Office, 1931. Special Collections, Arizona State University, Tempe.

U.S. Department of the Interior. *Annual Report of the Commissioner of Indian Affairs to the Secretary of the Interior. For the fiscal year ended 30 June 1929.* Washington, D.C.: Government Printing Office, 1929.

————. *Annual Report of the Commissioner of Indian Affairs to the Secretary of the Interior. For the fiscal year ended 30 June 1932.* Washington, D.C.: Government Printing Office, 1932.

————. *Fifty-ninth Annual Report of Board of Indian Commissioners to the Secretary of the Interior for the Fiscal Year 30 June 1928.* Washington, D.C.: Government Printing Office, 1928.

————. *Forty-seventh Annual Report of the Board of Indian Commissioners to the Secretary of the Interior. For the fiscal year ended 30 June 1916.* Washington, D.C.: Government Printing Office, 1916.

————. *Report of the Commissioner of Indian Affairs to the Secretary of the Interior.* Washington, D.C.: Government Printing Office, 1925.

————. *Statistical Supplement to the Annual Report of the Commissioner of Indian Affairs. For the fiscal year ended June 30, 1939.* Washington, D.C.: Government Printing Office, 1939. Special Collections, Arizona State University, Tempe.

U.S. Department of the Interior. Bureau of Indian Affairs. *Amended Constitution and Bylaws of the Hualapai Tribe of Hualapai Reservation, Arizona, Effective October 22, 1955.* Washington, D.C.: Government Printing Office, 1957. Microfiche 621 I 1228. University of Arizona Library, Tucson.

————. *Amended Corporate Charter of the Hualapai Tribe of the Hualapai Reservation, Arizona, 1955.* Washington, D.C.: Government Printing Office, 1955. University of Arizona Library, Tucson.

———. *Constitution and Bylaws of the Hualapai Tribe of the Hualapai Reservation, Arizona. Approved 17 December 1938.* Washington, D.C.: Government Printing Office, 1939. Microfiche 621 I 1251. University of Arizona Library, Tucson.

———. *Corporate Charter of the Hualapai Tribe of the Hualapai Reservation, Arizona.* Ratified 5 June 1943. Washington, D.C.: Government Printing Office, 1943. Microfiche 621 I 1254. University of Arizona Library, Tucson.

———. *Indians in the War.* Fact Sheet. Truxton Canyon Agency, Valentine, Arizona. Chicago: Office of Indian Affairs, 1945.

U.S. Department of the Interior. Census Office. *Report on Indians Taxed and Indians Not Taxed in the United States.* Eleventh Census. House of Representatives, 52nd Cong., 1st sess. Miscellaneous Codes no. 310, pt. 15. Robert Porter, Superintendent. Washington, D.C.: Government Printing Office, 1894. Special Collections, Arizona State University, Tempe.

## Secondary Sources

Adams, David Wallace. *Education for Extinction: American Indians and the Boarding School Experience, 1875–1928.* Lawrence: University Press of Kansas, 1997.

Alfred, Taiaiake. *Peace, Power, Righteousness: An Indigenous Manifesto.* Oxford: Oxford University Press, 1999.

Alfred, Taiaiake, and Jeff Corntassel. "Being Indigenous: Resurgences against Contemporary Colonialism." *Government and Opposition,* September 2005, 597–614.

Allen, John. *Lost Geographies of Power.* New York: Wiley-Blackwell, 2003.

Ambler, Marjane. *Breaking the Iron Bonds: Indian Control of Energy Development.* Lawrence: University Press of Kansas, 1990.

Anderson, Benedict. *Imagined Communities: Reflections on the Origin and Spread of Nationalism.* New York: Verso, 1983.

Anderson, Gary Clayton. *The Indian Southwest, 1580–1830: Ethnogenesis and Reinvention.* Norman: University of Oklahoma Press, 1999.

August, Jack. *Vision in the Desert: Carl Hayden and Hydropolitics in the American Southwest.* Fort Worth: Texas Christian University Press, 1999.

Badger, Anthony. *The New Deal: The Depression Years, 1933–40.* New York: Hill and Wang, 1989.

Basso, Keith. *Wisdom Sits in Places: Landscape and Language among the Western Apache.* Albuquerque: University of New Mexico Press, 1996.

Bataille, Gretchen M., and Kathleen Mullen Sands. *American Indian Women: Telling Their Lives.* Lincoln: University of Nebraska Press, 1987.

Bauer, William. "Working for Identity: Race, Ethnicity, and the Market Economy in Northern California, 1875–1936." In Hosmer and O'Neill, *Native Pathways*, 206–38.

Bender, Thomas. *A Nation among Nations: America's Place in World History*. New York: Hill and Wang, 2006.

Berkhofer, Robert. *The White Man's Indian*. New York: Vintage Books, 1978.

Berman, Teresa. "'All We Needed Was Our Gardens': Women's Work and Welfare Reform in the Reservation Economy." In Hosmer and O'Neill, *Native Pathways*, 133–55.

Bernstein, Allison. *The American Indian in World War Two*. Norman: University of Oklahoma Press, 1988.

Bieder, Robert. *Science Encounters the Indian, 1820–1880: The Early Years of American Ethnology*. Norman: University of Oklahoma Press, 1986.

Biolsi, Thomas. "Imagined Geographies: Sovereignty, Indigenous Space, and American Indian Struggle." *American Ethnologist* 32, no. 2 (2005): 239–59.

———. "'Indian Self-Government' as a Technique of Domination." *American Indian Quarterly* 15, no. 1 (1991): 23–28.

———. *Indians and Anthropologists: Vine Deloria, Jr., and the Critique of Anthropology*. Tucson: University of Arizona Press, 1997.

———. *Organizing the Lakota: The Political Economy of the New Deal on the Pine Ridge and Rosebud Reservations*. Tucson: University of Arizona Press, 1998.

Blackhawk, Ned. *Violence over the Land: Indians and Empires in the Early American West*. Cambridge, Mass.: Harvard University Press, 2006.

Bonvillain, Nancy. *Native Nations: Cultures and Histories of Native North America*. Upper Saddle River, N.J.: Prentice Hall, 2001.

Boxberger, Daniel. *To Fish in Common: An Ethnohistory of Lummi Indian Salmon Fishing*. Lincoln: University of Nebraska Press, 1989.

Braatz, Timothy. *Surviving Conquest: A History of the Yavapai Peoples*. Lincoln: University of Nebraska Press, 2002.

Bravo, Mario. *A View from the Hualapai Tribe: Common Threads and Shared Interests*. Fort Collins, Colo.: Rocky Mountain Forest and Range Experiment Station, 1993.

Britten, Thomas A. *American Indians in World War One: At War and at Home*. Albuquerque: University of New Mexico Press, 1997.

Brooks, James. *Captives and Cousins: Slavery, Kinship, and Community in the Southwest Borderlands*. Chapel Hill: University of North Carolina Press, 2003.

Brown, Jennifer S. *Strangers in Blood: Fur Trade Company Families in Indian Country*. Norman: University of Oklahoma Press, 1996.

Bruyneel, Kevin. *The Third Space of Sovereignty: The Postcolonial Politics of U.S.–Indigenous Relations*. Minneapolis: University of Minnesota Press, 2007.

Bryant, Kenneth L., Jr. *History of the Atchison, Topeka, and Santa Fe Railway*. New York: Macmillan Publishing, 1974.

Burton, Lloyd. *American Indian Water Rights and the Limits of Law*. Lawrence: University Press of Kansas, 1991.

Calloway, Colin, ed. *New Directions in American Indian History*. Norman: University of Oklahoma Press, 1988.

—————. *One Vast Winter Count: The Native West before Lewis and Clark*. Lincoln: University of Nebraska Press, 2006.

Campbell, Gregory R. "The Lemhi Shoshoni: Ethnogenesis, Sociological Transformations, and the Construction of a Tribal Nation." *American Indian Quarterly* 25, no. 4 (2001): 539–78.

Carlson, Leonard. *Indians, Bureaucrats, and the Land: The Dawes Act and the Decline of Indian Farming*. Westport, Conn.: Greenwood Press, 1981.

Carson, James Taylor. "Ethnogeography and the Native American Past." *Ethnohistory* 49, no. 4 (2002): 769–88.

Casebier, Dennis G. *Camp Beale's Springs and the Hualapai Indians*. Essex, Calif.: Tales of the Mohave Road Publishing Company, 1980.

Castile, George Pierre. *To Show Heart: Native American Self-Determination and Federal Indian Policy, 1960–1975*. Tucson: University of Arizona Press, 1998.

Castillo, Edward D. "Mission Indian Federation." In *Native America in the Twentieth Century: An Encyclopedia*, ed. Mary B. Davis, 345–48. New York: Garland Publishing, 1996.

—————. "Twentieth Century Secular Movements." In *California*, ed. Robert F. Heizer, 713–17. Vol. 8, *Handbook of North American Indians*. Washington, D.C.: Smithsonian Institution Press, 1978.

Chakrabarty, Dipesh. "Radical Histories and the Question of Enlightened Rationalism: Some Recent Critiques of 'Subaltern Studies.'" *Economic and Political Weekly*, 8 April 1995, 751–59.

Chatterjee, Partha. *The Nation and Its Fragments: Colonial and Postcolonial Histories*. Princeton, N.J.: Princeton University Press, 1993.

Cherniavsky, Eva. "Subaltern Studies in a U.S. Frame." *boundary 2* 23, no. 2 (1996): 85–110.

Child, Brenda. *Boarding School Seasons: American Indian Families, 1900–1940*. Lincoln: University of Nebraska Press, 1998.

Clark, Blue. "Bury My Heart in Smog: Urban Indians." In *The American Indian Experience, a Profile: 1524 to the Present*, ed. Philip Weeks, 278–91. Arlington Heights, Ill.: Forum Press, 1988.

Clarkin, Thomas. *Federal Indian Policy in the Kennedy and Johnson Administrations, 1961–1969*. Albuquerque: University of New Mexico Press, 2001.

Clemmer, Richard O. *Roads in the Sky: The Hopi Indians in a Century of Change.* Boulder, Colo.: Westview Press, 1995.

Cohen, Michael P. *The History of the Sierra Club, 1892–1970.* San Francisco: Sierra Club Books, 1988.

Collins, William S. *The New Deal in Arizona.* Phoenix: Arizona State Parks Board, 1999.

Connell Szasz, Margaret, ed. *Between Indian and White Worlds: The Cultural Broker.* Norman: University of Oklahoma Press, 1994.

———. *Education and the American Indian: The Road to Self-Determination since 1928.* Albuquerque: University of New Mexico Press, 1999.

Cook-Lynn, Elizabeth. *Anti-Indianism in Modern America: A Voice from Tatekeya's Earth.* Champaign: University of Illinois Press, 2007.

Cornell, Stephen. *The Return of the Native: American Indian Political Resurgence.* New York: Oxford University Press, 1988.

Cowger, Thomas W. *The National Congress of American Indians: The Founding Years.* Lincoln: University of Nebraska Press, 1999.

Cronon, William. *Nature's Metropolis: Chicago and the Great West.* New York: W. W. Norton, 1992.

Cronon, William, George Miles, and Jay Gitlin, eds. *Under an Open Sky: Rethinking America's Western Past.* New York: W. W. Norton, 1992.

Crosby, Alfred. *Ecological Imperialism: The Biological Expansion of Europe, 900–1900.* Cambridge: Cambridge University Press, 1986.

Cruikshank, Julie. *The Social Life of Stories: Narrative and Knowledge in the Yukon Territory.* Lincoln: University of Nebraska Press, 1998.

Crum, Steven J. *Po'I Pentum Tammen Kimmappeh: The Road on Which We Came. A History of the Western Shoshone.* Salt Lake City: University of Utah Press, 1994.

Cushing, Frank Hamilton. *The Nation of the Willows.* Reprint of *Atlantic Monthly,* 1882. Flagstaff: Northland Press, 1965.

Dale, Edward Everett. *The Indians of the Southwest: A Century of Development under the United States.* 4th ed. Norman: University of Oklahoma Press, 1976.

Dalleck, Robert. *Flawed Giant: Lyndon Johnson and His Times, 1936–1971.* New York: Oxford University Press, 1988.

Deloria, Philip J. "Historiography." In *A Companion to American Indian History,* ed. Philip J. Deloria and Neal Salisbury. Malden, Mass.: Blackwell Publishers, 2002.

———. *Playing Indian.* New Haven, Conn.: Yale University Press, 1999.

Deloria, Philip J., and Neal Salisbury, eds. *A Companion to American Indian History.* Malden, Mass.: Blackwell Publishers, 2002.

Deloria, Vine, Jr. *Behind the Trail of Broken Treaties: An Indian Declaration of Independence.* Austin: University of Texas Press, 1974.

―――. *American Indian Policy in the Twentieth Century*. Norman: University of Oklahoma Press, 1985.

―――. *Red Earth, White Lies: Native Americans and the Myth of Scientific Fact*. New York: Scribner's, 1995.

―――. *Spirit and Reason: The Vine Deloria, Jr., Reader*. Golden, Colo.: Fulcrum Publishing, 1999.

Deloria, Vine, Jr., and Clifford Lytle. *American Indians, American Justice*. Austin: University of Texas Press, 1983.

―――. *The Nations Within: The Past and Present of American Indian Sovereignty*. New York: Pantheon Books, 1984.

Denetdale, Jennifer Nez. *Reclaiming Dine' History: The Legacies of Navajo Chief Manuelito and Juanita*. Tucson: University of Arizona Press, 2007.

Dilworth, Leah. *Imagining Indians in the Southwest: Persistent Visions of a Primitive Past*. Washington, D.C.: Smithsonian Institution Press, 1996.

Dobyns, Henry F., and Robert C. Euler. *The Ghost Dance of 1889: The Pai Indians of Northwestern Arizona*. Prescott, Ariz.: Prescott College Press, 1967.

―――. "The Nine Lives of Schrum: The Pai Tokumhet." *American Indian Quarterly* 22, no. 3 (1998): 363–85.

―――. *The Walapai People*. Phoenix: Indian Tribal Series, 1976.

―――. *Wauba Yuma's People: The Comparative Socio-political Structure of the Pai Indians of Arizona*. Prescott, Ariz.: Prescott College Press, 1970.

DuMars, Charles, ed. *Pueblo Indian Water Rights: Struggle for a Precious Resource*. Tucson: University of Arizona Press, 1984.

Dunlay, Thomas. *Wolves for the Blue Soldiers: Indian Scouts and Auxiliaries with the United States Army, 1860–1890*. Lincoln: University of Nebraska Press, 1987.

Edmunds, R. David. "Native Americans, New Voices: American Indian History, 1895–1995." *American Historical Review*, June 1995, 717–40.

―――. *The New Warriors: Native American Leaders since 1900*. Lincoln: University of Nebraska Press, 2001.

Eley, Geoff, and Ronald Grigor Suny, eds. *Becoming National: A Reader*. New York: Oxford University Press, 1996.

Euler, Robert C. "Ethnic Group Land Rights in the Modern State: Three Case Studies." *Human Organization* 20, no. 4 (1961–62): 203–7.

Fanon, Frantz. *Wretched of the Earth*. 1963; New York: Grove Press, 2005.

Fay, George E. "Amended Corporate Charter of the Hualapai Tribe of the Hualapai Reservation, Arizona." In *Charters, Constitutions, and Bylaws of the Indian Tribes of North America. Part III: The Southwest (Apache-Mohave)*. Occasional Publications in Anthropology Ethnology Series 4. Greeley, Colo.: Museum of Anthropology, October 1967, 85–99.

Feld, Steven, and Keith Basso, eds. *Senses of Place.* Santa Fe: School of American Research Press, 1998.

Fisher, Andrew H. "They Mean to Be Indian Always: The Origins of Columbia River Indian Identity, 1860–1885." *Western Historical Quarterly* 32, no. 4 (2001): 468–92.

Fixico, Donald L. *The Invasion of Indian Country in the Twentieth Century: American Capitalism and Tribal Natural Resources.* Boulder: University Press of Colorado, 1998.

———, ed. *Rethinking Indian History.* Albuquerque: University of New Mexico Press, 1997.

———. *Termination and Relocation: Federal Indian Policy, 1945–1960.* Albuquerque: University of New Mexico Press, 1986.

———. *The Urban Indian Experience in America.* Albuquerque: University of New Mexico Press, 2000.

Forbes, Jack. "The Use of Racial and Ethnic Terms in America: Management by Manipulation." *Wicazo Sa Review* 11, no. 2 (1995): 53–65.

Foster, Morris. *Being Comanche: A Social History of an American Indian Community.* Tucson: University of Arizona Press, 1991.

Fowler, Loretta. *Arapahoe Politics, 1851–1978: Symbols in Crises of Authority.* Lincoln: University of Nebraska Press, 1982.

———. *Shared Symbols, Contested Meanings: Gros Ventre Culture and History, 1778–1984.* Ithaca, N.Y.: Cornell University Press, 1987.

———. *Tribal Sovereignty and the Historical Imagination: Cheyenne-Arapaho Politics.* Lincoln: University of Nebraska Press, 2002.

Fradkin, Philip L. *A River No More: The Colorado River and the West.* Berkeley: University of California Press, 1996.

Frazier, John, Florence M. Margai, and Eugene Tettey-Fio, eds. *Race and Place: Equity Issues in Urban America.* Boulder, Colo.: Westview Press, 2003.

French, Laurence. *Addictions and Native Americans.* Westport, Conn.: Praeger, 2000.

Garcés, Francisco Tomás. *On the Trail of a Spanish Pioneer: The Diary and Itinerary of Francisco Garcés in His Travels through Sonora, Arizona and California, 1775–1776.* Trans. Elliot Coues. New York: Harper, 1900.

Garroutte, Eva Marie. *Real Indians: Identity and the Survival of Native America.* Berkeley: University of California Press, 2003.

Goetzmann, William H. *Exploration and Empire: The Explorer and the Scientist in the Winning of the American West.* New York: Alfred A. Knopf, 1966.

Goldberg-Ambrose, Carole. *Planting Tail Feathers: Tribal Survival and Public Law 280.* Los Angeles: American Indian Studies Center, University of California, 1997.

Gooding, Susan Staiger. "Place, Race and Names: Layered Identities in *United States v. Oregon, Confederated Tribes of the Colvile Reservation*, Plaintiff-Intervener." *Law and Society Review* 28, no. 5 (1994): 1181–1230.

Griffin-Pierce, Trudy. *Native Peoples of the Southwest*. Albuquerque: University of New Mexico Press, 2000.

Hall, Stuart. "The West and the Rest: Discourse and Power." In *Formations of Modernity*, ed. Stuart Hall and B. Gielben, 275–332. Cambridge: Polity Press and Open University, 1992.

Hall, Thomas D. *Social Change in the Southwest, 1350–1880*. Lawrence: University Press of Kansas, 1989.

Hamer, John, and Jack Steinbring, eds. *Alcohol and Native Peoples of the North*. Washington, D.C.: University Press of America, 1980.

Harmon, Alexandra. *Indians in the Making: Ethnic Relations and Indian Identities around Puget Sound*. Berkeley: University of California Press, 1998.

Harring, Sidney. *Crow Dog's Case: American Indian Sovereignty, Tribal Law, and United States Law in the Nineteenth Century*. New York: Cambridge University Press, 1994.

Harris, Cole. *Making Native Space: Colonialism, Resistance and Reserves in British Columbia*. Victoria: University of British Columbia Press, 2003.

Harris, R. J., ed. *A Question of Place: Exploring the Practice of Human Geography*. Oxford: Blackwell, 1991.

Hawley, Ellis. *The Great War and the Search for a Modern Order: A History of the American People and Their Institutions, 1917–1933*. Longrove, Ill.: Waveland Press, 1997.

Hays, Samuel. *Conservation and the Gospel of Efficiency: The Progressive Conservation Movement, 1890–1920*. Cambridge, Mass.: Harvard University Press, 1959.

Hertzberg, Hazel. *The Search for an American Indian Identity: Modern Pan-Indian Movements*. Syracuse, N.Y.: Syracuse University Press, 1971.

Hine, Robert V., and John Mack Faragher. *The American West: A New Interpretive History*. New Haven, Conn.: Yale University Press, 2000.

Hinsley, Curtis, ed. *The Southwest in the American Imagination*. Tucson: University of Arizona Press, 1996.

Hinton, Leanne, and Lucille Watahomigie, eds. *Spirit Mountain: An Anthology of Yuman Story and Song*. Tucson: University of Arizona Press, 1984.

Hirst, Stephen. *Havsuw 'Baaja: People of the Blue Green Water*. Tempe: Walsh and Associates, 1985.

———. *I Am the Grand Canyon: The Story of the Havasupai People*. Grand Canyon, Ariz.: Grand Canyon Association, 2007.

Hobsbawm, Eric J. *Nations and Nationalism since 1780: Programme, Myth, Reality*. Cambridge: Cambridge University Press, 1997.

Holm, Tom, J. Diane Pearson, and Ben Chavis. "Peoplehood: A Model for the Extension of Sovereignty in American Indian Studies." *Wicazo Sa Review* 18, no. 1 (2003): 7–24.

Holt, Ronald L. *Beneath These Red Cliffs: An Ethnohistory of the Utah Paiutes.* Albuquerque: University of New Mexico Press, 1992.

Horsman, Reginald. *Race and Manifest Destiny: Origins of American Anglo-Saxonism.* Cambridge, Mass.: Harvard University Press, 1981.

Hosmer, Brian. *American Indians in the Marketplace: Persistence and Innovation among the Menominees and Metlakatlans, 1870–1920.* Lawrence: University Press of Kansas, 1999.

Hosmer, Brian, and Colleen O'Neill, eds. *Native Pathways: American Indian Culture and Economic Development in the Twentieth Century.* Boulder: University of Colorado Press, 2004.

Hoxie, Frederick J. *A Final Promise: The Campaign to Assimilate the Indians, 1880–1920.* Lincoln: University of Nebraska Press, 1984.

———. *Parading through History: The Making of the Crow Nation in America, 1805–1935.* New York: Cambridge University Press, 1995.

Hoxie, Frederick, and Peter Iverson, eds. *Indians in American History.* Wheeling, Ill.: Harlan Davidson, 1998.

Hundley, Norris. *Water and the West: The Colorado River Compact and the Politics of Water in the American West.* Berkeley: University of California Press, 1975.

Hurtado, Albert. *Indian Survival on the California Frontier.* New Haven, Conn.: Yale University Press, 1988.

Iliff, Flora Greg. *People of the Blue Water: A Record of Life among the Walapai and Havasupai Indians.* Tucson: University of Arizona Press, 1954.

Iverson, Peter. "Building toward Self-Determination: Plains and Southwestern Indians in the 1940s and 1950s." *Western Historical Quarterly* 16, no. 2 (1985): 163–73.

———. *Carlos Montezuma and the Changing World of American Indians.* Albuquerque: University of New Mexico Press, 1982.

———. *Dine: A History of the Navajo Peoples.* Albuquerque: University of New Mexico Press, 2004.

———. *The Navajo Nation.* Albuquerque: University of New Mexico Press, 1983.

———, ed. *The Plains Indians in the Twentieth Century.* Norman: University of Oklahoma Press, 1985.

———. *"We Are Still Here": American Indians in the Twentieth Century.* Wheeling: Harlan Davidson, 1998.

———. *When Indians Became Cowboys: Native Peoples and Cattle Ranching in the American West.* Norman: University of Oklahoma Press, 1994.

Jacobs, Margaret. *Engendered Encounters: Feminism and Pueblo Cultures, 1879–1934*. Lincoln: University of Nebraska Press, 1999.

Jacobson, Mathew Frye. *Barbarian Virtues: The United States Encounters Foreign Peoples at Home and Abroad, 1876–1917*. New York: Hill and Wang, 2002.

Jaimes, M. Annette. "The Hollow Icon: An American Indian Analysis of the Kennedy Myth and Federal Indian Policy." *Wicazo Sa Review* 6, no. 1 (1990): 34–44.

James, George W. *In and around the Grand Canyon*. Boston: Little, Brown and Co., 1900.

Jett, Stephen C. "The Navajo Homeland." In *Homelands: A Geography of Culture and Place across America*, ed. Richard Nostrand and Lawrence Estaville, 168–83. Baltimore, Md.: Johns Hopkins University Press, 2001.

Johnson, Rich. *The Central Arizona Project 1918–1968*. Tucson: University of Arizona Press, 1977.

Johnson, Troy. *The Occupation of Alcatraz Island: Indian Self-Determination and the Rise of Indian Activism*. Urbana: University of Illinois Press, 1996.

Johnston, R. J. *A Question of Place: Exploring the Practice of Human Geography*. Oxford: Blackwell, 1991.

Kaplan, Amy. *The Anarchy of Empire in the Making of U.S. Culture*. Cambridge, Mass.: Harvard University Press, 2005.

Keller, Robert, and Michael F. Turek. *American Indians and National Parks*. Tucson: University of Arizona Press, 1998.

Kelley, William H. *Indians: A Survey of Indian Administration in Arizona*. Bureau of Ethnic Research Annual Report 1. Tucson: University of Arizona, 1953.

Kennedy, David. *Over Here: The First World War and American Society*. Oxford: Oxford University Press, 2004.

Klein, Laura F., and Lillian A. Ackerman, eds. *Women and Power in Native North America*. Norman: University of Oklahoma Press, 2000.

Knack, Martha C. *Boundaries Between: The Southern Paiutes, 1775–1995*. Lincoln: University of Nebraska Press, 2001.

Knack, Martha, and Alice Littlefield, eds. *Native Americans and Wage Labor: Ethnohistorical Perspectives*. Norman: University of Oklahoma Press, 1996.

Knight, Rolf. *Indians at Work: An Informal History of Native Indian Labour in British Columbia, 1858–1930*. Vancouver: New Star Books, 1977.

Kramer, Lloyd. "Historical Narratives and the Meaning of Nationalism." *Journal of the History of Ideas* 58, no. 3 (1997): 525–35.

Kroeber, A. L., ed. *Walapai Ethnography*. Memoirs of the American Anthropological Association 42. 1935; Millwood, N.Y.: Kraus Reprint Company, 1976.

LaGrande, James. "Whose Voices Count? Oral Sources and Twentieth-Century American Indian History." *American Indian Culture and Research Journal* 21, no. 1 (1997): 73–105.

Lawson, Michael L. *Dammed Indians: The Pick-Sloan Plan and the Missouri River Sioux, 1944–1980.* Norman: University of Oklahoma Press, 1944.

Lemont, Eric C., ed. *American Indian Constitutional Reform and the Rebuilding of Native Nations.* Austin: University of Texas Press, 2006.

Levin, Michael D. *Ethnicity and Aboriginality: Case Studies in Ethnonationalism.* Toronto: University of Toronto Press, 1993.

Lewis, David Rich. *Neither Wolf nor Dog: American Indians, Environment, and Agrarian Change.* New York: Oxford University Press, 1994.

———. "Reservation Leadership and the Progressive-Traditional Dichotomy: William Wash and the Northern Utes, 1865–1928." *Ethnohistory* 38, no. 2 (1991): 124–48.

Liebow, Edward D. "Urban Indian Institutions in Phoenix: Transformation from Headquarters City to Community." *Journal of Ethnic Studies* 18, no. 4 (1991): 1–27.

Lobo, Susan, and Kurt Peters, eds. *American Indians and the Urban Experience.* Walnut Creek, Calif.: Alta Mira Press, 2001.

Lomawaima, K. Tsianina. *They Called It Prairie Light: The Story of Chilocco Indian School.* Lincoln: University of Nebraska Press, 1995.

Lone-Knapp, Faye. "Rez Talk: How Reservation Residents Describe Themselves." *American Indian Quarterly* 24, no. 4 (2000): 635–40.

Luechtenberg, William E. *Franklin D. Roosevelt and the New Deal, 1932–1940.* New York: Harper and Row, 1963.

Malach, Roman. *Mohave County: Sketches of Early Days.* New York: Graphicopy, 1974.

———. *Peach Springs in Mohave County.* Phoenix: Arizona Bicentennial Commission, 1976.

———. *Reflections: 100 Years of Truxton Country.* Tucson: Sunrise Graphics, 1988.

Mancall, Peter C. *Deadly Medicine: Indians and Alcohol in Early America.* Ithaca, N.Y.: Cornell University Press, 1995.

Manners, Robert A. *An Ethnohistorical Report on the Hualapai Indians of Arizona.* American Indian Ethnohistory: Indians of the Southwest. New York: Garland Publishing, 1974.

———. *Hualapai Indians II: An Ethnological Report on the Hualapai (Walapai) Indians of Arizona. Commission Findings,* comp. and ed. David Agee Horr. American Indian Ethnohistory: Indians of the Southwest. New York: Garland Publishing, 1974.

————. "Tribe and Tribal Boundaries: The Walapai." *Ethnohistory* 4 (Winter 1957): 1–26.

Martin, John. "The Prehistory and Ethnohistory of Havasupai-Hualapai Boundaries." *Ethnohistory* 32, no. 2 (1985): 135–53.

Mason, W. Dale. *Indian Gaming: Tribal Sovereignty and American Politics.* Norman: University of Oklahoma Press, 2000.

McClellan, E. Fletcher. "Implementation and Policy Reformulation of Title I of the Indian Self-Determination and Education Assistance Act of 1975–1980." *Wicazo Sa Review* 6, no. 1 (1990): 45–55.

McDonnell, Janet. *The Dispossession of the American Indian, 1887–1934.* Bloomington: Indiana University Press, 1991.

McGuire, Thomas, ed. *Indian Water in the New West.* Tucson: University of Arizona Press, 1994.

————. "Walapai." In Ortiz, *Southwest,* 25–37.

McLuhan, T. C. *Dream Tracks: The Railroad and the American Indian, 1890–1930.* New York: Harry Abrams, 1985.

McMillen, Christian. *Making Indian Law: The Hualapai Land Case and the Birth of Ethnohistory.* New Haven, Conn.: Yale University Press, 2007.

Meeks, Eric V. *Border Citizens: The Making of Indians, Mexicans, and Anglos in Arizona.* Austin: University of Texas Press, 2007.

————. "The Tohono O'odham, Wage Labor, and Resistant Adaptation, 1900–1930." *Western Historical Quarterly* 34 (Winter 2003): 468–89.

Menchaca, Martha. *Recovering History, Constructing Race: The Indian, Black and White Roots of Mexican Americans.* Austin: University of Texas Press, 2001.

Merriam, Lewis, technical director. *The Problem of Indian Administration.* Institute for Government Research. Baltimore, Md.: Johns Hopkins Press, 1928.

Metcalf, Warren R. *Termination's Legacy: The Discarded Indians of Utah.* Lincoln: University of Nebraska Press, 2002.

Meyer, Melissa. *The White Earth Tragedy: Ethnicity and Dispossession at a Minnesota Anishinaabe Reservation, 1889–1920.* Lincoln: University of Nebraska Press, 1994.

Mihesuah, Devon, ed. *Natives and Academics: Researching and Writing about American Indians.* Lincoln: University of Nebraska Press, 1998.

————, ed. *Repatriation Reader: Who Owns American Indian Remains?* Lincoln: University of Nebraska Press, 2000.

Miller, Jay, Colin G. Calloway, and Richard A. Sattler, eds. *Writings in Indian History, 1985–1990.* Norman: University of Oklahoma Press, 1995.

Miller, Mark Edwin. *Forgotten Tribes: Unrecognized Indians and the Federal Acknowledgment Process.* Lincoln: University of Nebraska Press, 2006.

Miner, H. Craig. *The Corporation and the Indian: Tribal Sovereignty and Industrial Civilization in Indian Territory, 1865–1907*. Norman: University of Oklahoma Press, 1976.

Morehouse, Barbara J. *A Place Called Grand Canyon: Contested Geographies*. Tucson: University of Arizona Press, 1996.

Nagel, Joanne. *American Indian Ethnic Renewal: Red Power and the Resurgence of Identity and Culture*. New York: Oxford University Press, 1996.

Nash, Roderick. *Wilderness and the American Mind*. New Haven, Conn.: Yale University Press, 2001.

Nunpa, Mato Chris. "Dakota Commemorative March: Thoughts and Reactions." *American Indian Quarterly* 28, nos. 1–2 (2004): 216–41.

O'Neill, Colleen. *Working the Navajo Way: Labor and Culture in the Twentieth Century*. Lawrence: University Press of Kansas, 2005.

O'Neill, Theresa DeLeane. *Disciplined Hearts: History, Identity, and Depression in an American Indian Community*. Berkeley: University of California Press, 1996.

Ortiz, Alfonso, ed. *Southwest*. Vol. 10, *Handbook of North American Indians*, William Sturtevant, gen. ed. Washington, D.C.: Smithsonian Institution Press, 1983.

Osburn, Katherine M. B. *Southern Ute Women: Autonomy and Assimilation on the Reservation, 1887–1934*. Lincoln: University of Nebraska Press, 2009.

Ostler, Jeffrey. *The Plains Sioux and U.S. Colonialism from Lewis and Clark to Wounded Knee*. New York: Cambridge University Press, 2004.

Parman, Donald. "The Indian and the Civilian Conservation Corps." *Pacific Historical Review* 40 (1971): 39–56.

Patterson, James T. *America's Struggle against Poverty, 1900–1980*. Cambridge, Mass.: Harvard University Press, 2000.

Pearson, Byron E. "'We Have Almost Forgotten How to Hope': The Hualapai, the Navajo, and the Fight for the Central Arizona Project, 1944–1968." *Western Historical Quarterly* 31 (Autumn 2000): 297–316.

Perdue, Theda. *Cherokee Women: Gender and Culture Change, 1700–1835*. Lincoln: University of Nebraska Press, 1998.

Peroff, Nicolas. *Menominee DRUMS: Tribal Termination and Restoration, 1954–1974*. Norman: University of Oklahoma Press, 1982.

Perry, Richard. *Apache Reservation: Indigenous Peoples and the American State*. Austin: University of Texas Press, 1994.

Peters, Kurt. "Santa Fe Indian Camp, House 21, Richmond, California: Persistence of Identity among Laguna Pueblo Railroad Laborers, 1945–1982." *American Indian Culture and Research Journal* 19, no. 3 (1995): 33–70.

Philp, Kenneth R. *John Collier's Crusade for Indian Reform, 1920–1954*. Tucson: University of Arizona Press, 1981.

————. *Indian Self-rule: First-hand Accounts of Indian-White Relations from Roosevelt to Reagan*. Logan: Utah State University Press, 1995.

————. *Termination Revisited: American Indians on the Trail to Self-Determination, 1933–1953*. Lincoln: University of Nebraska Press, 1999.

Pisani, Donald. *Reclaim a Divided West: Water, Law, and Public Policy, 1848–1902*. Albuquerque: University of New Mexico Press, 1992.

Pommershiem, Frank. *Braid of Feathers: American Indian Law and Contemporary Tribal Life*. Berkeley: University of California Press, 1995.

Prakash, Gyan. "Subaltern Studies as Postcolonial Criticism." *American Historical Review* 99, no. 5 (1995): 1475–90.

Prins, Harold E. *The Mi'kmaq: Resistance, Accommodation, and Cultural Survival*. Fort Worth: Harcourt Brace College, 1996.

Radding, Cynthia. *Wandering Peoples: Colonialism, Ethnic Spaces, and Ecological Frontiers in Northwestern Mexico, 1700–1850*. Durham, N.C.: Duke University Press, 1997.

Raibmon, Paige. *Authentic Indians: Episodes of Colonial Encounter in the Nineteenth Century Pacific Northwest*. Durham, N.C.: Duke University Press, 2004.

Ridington, Robin. *Trail to Heaven: Knowledge and Narrative in a Northern Native Community*. Iowa City: University of Iowa Press, 1988.

Rosenthal, Harvey D. *Their Day in Court: A History of the Indian Claims Commission*. New York: Garland Publishing, 1990.

Rosier, Paul. *Rebirth of the Blackfeet Nation, 1912–1954*. Lincoln: University of Nebraska Press, 2001.

Rothman, Hal K. *Devil's Bargains: Tourism in the Twentieth-Century West*. Lawrence: University Press of Kansas, 2000.

Said, Edward. *Orientalism*. New York: Vintage, 1979.

Saltman, Michael, ed. *Land and Territoriality*. New York: Berg Books, 2002.

Sando, Joe. *Nee Hemish: A History of the Jemez Pueblo*. Albuquerque: University of New Mexico Press, 1982.

Scharff, Virginia. *Twenty Thousand Roads: Women, Movement, and the West*. Berkeley: University of California Press, 2002.

Schwartz, Douglas. "Havasupai." In Ortiz, *Southwest*, 13–24.

————. *The Havusupai, 600 AD–1955 AD: A Short Cultural History*. Norman: University of Oklahoma Press, 1956.

Scott, James C. *Domination and the Arts of Resistance: Hidden Transcripts*. New Haven, Conn.: Yale University Press, 1992.

————. *Weapons of the Weak: Everyday Forms of Peasant Resistance*. New Haven, Conn.: Yale University Press, 1986.

Sheridan, Thomas. *Arizona: A History*. Tucson: University of Arizona Press, 1995.

Shoemaker, Nancy. *Negotiators of Change: Historical Perspectives on Native American Women*. New York: Routledge, 1995.

Sibley, David. *Geographies of Exclusion: Society and Difference in the West*. New York: Routledge, 1995.

Sider, Gerald. *Lumbee Indian Histories: Race, Ethnicity, and Indian Identity in the Southern United States*. New York: Cambridge University Press, 1993.

Silva, Noe Noe. *Aloha Betrayed: Native Hawaiian Resistance to American Colonialism*. Durham, N.C.: Duke University Press, 2003.

Smith, Andrea. *Conquest: Sexual Violence and American Indian Genocide*. Cambridge: South End Press, 2005.

Smith, Anthony D. *National Identities*. Las Vegas: University of Nevada Press, 1991.

Smith, Linda Tuhiwai. *Decolonizing Methodologies: Research and Indigenous Peoples*. London: Zed Press, 1999.

Smith, Paul Chaat, and Robert Allen Warrior. *Like a Hurricane: The Indian Movement from Alcatraz to Wounded Knee*. New York: New Press, 1996.

*Southwest Indian Newsletter* 1, nos. 3–4 (1951). Temporarily published by the Institute of Ethnic Affairs, Washington, D.C.

Spicer, Edward. *Cycles of Conquest: The Impact of Spain, Mexico, and the United States on the Indians of the Southwest, 1533–1960*. Tucson: University of Arizona Press, 1962.

———. *The Yaquis: A Cultural History*. Tucson: University of Arizona Press, 1980.

Spivak, Gayatri Chakravorty. "Can the Subaltern Speak?" In *The Post-Colonial Studies Reader*, ed. Bill Ashcroft, Gareth Griffiths, and Helen Tiffin, 24–29. New York: Routledge, 1995.

———. *A Critique of Postcolonial Reason: Toward a History of the Vanishing Present*. Cambridge, Mass.: Harvard University Press, 1999.

Stannard, David E. *American Holocaust: Columbus and the Conquest of the New World*. New York: Oxford University Press, 1992.

Stern, Steve J. *Domination and the Arts of Resistance: Hidden Transcripts*. New Haven, Conn.: Yale University Press, 1992.

———. *Resistance, Rebellion and Consciousness in the Andean Peasant World, 18th to 20th Centuries*. Madison: University of Wisconsin Press, 1988.

Sturm, Circe. *Blood Politics: Race, Culture, and Identity in the Cherokee Nation of Oklahoma*. Berkeley: University of California Press, 2002.

Taylor, Graham. *The New Deal and American Indian Tribalism: The Administration of the Indian Reorganization Act, 1934–45*. Lincoln: University of Nebraska Press, 1980.

Thomas, David Hurst. *Skull Wars: Kennewick Man, Archaeology, and the Battle for Native American Identity*. New York: Basic Books, 2000.

Thornton, Russell, ed. *Studying Native America: Problems and Prospects*. Madison: University of Wisconsin Press, 1998.

Todorov, Tzvetan. *The Conquest of America: The Question of the Other*. Norman: University of Oklahoma Press, 1999.

Townsend, Kenneth William. *World War Two and the American Indian*. Albuquerque: University of New Mexico Press, 2000.

Trafzer, Clifford. *As Long as the Grass Shall Grow and Rivers Flow: A History of Native Americans*. Belmont, Calif.: Wadsworth, 1999.

Trimble, Stephen. *The People: Indians of the American Southwest*. Santa Fe: School of American Research Press, 1993.

Trope, Jack F., and Walter Echo-Hawk. "The Native American Graves Protection and Repatriation Act: Background and Legislative History." In Mihesuah, *Repatriation Reader*, 123–68.

Trouillot, Michel Rolph. *Silencing the Past: Power and the Production of History*. New York: Beacon Press, 1995.

Trujillo, Octaviana V., and Jeffrey P. Shepherd. "An Enduring Voice in American Indian Education: The Arizona State University Center for Indian Education." *Journal of American Indian Education* 38, no. 3 (1999): 19–33.

Tyack, David B. *The One Best System: A History of American Urban Education*. Cambridge, Mass.: Harvard University Press, 1974.

Utley, Robert. *The Indian Frontier of the American West, 1846–1890*. Albuquerque: University of New Mexico Press, 1984.

Van Kirk, Sylvia. *Many Tender Ties: Women in Fur-Trade Society, 1670–1870*. Norman: University of Oklahoma Press, 1983.

Vicenti Carpio, Myla. "Countering Colonization: Albuquerque Laguna Colony." *Wicazo Sa Review*, Fall 2004, 61–78.

Vilarde Tiller, Veronica E. *The Jicarilla Apache Tribe: A History, 1846–1970*. Lincoln: University of Nebraska Press, 1983.

Wagoner, Jay J. *Arizona Territory, 1863–1912*. Tucson: University of Arizona Press, 1970.

———. *Early Arizona: From Prehistory to Civil War*. Tucson: University of Arizona Press, 1974.

Walker, Henry P., and Don Bufkin. *Historical Atlas of Arizona*. Norman: University of Oklahoma Press, 1979.

Watahomigie, Lucille. *Hualapai Dictionary*. Peach Springs: Hualapai Bilingual Education Program, 1976.

Watahomigie, Lucille, Jorgine Bender, and Akira Y. Yamamoto with Elnora Mapatis, Josie Manakaja, and Malinda Powskey. *Hualapai Reference Grammar*. American Indian Studies Center. Los Angeles: University of California, 1982.

Watahomigie, Lucille, Malinda Powskey, Jorgine Bender, Josie Uqualla, and Philbert Watahomigie, Jr. *Waksi: Wich, Hualapai Cattle Ranching*. Peach Springs, Ariz.: Hualapai Bilingual Program, 1983.

Watahomigie, Lucille, Philbert Watahomigie, Sr., and Josie Uqualla Steele. *Project Tradition and Technology: The Hualapai Bilingual Academic Excellence Program*. Peach Springs: Peach Springs Public School District, 1995.

Watahomigie, Lucille, and Akira Yamamoto. "Linguistics in Action: The Hualapai Bilingual/Bi-educational Education Program." In *Collaborative Research and Social Change: Applied Anthropology in Action*, ed. Donald D. Stull and Jean J. Schensul, 77–98. Boulder, Colo.: Westview Press, 1987.

Weaver, Thomas, ed. *Indians of Arizona: A Contemporary Perspective*. Tucson: University of Arizona Press, 1974.

Weber, David J. *The Mexican Frontier, 1821–1856: The American Southwest under Mexico*. Albuquerque: University of New Mexico Press, 1982.

———. *The Spanish Frontier in North America*. New Haven, Conn.: Yale University Press, 1992.

Weibel-Orlando, Joan. *Indian Country, L.A.: Maintaining Ethnic Community in Complex Society*. Urbana: University of Illinois Press, 1999.

Welsh, Herbert. *Report of a Visit to the Navajo, Pueblo, and Hualapai Indians of New Mexico and Arizona*. Philadelphia: Indian Rights Association, 1885.

West, Patrick C., and Steven R. Brechin, eds. *Resident Peoples and National Parks: Social Dilemmas and Strategies in International Conservation*. Tucson: University of Arizona Press, 1999.

Whatmore, Sarah. *Hybrid Geographies: Natures, Cultures, and Spaces*. London: Sage Publications, 2002.

White, Richard. *"It's Your Misfortune and None of My Own": A New History of the American West*. Norman: University of Oklahoma Press, 1991.

———. *The Middle Ground: Indians, Empires, and Republics in the Great Lakes Region, 1650–1815*. Cambridge: Cambridge University Press, 1991.

———. *The Roots of Dependency: Subsistence, Environment, and Social Change among the Choctaws, Pawnees, and Navajos*. Lincoln: University of Nebraska Press, 1983.

Wiley, Peter, and Robert Gottlieb. *Empires in the Sun: The Rise of the New American West*. Tucson: University of Arizona Press, 1985.

Wilkins, David E. *American Indian Politics and the American Political System*. New York: Rowman and Littlefield Publishers, 2002.

————. *American Indian Sovereignty and the U.S. Supreme Court: The Masking of Justice*. Austin: University of Texas Press, 1997.

Wilkinson, Charles. *American Indians, Time, and the Law: Native Societies in a Modern Constitutional Democracy*. New Haven, Conn.: Yale University Press, 1987.

————. *Blood Struggle: The Rise of Modern Indian Nations*. New York: W. W. Norton, 2005.

Williams, Robert A. *Like a Loaded Weapon: The Rehnquist Court, Indian Rights, and the Legal History of Racism in America*. Minneapolis: University of Minnesota Press, 2005.

Williams, Robert A., Jr. *The American Indian in Western Legal Thought: The Discourses of Conquest*. New York: Oxford University Press, 1990.

Wilson, Angela Cavender. "Grandmother to Granddaughter: Generations of Oral History in a Dakota Family." In *Natives and Academics: Researching and Writing about American Indians*, ed. Devon Mihesuah, 27–36. Lincoln: University of Nebraska Press, 1998.

Wilson, Waziyatawin Angela. *Remember This! Dakota Decolonization and the Eli Taylor Narratives*. Lincoln: University of Nebraska Press, 2005.

Wolf, Eric. *Europe and the People without History*. Berkeley: University of California Press, 1982.

Workers of the Writer's Program of the Works Projects Administration, comps. *Havasupai and the Hualapai*. Flagstaff: Arizona State Teachers College, 1940.

Worster, Donald. *A River Running West: The Life of John Wesley Powell*. New York: Oxford University Press, 2001.

————. *Rivers of Empire: Water, Aridity, and the Growth of the American West*. New York: Oxford University Press, 1985.

Young, Richard K. *The Ute Indians of Colorado in the Twentieth Century*. Norman: University of Oklahoma Press, 1997.

# Index

BIA. *See* U.S. Bureau of Indian Affairs

Cooney, Eldon, 131
Council of Energy Resource Tribes, 196
Cowarrow, 54–55, 57–58, 66
Coyote Jim, 46–47
creation stories. *See* origin stories
Crook, George, 39, 47–48, 57, 63, 108
Crozier, Hayney, 84
Crozier, Kate, 40–41, 46, 84, 97, 108, 137
Crozier, Maymie, 86
Crozier, Sam, 64, 92
cultural genocide, 4, 81, 123, 158. *See also* assimilation
culture and customs: acculturation and, 81–88; adaptation to reservation, 58; Anglo recognition of, 130; burial and sacred sites, 190–93; colonization and loss of, 3–8; festivals and events, 207; Hualapai Circle Dances, 129; industrial development impact, 189–93; preserving, xi–xii, 142; research methods, 209. *See also* Hualapai lifestyle/way of life

dam projects. *See* Colorado River
Davidson, Homer O., 106, 108
Dawes Act of 1887. *See* land allotment
decolonization. *See* colonialism
*Decolonizing Methodologies: Research and Indigenous Peoples* (Smith), 209
Deloria, Vine, Jr., 8
Denetdale, Jennifer Nez, 7
diabetes, 5, 209
Diamond River (Diamond Creek), 30, 35, 167
Dieguenos, 20, 22
disease and deaths: in boarding schools, 81–82; European introduction of, 26, 28, 213; government Indian policy and, 81; during Hualapai Wars, 25, 38; La Paz internment, 1–2, 42–43; reservation, 54, 60, 87
Dobyns, Henry F., 23–25, 43, 149
Dodge, Thomas, 146, 170

Douglas, William O., 113
drugs. *See* alcoholism and drugs

economic development: federal programs, 163–65, 184–89; Hualapai efforts at, 5, 16–17, 149–50; NPS and, 178; post-industrial, 197–203; railroad and ranching, 71–72; reservation housing and facilities, 153–55, 159, 169; sovereignty, 189–93; water rights, 203–7. *See also* poverty
Economic Opportunity Act of 1964, 164
education and schools: acculturation, 81–88; boarding schools, 7, 126–29, 146, 214; Chilocco Indian School, 97; Hackberry Day School, 82–83; public schools, 125–26; Valentine Indian School, 82–85, 100, 126
Elementary and Secondary Education Act, 164
employment and income, 40, 68–77, 139–40, 151–56, 159, 162–64, 182–85, 194, 197–201
Energy Fuels Corporation, 196–97
environmental pollution, 177, 184–86, 189–91
environmental racism, 17, 193
Euler, Robert C., 23–25, 149, 180
Ewing, Henry P., 65–66, 70

Fanon, Frantz, 8
farming and ranching, xiii, 3, 33, 41, 55–57, 70–72, 91–93, 102, 110–11, 136–37, 165–66, 195, 214
Festival of the Pais, 207
Fielding, Jean, 160
Fielding, Jim, 42, 55, 94, 99–104, 106, 108, 110, 113, 132, 140
Fielding, Suwim, 130, 136–37, 142, 147
Flies Away, Joseph T., 197, 199
forestry/timber industry, 58, 66, 139, 142, 148, 165–66, 168, 197

Fort McDowell Reservation, 189, 199
Fort Mohave, 31, 34–35, 37–38, 50, 82
Fort Whipple, 31, 108–9
Fowler, Loretta, 12, 101
frontier settlement. *See* colonialism

gambling, 78, 137, 199–200
Goldwater, Barry, 179–80
Gonzales, Onesimo, 205
Gorton, Slade, 17, 184, 187
Grand Canyon National Park, 16,
    166–69, 178, 198, 202–3. *See also*
    National Park Service
Grand Canyon Resort Corporation, 207
Grand Canyon West, 166, 198–203
Grant, Ulysses S., 92
Great Depression, 129–38, 140
Great Society, 155, 163–64, 185, 194
Grounds, Dave, 47, 131, 133
Grounds, Emma and Hamilton, 131
Grounds, William F., 56–57, 92
Grover, Dick, 120
Grover, Emma, 168
Grover, Indian, 79–80
*Gum-U: The Hualapai Newsletter*, 13

Hackberry, Ariz., 42, 48, 50, 52, 63,
    65, 75, 105
Hackberry Day School, 82–83
Halchidomas, 27
Halyikwamais, 27
Hamidreck, Edward, 131
Hamidreck, Evelyn, 159
Hardyville, Ariz., 31, 33–36, 50
Haskell Indian Nation University, 207
Haskell Institute, 168
Hatame (Peach Springs band), 46
Havasupai Reservation, 25
Havasupais, 20, 23–24, 27, 29, 65, 90,
    181, 193, 207, 229n3
Havatone, Delbert, 175
Havatone, Earl, 181, 196, 199
Havatone, Margaret, 151
Havatone, Roger, 84, 100–101, 136, 146
Havatone, Veronica, 151

Havatone, Wendell, 180, 194
Hayden, Carl T., 93, 103, 109–12,
    170–71
health. *See* alcoholism and drugs;
    diabetes; disease and deaths
Heneta, Johnnie, 84
Hitch Hitchi (Pais chief), 33–34, 38
Hobgood, Guy, 124–25, 134
Honga, Agnes, 84
Honga, Indian (Peach Springs band),
    42, 46, 136
Honga, Jane and Jacob, 126–27, 131,
    168
Honga, Lucinda June, 151–52
Honga, Monza, 191
Honga, Waylon, 199
Honga, William, 85
Honga, Wilson, 145, 153
Hoover, Herbert, 109
Hoover Dam. *See* Colorado River
Hopis, 19–20, 22, 25–28, 83, 126,
    189–90, 193, 212
Hualapai Alcohol and Drug Abuse
    Prevention Program (HADAPP), 156
Hualapai Charley, 32, 37, 39, 49,
    54–59, 66, 69, 77–78, 101
Hualapai Dam. *See* Colorado River
Hualapai Department of Cultural
    Resources, xiv, 191
Hualapai history: importance of
    preserving, xi–xii; intergenerational
    storytelling in, 1–2; oral accounts of,
    xiii, 13, 18–20
Hualapai History Review Board,
    209–10
"Hualapai Land Case," 107, 138
Hualapai lands: Pai origins story,
    20–25; railroads and ranching on,
    72–76; reclaiming, 45–54; removal
    and relocation, xii–xiii, 1–5. *See
    also* Hualapai Reservation; land
    allotment
Hualapai lifestyle/way of life: Anglo
    observations, 83; colonialism and,
    27–28; elders' role, 22, 25; land use,

49–50; nation-building and, 158–68; reservation, 60–66. *See also* culture and customs

Hualapai Livestock Protection Association, 165

Hualapai Mountains, 24–25

Hualapai peoples: band identity, 22–25, 38–40, 58, 60–61, 87; creating identity, 61–62; gender roles, 7, 85, 159, 214; misnaming of, 30, 61; off-reservation employment, 68–71; Pai origins story, 18–25, 213; in a postindustrial economy, 193–203; tribal census, 150; tribal membership, 143, 188–89. *See also* women

Hualapai Reservation: casino gambling, 199–200; establishment of, xiii, 5, 51–52, 54–60; land exploitation, 91–104; life on, 60–66, 121–26; population and changes, xiv; post–WWII politics, 138–43; railroad rights, 95–97, 104–14; ration days, 52–53; self-determination, 183–89

Hualapai River Runners, 16, 168, 183

Hualapai Skywalk, 17, 200–202, 216

Hualapai Tribal Council: approval of this book, xi, 208; confronting tribal issues, 15–16; post–WWII challenges, 138–43; teaching traditions, xiv; termination issues, 143–56. *See also* tribal government

Hualapai Tribal Court, 135, 137, 161

Hualapai Wars, xiii, 13, 24–25, 34–39, 58, 213

Hualapai Welfare Committee, 94, 106, 133

Hualapai Wildlife and Recreation Department, 166–68, 180

Hunter, Bruce, 136

Hunter, Edna, 86

Hunter, Timothy, 151

Hunter, Will, 84, 120

Hunter, Woodrow, 131

Huya, Jane, 46, 107

Huya, Philip, 84

hydroelectric power, 8, 16, 171, 175–77, 182, 203

Iliff, Flora Gregg, 83

Imus, Bill, 131

Imus, Carl, 136

Imus, Freddie and Norman, 131

Imus, Pete, 84, 120, 131

Imus, Queen, 46–47

Indian Blood Card, 189

Indian Child Welfare Act, 155

Indian Citizenship Act, 15, 116, 121

Indian Civil Rights Act, 161, 187

Indian Claims Commission (ICC), 25, 32, 145, 148, 154, 158, 182, 188, 215

Indian Community Action Program, 155

Indian Emergency Conservation Work, 130–32

Indian Gaming Regulatory Act, 199

Indian Health Service, 144–45

Indian Homestead Act, 124

Indian New Deal, 129–30

Indian Reorganization Act, 15, 64–65, 133–37, 211

Indian Rights Association, 5, 57, 106–13, 134

Indian Self-Determination and Education Assistance Act, 163, 184, 194–95

Indian Wars, 2–3, 51. *See also* Hualapai Wars

Inter-Tribal Council of Arizona, 145–46

irrigation. *See* water rights

Irwin, Jeannie, 160

Ives, Joseph C., 29–30

Jackson, Ina, 155

Jackson, Jeanne, 127–29

Jackson, Loretta, 191–92

Jackson, Robert, 165

Jeff, Frances, 86

Jewitt, Ovington (Mrs.), 86

Querta, Linda, 161
Querta, Sylvia, 196–97

racial classification, 188
racial discrimination: activism, 157–58;
among Indian groups, 132–33;
blood quantum, 3, 116–17, 143,
188–89, 193–94, 209; citizenship,
125–26; court system, 78; housing
and allotments, 123–24; "Indian
blood," 81; relocation programs,
151–52; reservation life and, 61;
in schools and hospitals, 125–26;
voting rights, 121
ration days, 40, 42–43, 52–53, 65, 70,
77–79
Redmen Self Dependent of America, 94
relocation. *See* termination and
consolidation
*Remember This! Dakota Decolonization and
the Eli Taylor Narratives* (Wilson), 9
*Report: Colorado River of the West Explored,
1857 and 1858* (Ives), 30
river-rafting, 16, 166–67, 194, 201–3
Riverside, Calif., 85–86, 97
Rocha, George, 155, 158–59, 162,
175–76
Roosevelt, Franklin D., 130
Roosevelt, Theodore, 178

Sampson, Indian, 47
Sanford Cattle Company, 72, 92, 102
San Francisco Peaks, 20, 192–93
Santa Fe Railway, xiii, 5, 14–16, 43,
50, 56, 71–76, 89, 96, 103–13, 123,
138, 151–52, 170, 214
Saujiname, Dickson, 85
Scattergood, J. Henry, 109–11
Schrum (Pais leader), 6, 24, 33–44, 49,
52–55, 65–66, 69, 77–78
Schrum, Bob, 41–42, 55, 94, 104,
106–10, 137
Schrum, Nora, 46, 107
Schrum, Ora, 86

Schrum, Virgil, 137
self-determination: congressional
legislation, 16, 184, 194–95;
defined, 103; government policy
toward, 129–37, 143–56; Hualapai
struggle for, 69, 88, 132; limitations,
158–68; politics and progress,
183–89; resistance, 91–104, 106,
114; water rights and, 168–82;
white encroachment on, 52. *See also*
national identity; termination and
consolidation
Seligman, Ariz., 48, 73–76, 105, 168
Sells, Cato, 105–6, 119
sexual abuse of children, 85–86
Shell, Charles E., 70, 72–73, 78–80,
83–86, 96, 115, 119–20, 124–25
Sherman Institute (Riverside), 85–86
Shivwits, 77
Sierra Club, 179, 202–3
Sinyella, Roy, 131
Sinyeoga (Pai headman), 58
slave trade/slave labor, 28, 188
Smith, Auggie, 25, 32
Smith, Ernie, 153
Smith, Jim, 46, 107
Smith, John, 46
Society for American Indians, 116, 157
Sonoran Desert, 1, 27–28, 77
Sookwana (Pai leader), 69
Soskourema (Pai headman), 54–55
Spanish Colonial era, 25–28, 213
Spencer, Charles and Synje, 51–52,
54–57
Spirit Mountain, 18–21, 23, 55–56, 212
Suathajame, Dan, 84
Sue, Mike (Peach Springs band), 46,
107
Sukwana (Cataract Canyon scout), 39
Sullivan, Wesley, 84
Suminimo, Grace, 128
Susanyatame, Ronald, 151
Susanyatame, Tom, 72–73
Swaskagame, Sam, 83, 118, 120

# About the Author

Jeffrey P. Shepherd received his Ph.D. from Arizona State University in 2002 and is interested in the historical intersections of colonialism and Indigenous nation building. In addition to his work with the Hualapai he is interested in the comparative histories of Indigenous peoples on the U.S.–Mexico and U.S.–Canada borders as well as historical memory within Native, Anglo, and Mexican communities in the Southwest. He has published in the *American Indian Quarterly*, the *Indigenous Nations Journal*, and various edited collections and has received grants from the American Philosophical Society, the Max Millett Research Fund, the Ft. McDowell Indian Nation, and the University of Texas at El Paso. He has also been a research fellow at the D'Arcy McNickle Center for American Indian Culture at the Newberry Library in Chicago. He is presently working with the National Park Service to write an environmental history of the Guadalupe Mountains National Park in West Texas. He teaches graduate and undergraduate courses on Indigenous, western, border, and public history at the University of Texas at El Paso.